OUT OF THIS WORLD

OUT OF THIS WORLD

An Anthology of the St. Mark's
Poetry Project
■ 1966–1991

Edited and
with an Introduction
by Anne Waldman
■

Foreword by Allen Ginsberg

■

Crown Publishers, Inc.
New York

A detailed list of acknowledgments begins on page 604.

Published by Crown Publishers, Inc., 201 East 50th Street, New York, New York 10022. Member of the Crown Publishing Group.

CROWN is a trademark of Crown Publishers, Inc.

Manufactured in the United States of America

Library of Congress Cataloging-in-Publication Data

Out of this world : an anthology of the St. Mark's poetry project,
    1966–1991 / edited by Anne Waldman : foreword by Allen Ginsburg. —
    1st ed.
        p.   cm.
    Includes index.
        1. American poetry—20th century.   2. American poetry—New York
(N.Y.)   3. St. Mark's Church-in-the-Bowery (New York, N.Y.)
I. Waldman, Anne, 1945–
    PS615.098   1991
    811'.540809747—dc20   90-28382
                                                                 CIP

ISBN 0-517-56681-8

Book design by Linda Kocur

10 9 8 7 6 5 4 3 2 1

First Edition

CONTENTS

Part I
Precursors
The Fifties and Sixties

Translations I

Part II
Beginning the Project
1966–1976

FOREWORD

St. Mark's has always been a culture church, and as a venue for poetry it has an old history. I first went to a poetry reading at St. Mark's in the thirties with my father, Louis, who was once secretary of the Poetry Society of America. W. H. Auden was a member of the congregation in the fifties, but long before that Isadora Duncan had danced there, Frank Lloyd Wright had lectured, Houdini'd given a magic show. There had been jazz in the late fifties, even theater.

Our postmodern era began with a series of open readings that took place in a basement, formerly a rare gay place, the Macdougal Street Bar, renamed The Gaslight Café by owner John Mitchell in '58 or '59—with LeRoi Jones, Gregory Corso, Ray Bremser, myself and Peter Orlovsky, José Garcia Villa, others. These were predated by a year by readings given by Jack Kerouac, Philip Lamantia, Howard Hart, Steve Tropp, and others at Circle in the Square, as well as at various lofts and parties. Initial events were so extraordinary that readings sprang up all along Macdougal Street, with Café Wha?, Café Figaro, Rienzi's; the first Gaslight Café reading was such an unheard-of event that it made the front page of the New York *Daily News*. In a way, it was an imitation of the San Francisco scene, supposedly brought west from Existentialist Paris, maybe ancient Rome.

The late 1950s New York readings, ignited by the San Francisco Renaissance readings, in turn continued the traditions of the "Berkeley Renaissance." The latter wave crested in 1948, with Jack Spicer, Tom Parkinson, Kenneth Rexroth, Robert Duncan, Philip Lamantia, Robin Blaser—a group of poets, an elite (not alienated, but an elite)—reading to one another in private houses, an intimate Buddhist anarchist hermetic circle that prepared the way for later generations. Grad psychologist Timothy Leary and hermetic artist-filmmaker Harry Smith were present, same community, same era. In 1955, our "famous" Gallery Six reading was held in a very small venue, an art gallery that was formerly a garage—maybe 150 people could fit in. The readings were thereafter carried on by the San Francisco State College Poetry Center.

Thus, the genealogy extends from San Francisco through the Gaslight to St. Mark's Church in New York. After the Gaslight, poets floated from joint to joint—from Circle in the Square to a couple of small cafés up and down the Lower East Side, then over to the Seven Arts Café on Ninth Avenue and 43rd Street, near Times Square. Seven Arts flourished for about a year and a half, with Ray Bremser, Janine Pommy-Vega, myself, Gregory and Peter, LeRoi, Jack Kerouac, Diane di Prima, Ed Sanders—and many other poets. As the "Beatnik" era ended, around 1963 or so, we wound up at The Metro, which was the final surge before the St. Mark's Poetry Project. The Metro was attended by everybody: Paul Blackburn was around, di Prima, Ted Berrigan, Frank O'Hara and Jackson Mac Low attended, and readings were for a long while organized by Allen DeLoach, who started a little "ditto" magazine, *Poetry at the Metro*. Later Ted Berrigan hosted the readings. Bob Dylan came once, I remember, to listen; regulars like Ishmael Reed, David Henderson and the Umbra group, A. B. Spellman, Steve and Gloria Tropp came to read. There had been an era of good feeling between blacks and whites, 1958–1962, when one literary center was LeRoi Jones's house with his wife Hettie Cohen. *The Floating Bear* magazine, an early mimeo edited by LeRoi and Diane di Prima, had circulated, as well as LeRoi's omniscient *Yugen. Evergreen Review* was flourishing and *Chicago Review* had begun printing Burroughs, Kerouac, Corso; after censorship troubles, the latter went independent as *Big Table* and fought Post Office censorship successfully in 1959.

The Metro suffered through two crises, which continue to this day, in one form or another. You had to have a "cabaret license" to have so-called "entertainment." In those days, the crucial questions concerned cost: forty, fifty, sixty thousand dollars, not to mention all the bureaucratic problems attached to a cabaret license—you had to put in an extra fire escape or an extra fire door, as well. The Metro was not a place with liquor, it was just a coffee shop with poets, and the real and legal point was freedom of speech.

Someone also wanted to hold a poetry reading in Washington Square Park. The police said no and refused to allow it; we defied the police and held the reading one Sunday. There were lots of European and Japanese camerapeople there, and the image of poets declaiming in the grass went all over the world. So-called "profanity" seemed the underlying problem—but again, the real issue was freedom of speech. This was the early sixties, but city regulations still insisted there could be no entertainment in the parks without a license, and bureaucrats said this was "entertainment," so you had to get a license. It was a classic First Amendment case. The ACLU intervened and said no, it's not "entertainment," it's public speech, free speech, soapbox.

Now, the cabaret-licensing problem was a hangover from a Draconian dope law that said that anybody who'd been busted, had any kind of conviction—misdemeanor or felony—couldn't get a cabaret license to play at a New York City café. That barred geniuses like Charlie Parker,

Thelonious Monk, and Billie Holliday from performing in New York clubs for decades. We abolished the poet's cabaret-license requirement through intervention of the City Council—by that time, we'd organized a public committee. Central to it was Ed Sanders, who then edited his elegant *Fuck You: A Magazine of the Arts*.

A New York City District Attorney, one Richard Kuh, had been prosecuting D. H. Lawrence's *Lady Chatterley's Lover*, Henry Miller's *Tropic of Cancer*, Jean Genet's *Our Lady of the Flowers*, and finally William Burroughs's *Naked Lunch*. By 1962, that censorship was broken by the courts, but Kuh went on to prosecute Lenny Bruce for his Greenwich Village nightclub act, and there was a strong literary reaction to that prosecution.

All at once came the emergence of underground films, synchronous with attempts at literary censorship, cabaret card licensing, Lenny Bruce persecution, underground newspapers like *The East Village Other* (which carried poetry) and *The Village Voice*, more or less at its height as a crusading bohemian paper. The literary, musical, and cinematic avant-garde, as well as civil rights, censorship, and minority problems, all came together at one point, one spot in time, in the early sixties. So it was a glorious ferment, as the old-fashioned littérateurs say, good as anything in the thirties or twenties. Race problems arose with the Metro proprietors, so we moved to St. Mark's Church—led by Joel Oppenheimer and Paul Blackburn.

St. Mark's has become my church, my religion place. I've been living nearby on the Lower East Side for thirty-five years. Certainly by the sixties it was my church in the sense that that's where my community was, my Sangha, my peers. I could pass out information, find out the latest gossip, what's new, follow the latest art spurt. It was part of my education, part of my resources. Networking in that open community was intricately involved with private and public life. High-school kids coming to the church could enter a very sophisticated atmosphere and get an education they wouldn't get in grammar schools or even colleges: education in the advanced standards of Bohemia.

Officially, The Poetry Project began in 1966. According to Anne Waldman, the sociologist Harry Silverstein applied for the founding grant, through the New School for Social Research across town. Money came through the Office of Economic Opportunity (OEO) under Lyndon Johnson, for a pilot program to help "alienated youth" on the Lower East Side. So the church started housing the Black Panthers' breakfast program, the Motherfuckers' dinner program.* Anne remembers "huge

*Motherfuckers: a black skirt and shirt psychedelic anarchist lunatic fringe left-hand politics commune-romantic nuisance youth extremists of the late sixties.

pots always cooking"; there was a child-care project too. The Lower East Side hadn't any counterculture center, and given the alienation of different minority groups, some center was needed with sensitive antennae for white, black, brown, and hippie post-Beat groups.

One interesting fringe benefit of this gathering was the margin of old bohemians left over from the thirties and forties still living on the Lower East Side and in the Village—antique "delicatessen intellectuals." Politically, there were remnants of the Old Left among the poets. Another node on the Lower East Side at that time, older than The Poetry Project, was the War Resisters' League. The war was central to everybody's preoccupations in the sixties. Many of the poems of the time expressed outrage or sympathy or violence or fright or grief. Primarily grief or fear. So there was a community, a forum where people could articulate their relationship to the big national problem of the Vietnam War and the hyper-militarization of Whitman's America. Questions of ecology had also entered into poetry through the 1950s San Francisco Renaissance; Kerouac and Gary Snyder and Lew Welch used their verse as a vehicle for expressing fright or shock or information for all mankind on the planet. Sixties mouths could meet people who had been pacifists in World War I, people who knew Catholic worker saint Dorothy Day. You got a taste of prior eras, prior movements, prior communities and their moments of glory: publications, parties, social activities, and love affairs, decades old.

For a person without an extended family in New York—my brother was living on Long Island, my father in New Jersey, and my mother was dead—St. Mark's served as immediate neighborhood community and family. "Rootless cosmopolitans," urbanized, sophisticated artists and writers gathered at The Poetry Project. It served and still serves to formulate local public opinion. Barriers were removed between inner and outer, between subjective worlds and objective social worlds. Here was space where people could proclaim to society what they wanted— and in a church, which lent their address proper dignity.

Liberation of the word. Liberation of minority groups, questions of race. The famous "sexual revolution." The celebrated women's liberation—women writing and reading brilliantly, led by poets Anne Waldman and Diane di Prima, Alice Notley, Maureen Owen, Denise Levertov, Joanne Kyger, also Diane Wakoski and Rochelle Owens and Carol Bergé, others. At least in my circle these were among the stars who gave expression to new independence. There were angry denunciations, manifestos, gay liberation performance pieces; there was romantic love poetry, there were prose poetry journals like Taylor Mead's excellent *Diary of a New York Youth* (Kerouac liked Mead's free style and frankness). *The World* mimeo publications were acknowledging the changed role of sex, and all these themes could be expressed—even put to music. None of this was particularly "committed" poetry, *engagé* in the old Marxist or newer Existentialist sense. Put simply, the mode of poetry was subjective, so that any rumination that might engage you alone in bed would enter your poetry, and that could include what you read in *The New York Times* or saw on television or heard on the radio or thought in bathtub solitude or saw on the streets if you were tear-gassed. Very often, while making national pronouncements in poetry, I wondered if the FBI sat in the audience listening (as they did later in Chicago in '68).

Beginning with Great Society sixties Johnson policies, followed by Carter's, the government spent a great deal of money on the arts through OEO, as it had through the 1930s WPA. In 1966–68, money was spent on art. With that came some democratization of the intelligentsia, and some local poverty workers became intelligentsia. Everyone realized that heretofore this subsidy money for the arts had been going to institutional millionaires who operated symphonies and museums. Suddenly, small, decentralized, individual community projects could be subsidized by the government. There was a big push for minority and multicultural arts, bohemian arts, for individual arts, for poetry readings around the country, poetry in the schools, little magazines with their Coordinating Councils, and a number of strong provincial centers of poetic activity.

Monday-night readings at St. Mark's were open to everyone. And then, for bardic soapbox stars of their own romance, subjectivity, passions, and political prophecy, you had the Wednesday-night readings. On New Year's Day readings, everybody in the community would come out, perhaps two or three hundred people, to do a one-, two-, three-, or four-minute shot—maybe their most intense perception of the year, or the one piece they'd prepared that they could show off to the entire community, and that would include everybody from John Cage up to Grand Master Xylophone. Yoko Ono came once, completely dressed in white, and breathed into the microphone with her "Formula in Awe of the Air"—was that it?—a piece mostly of silence. The audience was, and is, a regular community, unlike those at university readings—this audience had been going to the same place to hear readers for ten, twenty years, so accumulated much granny wisdom about poetry, familiarity, and gossip. The audience, totally attuned, might know prior work from prior readings. Let's say Robert Creeley comes and reads a special poem dedicated to René Ricard, or I read an epilogue to "Kaddish" in the form of "White Shroud," hearers know these texts resonate with old history, because everyone's familiar with earlier texts and styles.

In later years, St. Mark's became a cradle for some higher rock 'n' roll, New Wave, and performance language. Patti Smith, Jim Carroll, William Burroughs, Laurie Anderson, Lou Reed, Philip Glass, Steven Taylor—all were at one time either apprentice poets at St. Mark's or participated in year-round activities or performed occasional work. So it had tremendous impact on the centralized progression of rock 'n' roll intelligentsia. Interestingly enough, St. Mark's was only ten blocks away from CBGB's, the bedraggled punk mecca of the early eighties.

With the age of Reagan, a deliberate, Federal concerted anti-democratic attack on small, individualistic, community-led arts groups began. The present attack on the NEA is an attack on decentralized initiative and diversity. "Why should the general public support, with taxpayers' money, dirty poems, anti-American poems, 'immoral' poems?" Kill the classic U.S. avant-garde that helped with the Cold War in Eastern Europe! "What good is this avant-garde? Why should the public be forced to pay for it?" This is the voice of the demagogue bureaucrat and can be answered simply:

The avant-garde has a healthy role to play in any culture. The Green Revolution and notions of ecology were proclaimed by the avant-garde in America before scientific popular notions of ecology became part of majority opinion. The green movement was fostered in 1950s poetry by savants like Gary Snyder and Michael McClure. More poignantly, it was the avant-garde, the very same artists who would be censored by the so-called "anti-Communist" fundamentalists in America, who were censored in totalitarian Eastern Europe. Deconstruction of the German, Czechoslovakian, Hungarian, Bulgarian, and Romanian Communist bureaucracies was spearheaded by members of the literary avant-garde who were allied, historically and by personal connection, to the very same avant-garde here in America censured by neo-conservatives. Ed Sanders and his band, the Fugs, with their "Coca-Cola Douche" or "Police State Blues," would never be subsidized under the demagogue censor's 1990s NEA new rules, nor would The Mothers of Invention, led by Frank Zappa, or Andy Warhol's Velvet Underground, Lou Reed, Dylan, Burroughs, Kerouac be approved—though all are heroes now in free Czechoslovakia. For myself, my own poetry has been chilled off public broadcast in parallel censorship by the Federal Communications Commission.

The age of Reagan-Bush, then, cracked down on the liberation of the Word, lowering St. Mark's NEA grants funds as well as diminishing funds previously granted to other decentralized arts groups, including Intersection for the Arts in San Francisco. In 1989, St. Mark's funds were reduced to $5,000, not enough to pay one person to move chairs for a year. Neo-con politicians are talking as if they had a monopoly on God, with gas-bag "moral majority" and "born-again" political groups hyping money off airwaves for promotion of what the American Founding Fathers denounced: the domination of State policy by an intolerant Church. These neo-con cults try to make the nation legislate parochial Church morality, aiming to restrict political humor and liberty of expression. The Bush Era's permissive manipulation of fundamentalist political mania has already led to withdrawal of appropriate subsidy and encouragement for the spiritual liberation that the St. Mark's Poetry Project manifests. Either way poets rather than fundamentalist betrayers of the spirit will win the world, because the planet needs imagination, the avant-garde spirit of poetry, to survive.

—ALLEN GINSBERG

I remember Charles Olson's reading at the Berkeley Poetry Conference in 1965. His words and phrasings were the runic in-head squabbles and gestures of a blazing, overactive mind. There was a painful quality to his inability to completely enunciate his volcanic passions, as he struggled to bridge the gap between insight and articulation. His friends and colleagues in the audience would support him as far as he cared to go. I remember feeling his vulnerability and exposure on this occasion. This fragility seemed ironic considering Olson's physical size and stature as a poet. Breathing heavily, his huge frame swaying, he was at once a hermetic scholar, mad scientist, and the breath of some untamed wind dancing and coming apart before our eyes.

I remember vowing then and there that, beyond the practice of my own writing, I would work for and be part of a literary community that would honor its members and provide a network for their ongoing writing. Forums for poetry, outside of occasional academic gatherings, were scarce at this time, for the most part operating irregularly out of bars, coffeehouses, bookstores, and people's homes. Poetry needed a larger arena; the community needed it as well. The few small-press publications around New York, for example, didn't seem enough to convey the creative energy building in the mid-sixties. Beyond the idea of publishing was the urge to get up and sound the words on a stage without fancy lighting, props, or rehearsals. The rawness of that act, however indulgent it might seem, could be glorious.

I had grown up on Macdougal Street, the daughter of bohemian parents who had met in the artistic milieu of Provincetown. My mother had been an early "drop-out," sailing off to Greece upon marrying the son of the celebrated Greek poet Angelos Sikelianos, and living there a decade. My father, a former "swing"/jazz piano player, had also had an earlier marriage, to the daughter of a labor journalist, Mary Heaton Vorse. As College Secretary at Pace University, he had hosted Allen Ginsberg on the occasion of his reading there in the 1950s. My mother wrote poetry and translated the work of Sikelianos into English. During high school I frequented the cafés along Macdougal, and I remember seeing Gregory Corso, quintessential *poète maudit*, a block from my front door, and being struck by his "poetic aura." My mother took me to hear Robert Lowell at New York University and encouraged the development of a "good ear" for poetry.

Donald Allen's historic anthology, *The New American Poetry*, published in 1960, brought together what for me was most exciting in post-war American poetry. In that collection, the contributors are divided into five groups: those associated with Black Mountain College, *Black Mountain Review*, and *Origin* magazine; the San Francisco Renaissance; the Beat Generation; the New York School; and a loosely connected group, defined by their "own original styles and new conceptions of poetry," who were also associated with some of the writers in the aforementioned groups. Many of the poets in Allen's anthology had gathered in Berkeley at the Poetry Conference in 1965.

I was in college then and returned to Bennington for a final year, where I edited the college's literary magazine, *Silo*, and founded *Angel Hair* magazine and books with Lewis Warsh, a young New York poet. We had met after the Robert Duncan reading at the Berkeley Conference.

What had struck me was the startling individuality of the work, the poetic stance, and the energy of each writer I witnessed at Berkeley. Yet, with the exception of Lenore Kandel, where were the women poets? Out of a total of forty authors in the Allen anthology, only four were women. I took this as a personal challenge. The new poetic community must invite women's writing. Still, as a fledgling writer of poetry, I was nurtured and inspired by these parent, though largely male, sources. William Carlos Williams had declared that each new generation of writers must move the practice forward at least an inch. He wrote:

> Forward is new. It will not be blamed. It will not force itself into what amounts to paralyzing restrictions. It cannot be correct. It hasn't time. It has that which is beyond measurement, which renders measurement a falsification, since the energy is showing itself as recrudescent, the measurement being the aftermath of each new outburst.

Ezra Pound admonished, "Make it new!" Gertrude Stein had said, "Anybody that creates a new thing has to make it ugly." I took these as urgent commands to get on with my own work, however raw and crude it might be, as well as to help create a forum for younger writers, which would simultaneously honor the "elders." The only criterion for judgment would be whether the work truly "breathes," (in Emily Dickinson's sense of the term). William Carlos Williams had also written:

> Poetry is language charged with emotion. It's words rhythmically organized. . . . A poem is a complete little universe. It exists separately. Any poem that has worth expresses the whole life of the poet. It gives a view of what the poet is.

> In poetry you're listening to two things . . . you're listening to the sense, the common sense of what it says. But it says more. This is the difficulty.

I had experienced the poem as a "complete little universe." I felt the poems of Olson or Duncan, Robert Creeley or Denise Levertov, Frank O'Hara or Allen Ginsberg, expressing what those poets are. I could hear the sense. But the ineffable quality and difficulty of "it says more" was what hooked me. It was a great pleasure to be in the presence of the poet, to follow the voice and breath and rhythms, to participate in the ritual enactment of the poem. There was something sublime in that *difficulty*. You couldn't neatly sum up the experience and take it home with you. You couldn't pinpoint it, name it, own it.

During my nonresident term away from Bennington I worked in New York at radio station WRVR, which operated out of Riverside Church. I hosted a poetry series on the air and helped with the production of two short Sam Shepard plays. I remember moderating a panel that included John Ashbery, John Perreault, Ted Berrigan, and Peter Schjeldahl, who were the respective editors of *Locus Solus, Elephant, "C" Magazine*, and *Mother* magazine. The topic was "the little magazine," and as nervous as I was, it was somehow reassuring to hear that these editors faced the same challenges as I was facing with *Angel Hair*. Williams had written something, too, about the publishing of a little magazine being like climbing into bed with other poets.

On the subway, as we headed downtown from the radio panel, Ted Berrigan playfully put me down for deferring to John Ashbery and giving him more air time. He called me a snob! I felt delighted to be striking up friendships with writers I admired, whose work I was avidly following in the magazines we had been discussing. My old high school friend Jonathan Cott had been sending copies of *"C" Magazine* to Bennington. I remember the excitement of finding the 8½-by-14 mimeographed and stapled product crammed into my mailbox; fresh work from Edwin Denby, Joe Ceravolo, Ron Padgett.

After graduating in June of 1966, I moved to 33 St. Mark's Place and shortly thereafter heard that St. Mark's Church was hiring artists for a new arts project to be administered by Harry Silverstein, a sociologist from the New School of Social Research. He had successfully landed a grant from the Office of Economic Opportunity to work with alienated youth on New York City's Lower East Side. St. Mark's Church was the obvious choice for such a venture since writers, jazz musicians, and filmmakers had been active on the premises since the early sixties. I had a membership card to the film series run by John Brockman, where I saw first rushes of Andy Warhol's *Sleep*, with enigmatic shots of poet John Giorno dozing for hours and hours and hours. I had also performed in a play of Ralph Cook's, playing a cheerless neurotic, and had been heckled by Sam Shepard and Charles Mingus, Jr. Paul Blackburn had moved the poetry reading series from The Metro coffeehouse on Second Avenue to the parish hall of the church. Like a real trooper, he lugged his old Wollensack tape recorder to every reading, dutifully recording the evening and passing the hat for the featured reader.

The time was ripe for a flourishing of activity in theater, film, and poetry, and a noncommercial community space was needed to showcase new experiments and discoveries. The aesthetic sensibilities of the so-called New York School (John Ashbery, Kenneth Koch, Frank O'Hara, James Schuyler, Barbara Guest) held a particular attraction for younger poets. Their work—subtle, witty, urban, visual—included the playfulness of the Surrealists without the ideology. It didn't complain or call attention to itself. It was anti-provincial. I enjoyed the "talk" of these writers as I got to know them better, and also appreciated their interaction and collaborative work with the New York painters. The New York School shaped the "local environment" through literary and art magazines, readings, openings, and parties and provided, in a sense, the matrix for The Poetry Project. A new generation, picking up on the work of these "elders," began to experiment further, extending the modernist line. Such collective energy resulted in a new downtown scene, an especially welcome facet of which was its inclusion of young women writers.

The Reverend Michael Allen hired me, along with Joel Sloman and Sam Abrams, to assist Joel Oppenheimer, who was to direct The Poetry Project. Reverend Allen was the Episcopal rector of St. Mark's, who had recently returned from riding freedom buses in the South. He was then preparing for a trip to Vietnam with Joan Baez.

We decided to call our new venture a poetry "project" because we saw it as an ongoing event requiring hard work and perseverance. We also had in mind the sense of an outward *projecting*, "to direct one's voice to be heard clearly at a distance." Public readings were at the heart of the plan.

Another important aspect was the publications, the one-shot *Genre of Silence*, which Joel Oppenheimer edited, and the more regularly appearing *The World*, a mimeographed magazine. Joel Sloman, editing the first issue of *The World*, sent stencils to contributors, inviting them to type their own poems, which we then mimeographed. Joel and I wound up having to retype a lot of them. I went on to edit or co-edit twenty-eight issues of this magazine. It has since run to forty-one issues under a series of guest editors. Later publications included *The Poetry Project Newsletter*, numerous publications from writing workshops sponsored by the Project, and, more recently, *Poetry Project Papers*.

Generally, a little magazine is a volunteer publication of unpredictable appearance that springs up almost spontaneously as the need arises, i.e., wherever people are writing without an outlet for their work. It takes considerable effort to put out such a magazine, but the impulse comes from necessity rather than from the expectation of rewards. The only reward an editor can hope for is the occasional approval or gratitude of a comrade. Because of this lack of material compensation most little magazines can't expect a long life span, yet a few manage to survive. *The World* is such a magazine.

There were few little magazines in New York in 1966. The most significant of these—"*C*" *Magazine*, Diane di Prima and LeRoi Jones's *Floating Bear*, and Ed Sanders's *Fuck You: A Magazine of the Arts*— were phasing out. *The World* seemed to fill a real need.

By 1968, as the initial two-year grant from the Office of Economic Opportunity was running out, the Project was sustained by small grants from the Noble Foundation and the Kaplan Fund, and a few individual contributions. Greater solvency was enjoyed in the seventies and eighties with support from The New York State Council on the Arts and The National Endowment for the Arts.

Over the years *The World* had received continued support from the Coordinating Council of Literary Magazines. Friends and neighbors from the Lower East Side community often helped with collating and stapling, at times when a single editor would have been tempted to throw the switch for the last time on the leaky mimeo machine and never again enter the stamp line at the Fourth Avenue post office.

The writing in this anthology, selected primarily from issues of *The World*, represents an extraordinary variety of "voices" spanning nearly two and a half decades. Most of the contributors to this collection have participated in the activities of the Project as guest readers, workshop teachers, lecturers, directors, assistant directors, secretaries, artists-in-residence, and board members. In a general sense, the writing here stands outside academic conventions and celebrates the "outrider" tradition.

I have divided the book into three sections. The first contains work by the so-called precursors, or elders, writers who had achieved some prominence by the time the Project began and were, as mentioned, an inspiration for my own work and that of many younger writers at the time. The second section includes work of writers active during the first decade of the Project's history, those who came into their own in the seventies and were, in a sense, the "founders" of the Project. The third section presents work from a second and third wave of writers, who came to the Project later, not necessarily younger, but a younger generation in the Project's history. These are not hard and fast divisions; the intention rather is to give a sense of lineage, a notion of the relationship of the writers to the Project.

Between each section are short selections from the translation issues of *The World*, edited by Ron Padgett and Danny Krakauer respectively. These convey the attraction and value that poets of these pages have so often found in the challenge of recasting acts of one language into another.

The Contributors' Index presents biographical and bibliographical information, as well as statements by authors on their own personal involvement with The Poetry Project and St. Mark's Church. It provides an entertaining compendium of anecdotes and appreciations.

What struck me most in editing this anthology was the common ground that The Poetry Project, with its publications, workshops, and various reading and lecture series, has provided for the broad range of writers represented here. So many have found at the Project an oasis of artistic encouragement and opportunity, and I am reminded of the memorial to W. H. Auden, Paul Blackburn, and Frank O'Hara dedicated in the St. Mark's churchyard on April 30, 1975. There are three flowering trees and a plaque that, quoting Auden, reads: "Thousands have lived without love, not one without water."

—ANNE WALDMAN

Precursors
The Fifties and Sixties

"I don't want

my poems lisped on

the numbered

tongues of children.

May they be part

of the world and sight

by which we become

the eye and defy

questions with our beauty"

—Frank O'Hara,

"Variations on a Theme by Shelley"

HELEN ADAM

Deep in the Sub-Way

_____

Deep in the sub-way I sit lonely
Riding the B.M.T.
Far, far away, on the sands of Coney
Frolics the salty sea.

"Straight is the track to Coney Island"
Wheels in the darkness sing.
"Far, far ahead the waves run shining
Under a sea gull's wing."

Where are those sands of distant Coney,
Wished for so long in vain?
"Past Borough Hall and DeKalb Avenue station"
Sings the shuddering train.

"After Neck Road, in the early morning,
Out beyond Sheepshead Bay,
Cool and remote lie the sands of Coney,
Empty at break of day."

So many miles, so many stations,
Before I reach that strand,
Where the small waves, quietly breaking,
Flit up and down the sand.

I, in whose heart the North Sea echoes,
And the Pacific roars,
Why should I crave the sad Atlantic
Splashing on Brooklyn's shores?

Splashing on shores by millions trampled,
Still it's sublime to me.
Cluttered with garbage, spoiled, polluted,
Still it's the sea! the sea!

Under the city darkly I travel,
Locked in a lurching car,
Dreaming of sea waves, deep in the sub-way.
Coney so far, so far.

■

DAVID ANTIN

A Story

Stefan and Tadeusz traveled north in a closed cattle car for two nights and two days. When they arrived they had no idea where they were. Only they were marched to a large wooden barracks where they were given sleeping quarters in a chicken-wire frame and slept three tiers high. From the salt tang in the air and the fact that they had traveled north they thought they were somewhere on the coast of the Baltic.

. . . . .

One was a schoolteacher and the other a mechanic. Stefan had soft hands but Tadeusz didn't mind hard work. Yet the concrete was hard on his fingers. They were put on a routine latrine job. But one day they stumbled on an open door.

. . . . .

It looked just like a little aeroplane and Stefan wrote home to complain about the weather. He said the climate was severe and that Aunt Katya wouldn't like it here.

. . . . .

In the laundry shed a voice above them murmured, "How long has it been since you knocked the head off the bottle?" It came from Stanislaw Obrebski. In a locomotive driver from Stettin. At the mouth of the Oder. He carried the news to Rafal.

. . . . .

Soon the French girls were watching trains on the Vistula. They were the first to pass the name.

. . . . .

By train to Danzig. In a shaving brush. Stowed away on a coal boat to Gotland. Thence to London.

. . . . .

Peenemünde. Peenemünde. Peenemünde.

. . . . .

In the forests about Warsaw footsteps fell at the fringe of the thicket. It was Molda from Blizna-Pustow.

. . . . .

At Sarnaki by the River Bug. Near Wyszkow. A small boy cried, "Father, Father, a little plane flew over the river." "In which direction, Sigismund?" The little plane flew south. "Father, Father, another little plane flew over." "In the same direction, Sigismund?" "Yes, I found it by the river."

. . . . .

Sigismund's father called upon Andreas to drive his cattle into the river. "Andreas, drive them into the middle. Let them churn up the mud." As this was going on a Mercedes drove up with three officers inside. "Did you see a little aeroplane?" they inquired. Everyone had seen it. Otto was positive it was headed for Sokolow, due east. Andreas said it had clipped the trees. This was due south. And Sigismund's father took the officers aside. "To be perfectly frank, Hauptmann, it passed over these trees." (This was due north.) "You are an imbecile," the officer raged.

. . . . .

An ex-Polish air officer named Wlodek crept out of a hedge and guided them to their airstrip rendezvous. All of this took effrontery and consummate nerve. The focal point was a woodcutter's cottage, where they waited for the first few bars of Chopin's *Opus 15*. "That's our signal," said Wlodek. "They will be here tomorrow." They spent the rest of the day trying to contact the Polish Home Army.

. . . . .

Everyone worked like a madman. Those without shovels dug with their bare hands. They found planks to form a ramp out of the muck, and at the height of the activity a sentry crept by with the news, "There's a German patrol on the way." But gradually the Dakota was hauled out of the morass and the pilot found higher and drier ground. The packages and passengers were stowed away, and she skimmed off like a bird to Brindisi. They say that the Polish patriot is living in the United States today.

■

JOHN ASHBERY

In a Boat

Even when confronted by the small breakwater
That juts out from the pebbled shore of truth
You arch your eyebrows toward the daytime stars
And remind me, "This is how I was. This was the last

Part of me you were to know." And I can see the lot
Ending in the wood of general indifference to hostility
That wants to know how with two such people around
So much is finishing, so much rushing through the present.

There was a tag on the little sailboat
That idled there, all its sails rolled up
As tightly as umbrellas. What difference?
The orange shine stood off, just far enough away

Not to catch the commas and puns as you spoke
This time in defense of riders of the squall,
Of open-faced daring, not just to the empty seas
But for the people swathed in oilcloth on the beach.

"It is no great matter to take this in hand, convince
The tips of the trees they were rubbing against each other
All along. Each contrives to slip into his own hall of fame
And my common touch has triumphed. The doorpost shall turn again
    and again."

■

Ignorance of the Law

I have it on good authority
Usually reliable sources have
Stained the anonymity of the law and still it empties
Everywhere. There are names like Bill and Ken;
We are flattered to own our own, yet it becomes a tributary
Of the wall of the law.

Some days it looks like a sign for everything is all right,
Others it arpeggios into early twilight and silence.
Each day suffers its humiliation,
The nights are silent
And morning is merely quiet,
A time to pick over, salvage,
Light the small fires.
And truth burns smoky, being green.

And if during the middle of the day a hush comes
That seems to ask what all this fuss is about anyway,
Beware the rising stair, cloud-capped,
That is not a jumping-off place.
A messenger will meet you there,
The good news skewed with the bad in his quiver,
And vanish after a one-liner. O our breakfasts
Were impossible too. Finally what we were driven to
Became erect and noble. Built of cheap materials
But the line knows its own dignity, isn't just idle pathos.

Came to that opus, the whole hill,
Welling, backing down
Into its own froth, a sign for many
Who were otherwise too tired to notice
On the subway going home, forgetting that in another ten years
It would have receded into the flank like

It's over now. The season with its insects
Fades like a newsreel, the cheering beside the point.
At the terminal of the sun a few of the brainwashed
Still loiter, but it is late,
The smells of cooking are strict and pointed like a compass
At the lateral town that seems like a bargain now.
It was always there, waiting there.

Forgive us our enemies, what we do to them,
Help us make change for those who do not entirely see us.
Make us visible. Lead us to the jackpot of redemption,
The bonanza of enlightenment, seeing as how we wheeze and waver,
For such examples, while not unknown,
Are altogether rare.

■

Sleeping in the Corners of Our Lives

So the days went by and the nickname caught on.

It became a curiosity, but it wasn't curious.
Afternoon leaves blew against the stale brick
Surface. Just an old castle. Enjoy it
While you're here. And in looking for a more convenient way
To save one's soul, one is led up to it like a season,
And in looking all around, and about, its tome
Becomes legible in the interstices. A great biography
That is also a good autobiography, at the station;
A honeycomb of pages with listings
Of the tried and true, that radiates
Out into what is there, that averages up as wind,
And settles back into a tepid, modest
Chamber with its mouse-gray furniture, its redundant pictures.

This is tall sleeping
To prepare you for the soup and ruins
In giving the very special songs of the first meaning,
The ones incorporating the changes.

■

JOHN ASHBERY &
KENNETH KOCH

(A Conversation)

KOCH: John, do you think we both might be too much concerned with matters of taste? Or don't you think it's possible to be too much concerned with it?

ASHBERY: What else is there besides matters of taste?

K: How would you change that statement if you wanted to put it in a poem? I think that statement would seem too pompous to you to put into a poem. Or too obvious.

A: I would not put a statement in a poem. I feel that poetry must reflect on already-existing statements.

K: Why?

A: Poetry does not have subject matter, because it is the subject. We are the subject matter of poetry, not vice versa.

K: Could you distinguish your statement from the ordinary idea, which it resembles in every particular, that poems are about people?

A: Yes. Poems are about people and things.

K: Then when you said "we" you were including the other objects in this room.

A: Of course.

K: What has this to do with putting a statement in a poem?

A: When statements occur in poetry, they are merely a part of the combined refractions of everything else.

K: What I mean is, how is the fact that poetry is about us connected to the use of statements in poetry?

A: It isn't.

K: But you said before—

A: I said nothing of the kind. Now stop asking me all these questions.

K: I'm sorry.

A: Now I'll ask you a few questions. Why are you always putting things in Paris in all of your poems? I live there but it seems to me I've never written anything about it.

K: Isn't "Europe" mainly set there?

A: No. Reread that poem. It all takes place in England.

K: What about the gray city and the snow valentines and so on? Even though the main part of the narrative obviously takes place on the flying fields of England, the real psychological locale of the poem always seemed to me to be in Paris. No? Where were you when you wrote it?

A: In Paris. But there is only one reference to Paris in the entire poem.

K: Well, I wrote "Ko" in Florence.

A: I wish you would answer my question and also explain—

K: And there is only one reference to Florence in it, but the way things come together and take place always seemed to me very dependent on the fact that it was written in Florence. What did you want me to answer?

A: Let's ignore for the moment at least your enigmatic statement that the way things come together reminds you of Florence—

K: I did not say that.

A: Anyway, I wish you would explain for me and our readers—

K: Listeners.

A: —why we seem to omit references to the cities in which we are living, in our work. This is not true of most modern American poetry. Shudder.

K: Hmm. I guess we do. I did write one poem about New York while I was in New York, but the rest of the poems about America I wrote in Europe.

A: I repeat, why we seem to omit *almost* all references—?

K: I find it gets to be too difficult to get through my everyday associations with things familiar to me for me to be able to use them effectively in poetry.

A: Snore.

K: I myself am bored by my attempts to make abstract statements and wish I could do it as facilely as you do. I'm going to cut out my previous statement. What made you snore?

A: Well, if you're cutting out your statement, then my snore naturally goes with it, I suppose.

K: Maybe I won't cut it out. Or I might just keep the snore.

A: It sounded too much like the way all artists talk when asked to explain their art.

K: Yes, I agree. I dislike my statement. Why do you suppose we are so bothered by such things?

A: It's rather hard to be a good artist and also be able to explain intelligently what your art is about. In fact, the worse your art is, the easier it is to talk about it. At least, I'd like to think so.

K: Could you give an example of a very bad artist who explains his work very well?

A: (Silence)

K: I guess you don't want to mention any names. Why don't you want to mention any names, by the way? Especially since I once heard you say that names are more expressive words than any others.

A: Some people might get offended. I don't see the point of that.

K: Do you mean you're afraid?

A: No. Just bored in advance by the idea of having to defend myself.

K: Have you ever been physically attacked because of your art criticism?

A: No, because I always say I like everything.

K: Would you say that that is the main function of criticism?

A: If it isn't, it should be.

K: How can one talk about what should be the function of something?

A: Our problem seems to be to avoid it.

K: To avoid what?

A: Talking about what you said.

K: Let me go back a little.

A: That's always a mistake.

K: All right, I'll take you at your word. But we were getting on to something interesting—but it went by so quickly.

A: This is true of much great poetry.

K: And even truer of the rest of it. I was thinking today as I drove over here what my poetry could possibly do for me or for anyone who reads it. I thought it might make people happy temporarily.

A: That's a pretty tall order.

K: I know. I was just going to change the word from "happy" to something else.

A: I'd be interested to know what you were going to change it to.

K: Maybe to "pleasantly surprised."

A: Now you're talking!

K: I was thinking about that and about what seemed the uselessness of it all. In fact, I think about that a lot.

A: Is Joseph Dah your ideal?

K: In which phase? As an action poet or as a regular poet, which he becomes after the death of Andrews?

A: As an action poet.

K: I was thinking about that in the car today, though I didn't think about Joseph Dah. I was wondering if there was some way to make one's actions as varied and interesting as poetry. I then thought probably not, since I would get too tired, and also there is the problem of getting older and weaker. This made me think about whether it really was possible to retain some degree of strength and youth in one's poetry even though one's body is getting weak and old. Then I wondered if there was any point in doing this. I thought that if I was wondering if there was any point in remaining young and strong and in being great and happy, then I must be bothered or depressed about something else, since in what I have usually considered my normal states I am very interested in these things. Thinking thus, I drew into the Hazans' driveway and we began this interview.

A: Do you have any idea about how you could make your actions more varied than they are?

K: Absolutely none.

A: Your witness, Mr. Defense Attorney.

K: You're a wit and I see that you are obviously going to win this interview.

A: I don't like to think that I might have wit. It's the one chink in my nonexistent armor.

K: Your last remark would indicate that you don't have to worry too much about it.

A: I'll pass over your use of the subjunctive and return to the "problem." What is the nature of our poetry? I mean, first, is it poetry? And second, does it have a nature?

K: A third question might be whether your poetry and mine are sufficiently similar to be discussable as "our poetry." Let's just say they are; otherwise we'd have to make too many distinctions as we went along.

A: Can you think of an example of poetry?

K: Yes. Though it depends on what you mean by the word. There is, after all, a certain well-deserved opprobrium attached to it.

A: Mmmm. But just what is this opprobrium and who deserved it? I was reading recently in a book by Jean Paulhan that ever since the nineteenth century poets have been contemptuous of poetry and novelists of novels. In fact, somebody—I believe it was Sainte Beuve—once criticized somebody else—Balzac, I think—by saying, "Ça tombe dans le roman"; and Victor Hugo prided himself on not being "just a poet." On the other hand, you hear a lot of painters these days say that the only thing that interests them is painting. Since I brought up the subject of paintings, I would like to mention that the spaces between things seem to be getting bigger and more important.

K: Do you mean in painting or in life?

A: We'll work this out later. Meanwhile, I once read that as music becomes less primitive and more advanced, the intervals between the notes get bigger. Compare the "Volga Boatman" with the Love-Death from *Tristan and Isolde*. A lot of our good painters seem to rub out most of the picture these days. It gets harder to make the connection between things. Now I'd like to quote a line of your poetry in order to prove this. (Long silence.)

к: Why don't we use some of your lines instead?

а: Okay. Toss me my book.

к: Do you mean you couldn't find any examples in my poetry?

а: Mmmm. You cut out all of your incomprehensible poems.

к: No, I didn't. What about "January 19th"?

а: *"Lorna Doone fizzled the dazzling icicle pencil by sheer blue shirts."*

к: What are the spaces in it?

а: The words that would explain the relationships between these various things.

к: You mean that would explain how one could fizzle a pencil by shirts?

а: That's right.

к: Could you please give me an example from your own poetry, to make it clearer?

а: I think it's already clear enough but I will if you insist.

к: It is quite brilliant.

а: Nonsense. *"Night hunger/or berry . . . stick."* This isn't such a good example as a matter of fact.

к: Why?

а: What with the prevailing climate in poetry, these lines seem perfectly crystalline to me and should to any reader with a normal I.Q.

к: When you say "crystalline," do you mean that the lines mean only one definite thing?

а: Well, not more than about four at the most.

к: It does seem obvious. A man is hungry for berries at night and goes out to get them with a stick. Or else he goes out to get them and he is touched on the face by a stick—part of a branch. Or the berry itself is hungry at night and looks to the stick for refreshment, which it does not get from it. Or the berry is so hungry at night that it dies, its whole branch dies and later becomes a stick. Or a man is hungry for berries at night, goes out to get one, and it sticks to him. Or the berry gets so hungry at night that in its hunger it attaches itself to something else and gets stuck to it. These seem to me just a very few of the meanings related to all the possible meanings as our galaxy is to the sum total of all galaxies.

а: Since none of these meanings is very interesting, what was the poet's point in making it all so ambiguous, assuming that this itself was not the point? I mean making it ambiguous so as to conceal the apparent lack of interest in the various ideas expressed.

κ: Well, if you are following the poem and if you come to a place where you don't know if you're a man or a berry and you keep going along anyway, then you're having a mystical experience. Lines like these enable the reader to escape from his ordinary consciousness of himself. Aside from which, it's very enjoyable to feel like a berry or a stick or a person you know nothing about.

A: I don't know as I'd care to feel like a berry, let alone a stick, and I too often feel like a person I know nothing about.

κ: What's his name?

A: If I knew his name, I'd know something about him.

κ: Go on with what you were saying about your line. What's your answer to your question?

A: No, I was just wondering if ambiguity is really what everybody is after, but in that case, why?

κ: People seem to be after it in different ways. Actually one tries to avoid the Cleanth Brooks kind, no? It seems an essential part of true ambiguity that it not seem ambiguous in any obvious way. Do you agree?

A: I don't know. I'm still wondering why all these people want that ambiguity so much.

κ: Have your speculations about ambiguity produced any results as yet?

A: Only this: that ambiguity seems to be the same thing as happiness— or pleasant surprise, as you put it. I have a feeling that since I am assuming that from the moment that life cannot be one continual orgasm, real happiness is impossible and pleasant surprise is promoted to the front rank of the emotions. Everybody wants the biggest possible assortment of all available things. Happy endings are nice and tragedy is good for the soul, etcetera, etcetera.

κ: You speak after my own heart, but you speak more as an aesthetician than as a man. Perhaps there is really no distinction between the two, but some pleasures do free one from desiring others.

A: Name one.

κ: The pleasure of relief from pain frees one temporarily from the desire to suffer.

A: So the desire to suffer is a pleasure?

κ: No, desire is a pleasure. But suffering is accounted a pleasure by many. Let me put it another way. Relief from pain frees one momentarily from the desire to take great risks involving pain but which might lead to some small pleasure.

A: I think that ambiguity includes all these things.

κ: An obviously evasive answer, but I'm afraid we're off the subject anyway. A better example is that if one is passionately in love, one does not desire a lot of other people. In fact, love sometimes makes people indifferent to pain and even death. I know this is true, both from books and from experience.

A: I won't embarrass you by calling attention to the obvious flaws in your argument. Getting back to my favorite theme, the idea of relief from pain has something to do with ambiguity. Ambiguity supposes an eventual resolution of itself, whereas certitude implies further ambiguity. I guess that's why so much "depressing" modern art makes me feel so cheerful.

K: Could you go back now and explain what you felt when you wrote those lines about the berry?

A: Afraid not. I had even forgotten the lines, let alone having written them. And this has some bearing on our topic of discussion.

K: Many poets don't ever forget what they've written. I can see our forgetting our lines either as good or as bad. Do you forget any place in which you've lived or anyone you've liked very much? I mean within the last five years.

K: I don't quite see what the point of that is. I mean, writing a line of poetry isn't the same as living someplace.

K: I was just thinking of how your forgetfulness might be criticized—that is, from the point of view that what you write doesn't mean enough to you for you to remember it. I don't agree with this criticism at all. I just thought my remark might stir you into explaining why you don't necessarily remember your poems.

A: If you don't agree with this criticism, then perhaps you'd be kind enough to explain why, since I fear it's a very telling one.

K: I don't believe that you do. If you did, you'd memorize your poems.

A: It seems to me that forgetting plays a bigger role in our poems than either of us is willing to own up to. Not only do we forget the place where we live, as I pointed out earlier—

K: You did not say that. You said we didn't write about the place in which we live.

A: Well, we might just as well have forgotten it, for all the difference it makes. Also, what about sex, which seems to make no appearance in either of our works—that I can think of at the moment?

K: Do you mean the details of sexual intercourse? Practically every poem either of us has written seems to me to be about love in some form or another.

A: Well, so what happened to those details?

K: I hope they are still there.

A: Look again.

K: Yes, I've just gotten word that they are still there. On the other hand, there are a number of things that would not be there at all if we didn't write about them.

A: Does this mean that you think these things are important?

K: What things?

A: Whatever it is that's there.

K: Do you mean the things we write about or the details of physical love?

A: The things that wouldn't be there unless we wrote about them, blockhead.

K: It is you who are a blockhead for not making your questions clearer.

A: Maybe this has some bearing on the topic of our discussion.

K: In what way?

A: I can't remember what it was that we were talking about.

K: You seemed to be talking about ambiguity, and then you seemed to think that being a blockhead has something to do with it.

A: I think we should clear up the question as to whether ambiguity in our work is the result of modern life's having made us so ashamed of our experiences that we cannot write about them in any other way, or whether we feel that if we turn quickly around we'll discover something that wouldn't have happened otherwise.

K: The first possibility you mention I don't understand—how can "modern life" make us ashamed?—but the second is very appealing. I don't feel, by the way, that what I am after in my work is ambiguity.

A: What do you feel that you are after?

K: Guess.

A: I give up.

K: Do you mean to say that you have been reading my poems all these years thinking, "Ah, there he's succeeded in getting that ambiguity he's after" and "Oh, there he hasn't"? I mean, you don't really think that a main aim in my poetry is to be ambiguous, do you?

A: Well, it would help if you would consent to give a straight answer to my last question.

K: I think the difficulty of my doing so has considerable bearing on the topic under discussion.

A: Since you refuse to reply unambiguously, I must conclude that ambiguity is the central thing in your work.

K: I have always liked your poetry, but your command of logic leaves me speechless with admiration.

A: Perhaps this has some bearing on the topic of our discussion.

K: I don't see how.

A: I assume that you were being ironic when you said my command of logic left you speechless with admiration. Therefore poetry is not logical or is not necessarily so.

K: What you say is very unclear, but I suppose you mean that since I find one of your remarks illogical and since I like your poems, that therefore I must like poems that are illogical. But I don't find your poems either logical or illogical. If you want this interview to have the logic of a poem and not ordinary logic, we will have to start over again.

A: If you don't find them logical or illogical, then what do you find them?

K: Your question doesn't make any sense.

A: Neither does your poetry.

K: Do you think there's only one way of making sense? We seem to be trying to trap each other into making pompous statements.

A: Yes, we seem to be determined both to discuss poetry and not to discuss anything at all. This is probably what we do in our poetry. I only wish I knew why we feel it to be necessary.

K: I should think if we really wanted to know why we felt it to be necessary, that we could probably find out. I don't think we really care.

A: You're right.

K: Perhaps there's an element in our poetry of not wanting to be too definite, not wanting to name things too clearly, in order that nobody else can possess any one of them independently of the whole poem. But the statement I have just made, although it seemed rational to me when I made it, now seems to me to make no sense.

A: Does this ever happen to you when you write poetry?

K: Constantly. It's very exciting when it does; if one writes fast enough when this is happening, one can catch the movement of the mind, which is, I think, something I care about very much, more than ambiguity, for example. Of course, it's true that the mind perceives everything ambiguously. I think we may be close now to an answer to our problem.

A: Why does catching the movement of the mind seem important to you?

K: I knew you'd pick up that bit of critical gibberish. But I rather think you know what I mean and that you are stalling for time.

A: Whenever I read a sentence, including a line of my own poetry, I am beset by the idea that it could have been written any other way. When you are conscious of this when you are writing, it can often be very exciting. I respond to works of art that express this idea, such as the music of Busoni, the main element of whose style is that it didn't necessarily have to sound this way.

K: Do you think the kind of art you and I like and create might be called "evasive"? Do you think we like the feeling of ambiguity and multiple possibilities partly or wholly because we don't want to be pinned down to anything we've done or are about to do?

A: Possibly, but I think that if we like things that are evasive, it's because there is no point in pursuing something that is standing still. Anything that is standing still might as well be dead.

K: What about overtaking something that's moving clearly in one direction or meeting something head on? I mean, why this passion for two things at once? Obviously, it corresponds to reality. One sleeps and is in bed at the same time. But why is this so important to us and other artists?

A: I don't understand what you mean about sleeping and being in bed at the same time.

K: Oh. That was just an example of how simultaneous actions or states in reality correspond to those in art. I mean, all aesthetic attitudes or ideas correspond to the real state of things. We could just as easily be so warmly interested in the concreteness of everything, or in its human or divine qualities, as we are in its ambiguity and multiplicity.

A: But all these things you mention do constitute multiplicity. It seems necessary to illustrate this fact by examples.

K: Would you say that's why you write poetry?

A: Yes.

K: For whom do you do this illustration?

A: For the average reader.

K: Do you expect to help him in this way?

A: No, I expect him to help me.

K: How?

A: By drawing my attention to the fallacies of my approach.

K: Has any average reader ever done this for you?

A: No, but I'm still hoping that he will. That's what keeps me going.

K: You would say that you write, then, chiefly in the hope of being corrected?

A: I think I've made myself sufficiently clear and would welcome a few statements from you. How about criticizing some of my poetry, for instance?

K: Which one?

A: Well . . . "The Suspended Life," for instance. I rather like this poem, but I don't like the first part so much. As often happens, it was necessary to write it in order to get to the more interesting part, but by that time the uninteresting part had gotten thoroughly enmeshed with the rest and could not be removed without causing its collapse.

K: Which part do you mean by the first part? I think the whole poem is terrific.

A: The part up to the first space.

K: Why do you like the first part less?

A: The lack of connection between the sentences doesn't refresh me. Also, there are too many things like your work. Such as the "tooth weather information clinic" and "the button's pill." I am more interested in the conversation in the middle, and I only really like the landscapes at the end.

K: I think "And sudden day unbuttoned her blouse" is one of the prettiest lines in the world. I'd like to talk about "Europe" for a moment. It seems to me to present a whole new way of relating words to experiences and to each other. Since many people find it very hard to read, could you give them any suggestions for making it less so?

A: No.

K: Were you consciously trying to be ambiguous in "Europe"? Were you conscious of having big spaces between things?

A: I guess so. I was trying to conceal the plot of a book I picked up on the quai called *Beryl of the Biplane*. At the same time I heard a piece on the radio by an Italian composer who had taken a recording of a poem by Joyce and transformed the words until they were incomprehensible but still gave an idea of the original. I got the title from the name of a subway station in Paris. It seemed to me that I was at last permitting myself to allude to Europe, which had been my center of activity for several years, but by merely listing a lot of things and situations that could be found in most other places as well and by keeping the ceramic title of the subway station firmly in mind, it seemed to me that I could convey the impression that Europe was just another subject, no more or less important than a lot of others. I suggest that you not ask me why I was doing these things.

K: It seems clear enough why. You didn't use any cut-ups in writing "Europe," did you?

A: Yes. I used some passages from *Beryl*. I think I might also have put in a few words from an article in *Esquire*, as well as a mistranslation of something I saw written by an automatic toy in the museum at Neuchatel—"des mécanismes précis nous animent," which I misread as "nous aiment."

K: There's no key to understanding the poem, of course, no hidden meaning?

A: No, it's just a bunch of impressions.

K: Why is the idea of keys and hidden meanings not appealing to you?

A: Because someone might find them out and then the poem would no longer be mysterious.

K: I feel the same way. Do you use any deliberate methods to make your poems mysterious?

A: I don't know, but it just occurred to me that detectives and detective work crop up quite often in our poems. As, for example, your sheriff searching for a walnut; a poem that I have always found beautiful without knowing why. Perhaps it's because the idea of someone searching scientifically for something is beautiful, even though I have no desire to imitate that person.

K: I think what I was feeling when I wrote those lines was that the frenziness of the search for the walnut was like the emotion I felt for the woman the poem is about. I wasn't thinking of a scientific search, actually. Could you tell me why the figure of the janitor occurs so often in your recent work?

A: Possibly because of "The Janitor's Boy" by Nathalia Crane. He's a love-death symbol. On page 93 of *Ko* is the memorable line, "*Some towns of course are famous for two things.*" This seems to be typical of your habit of making an absurd abstract statement as though there was no point in trying to make any other kind. I find this typical of the defeatist attitude which pervades your work and which I greatly admire.

K: Such statements seem to me not so much defeatist as affirmative. I feel that we need a lot of new things to think about.

A: I'll accept that. It seems to me a reasonable place to end this interview.

■

PAUL BLACKBURN

Sonofabeech

_____

The sea is great tonight, full
            tide, the moon
flashing all over the Narrows.
On the Brooklyn side the lights move
down Belt Parkway at 60 mph, and are gone
the shell of the Verrazzano Bridge stands
slim and black across the neck of the bay.

Only from the long line of spray
            at Rockaway, where the sea cracks up
                        on the moon-dark sand,
                                    LISTEN!
you can hear the grating roar of
beercans that the waves draw back and fling
at their return upon the crapped-out lovers,
            stop, go
            again, and then hang back once more
the dull-assed cadence slow and bring
the eternal note of hangup in.

Ginsberg, long ago, heard it off the Tangier beach
and it brought into his mind the turbid ebb and flow
of water in his toilet bowl in East 2nd St.
It brings also to our minds a thought
hearing it by this Far Rockaway.

The sea of cunt was once too at the full
and round the Manhattan Island shore
lay like the folds of a great shining used condom
the financial district full of sperm.
But now I hear only its long withdrawing squush,
bored in the sunrise, retreating to death in the nightwind,
down the small-breasted ex-virgins, drear and naked fingers of the
      world.

O love, let us be true to one another,
for the island which seems
to rise before us like a land of dreams, each
one so various, so beautiful, so new,
hath really her second diaphragm, or takes Enovid, or
hath a good abortionist in Delaware:
and we are here as on that darkening square of bed
swept by confused accordions of polak, wop, and kike,
where ignorant mick and aeshkenasz get smashed by night.

■

PAUL BOWLES

from *Points in Time*

She dreamed of a hawk that hovered. An omen, the others said. And when they went down to Asana a beggar stopped them at the entrance to the town. He raised his finger and spoke.

Pay heed to the wind that moves above this place.

The woman saw his face and thought again of the hawk. She sat before him in the dust. Behind, the walls, and higher were the hills, white and hard in the noonday sky.

The drums you hear are not those of our people. Nor are the hands that hit the skins.

And they did not enter Asana, but turned southward over an empty plain, and two days afterward they came to the bank of a river. Here they rested. Of Asana no wall remains.

■

RICHARD BRAUTIGAN

Love Poem

It's so nice
to wake up in the morning
    all alone
and not have to tell somebody
    you love them
when you don't love them
    any more.

■

30

R A Y   B R E M S E R

Rolling with the Wind

---

cylindrical empressario roll on by me barrelling!
    the dusty, august & impressive totempole turns to stare!
what is this rolly-ol, this fat around the pillow case
    i sudden see &, captured by momentum, join the fare?

        (it's my olden rollerskates
          tonight transports me; i
          the former phantom of New York;
          i the latent prisoner of speed
          whipped around pylons otherwise
          totempoles, whose seventy thousand
          countenances repell & disinherit me!

THIS IS A BANKED TRACK AROUND WHICH
SHOOT 20 PERCENT INSANITY FOREVER!

        (Van Cliburn play
           Tchkowski on enormous
             symphonic piano accompanied
               by timpani & flute . . .)

        I am a DEAF & A DUMB
          MUTE; *allatime gibbering* . . .

once go-round; two around, thrice go-round, four . . .
a mile in Just this number/two times more!
on the left-bank is old rolladium heros;
    The Jersey Jolters! Detroit's Death Defying
          devils . . . now the graceless
            intercom/startles the vague
              steel skating-rink with court-list:

criminal court, part 1-A; criminal court, part 1-B;
Bronx County Supreme Court, part 83; Manhattan
Arrest Court; Night Court; Gamblers Court; general
sessions, part 2-A; part 2-B; part 3-A; B,C,D, & E;
Felony Court; Magistrates Court; Supreme Court Clinic;
Domestic Relations Court; special sessions, 1-A;
special sessions, 1-B; 1-C; 2-A; 2-B; 3! Richmond
Superior Court, part 1700; charges, F.O.A.; 3305;
1751; homocide; lethalcide; sunnyside 6-5000! this
is Pennsylvania! Hartz island! Rikers! Sing Sing!
Auburn; Dannemora; Attica; Great Meadow; Bellevue;
Matawan; Central Islip; Pilgrim State, oblivion . . .

still, the robin goes around, the bank of track is
45 degrees . . . the Washington Jets Bake birthday-cake &
knew you were coming . . . a banjo strumming;
    (Thelonious Monk plays
     rootie tootie—i am deaf
      and dumb & (one miles run, keep
       running O cylindrical empressario on
       the go!

■

WILLIAM S. BURROUGHS

"a man of letters
une poème moderne . . ."

a man of letters une poème moderne purred back his young
    American friend
am sure control machine gives you pain lighted length of time
    hysterical reactions
for he had a mouth injury one ugly story related pretty baby please
the countess inert and repulsive approached some entrail throw
    latterly in
exorable down spiral modest obscene old man of letters placebo
    tablet the
druggist pushed into the electric psychiatrist fierce as the desert
    vulture
sniffed the cocaine up viciosos something of an ancient cave
    painting with
human blood has been found interesting theory from the shop keeper
    he purred
out eyes narrowed to grey slits why that's deadlier than cocaine suck
riches from phosphorescent stumps a good claret yes sir oui oui
    Beaujolais
on the darkened dance floor flickering closer with the knife people
    die
believe it very long and before that most of them do how the recipe
    discreetly
seasoned fell into our hands I don't know Japanese person sometimes
    le comte
emitted a sharp cold bray of laughter died when their batteries an
    inch from
the wall he enjoys quality job you're fired gave out a son malheur
    his foot
men stepped closer pretty little blue eyed teen ager pass it on craps
    last
house mountain lake the pack around and maybe boy holds up a
    string of trout

■

GREGORY CORSO

Holiday Greetings

---

last night was at its nightest
the moon full-mooned a starless space
as sure as snow beneath snow is whitest
so shall the god surface the human face

■

"Beauty swells within me"

Beauty swells within me
I look down and O
My feet of mountains!
Above the clouds breathing
Epical gulps of starched air
I've a belly—
Like all India in solo pregnancy—
Belching thunderous wisps
Of laborious poesy

■

An Egyptian Mistress' Loveglyphs

O Potter
who wheel'd the proto-egg
how so lovely a man you were
when so young a boy

And those hands!
How often in anatomical class
(the true reason why
I choose Thebes over Memphis)
I'd fancy their divine rapes
whenever they rose to gesticulate
the air into pharaonic shapes

But all the years it took
to chip the god from your eyes
Chip chip year after year
until the shape
like a ton of sun
did finally materialize

■

For Ignorance

I owe nothing to the Phoenix
The Empress has been paid
Let the Fool try and collect
The Knight deserves what's owed him
The Wanderer will settle for a mere token
I say pay the player and be spared his hysteria
The Dealer will do the paying hereafter
As for the Magician death is a debt twice paid
Screw the Hangedman's aleph legs
The Earl of Reverse has dealt
    the Ace of Cups a rat
The Comte St. Germain knew where to go
    which is more than can be said
    for the Marquis and Balsamo—

■

ROBERT CREELEY

Echo

_____

Pushing out from
this insistent

time makes
all of it

empty, again
memory.

■

"Bolinas and Me . . ."

_____

For Stan Persky

Bolinas and me.
Believe me.

Roy Kiyooka
not here

says that.
Say this.

The human,
the yearning,

human situation
wanting something to be,

which is.
What's wanted?

Let the man put the gas in
your car, John, e.g.,

complete doing what
you wanted him to.

Have *done* with it?
Ham on rye.

The sea, the drive
along the coast in L.A.

I remember Joanne. I
want to. She's

lovely, one says.
So she is. So

are you too.
Or one. Have

done with it.
You see that

line or rocks out there?
Water, waves, two

dead sea lions,
says Peter. He's

lovely. All of them.
Let's walk down

to the beach, see
the sea, say.

If you love someone,
you'd better believe it,

and/or you could,
could write

that all night,
all right. All wrong.

All—isn't enough.
I want to get going. Here's love.

Drive home, up through the mountains,
dense fog. See the car lights

make way of it. See
the night, all around.

Bleed, into the toilet,
two nights, two days,

away from whatever,
go home, and stay there?

I want to walk around here,
look at the people, pretty,

look at the houses, stop in
the bar, get the mail, get

going again, somewhere.
One, two, three, four.

Husbands and fathers.
Sweet love, sweet love.

The kids come
by on bicycles, the little,

increasingly large
people, in the rain.

The liquor store lights
shine out in the night,

and one is walking, going,
coming, in the night.

Holy place we stand in,
these changes—Thanksgiving,

in the circle of oaks,
the sun going west, a glowing

white yellow through the woods.
To the west all the distance.

Things move. You've come here
by one thing after another, and are here.

Flat thoughts in recalling
something after. Nostalgic twist

of everything so thought—a
period of thought here.

Hair falling, black tangle,
standing in front of the fire,

love dancing, silent, a figure,
a feeling, felt and moving here.

After all it speaks
less in saying more. It, it—

the hunk of wood is
not burning.

Marriage burns, soars—
all day the roar of it

from the lovely barnspace.
The people, the plentitude of all

in the open clearing, the sunlight, lovely densities. I am

slowly going, coming home. *Let
go, let go of it.* Walking

and walking, dream of those
voices, people again, not

quite audible though I can
see them, colors, forms,

a chatter just back of the ear,
moving toward them, the edge

of the woods. Again and
again and again, how

insistent, this blood one
thinks of as in

the body, these hands,
this face. Bolinas sits on the ground

by the sea, sky
overhead.

■

FIELDING DAWSON

On Writing Novels

One of no doubt many ways to regard writing novels is, for those as myself who enjoy brevity, to regard the necessary bulk—involving terrific detail and a continuity beyond our habit—as a reach to our most extreme limits, a stretch of the mind as happy as the body after a long, deep sleep, in awareness of the day ahead, so the intellect alert is as the body alert—to new action.

Aside from the usual "form of the novel" dogma, there are, it seems, two primary considerations. One in the form of a warning: keep characters few, and distinct. The other is—an absolute must IF the desire is for a compelling tale (if not, none of this matters)—never fail the awareness of each character's point of view: this is the heart of the matter of writing novels. Good story, location, description, dialogue, plot, are the stuff of standard, hackneyed formula, and indeed useful. But distinct voices, each with an individual point of view, is the fulcrum, and in the end, the tale itself.

Action evolves from character, which creates the form and arrangement of narrative on the page, thus the whole.

I don't write how I do it because I'm pretty sure I'm doing it wrong, so I shan't pass on wrongs. The way to do it right is to consider beforehand a viable outline—or tale—involving a few characters with their point of view. Yes, this is the formula, practiced since Defoe, but the formula has grown stagnant, and needs a change. Pretty words for a skull-cracking task, more often than not thankless at best while in process, and in the exhilaration of completion, terror of failure, for it has to work.

The essential problem involves the human paradox of the stretch of the imagination to the limits of creative capacity made readable and compelling: the farfetched made routine, the fantastic plausible, and if you read me right you'll see this paraphrase of Melville, to further which, writing novels is twin to writing plays; thus, fiction (if the intent is realism, none of this matters) is of theater, where action evolves from the characters presented, each of whom has a point of view. And if each point of view is different, or unique, one understands the thrill of someone agreeing with someone else.

The standard formula practiced by ex-journalists and academicians is first of the story, the plot. Next get characters to fit, give 'em appropriate detail, describe scenes of action, add dialogue.

I say story comes from character, and from character comes theater, from which the novel emerges and so too the screenplay, and, over and over I've said it, but here with a twist, neat and nifty to place point of view so high on the list, but how to be at ease writing it? Write essays.

The essay is the sublime point of view. Thus, with a few characters involved, using theater, we may establish—no matter how incredible—interesting, solid voices of reason or unreason that form different points of view, discovered through writing essays, which have to be written to be discovered, which is why the essay is the root of the novel, and the writer the victim of the art; like pouring water on a sleeping cat, one never knows quite what will happen, all hell breaks loose, be aware that writing novels is an act of forethought, thought and afterthought, with an ear for the stage, an eye for vision, a taste for nothing but the finest prose, a smell for the worst, and that beautiful, open, endless tingle, in the space of what lies ahead, which, I say, at full, yet exact, end shall be left intact.

Hear every word, and their patterns. How? Read William Carlos Williams (Paterson I-II) out loud—note his line breaks!

Keep syllables on the mono line, make it a discipline. Beware big words. Create original voices. Reject thoughtless language: whatever, share, enjoy. Have a nice day.

Never write like people speak because people speak gibberish, or, if that's the desire, catch all the stammers, stutters, slips, changes of mind, bad syntax, advertising catchphrases, hums, spittle, unhs, nnnhs—our common spoken language *is* nonsense. Learn how black, Chicano, Spanish, and Orientals speak English (American); it is *not* as Eddie Murphy speaks: white hacks write his script. And this is why writers cheat, take shortcuts and create a false drama, because to actualize our common language is too much work, and a paradox on top: the people who speak it are too ignorant and lazy to write it in context, and we're too educated and lazy to try. But in any event, no matter, the tale we tell must be compelling, period. Chandler invented a language to work it his way. He was a poet, in the beginning, and an essayist.

Hear every word, and their patterns. Word, sentence, paragraph, chapter, book, section or part, to the entire completion of the narrative, and type the words, lower part of the page, at center: The End.

Lean to understatement—with passionate exceptions—as a rule, to be without fail rewritten, as passion is, for the difference between writing and speech in writing is written, and rewritten and speech can't be. That's explanation, and we know that drag—unless that's the mode! If so, pursue that form, with those demands, from that stammer or press secretary point of view.

And last, take a tip—or two. First, while writing the novel, read a book that keeps continuity and doesn't interfere: I read Dickens's *Pickwick Papers* while writing *Ladder*, and early Eric Ambler and again Chandler while writing *Spitfire*, two masters of prose style that encouraged, without interference, my work. Know, however, that a new prose will be rejected, as mine is, and that its fate stands in the glare of the road ahead, into which we write.

■

EDWIN DENBY

Sonnet

You can have the measurements O.K.ed, mailed,
Talk with the bank, and get the building faced,
Carry it on the books, and when the firm's failed
Pedestrians still go by the slabs as placed.

Pride shifts from this accomplishment to that,
Leaves old killings and half a city built,
The noise that smoothed it like a swimmer's fat
Disintegrates into Sunday bits of dirt.

Measurements however in straight angles to
The pavement and a standpipe do not so move,
As if the mind shifts slower than people do
And keeps widening the space between love and no love.
This widening like a history mystery
Is what Rudy's camera takes in the city.

■

"An eye is wide and open like a day"

An eye is wide and open like a day
And makes a sign in an American field,
The field of lettering, which reaches each way
Out to the section-line and does not yield,
Stops simply at that imaginary line
That begins a like life in a like square,
A neighbor's other name and other sign,
From here (like) you can see Ray's silo over there.

■

44

In Salzburg

Fingers broke heavily a table-top, cold
the fleshfalls, skins displaced, baring kinks, frequent cut,
square, plane surface,
on forks, on tumblers of liquid, cheap, on news,
on peak, on backward,
feels the rollers for ill knuckles, benefit, side,
feels almost green color, like a nose, or a,
flings wet cloths, muffed through
for a chair leaned there heavy square table
weighing.

■

In Shepherds Bush

Very carefully, I wrap the metal foil
                              around each finger
      and cast it in the stuff.

The foil is paper thin
                  and then I make it thinner.
            with my other hand's fingernails.

Sometimes the foil splits in a lovely Egyptian way.

(It came clothing chocolate.)

(I am very careful to peel it off carefully.)

I have finished all five fingers
                        and lay them on the brown table
         I am sitting at.

Now I arrange them the way they are
                        supposed to lie down.

Thumb first, then the index finger,
                        etc.

I am stricken with fear.

What if I get killed going home from here?
                              and all that's left
                  of
                  me
               are these thin casts
                  of my fingers
                        on
                  my right hand.

      I am left handed.

■

DIANE DI PRIMA

Poem in Praise of My Husband

I suppose it hasn't been easy living with me either,
with my piques, and ups and downs, my need for privacy
leo pride and weeping in bed when you're trying to sleep
and you, interrupting me in the middle of a thousand poems
did I call the insurance people?   the time you stopped a poem
in the middle of our drive over the nebraska hills and
into colorado, odetta singing, the whole world singing in me
the triumph of our revolution in the air
me about to get that down, and you
you saying something about the carburetor
so that it all went away

but we cling to each other
as if each thought the other was the raft
and he adrift alone, as in this mud house
not big enough, the walls dusting down around us, a fine dust rain
counteracting the good, high air, and stuffing our nostrils
we hang our pictures of the several worlds:
new york collage, and san francisco posters,
set out our japanese dishes, chinese knives
hammer small indian marriage cloths into the adobe
we stumble thru silence into each other's gut

blundering thru from one wrong place to the next
like kids who snuck out to play on a boat at night
and the boat slipped from its moorings, and they look at the stars
about which they know nothing, to find out
where they are going

■

Night Life in Casper

Sore throat, sore head & soul; let's go
dancing tonite sez Frances (knowing
I loved to dance) Mike Hanna
picks us up, we go to
the Holiday Inn! funky
cocktail piano, funky cocktails
pernod & water for me; beer
& tomato juice for Mike; harvey
wallbangers for Frances. A lot of
talk w/a nice NY Jew who lives
& politics in Casper (unsuccessfully)
More talk w/his smart but alcoholic wife.

Let's try
the Ramada, sez Frances, we do.
Two fat & funky country western people.
A navy career man from Colorado tells us
about the Communist Plot.
Mike Hanna rhumbas.
I dance free form, San Francisco
style. I ache
all over; demand to go home; take baths.
Make fires; try to get warm.

October 24, 1972

Waikiki Room, Minneapolis

curried shrimp (not very good) again!
no need to eat another cow!
Europe around me: accents, paranoid talk
of escape from Poland during ww ii
of fear of now returning—had he killed
that border guard? Waiter polite
& reassuring—brings him saddened waitress
w/a cracked diamond. Polish lawyer
assumes professional role—his turn
to be reassuring. All my guilt
at not being wasp in Wyoming, not agreeing,
voting for McGovern, recognizing
myself in all those Indians & girls
locked up at Sheridan, begins to drop away.
it's ok to be me! Even if
I forgot to get a ticket before I went
for my buffet. It's OK
to be dark, remember other languages,
wear a long skirt, dont have to slink
(in yr soul, while wearing a brave front)
before those dumb, steer-like, castrated
                              but mighty
oil-lords & politicians, judges & legislators
whose frightened wives are drinking themselves
                              to death
all over beautiful Wyoming.

O wonderful eastern city, Minneapolis,
                    gateway
to two worlds, I feel the net of anglo-
                    America melt
as I sign my check, saunter to elevator
unpack my Buddha, let the chilly wind
from Mississippi blow thru my
dusty room.

                              October 26, 1972

49

EDWARD DORN

You can't fall out from
an *at ease* position

───────────────

Looking through the hole
he sees a man lying crushed
beneath a truck
composed of yellow plastic
and beside him is a dirt popsicle stick
or is that a flat finger
caught in a golden paperclip
wrapped in a package
of unfocused attribution

Now the man has been silent
for a long time
It is pointless to guess what
he can do
for he is plastic too

■

Paranoia, Incorporated

───────────────

(a conversation

Do you see any agents
& instrumentalities of the state
Out There?

Yes my liege, they are
Everywhere
the Instrumentalities
Out There!

■

50

The history of futures

The long horn was an automotive
package of hide & bones, a few hundred
pounds of dope that delivered itself
entirely free of moral inconvenience
otherwise known as fat
yet with a memory fresh enough
to respond

The Bloody Red Meat habit
dates from about 1870
Before that we were a Sowbelly Nation
Beef is the earliest element
of the energy crisis, a typical
Texas result

Importations from Argentina
are meant to satisfy
the Bloody Red Meat habits
of our best friends—you don't
want your best friend eating guts
and shit like that!

With foodstamps we have pure script
Which brings us
to a truly giant dog
the most immense friend conceivable
A Fenrir created by beef heart
And there you have your apocalypse, Ladies & Gentlemen
One morning he gulp; swallows the Sunne

■

Electric Hat

Pictured in my window
the sunne is shining down
flashing on a foot of snow
rollin like a fresh white sheet
all the way to the street

Then a man comes into view
pulling a loaded sled
out of the sunken confines
of the black overwhelming avenue
He is keeping his head warm
with an electric hat

■

Executioner, stay thy cold blade

As knowledge grows
it becomes apparent
that the brain
is a machine
of a type
very different
from those made hitherto
by the thotfull
    efforts of man

Its success is largely due
to the richness
of its parallel circuits
and its redundancies

This makes it very difficult
to assign particular functions,
especially
by the technique of removal

■

L A R R Y   E I G N E R

a plane in the hot sky

———————————

    raw sunny days
    cool cloudless nights

        Got up   there   pretty early as
        time goes

         all kinds
           of traffic   you shdve
               see

                Put shirt on or sweater with a hand
   and a fist but not a stocking. hm. It just takes
  the thumb and 1 or 2 fingers,   more hardly does
work.   Nothing possible if too tight

    Again we're living near an intersection, corner.
Not busy. Trees. Four different houses. No gas.
Behind and before walk lawns curbing retains.
White street at any level;   Cast away
things far away out of sight,   on a dark sea
  out of light.   the sun comes out
                                  among leaves
    on the roof a man
        to the delivery boy   working

        on a curtain of sound
      from next door

          it's a waterfall enough
        over time

a plane in the hot sky
      I didn't get what they were saying
the warm earth

    t h o s e

bad times

    not thinking

        much

          now

    ■

KENWARD ELMSLIE

Easter for Anne

---

        movies in my head
pesky Eskimo-ies
won't play Loews
        audience fled
        too much amphed—

as in congradulations.
Anne, congradulations.

The Bijou
want squeeze you.

It's a vestigial age
that can cram onstage

jewels and gams
     femmes

       gems
     femmes

that's us up there
moving through wild air

where Jackie Curtis
shows what hurt is

love and pain
singing in my brain

The Man That Got Away
waking up make-up on today

■

Hand

The hand, wizened but sprightly, circled the round toolshed, hunting for Romulus and Remus in what it took to be the total chaos of Outer Space. The dissonance that sounded like time moving backwards, faster and faster, was actually the racket some pals of the Dawn Brigade (out scrounging for circuits) were making, hurling hard balls of mica at zombies (this is what's so ironic)—victims of amnesia (this is what's so ironic) but elephant-sized, standing in the endless swamp.

■

WRJ

Real big haw haw mistake. Stick accordion-pleated bits of paper under laces. Boots.

Outfit.
Local outfit.
With a local outfit.
He's with a local outfit.
Partic. if he's with local outfit.

Every person developed a tricky double nature, and an awareness of how crazy destiny really is swept through just about everyone.

"Roberta."
"Roberta" Grand.
Ex-All-America Grand.
Grand Family. Grandson.
Grand Family. Grandson. Al Grand.

Seven summers running, farmers complained. Bring back cows, crows, rows. Not quarrels haw haw haw. Betcha thot—

Al's graduation present from "Roberta" was a take-out food place franchise on the thruway. Above long-horn skull red neon arms baste red neon carcass (blinky bones) with 1-2-3-4-5 baste sequence, blue neon juice driblets arc up and down, up and down: same time. Same time red neon lips open wide 1-2-3-4-5 sequence plus tongue that looks real comes out and licks upper lip then down to lower lip plus Good God let's eat song come out with big celebrity singer walking along to tip of tongue (looks real). She's The Mither Sister Cass whose Car-Cass Chain is all over country. Right under tongue, two horizontal red neon arms. Hands almost touch. One has yo-yo. One has I.D. bracelet: Al. Biff never did find out what Yo-Yo Champ Prize was. Mayor drowned out by garbage disposal unit parade. Nice of Mither Sister Cass, the added neon and all. Downpour. Everyone scrambled for safety and drove off. Biff & Al laughed so hard their stomachs hurt. Curl up in red mud. Lie there, laugh away. Snail-pace landslide. Franchise bldg. edges onto thruway. Neon speed-up, maniacal basting, arcs go nuts. Yo-yo! Who's Champ now, Yo-Yo, haw haw haw. Their cocks start to stiffen and they forget they're in rags and pals.

Al.
Back to Al.
Out trout-fishing with the regular team when he looks down and sees paper flowers, a whole garden coming up out of the clear pool, attached to each other with strings, plus a flag with one word on it: FLAG. Haw haw haw goes the whole gang.

THE TINSEL OF RELIGIOUS VOCAT	THE TINSEL OF RELIGIOUS VOCAT
THE MYSTIQUE OF FOREI SEAPORT	THE MYSTIQUE OF FOREI SEAPORT
NO LONGER CONCERNED THE YOUNG	NO LONGER CONCERNED THE YOUNG
THE DREAM MATES BOBBED FOR MU	THE DREAM MATES BOBBED FOR MU
OLORED APPLES INJECTED WITH S	OLORED APPLES INJECTED WITH S
IN-CROWD OF SIX-FOOTERS RELEN	IN-CROWD OF SIX-FOOTERS RELEN

Rough talk turns to sweet talk as the shadows lengthen. Biff sticks the one shuttle-cock in the whole local area for miles around in his hair and prances around like a road-runner (score tied too). Whole team bombards him with small pieces of reject coal they'd picked up walking along the trestles earlier in the day on the way to the out-ing. Hour after hour, Biff'd sped by them in his green roadster, with the co-ed mannequins roped into position in the rumbleseat, so he'd seem popular. Biff wasn't even looking at the road. He was too busy kissing someone who was deliberately keeping out of sight in the front-seat, just running the tip of his tongue along the blond eyelashes glinting in the sun, back and forth: his passenger's head was propped up against the steering wheel, facing him.

As his contribution, Al recited a list of pet peeves. Coffee. All up and down Main Street, trumpet vines cover up the upstairs windows: leaves.

Coffee.
Blows on coffee.
Al blows and blows on coffee.
Al gulps down a big swallow of coffee.
Waitress comes by and fills up cup with more coffee.
Ooga-ooga. Pause. Ooga-ooga. "What's the rush? Finish your coffee!"

Another time, peeped thru keyhole of Biff's weekend cabin, only to see an eyeball—staring—back—at—him! Eyeball goes away. "Roberta." "Roberta" struggling with back zipper, with one hand. Other hand, holds onto droopy string bag, empty. Floor covered with groceries. T.V. on kitchen table, but Biff blocks screen taking off jockstrap.

■

At the Controls

Though I'm not a woman
falling in love overnight
leaving nothing for the children to quarrel over

    L   equals the old El, rattling through my dreams.
    o   equals multiple-choice olive grove
    v   equals vicuña we snuggle over and under, got shredded,
    E   equals eggs in the morning, easy over

        pyramids, scrambled eggs, hallway, smelly eggs,
        morass, bus, bus depot eggs,
        grease-monkey always smiling up at me eating my eggs,
        on my pants, field, dinosaur eggs,
        flying down to Rio, handsome, huevos,
        g'wan, the siding, open transom eggs,
        dawn, sunny side up, showered at the Y,
        second balcony, rooftop, back of truck,
        scrambled egg sandwich, oeuvres, gallery eggs,
        Bogotá, dried wartime eggs, car, rented car,
        hotel eggs, motel eggs, motel eggs, hotel eggs,
        Harlem, boxcar, yachts riding out the storm,
        eggs on the rocks, crack,
        sleep, cracks,
        bed, bed eggs,
        sleep eggs
        closing out intruders

                ■

ALLEN GINSBERG

Bixby Canyon Ocean
Path Word Breeze

Tiny orange-wing-tipped butterfly
fluttering sunlit
from violet
blossom to violet
blossom

Ocean is private
you have to visit
her to see her
Garden undercliff
    Dewey Pinks,
        bitter Mint,
  Sea Sage,
       Orange flaming
          Paintbrush
   greenspiked fleurs,
  Thick dainty stalked
        Cow Parsley,
  Starleaf'd violet bushes,
  yelloweyed blue
      Daisy clump—
red brambled mature sour
         blackberry briars,
yellow budded
      Lupine
    nodding stalkheads
    in Sunwarm'd
       breezes
by the brooks tricklet
    wash in the ravine
        Bridged with cloud

Ruddy withwine morning
        glory's tiny tender
                        cowbells,
        guarded by poison oak sprigs
                        oily hands
Green horned little
            British chickweed,
waxlight-leafed black
                seed stalk's
    lilac sweet budcluster
Ah fluted morning
    glory bud
            oped
& tickled to yellow
        tubed stamen root
        by a six legged
            armed mite
        deeping his head
        into sweet pollened
                        crotches,
Crawls up yr veined
        blossom wall
        to petal lip in
            sunshine clear
        and dives again
        to your tongue-stamen's
            foot-pipe, your
        bloom unfolded
        to light—

        Above ye the
        Spider's left
        his one strand
            catgut silk
                shining
                    bridge
        between
            cookoospitted
                mint leafheads
        & newgreen leafsprig'd
                seedy lilac

Granite Sagely
    Browed above the Path's
        black pepper peapod marge—
Grey rock dropping
    seed,
withered bush-fingers
        tangled up
        stoneface
    —cracked with
        green stalk
                sprout—
Brooktrickle deep
    below Airplane
        Bridge
                Concrete
    arches balcony'd
    Pendant over
    Oceancrash
        waves
falling empty eyed
    breathing water
                wash afar

Morning Night shade
    in alder shadow'd
Pathside—Nettle plant
    Leaf-shoulder
    vegetable wing'd
    baby faces,
        green earmouths
                sprouting
    Celery handspread
        Heal-All mudras
    open asking why me.

Sunlight trembling
        branch-leafy willow,
yellow haired wingy bee's
            black horn
bowed into threadpackt mauve
        round thistle mouth,
    dewey web throat

> green needle collar'd,
Symmetric little
> Cathead erect
> electric thorn'd
> under giant hogweed
> stalked parasol blossoms—

Ash branch's tender
> pinecone cluster
> proffered by leathery
> sawtooth rib leafs

red browed beedle
> perched on Egyptian
bridge of Spider fern's
> soft-jointed spike-sticks
Brown water
streaming
> underbrush
sparrowsong
> winged brown
> whistling above
cold water pebble
> silver pour . . .
Shrowded
> under the
Ash spread, on
> damp leafwither,
shield tubes
> & condensers
> of small Sony
> TV machine enwired
> rusty w/resistances

giant grass
> leafspears
morning glory hillside
> perched over clearing
All branches lifting
> up
> papery seedhusks,

parasolspiked Fern
       Tramping together
           upright pushing
               a thistle aside,
      groundwheat leaned
      by beach path—

Oh ocean white-
      waved pouring
   foamy noises over
      rocky sandshore
Chevrolet writ
  on radiatormouth
Set above
        Private Land
Do Not Enter
   incised wood
      Sign-beams

Frying chickens from
   Arkansas!
Musselshells'
    Briared graveyard
       footplot—
Dewey round bushes
   guarding ocean
      path with
 myriad greenstar'd
    leafarms
  cradling white-walled
        dewdrops

Telephone
   pole trunk
stuck
   out of old
   landslide head

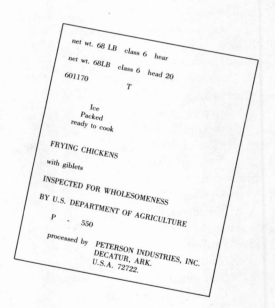

net wt. 68 LB   class 6   hear
net wt. 68LB   class 6   head 20
601170   T

Ice
Packed
ready to cook

FRYING CHICKENS
with giblets

INSPECTED FOR WHOLESOMENESS
BY U.S. DEPARTMENT OF AGRICULTURE
P   -   550

processed by   PETERSON INDUSTRIES, INC.
DECATUR, ARK.
U.S.A. 72722.

Covered with iceplant
green lobsterclaw
  trefoil solid
        edged,
pinked with
hundredfingerpetaled
  Sea vine blossoms
Dry brown kelp
  ribs washed
  in a heap at
  streamside in
    wet brown sand
    to listen to
      oceanroar
    and wait the
    slow moon
      tide.
Stream water
  rushing flat through
beachmound
  Sand precipices,
tiny wet arizonas
flood lips
      —cliffs
cradling the last
  greysmooth boulders
  shat by the rains
pissed out
  by spring storm
    from
the forests
      bladder
      hills
  Small granite
  blackpocked
    hearthstones
  washed to last rest

Ocean wavelet's
            salt tongue
            touching
            forward thru
             sand throated
            streambed
             to lave foam &
            pull back bubbles
            from the iron
         Car's rusty
               under carriage
                  kelp pipes
                     & brown chassis,
                  one rubber wheel
                     black poked from
                        Sand mattresses
                           rock wash

O Kerouac
         thy broken
         car Behold
      Digested in
      Saltwater
            sandbottom
      giant soulless
         Chicken
            sea gizzard filled
               with unthinking
            marble rocks—
      Poured down
         road in
            avalanche!
      to the granite
         snout of the
                  seacliff

O see the great
            Snake kelp's
      beet green head still lettuce-
                  haired
            stretch forth
                  a fingerthick tailroot

66

above seaweed broider
            wavelets
      rushing foam
                  tongued—
Was that kelp
      Intelligent
Einstein hairleafed
      faceless bulbhead

Oh father
      Welcome!
   The seal's
      head lifted
   above the wave,
   eyes watching
      from black
            face
   in waterfroth
            floating!
Come back again!

Huge white
waves rolling
in grey mist
birds flocking
   rocks foamed
   floating above
   the
      horizon's
         watery
            wrinkled
               skin
   grandmother
      oceanskirt
         rumbling
            pebbles
   silver hair ear to ear.

May 28, 1971

■

Wyoming

A mountain outside
a room inside
a skull above

Snow on the mountain
flowers in the room
thoughts in the skull.

■

Mugging

Tonite I walked out of my red apartment door on East 10th street's
     dusk—
Walked out of my home ten years, walked out in my honking
     neighborhood
Tonite at seven walked out past garbage cans chained to concrete
     anchors
Walked under black painted fire escapes, giant castiron plate
     covering hole in ground
—Crossed the street, traffic lite red, thirteen bus roaring by liquor
     store,
past corner pharmacy iron grated, past Coca Cola & My-Lai posters
     fading scraped on brick
Past Chinese Laundry wood door'd, & the broken cement of stoop
     steps to For Rent hall door painted green & purple Puerto
     Rican style
Along E. 10th's glass-splattered pavement, kid blacks & Spanish
     oiled hair adolescents' crowded house fronts—
Should I have brought a harmonium chant N.Y. blues at Ramsey
     Clark Poetry Rally?—
Ah, tonight I walked out on my block N.Y. City under humid
     summer sky Halloween,

thinking what happened Timothy Leary joining brain police for a
season
thinking what's all this Weathermen, secrecy & selfrighteousness
beyond reason—
Walked past a taxicab controlling the bottle-strewn curb—
past the young fellows with their umbrella handles & canes leaning
against the ravaged Buick
—and as I looked at the crowd of kids on the stoop—a boy stepped
up, put his arm round my neck
tenderly as I thought for a moment, squeezed harder, his umbrella
handle against my skull,
and his friends took my arm, and a young Puerto Rican companion
tripped his foot 'gainst my ankle—
and as I went down shouting Om Ah Hum to gangs of lovers on the
stoop watching
slowly appreciating, why this is a raid, these strangers mean strange
business
with what—my pockets, bald head, broken-healed-bone leg, my
softshoes, my heart—
Have they knives? Om Ah Hum—Have they sharp metal wood to
shove in eye ear ass? Om Ah Hum
& slowly reclined on the pavement, struggling to keep my woolen
bag of poetry address calendar & Leary-lawyer notes hung from
my shoulder
dragged in my neat orlon shirt over the crossbar of a broken metal
door,
dragged slowly onto the fire-soiled floor an abandoned store, laundry
candy counter 1929—
now a mess of papers & pillows & plastic covers cracked cockroach-
corpsed ground—
my wallet back pocket passed over the iron foot step guard
and fell out, lost void, taken by fingers, stole by God Muggers—
Strange—
Couldn't tell—snakeskin wallet actually plastic, 70 dollars inside my
last bank money for season,
old broken wallet—and dreary plastic contents—Amex card & Manf.
Hanover Trust Credit too—and business card from Mr. Spears
British Home Minister Drug Squad—my draft card—my
membership in ACLU & Naropa Institute Instructor's identifica-
tion
Om Ah Hum I continued chanting Om Ah Hum
Putting my palm on the neck of an 18-year-old boy fingering my
back pocket crying "Where's the money"
"Om Ah Hum there isn't any"

My card Chief Boo Hoo Neo American Church New Jersey & Lower
    East Side
Om Ah Hum—what not forgotten crowded wallet—Mobil Credit,
    Shell? old lovers addresses on cardboard pieces, booksellers
    calling cards & all—
—"Shut up or we'll murder you"—"Om Ah Hum take it easy"
Lying on the floor shall I shout more loud?—the metal door closed
    on blackness
one boy felt my broken-healed ankle, looking for hundred-dollar
    bills behind my stocking weren't even there—a third boy untied
    my Seiko Hong Kong watch rought from right wrist leaving a
    clasp-prick skin tiny bruise
"Shut up and we'll get out of here"—and so they left,
as I rose from the cardboard mattress thinking Om Ah Hum didn't
    stop em enough,
the tone of voice too loud—my shoulder bag with 10,000 dollars full
    of poetry left on the broken floor—

November 2, 1974

■

The Little Fish Devours the Big Fish

WHEN THE TROOPS

GET THEIR POOP

AT FORT BRAGG

HOW TO FRAG

SANDINISTAS

LEFTIST NICAS

OR GO BOMB

GUATEMALAN INDIANS

MAKE A TOMB

FOR MEN & BOYS

ENDING JOYS

OF VILLAGES

AND PILLAGE

OR BURN DOWN

TO THE GROUND

LITTLE HUTS

WHERE PIGS RUT

THIS COSTS MUCH

TAX MONEY AS SUCH

FOR AN ERROR

OF RED TERROR

HYPOCRISY

IS THE KEY

TO SELF DEFEATING

PROPHECY

YEVTUCHENKO

ERNESTO CARDENAL

ALLEN GINSBERG

ROCK 'N' ROLL

SENTIMENTAL

& RELIABLE

& POETICAL

THEREFORE URGE
WASHINGTON
& HAVANA MEN
TO RELAX
& REFLECT
THAT THE AXE
ON THE NECK
OF NICARAGUA'S
A BIG ERROR
OF WAR FEVER
DOUBLE BIND
MAKES US BLIND TO
SELF FULFILLING
PROPHECY—
IF YOU'RE WILLING
LOSE YOUR EYE
& YOUR EAR
MAD WITH FEAR

HYPOCRISY
IS THE KEY
TO SELF FULFILLING
PROPHECY

YOU CAN BET
MARXIST THREAT
STARTS WITH THAT
SELF FULFILLING
PROPHECY
IF YOU'RE WILLING
TO ADMIT
THAT THE THREAT
OF INVASION
OF A NATION
MIGHT CAUSE THEM
GREAT ALARM,
MAKE THEM ARM
TO RESIST,

MOBILIZE
TO INSIST
THEY WILL FIGHT
BACK ALL RIGHT
THEN TO CONDEMN
THEIR ARMED MEN
AND NOT MOLLI-
FY THEIR FEARS
IS SHEER FOLLY
O MY DEARS!

HYPOCRISY
IS THE KEY
TO SELF FULFILLING
PROPHECY

UNITED STATES
YOU'RE THE GREATEST
SUPERDICK
YOUR BIG STICK
& BIG MOUTH
NORTH & SOUTH
CAUSES FEAR,
ARMIES NEAR
AND ARMIES FAR
OR ARMY TALK
WHEREVER YOU ARE
MAKES FOLKS HERE
THINK YOU'RE QUEER,
BIG GUN BOATS
THAT YOU FLOAT,
BIG RUMORS
THAT YOU DOTE
ON WILL BE QUOT-
ED IN MANAGUA
SANTIAGO
BUENOS AIRES
& HAVANA
AS MORE DREAD
THREAT OF WAR

AND CENTRAL
AMERICA WILL
MOBILIZE
MILITARIZE
AND DEVISE
A DEFENSE,
IT'S COMMON SENSE.
THEN TO COMPLAIN
THAT THEIR PLAN
TO FIGHT BACK
IS A PAIN IN THE NECK
OF THE PENTAGON—
IS CRAZY MAN
WASHINGTON
IS CRAZY, MAN.

HYPOCRISY
IS THE KEY
TO SELF FULFILLING
PROPHECY—
IF YOU'RE WILLING—
COSTS AN EYE
AND AN EAR
MAD WITH FEAR

11PM Intercontinental Hotel Bar
Managua Nicaragua January 25 1982

■

BARBARA GUEST

Oh Laudanum

This ridiculous valium
this semi dosage for mini hysteria
this fragment
this paper chase!
this hare!

O those white chickens don't flutter
there is not a head cut off
the airplane did not crash
I am not alone at the bottom
of wherever the rabbit . . .

Elizabeth Barrett Browning!
I need you now
I need your laudanum
your velvet chaise
even Florence and its statuary
I would exchange for this loose masonry

Here!

where it rattles around
and there is only a surreptitious yellow
valium
to cause the air to hesitate

Elizabeth
there are circles under my eyes, also
and there are rims to my feelings

I have difficulty crossing bridges
even the front gate is subterranean
I wish you were here to take the subway
then I'm sure you would share
that spoonful of laudanum

we would not discuss sonnets
or politics or the difficulty
of hair hanging loose
or where silk parries the skin
or even the Italian aristocracy

I can see that spoon in your hand
the drops one after the other
filling it

later with dropping eyes
we might regard one another,
and heavy with the gaudy flower
listen dolce e lento
to melons sliced in the near room.

■

DONALD HALL

7 Poems

You hate animals
that kill birds.
I see you under low leaves,
eyes fixed.

. . . . .

When you woke you turned
over to me, kissing. I thought
you were Lynn Redgrave, out of the play
the night before. I was embarrassed,
I hardly *knew* you!

. . . . .

We walked in small streets
finding green balconies, and turned
into a green and yellow
alley of artichokes, pears
in triangles, tomatoes and lettuces;
crabs moved
gradually, half-certain.

. . . . .

Morning in bed, then
three hours apart. I carry you
in the sudden twitch
of my shoulders.

. . . . .

Taste cold
as if you ate stone.
Wear cold
as a skin
to keep in the blood,
the pulse
of the spirit which digs
itself a hole, leaves
and dead grass
loosely together above it,
against the snow.

. . . . .

This sadness!
I wrap myself in it like bedclothes
that give off cold.
I take walks in it.
There are no rabbits in it.
For an hour
it was a small room with no doors
where I lay still.
Then I was not waiting for anything
and the room opened
to my big empty house full of doors.

. . . . .

The radio keeps talking.
It tells me news and weather
and feelings
about products and sadness,
boxes and boxes of sadness
available in the neighborhood
of last year's flies.

■

Story

"Mama, show Billie-Jean how you can sit on your hair."

"Mama, let me brush your hair."

Until my grandmother was an old woman, she pulled her hair into a bun at the back of her neck. At night when she let it down, it fell to her knees. Her daughters were always after her to let them brush it. They took it as a personal treasure. And one of the things she hated most in the world was to have her hair messed with. She was tender-headed, but she was also tender-hearted and she'd sit with her teeth gritted after the tangles were out and let one or another of her girls brush the hair that at first was raven black, then salt and pepper, then gray; and by the time it was gray, it was me . . . "Grandmama, let me brush your hair." And when she couldn't stand it a moment longer, she'd snap, "That's enough now!" and take the hairbrush . . . and as quickly she'd smile and be her own gentle self, the snap being a reflex and not anger. It was always a gift to brush her hair.

She was a scant five feet tall and worked as hard as a full-sized man. Especially after she married her second husband who lost everything that came to his hand. He had red hair and a mean disposition.

In Texas when you say of somebody, "He married a redheaded woman" or "She married a redheaded man," you're saying "Look out!" Maybe nobody says it when the redhead's a gentle one, and that's the discrimination. Maybe that phrase itself is a kind of word for redheads who are bad-tempered. Whatever. The fact is: The second time around, my grandmama married a redheaded man who was as sour as she was sweet. It must have been a surprise to her. Her first husband, Mr. Hall, had been a good husband, a good father, and a frugal man.

"The first thing us kids learned about the old man was not to walk in kicking distance," my mother said.

There were thirteen kids in all, lumping together the ones my grandmother had by Mr. Hall, the ones the old man had by his first wife, and the ones they had together. At least the old man didn't show any preference for his own. He was as bad as he could be to all of them.

My mother stood up to him when she was twelve. She was a substantial twelve-year-old. The old man had Sis in the kitchen and was mad at her about something. Sis was the first child he had with my grandmother . . . a sad, scrawny thing all her life . . . she ended up married to a squint-eyed mechanic named Jack who took up where the old man left off. Anyway, "He was hitting her with his fists just like she was a man." She must have been about eight, and my mother picked up a piece of stove wood and said, "You old son-of-a-bitch, if you hit her again, I'll kill you!" And he laid off.

I meant to talk about my grandmother, but it's hard to avoid the old man. By the time I really remember him, he had taken to his bed to die.

He was about twenty years older than my grandmother. She was in her twenties when they married. I must have been born when he was around sixty and he went to bed when he was sixty-three. He didn't pass away until he was in his nineties, so there was some small margin of error there, which nonplussed him not at all. He had a running, full-scale deathbed scene for more than thirty years.

My mother and her sisters would go to Abilene for a visit and would invite Grandmama to come home with them for a while. There were always other people in the house who could tend to the old man.

She'd say, "Well . . . Papa *has* been feeling a little better lately. I'll go ask him."

There'd be a roar from the next room.

"You're doing what no woman has ever done!" he'd yell. "You're leaving your husband on his deathbed. You go right ahead, but know that I won't be here when you get back!" That was his constant theme . . . for thirty years. And Grandmother would come back to say, "Papa isn't really feeling well enough for me to go, honey."

My memory of him is mostly that if he wanted anything, he'd start swearing at the top of his lungs and my grandmother would rush to him saying, "Yes, Papa?"

He wore long-handled underwear for pajamas and at times he'd undertake a minor trip away from his bed, big pooches like air bubbles in the long-handles at the knees and elbows and seat. He'd stomp to the bathroom or the kitchen, glaring and swearing at anyone he met. There was always a sense of scurrying when the old man moved around. Everybody getting out from underfoot.

Apart from the scene in the kitchen, he only got his comeuppance three times that I know of.

The Ku Klux Klan got after him one year when he had made a crop and had money in the bank and was sending my Uncle Marion to school barefoot after the snows had started. One morning there was a note on the kitchen screen door: "Get your boy some shoes. KKK." He paid no attention and three days later a note on the door said, "We're coming for you tonight. KKK." And he took Marion into town and bought him some new shoes.

The second time was: In Texas in the summertime when it's really hot, the practice on farms is to pull the metal bedsteads out of the house and set them up under trees or on the side of the house opposite to where the sun rises, and everybody sleeps out. Well, the old man always woke up before anybody and he always took it personally that the others were still lying there after he slung his legs over the side of his bed. So he woke them by swearing at them. There was a time when he was making Sis his particular scapegoat and he'd jump her every morning. My mother had taken Sis on as her special charge and one night she told her, "Tomorrow morning when the old man starts swearing at you, tell him to go to hell and take out across the sticker patch. I'll bring you something to eat in the orchard."

I want to describe a sticker patch for anybody who's never seen one. In some parts of the Texas plains the stickers are the only green things in sight. They flourish no matter what. They lay out huge and uneven and absolute. It's possible for kids who go barefoot to memorize their local sticker patches like a geographer memorizes maps. It saves time to be able to traverse a sticker patch's bald spots instead of having to go around it.

The next morning in gray dawn the old man started raking the air with his daily message and Sis swung her own skinny, kid-legs over the bed, mumbled, "Go to hell," and set out running with the old man hard on her heels. She hit the sticker patch and immediately shifted into an intricate series of little hops and jumps like Liza across the ice. The old man hit the sticker patch right after her. His momentum overrode his tender feet and carried him five or six or ten feet into it before he was stopped. Like a cripple, a different man, he turned to start the long, hobbling way back, picking his way step by step, walking on the sides of his feet. My mother took Sis some cold biscuits and preserves to the orchard and Sis came home for supper, coming in quietly to take her place. The old man didn't say a word.

The third time was, he did finally die. Most of his "mourners" had tightly pursed lips while the preacher talked about his virtues. But my grandmother really cried. She really had loved that mean old fool.

■

ANSELM HOLLO

he she because how

---

one a.m.
      and she has been sleeping
two hours
      is still asleep

didn't marry him "only to sleep"
but does now
      sleep

because she's tired because
he's been unkind? because

feeling her bones through her sleep
on the floor in their other room

because she's her kind of woman
because he's his kind of man

and because he's his kind of man

and because she is sleeping
      he's writing
moving a few of his smaller bones

words like love and hurt
kindness unkindness blindness
ecstasy jealousy anger
sweetness
      that too
sweetness of making it with you

how do these words hang together
how does his hand move the pen

how do he (plus) she (equals) it hang together
on their still beautiful
(though in his case
                        slightly bent) frames?

two a.m. questions
now make him sleepy too

he'll go wake her up

they won't feel the same

                        ■

In the Mission

For Robert Creeley

god

his
followers
started the place but

god
is not what you think
in the mission

                . . . . .

as the song
goes: "the _good_
times, the _bad_
times"

god knows
back there,
in his snug chair
on the favorite floor

of his perishing tower
wistful
sniffing
a flower:

"*reminds* me of
all of them"

      . . . . .

be a hundred and ten
go to sleep.
say,
"au revoir."

      . . . . .

she used to be angry,
but now she is sleeping:

"oh let me dwell in
comfortable-looking
hole in your facial cheek"

      . . . . .

see see

five short yellow
daffs—narcissi—
whatever they are,

flowers of spring
tra-la, suddenly
in this lone kitchen sing

a scent sweet, it says
"si, si"
. . .

. . . . .

most of life not
that way,
yet one remembers

when it has been, been seen
& heard & felt, & smelled
that way.

. . . . .

c & w

life is complicated
drains are roaring
percy b. shelley
was fond of soaring

in walks a minimalist
he says "that's boring"
he needs to be kissed
by someone complicated

another sweet
big head
to remain entertained
& a bit more alive than dead

. . . . .

high cloud

populous raft of confusion
drifting across the sky
while fur turns gray

. . . . .

rimas: almost eighteen

i haven't lost my mind, you know
although i think, believe, i've found
a woman, most intelligent, most kind
with whom i then proceed to fight
on what i thought was an auspicious night—
about what, neither of us know.

there is the rain, there is the snow,
the dew, the fog, the mist, the glow,
the atmosphere containing us
& the necessity to catch the bus.
hers. mine. possessive forms of action
giving one little or no traction.

so, let it slide, & let's abide, & sigh
as dawn is drawing nigh & fires are lit again
throughout the camps of busyness & gain.

  i love her eyes: love them when they look at me,
  her mouth when it moves, even when not speaking.

   . . . . .

in the summer, he said, i write short

   . . . . .

now that people are wearing hats again
one can tell them go shit in your hat again

   . . . . .

make her laugh: the world
seems like it's staying

   . . . . .

"they only made one of these.
so you deserve it?"

· · · · ·

who's here?

2 powerful democrats
many united beefworkers
some undecided youths
"just white poet trash"
      —the decisive instrumentality

· · · · ·

a high note

leaves one at a loss
for an appropriate quote

& so, remembering, one says "hello"
& says, into dark air, "you're very nice"

rolls over, hugs
oneself, & wants you back

· · · · ·

back in new york

"my sister, life"—last time i saw her
i begged her not to be as literal as me;
old flames, old blames—none there
that precious funky afternoon: yes,

some lives work: somewhere in here's
this romantic boy, writes letters in his head
& in his heart—which are the faces
he makes, in there, inside himself.

& once in a while, he jumps up on the shelf,
& sits there: looking at you: eyes all one color.

. . . . .

whitman's secret

you're not gonna sleep
anyway
you're just gonna lay
around & curse

so why not stay up, brother,
& think about everything

& i mean *everything*

. . . . .

her face, absolutely
two sides

& sometimes, in motion,
unearthly harmonious

. . . . .

"to bed, to bed,
as lady macbeth said"

there was a time
one thought that was funny

an amusing
rhyme

. . . . .

ferocious sociopath
rubs ace of hearts
against his crotch, for luck

un poco buzzed, observing water's descent
upon phenomena, thursday, also césar
vallejo's "bad day"

. . . . .

clarification

not
buying
you:

just
buying
you

a
drink

. . . . .

a kind of vow

make me
a pillow
& i'll
sleep on it
as long as it
takes me

. . . . .

proofreading discovery

inextricably
interwoven

became

methodically
intentional

. . . . .

shiva
takes it
apart &
down,

puts it
together
again
in the ground—

("aahh-yess, shee-vah take it apart 'n . . .")

         . . . . .

not going to read
any of these
to anyone
over the phone
tonight.

tonight is the night
anyone's under the covers
with their lovers
present or not,
present or not.

8:81—8:82
Yerba Buena
a.k.a. San Francisco

■

ROBERT KELLY

(Vera Historia)

———————

particularly the shit
of style
          now for to my
certain knowledge 30 years
the slick blackhaird of
New York have whipped
small combs thru hair
& gazed
thereat
in every circumstantial glass

now pussy is the aim of this
wild root of their secret
smearings
          or even that shy
internal box
a boy may nurture
self-contained:
                    Ganymede too
slabs his onyx hair

                    & even lord
Poseidon when he turns
into a great white-wingd
stud-goose & drives
his waterbolt up Leda's ass

is sleek of feather
(Helen's father,
                    own uncle
to the motorcycle twins,
enemy of simple
halfcocked travellers

who propped up Helen
in the world to show

if a man will follow pussy
just how far he must go

■

The Tower of Babel

Certain men decided to build a tower that would reach heaven.
Week after week they toiled on the plain where bedrock, the
planet's primary shield, offered surest foundation. The tower
rose ever higher and the works ran smoothly. One day heaven
looked down and saw the building coming closer to it. Heaven
grew confused and disorganized. The former unity of its
purpose and consistency dissolved.

Heaven fell. Great flecks and patches of heaven dropped,
landing on the tower and its builders. "We have reached
heaven!" some cried. "Heaven is all over my hands!" one
of them noticed.

There seemed to be no further point in completing the tower.
Or, more precisely, it was not generally realized that the
tower had never been finished; even the canniest builders
tended to confuse the structure itself with the conscious
goals they happened to have had in mind. So far as we can
tell, the tower still stands unfinished, and no one can say
where it actually could go.

■

KENNETH KOCH

The Gold Standard

A mountain shrine in China. Enter two monks.

FIRST MONK:

Sit down. Now let us rest the burden here
Of our exhausted mortal parts and speak
Of things we do not understand. Commence.

SECOND MONK:

Oft have I wondered when I hear men say
That in their land the currency is solid
Because it rests upon a base of gold.
They call it . . .

FIRST MONK:

The gold standard—

SECOND MONK:

Yes, that's it!
And often on some lonely winter night
Which freezes traveler and his poor mount
Who, wandering down some valley side, know not
Which way to turn so as to find their rest,
Oft have I heard men's conversation turn
To gold and to that system too whereby
The currency of any nation may
Be given a solid base.

FIRST MONK:

By the gold standard.

SECOND MONK:

Yes, that's it. But you who seem to understand
Such fiscal matters, tell me now and briefly
What this gold standard fiscal system is.

FIRST MONK:

That I shall try, though of success be never sure
Till it has come unquestioned. Shall not I
Use for example the United States
For there I know the gold is in Fort Knox
And all their currency is based on it.

SECOND MONK:

It's well. Proceed.

FIRST MONK:

Proceed to it I shall.
But where shall I begin? Perhaps with coin,
Yes, that is where I should begin, because
It's there the question rises. Let me see.
If I have here a token in my hand
Of wood or metal, and we say that it
Is "worth five dollars," then what can we mean?

SECOND MONK:

What is a dollar? Tell me that before
You carry any further this great theme.

FIRST MONK:

It is the coin of the United States.
One says one dollar, two dollars, five dollars,
Ten dollars, twenty dollars, ninety dollars,
And so on to a billion. As for smaller
Denominations, they are parts of dollars—
A nickel, for example, is one twentieth
Part of a dollar, and a dime one tenth.
A penny is a hundredth part, a quarter
A quarter part as one might well expect.
There is among the coins also another,
The half dollar—and now my list's complete.
So when I say one dollar now you will
Know what I mean? or when I say a dime?

SECOND MONK:

> Perhaps I'd better have a record of it.
> Have you a plume? I'll write these figures down.
> Yes, now, that's it, I think I understand
> And if I do not I can look that up
> Upon the list which I forget to know.

FIRST MONK:

> Fine, now we have the list and have begun.
> Thus to more difficult matters. If I have
> A token in my hand of which 'tis said
> That is five dollars, in what sense can that
> Be said to have a meaning? that is to say,
> Why should you give me, if I give you this,
> This token that I say is worth five dollars,
> Why should you give me rice, and fish, and ink?

SECOND MONK:

> Because you are my brother, Cho Fu San,
> And I would not deny you anything.

FIRST MONK:

> I asked here for a monetary reason.
> I know, Kai Fong, there is not anything
> We'd not do for each other—but if I,
> A stranger to you, held this token out,
> Why should you give me meat or fish for it?

SECOND MONK (smiling):

> Why, I would recognize you, Cho Fu San—
> That scar upon your hand which healed the cut
> You got in gathering branches in last year
> So we could make the fire at Ho Ku Temple
> Where they had for a time run out of fuel.
> You were much praised for that. Could I forget
> A deed so noble or a hand so marred
> By what it did for selflessness? Besides,
> Even if you had no scar upon that hand,
> What if I did not know your name or face,

What if you came to me and asked for fish
And held a token out—would I not give?
Is not our duty still toward all who need?

I now perceive
How far the concept of all payment is
From your enlightened soul. Yet I'll explain
In a more fundamental way, so that
You may perceive it clearly—for, who knows?
Such knowledge may empower us some day
To do some good we do not know of now.
Attend! You know in the non-priestly world
That men instead of bartering, that is,
Giving a fish for rice, or trees for seed,
Or wives for cattle, or spun silk for tea,
Have worked a system out in which there is
Some kind of general substance which is used
To represent the barter value of
Each kind of thing one needs.

SECOND MONK:

I do not know
Exactly what you mean by "value," brother.

FIRST MONK:

How not?

SECOND MONK:

Well, if I give you green tea leaves,
Say half a pound of them, and you give me
In fair exchange three pounds of rice, shall not
We say, then, that the "value" of a pound
Of rice can be computed at one third
A half pound of green tea?

FIRST MONK:

That is, one sixth,
Yes, one sixth of a pound of green tea leaves
Would be the "value" of a pound of rice.
You seem to understand the concept.

SECOND MONK:

Wait! If another brother, passing by,
Has urgent need of rice, and offers me
Six pounds of green tea leaves for what I have,
What is the "value" of the green tea then
And of the pound of rice?

FIRST MONK:

The pound of rice
Is worth six pounds of green tea leaves.

SECOND MONK:

Then you,
If you should wish to buy your own rice back,
Would find that with your half a pound of tea
You could buy but one twelfth of a pound of rice.
If then you wished some tea along with rice
And tried to purchase some green tea from me
At what we had agreed to be the "value"
Of half a pound of tea, you would receive
For all your rice but one twelfth of one sixth
Of one pound of green tea, which is, I think,
One seventy-second of a pound of tea.
Then if you tried to buy some rice from him
Who had the rice you sold him, and perhaps
By chance had now some more, for all your tea
You would receive, I must take plume and paper,
One seventy-two times six, four thirty second,
One four hundred and thirty-second part
Of a pound of rice is all you would receive.
Then if you wished—

FIRST MONK:

Stop, brother! you are driving me insane!
I have not followed you, I am all lost
In these fine figurings. Let me begin
Another way, that all shall not be lost.

SECOND MONK:

Lost surely to you were much rice and tea
In what I figured out, which I imagine
Was accurately tuned to what you'd said.
Perhaps all currency is chaos—

FIRST MONK:

No,
Let me explain again. At least I'll try.
For night is going past.
And we, in this part of the subject, are
Still far from understanding what the "base"
Of currency may be, and how a standard
Of gold or silver can sustain its value.

SECOND MONK:

But "value"—

FIRST MONK:

Kai Fong, I said that I would try.
I know that "value" is not clear just yet
And yet it is an ordinary concept
Which I am certain we can understand
Together, let me but find the proper words.
In the example that you gave just now,
You spoke of two discreet ideas of value—
For me, the rice was worth less than the tea,
And so for you, at the time of our exchange.

SECOND MONK:

Yes, I can vouch for that. For you gave me
For three whole pounds of rice only one half
A pound of green tea leaves.

FIRST MONK:

But this was done
By our agreement; we did not dispute
The value of these things.

SECOND MONK:

Yes, for the sake
Of finishing our discussion, let us say
That we agreed, although I do not remember
How we agreed, or why.

FIRST MONK:

Then let us say
That we agreed and that there was a reason
We came to this agreement, which was this:
That there is only a given amount of rice
In China and a given amount of tea.

SECOND MONK:

The man who can find out such vast amounts
Must be some sort of Buddha at the least—
For who could know such things?

FIRST MONK:

Why, men may go
To all the villages and ask each man
How much of rice he has and how much tea.

SECOND MONK:

But this would take a thousand thousand years.
China is vast.

FIRST MONK:

True—and perhaps there is no need
To go to every village in the country—
Perhaps it is enough to know how much
Rice and tea there are in one's own village.
Then, if one finds there are ten thousand pounds
Of rice, and fifteen thousand pounds of tea,
One can compute that for one pound of rice
One should receive a pound and a half of tea.

SECOND MONK:

Yes, I have checked it with my plume
And paper, and I find you are correct.

FIRST MONK:

Thus can each village figure for itself
The price of rice in tea or tea in rice.
Then if, say, Village Chu should be the one
In which one pound of rice is worth of tea
One pound and a half, and if in Village Cheng
There were eighteen thousand pounds of rice and nine
Thousand pounds of tea, so that for one
Pound of rice one got one half pound of tea,
Then it would be in the interests of the men of Chu
To take their tea to Cheng and sell it there;
So men of Cheng would sell their rice in Chu.
Eventually there would be established
A common rate for rice and tea which was
Observed in Cheng and Chu.

SECOND MONK:

Which I suppose
Would be—let's see—the total of the rice
In both towns is twenty-eight thousand pounds,
Of the tea twenty-four thousand—both can be
Divided, seven to six. Yes, tea would be
Worth one and one sixth pounds of rice per pound.

FIRST MONK:

See what a brilliant light the moon throws now
Upon our humble floor of straw and reeds!
So man by guidance of superior light
May understand his world.

SECOND MONK:

And we may see
How little we have fathomed yet of all
We have set out to know. Distant still seems
The goal of understanding this our subject.
For what has gold to do with where we are now?

FIRST MONK:

If it is decided
That for one pound of tea one can receive
One and a sixth pounds of rice, then one can say
Let this wood token serve to represent
One sixth of a pound of rice. With six of these
One can obtain a pound of rice, with seven
One can obtain a pound of tea.

SECOND MONK:

Buy why
Would anyone take that which "represents"
In change for that which is? A sketch in ink
May "represent" this mountain, yet I would not
Take it in fair exchange.

FIRST MONK:

Of represent
Two meanings are there—other is the one
I took than that which you have understood.
And yet it serves to introduce the next
Step in the argument that binds us here.

SECOND MONK:

I wished to know, since I cannot eat wood
But must eat rice, why I would take this wood
And give good rice for it.

FIRST MONK:

The reason is
That for "this wood," if given in a trade,
You could receive the same amount of rice
You traded for the wood. Or, if you wished,
Six-sevenths of a pound of tea.

SECOND MONK:

And yet,
What if I traded all my tea for wood
And all my rice for wood, then had much wood,
A thousand thousand thousand pounds of wood,

And what if no one wished to have my wood,
Would I turn termite then to eat my wood
Or would I simply starve for lack of rice
And die of thirst for lack of steaming tea
Which fills the soul with purpose and delight
And reverence for all being? I should not,
I think, give any of my rice for wood
Or any of my tea.

FIRST MONK:

The deepest shades
Of ebony-black night by now are past;
Some stars are gone; few others through the fog
Are shining still; much time does not remain
Till we once more, at dawning, must descend
Into the hills and valleylands below.
I wish, before that come, that on this night
Some further understanding yet might be
Generously given us by One above.
Perhaps I see a way: what if this wood,
Which I agree with you necessity
Would not require to be desired by many
And certainly not all, what if this token
Were made, instead, of gold?

SECOND MONK:

A thing of beauty!
A rare thing also! I would gladly give
Some tea or rice for it, for then I could
Carve a sweet Buddha from it which I'd place
In great Gautama's honor in some shrine!

FIRST MONK:

We have not yet
Arrived at this great argument's full course!
New difficulties show at every turn
And we must show brave hearts to carry on!
What if you did not make a statuette
Of all this gold you had, but if you kept it
And used it, some perhaps for sculpturing,

Both other pieces of it to buy tea
And rice and clothing, to acquit yourself
Of every human need, nor be obliged
To carry rice and tea around with you
To barter for each single thing you wanted?
Would that not be a great convenience
And joy and boon to man?

SECOND MONK:

I think I see.
The gold would "represent" the rice and tea.
Yet also have a value of its own.

FIRST MONK:

Yes, and all persons would agree on it.

SECOND MONK:

What if some person should not care for gold?

FIRST MONK:

Why, he would learn he could get tea for it,
So he would treasure it as he did tea.

SECOND MONK:

I think I see. So by a general process
Of village into village, state through state,
The general value of a pound of tea
Is fixed, as is the value of an ounce
Of gold: but how is gold distributed?
What if a man have only rice and tea?

FIRST MONK:

Why, he can sell some rice and get some gold.

SECOND MONK:

But what if no one in the country round
Have any gold? what would they use for money?
Would they go back to bartering again?

FIRST MONK:

    I do not know. Perhaps the government
    Would have in every village people doing
    Governmental jobs for which they'd pay them
    In quantities of gold, then gradually
    This gold would be distributed about
    So that each person had some, and each town.

SECOND MONK:

    If gold were scarce, might not men hoard it then
    And melt it into ingots, from which they
    Might mould great Bodhisattvas fair as heaven?
    And if sufficient number acted so
    There would not be much gold about, and so
    Men would go back to barter once again.

FIRST MONK:

    Too true. The only answer then would be
    To find more gold and turn it into coins.

SECOND MONK:

    And these, in turn, when hoarders got to them
    Would vanish into Buddhas. And besides,
    The supply of gold, you said, was limited.

FIRST MONK:

    We may be closer than we thought we were
    To the chief subject of our argument—
    Which is how gold which is not used can give
    "Value" to coins and paper bills which are.
    Where we are now, it seems to me, is this:
    That there are serious reasons for not using
    Gold as currency, and one is hoarding.

SECOND MONK:

    What might another be?

FIRST MONK:

Gold wears away.
It is a metal generally soft.
With constant use the wealth of any nation
Would gradually decrease, a sorry thing.

SECOND MONK:

So paper, then, and other things are used
In place of gold—but since they have no value,
Or do not have the value of the gold,
Why do men count them as if they were gold?

FIRST MONK:

That is the mystery of the gold standard,
Which now we must attempt to understand.

SECOND MONK:

Cho Fu San, I had a thought.

FIRST MONK:

What is it, dear Kai Fong?

SECOND MONK:

It did occur to me that I have heard
That the United States no longer used
What we have called gold standard, but instead
The silver standard for its currency.

FIRST MONK:

Your words ring true.
I do remember that that is the case.
I had forgot. Yet still we have not lost
These precious hours of night, for I perceive
We have but one more step to understand
Once we have seen what the gold standard is.

SECOND MONK:

What is it, Cho Fu San?

FIRST MONK:

To understand
How the gold ingots buried in Fort Knox
Can guarantee the value of the paper
In silver, which I think should be quite clear.
For once one knows how much a pound of silver
Is worth in gold, then one can calculate
How much a piece of paper backed by gold
Embedded in the earth is worth in silver.

SECOND MONK:

I take it that the silver is not buried
Instead of gold because, being less precious,
They would need more of it, a great deal more,
And thus would have to dig a larger cavern
And labor terribly to carry down
Into the cavern so much weight in silver.

FIRST MONK:

And, besides,
The huge amount of gold now buried there
Would have to be transported to the surface—
And what, exactly, would they do with it?

SECOND MONK:

Why, they could give it in exchange to those
Who gave the silver that they placed in earth.

FIRST MONK:

Would people give the silver? I believe
That they would bury governmental silver.

SECOND MONK:

How would the government obtain this silver?

FIRST MONK:

From silver mines belonging to the state.

SECOND MONK:

Has it much silver now?

FIRST MONK:

I do not know.
In any case, the gold is buried still
And it is used to guarantee the value
In silver of the paper and the coins.

SECOND MONK:

Dear Cho Fu San, some aspects yet unclear
Are to my spirit. Why should I accept
A piece of paper for a pound of rice
Because some gold is buried in the earth
Which I can neither use, nor hoard, nor see?

FIRST MONK:

I think perhaps that you would have the right
At any time to give the government
The piece of paper and receive the gold.

SECOND MONK:

What? would they dig it up? Suppose each person
Should trade in all his paper bills for gold?
Then there would be no ingots in the earth
Nor any paper bills. Then we should have
Gold coins again—

FIRST MONK:

Perhaps this is the reason
The country has gone on the silver standard.
The gold remains to guarantee the value
Of coins and paper money, but one cannot
Obtain the gold in fair exchange for it,
But only silver.

SECOND MONK:

Where, if not in earth,
If not in some voluminous Fort Knox,
Is all the silver kept which would be needed
To give to everyone in fair exchange
If all decided to turn in their money
For silver bars?

FIRST MONK:

Kai Fong, I do not know.
Besides, if all these silver bars existed,
What need would be to have the buried gold?
For silver itself would guarantee the value
Of every coin and bill?

SECOND MONK:

O, Cho Fu San,
Our cerebrations now must reach an end.
The morning rises, and the mist that clears
Reveals a lightsome snow which promises
A perilous descent. Come on, old friend—
Let those who need possessions puzzle out
The snaggles of this argument. For us,
Who live by other lights, what we have learned
This evening seems enough.

FIRST MONK:

I come, old friend.
The trail is difficult.

SECOND MONK:

Here, take my arm.
We shall find other shelter once below.

■

RUTH KRAUSS

Artaud, Reverdy, and Myself

---

my warm heart
your cold hand
and a bird is flying I
remember
the world
is round you would say someone smiled and it kept on
going a man is speaking an ocean is approaching my
warm heart your cold hand and a bird is flying I

■

MICHAEL McCLURE

The Cloud

_____

For Stan and Jane

WHAT I KNOW IS LIKE
A CLOUD.
I am rushing into
it
as it swells out
behind me
in expanding billows of information
like a green sweater
embroidered with red roses
floating
on blue waves
lapping
in the surf
from
reflected
star
to
star

while motorcycles roar
and I smell
the leather bindings
of old books.

■

Elves

WE
DO
NOT
BELIEVE
that all of the oil that is burned
and the mountains of food
to be consumed
or the construction
of the huge ceremonial
vehicles
will broaden
our knowledge
of
poetry!
We ask for the rainbow
and
the keys
to Elf Land.
Keep your fucking war!

■

.

First Poetry Streak

GREGORY CORSO
your naked
torso
is not a bore.
so
here you are
streaking
at St. Marx!
(You're even in good shape.)
We're larks
of prestige.
We're grapes
speeding past
at 50,000 miles per hour
with our noses
in the press.
The stars forget to dress
and they run naked
as an ape
or cherub
through all the old
cathedrals.
Death to doldrums,
there goes mooning,
beamy
Corso!

■

Stanza from "Xes"

VEILS ADRIFT WE SLIP WITHIN—UNKNOWING.
GRUNTS HURLING FRAG GRENADES. Monk
tranked at his piano.
Dreamers in the painted caves.
GALAXIES ON WALLS. CREATURES
IN THE EYELID.

BINS OF MONEY, OBJECTS,
PLASTIC ARE NO ACCOLADE!
Nor rest, nor sleep, nor ease!
The fork,
the new path,
is back
at the barbarous
DISTORTIONS.

THOU KNOWEST
NO MACHINE

can do this. No

program

no
new knowledge
in the timeless

SLIPPING . . .

■

JACKSON MACLOW

5 Poems for & from Louis Zukofsky
1 May 1963

Z 1.

NOT ELECTRIFIED.
EXCHANGE.
CORN MAYBE?

WHAT IS MONEY? CLOCKWORK.
TIES BETWEEN PEOPLES.
CONGEALED IN MONEY.
MORE OF IT THOUGH.

TO BE ALIVE.
DEAD.
TERRIFY YOU.
ALONE.
WATCHING.

SHORT-CHANGED.
SILLY DEATH YOURS.
SARABANDE NO LOUDER THAN BEFORE.
LONG IT WILL TAKE.
SOMETHING ABOUT THE BEGINNINGS.
OVERNIGHT.

Z 2.

WHAT OTHER FLOWERS?
MAID-IN-THE-MIST, SON.
STRAWBERRIES SO PLENTIFUL.
COAT OF MAIL, HORSE BEHIND HIM?
NOT ME.
PEACHES.
SCAMPERS IN RIGHT, FRUGAL, TOO.

DEAD AND THE LIVING.
FERRET ME?
SECONDING ATTENDANT'S SKEPTICISM.
YOU CAN'T FRY ME.
BEHIND, YOU, THE FUTURE.
A RELATION. DUMBNESS. HANDS.
SHINNING. HEARD STUMBLING.
HARPSICHORD RED LANTERN.
IN A PAUSE OF THEIR DANCE.
DUSTER.

HAVE I ESCAPED FROM DEATH?
DON'T MATTER.
THE LAMP GOES OUT.

Z 3.

GETS DOWN FOR A MOMENT ON ONE KNEE.
WHAT'S TROUBLING YOU?
AREN'T YOU DEAD?

LISTEN.

WE WERE GOING SOMEWHERE,
STEPPING OFF SOMEWHERE.

REMEMBER? FROM ANOTHER WORLD.
SAD RECOGNITION.
WE'RE GOING TO A WEDDING.
AFTER THE DREAM CURTAIN FALLS.

Z 4.

THE MUSIC OF MOZART.
THREE LEVELS.
THE GARDEN TABLE.

AMONG THE NEWCOMERS.

GRACE, GRACE.
PROJECTS THOUGHTS. NOW.

Z 5.

A KIND OF PHOENIX WE HEAR.
UP THE STAIRWAY. STAIRHEAD.

TAKEN CARE OF.
LIVE TO SEE IT.

STAIRHEAD.
WHEN I WAS SMALL, A WALK-UP.
DANCING, I LOVED IT.

TOO MANY RELATIVES, GIRL.
LAUGHS LIGHTLY.
SMILES AGAIN. "I'M NOT TRYING."

CARRYING HER TRAIN, GIRLS.
YOUR EYES ARE SOFTER.
FATHER ON THE STAIRHEAD.
DOCTOR & NURSE GO DOWN THE STAIRWAY.

WALTZING TOGETHER NOW.
BEAUTIFUL.

■

HARRY MATHEWS

Milk Plasma

For Elizabeth Baker

"My name is the Norway lobster. I not only invented an eight-pointed star but I have counted the three milestones." Answer: Bollinger champagne wine.

"I am called the bucranium. Not only have I revived the stone candle: I have uncrossed the guns so they point like quills towards the one-handed clock." Answer: Tequila Eucario Gonzales.

"Turtle and elephant are my names. Not only have I breakfasted with the dragon, but I have also dreamed of volutes followed by successions of volutes." Answer: MacGonigal's Highland malt.

"My name is the parrot vulture. Not only did I tape the beard-headed horse but I have bedizened gryphons." Answer: Old Bush.

"They call me bookish cow. Not only do I rise on the wings of observant gratulation, I also spat on bell cocks." Answer: Marie Brizard London gin.

"I have been hailed as the oblong pulpit. Not only do I drag my scales through the ear-axis but by turning them up through the beard I also stuff out the mouth with fangs." Answer: Yellow chartreuse.

"Does acanthus suit me as title? Didn't I inscribe and decipher, in a spirit of clemency, Justice's indescribable, innumerable rolls? I also bewitched the little siren on her golden, gold-colored lion." Answer: Ballantine's ale.

"I'm called hooks. I have not only deambulated in the dwarf gallery and hung from squinches, I have also clipped the hooks of the madman of the Capuchins—the one they call Emily." Answer: Cacique rum.

"Some call me ASTRONOM. Not only can I bake bricks into volutes, I can also crack milestones into mountains: the very same." Answer: Campari *bitter*—

Mrs. Cinvella resumed her skewers.
These verses follow the cream form.

■

HILDA MORLEY

For Simone Weil

———————————

Would you
             perhaps
write for the poor
               the old
woman who cannot cross the street
                           for weakness

and whose shoes are
misshapen damp rags
                     between whom and her life there stands
no screen, no muffling
element
         nothing at all
beyond reality

         Empty branches
cross the sky in leadings and where
leaves and snow also have fallen
away
      are unburdened!
                    they scarcely
move but are always in
motion,
         reaching
tensely to each other for what
they find: not in loneliness but bound together
to themselves)
               A severity
not strait nor grey
                    except the grey
of light,
         the deeper almost blue
which moves most often
in bending

■

FRANK O'HARA

"Now it seems far away and gentle"

Now it seems far away and gentle
the morning miseries of childhood
and its raining miseries over the schools

Alterable noons of loitering
beside puddles watching leaves swim
and reflected dreams of blue travels

To be always in vigilance away
from the bully who first broke my nose
and so I had to break his wristwatch

I hit him
      it fell off
              I stepped on it
and he
      will never again know
                 the time

A surprising violence in the sky
inspired me to my first public act
nubile and pretentious but growing pure

As the white-caps are the wind's
but a surface agitation of the waters
means a rampart on the ocean floor is falling

All will soon be open to the tender
governing tides of a reigning will
while alterable noon assumes its virtue

■

119

Variations on a Theme by Shelley

1

We live in an opal or
crystal ball. The sun's
an eye, against it clouds
crowd like Spanish castles
on a mountain. Everywhere
colors dampen cling and from
our heat slide into the sky.

2

The shifting roses
of brick and iron
bleed the earth as
we erect trellises
ladders and trees.

3

I don't want my poems
lisped on the numbered
tongues of children. May
they be part of the world
and sight by which we
become the eye and defy
questions with our beauty.

■

"How poecile and endearing is the Porch"

How poecile and endearing is the Porch
it lingers there in the dying light
a school of fish, sacred and wise
Sappho is teaching Socrates is
teaching Virgil is teaching Nadia
and Ned everyone is teaching someone
this is Greek civilization! Come on in

■

FRANK O'HARA & BILL BERKSON

Reverdy

Reverdy is not like Chopin. He is a long city street with small musical houses on it.

There is a word "redacteur" in French of which I cannot recall the meaning.

Here are two cups, a Keats, a comb and a brush, four packs of cigarettes, an ashtray labelled "Chance," two boxes of matches, a rope, *Always Love a Stranger*, a wire brush, and a carved piece of wood which I cannot understand. This is where Reverdy still lives, inexplicably as ever.

What strikes the eye hurts, what one hears is a lie. What is written struggles through, and then has struggled through and is white. The snow lasts because of the sun. Never letters, always messages.

Here we are getting ideas like the French. Yippee!

We discovered many years ago that in French you *can* say anything . . . except certain things which Eliot, Valéry, Claudel, Béranger and others have said. Yippee!

Reverdy is not a cubist. Who ever was? One hundred Americans a day are accused of cubism. "The pubic area of the male is not a thing of beauty." "The public area of the female is not a thing of beauty." (These are two American sayings, showing a lack of Reverdy.)

Picasso is fire, Reverdy is flint. In America flint is used for arrowheads as well as tinderboxes. Do you like to hunt for what you eat? Are you a cannibal? Is there order outside of insanity or just a maelstrom of velleities and mistakes? "Je suis las de vivre dans le pays natal." When you get to the maelstrom, let me know. If you have to pick the ashes off your cigarette, you are born to any given work of modern art. We no longer know what wires are wrapped around us than what air we breathe. We no longer care who is next door; we know how they feel about us. One drinks more than one thinks. There is no sense in coming home "early." We are already in the maelstrom, which is why we don't "know" it. I want to get up "early."

In America there is only one other poet *beside* Reverdy: William Carlos Williams.

They are both alone. How do you feel about titles like "THEY ARE BOTH ALONE," "WAKE UP AND DIE," "YOU DIE WITH YOUR EYES OPEN, DON'T YOU?" AND "CHAIR VIVE, POEM?"

We have made ourselves cretins for Reverdy's sake.

We must all pretend to feel fine or get shot like a horse.

1961

(Written for the French of John Ashbery)

■

JOEL OPPENHEIMER

The Clash

when i was fifteen i read spenser.
two weeks later, in a poker game,
drawing kings over queens, i named
it the *bower of bliss*
                 this knowledge,
of course, came far too early, yet
how was i to know this
                 and now i have
seen women do terrible things, and
known myself also—i have come now
to so many terrors of the clash between
us i do not know what i believe, and still,
and still, and still.

■

In the Beginning

i have few clothes and
many books, you bring
few clothes and many
books, still, have no
doubt of it, the one
closet won't be enough,
and tho in our world
there is always room
for one more book
somehow the clothes
will be a problem. tho
in bed there is no
ending the combinations
there will not be room
in one closet for two
suits four dresses two
raincoats two winter coats
and your new spring topper—
if they still call them
that—and the shoes, my
god the shoes, what in
hell to do with all of
them, not even a plastic
shoe bag hanging on the
door of the closet—we
will move to a bigger
place, two closets, lugging
the books and the bed.

■

PETER ORLOVSKY

Love Poem to
A.J. Mustie

Who, Last night I went
down to A.J.'s grave & tickled
his Kind peasefull Feet—he said
Peter—"Stop Fooling around"
and remember when I was in
court sitting on the late afternoon
of May 15th 1965—on the Frunt
Right Hand side—
the Negro Judge asked me
How do you Plee—arm Forces
day Parade the Smart
c.n.v.a. told me to sit down
in frunt of the Arm Forces Day Parade
and I was shy & Timed and said
yes can I bring my Finger
simbles & sing Hare Krish—okay
but not to louang and just so
Long as it dont interfear with
the Aim of the Sit Down in frunt
of the Armed Shouldges March.
It was my first and only so far
sit Down attempt—
and maybe A.J. is speaking to
me from his grave saying—
Peter—Please Peter—work
on your 641 muscles and
Then work on yr arms—that
combo of Trycept—bi-cept
& Deltoid in the upper Arm
get them big & strong and well
Defined with some Separation
and controll & pack some

added energy streangth
between the split Bi-cept
muscle—and get the full
Try cept muscle to surface
so the whole try-cept muscle
appears in 6 dimension of sight
streangth—not muscle but
something more stronger than
sight streangth—
work on the Arms of your Arms
so that the Army will know
that Arms are arms and not guns
or Bombs but Arms are Arms
Just as Armys are Armed with
Arms of Bicepts & trycepts & the
stripes of the down flowing Deltoid
muscle
Yes, I am going back to the
Land of my arms—when I was
15 to 18 teen my brother Julius
installed in me a growing desire to
develope what mother Nature so Loveingly
gave me—
So I became a trying 185 lbs
barbell set with no stand for
Thigh squatts exercises—
well in short—tho I worked out
in the Hill of Northport—1 to 2 to 3 hrs
3 times a week—and maybe a little
extra on Sat & sunday or not if I
was to lazey or if I dident
Jerk off or Pull of my meat
as it was told to me
or masturbation—in short—
I couldent stop masturbation
asIhavenow
it was always a drain of energy
to put it simpley—I'd jerk off
& when it came time to go thru
my exercises ruteen I dident
spend the 2 or 3 hrs it takes

to finish the Schedual—I
usualley ended with squats
3 sets of 10 repetitions
that makes 30 squats about
& then when I got 18 teen
I went back to my old Neighboar
hood Looking for Julius in
Flushing down Bowne Street in 1950
into a back yard whearlots of weights
and a good bar were, I put them all
400 lbs just about maybe 385 or
390 and tried to Dead Lift them—
well it was a strugle & I dident think
I could Lift it off the ground &
then I said come on Peter
you better do it—
and as I got my back straight
with the 390 above my Nees my
back started to snap
its Spine fingers of Pain that
said to put it down & dont do
this again untill you
slowly work up to handle this
weight—dont be a fool Peter
You are going to ruin yr back
at 18 teen and then kiss all yr
barbells goum by by Charle—
Mother Nature Dosent like you
going greedey after strength
at so young an age—she
has a way of handeling yr
backif you get too greedy for
strength—
So A.J. Mustie—I only wished
I had the simple Intelegence to
of learned more from you when you
were living & seek you out on peasefull
ways to stop Arm Forces Day
March Parade Down 5th Ave
of May 15 teenths of 70ees
and 80ees and 90ees and

2,000ands—I think I'll go and
attend this March from now
on so come this next May 15th
or whenever it is in May, I'll
be there displaying my both
upper bare arms to show
my Progressive Build up—
Yes—Dear A.J. I'll try
to make up for my past
Lazeyness—it's the memory
of you in Court trying to
back me up so I dont get
scard—all the Public assistence
Lywer, a woman would say to
me was why dont I get my
Ponneytail cut—when I
wanted to Plead Not Guilty
they advised me to Plee Guilty
and told me to—that to
plead not guilty—lets not
talkaboutthat but about yr
hair—and I fell for
this pitch—I got finned
$25 that Kind CNVA funded
and Dear A.J. Did you pay my
Fine or did I. Why were you
in court that evening—I dident
know you would appear—
I just happen to pear over
my right shoulder when
I was brought to stand
before the Negro Judge
it was really a kind surprise
yr silent presence in
May 1965

■

"Any Haig-type person"

Any Haig-type person
who thinks of starting another Vietnam-type war in El Salvador
will be cooked in the heart attack soup pot tomorrow morning

6 A.M. sharp,

So says my Mont Blanc pen.

. . . . .

Of course it's not nice to wish anyone a heart attack, not
even Kissinger. The poverty must be fantastic in El Salvador,
as the lady mentioned probably a lot of disease too. I guess
it's a place where you can die very fast.

But the big blue sky shines
very
tenderly
no matter who's dying or living under it.
There was in the *New York Times* an interesting report about a
week ago that said the real problem in El Salvador, in Central
America, was poverty & Uh, poorness, that the malnutrition &
poverty & sickness were the main reasons that caused people
to . . . that had very little to do with Marxism or Communism, or
that the vast difference between the rich & the poor. . . .

I think I saw on tv
David Susskind interview
a young doctor in El Salvador
and the doctor said: something like 40 miles north of El Salvador
is a small city where 10,000 mostly young kids live
that's considered an open fire zone for the Salvadoran government
although most of the population is extremely young . . .

40,000 brand new sinks, 40,000 pianos.

■

JEROME ROTHENBERG

from *Conversations*

(I)

Were you sleeping today?
(Yes.)
And yesterday?
(Also.)
And will you be sleeping tomorrow when the moon
comes back?
(I will be watching the moon.)
Will you be watching the moon forever?
(That question needs no answer.)
Yes.
(The light is dark.)
Yes.
(The light is at a certain distance from the moon.)
Hello.
(The moon is not the moon. My arm is dark.)
Hello hello.
(My arm is not the moon. The moon is hidden.)
Yes.
(Your voice is sleepy.)
We haven't slept in days.

(II)

Forget Jerusalem.
(He forgot it.)
Forget Detroit.
(He forgot Detroit.)
The boat is waiting for us, mother's waiting in the
boat, & there's always room for more.
(He bent down to get under the rope.)
Nice spring day we're having.

(Yes.)
There were seldom days like this when we were young.
(I don't remember.)
Yes.
(Well certainly.)
Forget Detroit.
(I don't remember.)

(III)

A penny.
(Two will get you candy.)
I want a rope.
(I want a pair of bright suspenders.)
I want a rope to swing from.
(I want to suffer, I want to fall on my face like a pig.)
I want you to.
(I want to see someone stop me.)
I'm too cautious.
(I'm not too cautious & I believe in God.)
It's good to be a brother.
(Kiss me.)

(IV)

I can't bite what I can't remember.
(What?)
I can't remember what I can't bite.
(You may be right.)
I can't cry, I can't try, maybe I can't die.
(Maybe you can't try.)
Maybe I can't try more.
(Or maybe before.)
Maybe I can't before I won't remember.
(Maybe the same.)
The same way everyday but today.
(Maybe tomorrow.)
Maybe two Mondays from now.

(V)

On Monday I decided to love those who hated me.
(I will reward you.)
On Tuesday I avoided the eye of a needle & started to sing.
(I will sanctify you.)
On Wednesday I who was small felt that I was growing
larger & larger until I filled the world.
(I will give you my turban for a crown.)
On Thursday I considered no garment beneath me.
(I will make every day a new Thursday.)
On Friday I waited for the revelation of Saturday.
(I will establish my covenant with your seed.)
On Saturday I slept with the floor.
(I will replenish your children who come after you.)
On Sunday I saw no more colors.
(I will enhance you, I will teach your name to your enemies.)

■

JAMES SCHUYLER

A Penis Moon

───────────

twas the night before Columbus Day, '70
and the humidity gave a semblance
of warmth to a day not unchilly, even somewhat clammy.
Some listless starlings pecked in a lackluster way
among the leaf litter: from elms, which crumble in the stillness
                                                    as you look.

A cloud kissed me.
The moon came up like a white spitz
going downtown to get the paper.
A rabbit named Spatsy hops in its cage.
He is eating a pear.
I had a thought, that life should not have uses
saying, "But what *good* is it?" just
"accept with pleasure"ness
then I saw a face

and what use is it, hankering
for what you can't won't ever have?
Here is the spitz, back from Silver's
with the paper. It is the wrong paper.
Shall we beat the dog, or praise him?
Reading of discoveries by woolly moonlight,
it rises today, attentive as one rabbit ear.

■

Letter to a Friend:
Who Is Nancy Daum?

All things are real
no one a symbol:
curtains (shantung
        silk)
potted palm, a
bust: flat, with pipe—
  M. Pierre Martory
a cut-out by Alex Katz:
dreaming eyes
        and pipe
contiguous to
en terre cuite
              Marie
Antoinette
her brown and seeming
living curls
and gaze seen as
reverie: *My Lady*
of My Edgeworth
("Prince Albert in
  the can?" "Better
  let him out, I . . . !")
pipe dream. Some
vitamins; more
Flying Buzzard
        ware:
a silver chain—my
silver chain
from Denmark from
you by way
of London—
(I put it on: cold
and I love it
its weight:
        argento
          pessante)

a *sang de boeuf*
        spittoon
or Beauty bowl,
a compact
with a Red Sea
        scene
holding little
pills (Valium
for travel strain),
this French
        lamp
whose stem of
    glass
Lights softly
                up
entwined with
autumn trees
(around the base
        are reeds)
its glass shade
        slightly oiled
as is the dawn
above a swamp
lagoon or fen where
        hunters lurk and
        down *marc* or *cognac*
or home-made rotgut
    of their choice,
I—have lost
        my place:
No, here it is:
        Traherne,
*Poems, Centuries
    and Three
            Thanksgivings,*
a book beneath
    the notebook
in which I write.
        Put off the light—
the French lamp
    (signed, somewhere)

And put it on:
the current
          flows.
My heart
beats. Nerves,
   muscles,
the bright invisible
red blood—*sang*
d'homme
   helps (is
that the word?)
   propel
this ballpoint
          pen:
black ink is
   not black
       blood.
Two other books:
The Gay
          Insider
—good—*Run*
Little Leather
Boy awaits
assessment
on my Peter Meter.
A trove of glass
   within a
   cabinet
near my
       knees
I wish I were on
my knees
embracing
   yours
       my cheek
against the suiting of
          whatever
suit—about now—
or soon, or late—
(I'm not prompt,"
   you said, rueful
       factual

"I" I said, "climb
walls")
O Day!
   literal
and unsymbolic
        day:
silken: gray: sunny:
   in salt and pepper
tweed soot storm:
guide, guard
      be freely
        pierced
by the steel and
gold-eyed
needle passes—stitches
—of my love, my
        lover,
      our love,
his lover—I
        am he—
      (is not
at any trick
each and every life
at hazzard: *faites
vos jeux,*
      messieurs)
. . . Where am I?
      en route to
        a literal
Vermont. It's
            time
                to
—oh, do this
        do that—
I'll call.
Perhaps we'll
   lunch? We
already
said goodbye a
long farewell
for a few weeks parting!

My ocean liner,
   I am your
tug. "Life
is a bed
         of roses:
rugosas,
nor is it always
      summer."
Goodbye. Hello.
               Kiss
Hug. I
      gotta
run. Pierre
Martory,
his semblance,
smokes a St.
            Simonian
pipe and thinks.
Mme. de Sevigne
-type thoughts.
He was, when
            posing,
perhaps, projecting
A Letter to a Friend.
         (signed)—
all my
—you know—
      ton
            Dopey.
P.S. The lamp is
  signed, Daum,
      Nancy.
Hence I surmise
   she made
or, at least
         designed it.
Who *is* Nancy Daum?

■

Smothered in
Fox Grape Leaves

What's that tree with orange lumps?
I can't get close enough to tell.
A water skier passes
On Noyak Bay. Background,
the North Fork. Still, gray,
too hot. A breath comes off
the water: what a mercy
to be here, not in New York.
Near my foot, a yucca
holds its seedpods erect:
a candelabrum in an Art Nouveau church.
Here comes a white cat
to see me. No, it's headed for
a tangle of bittersweet,
honeysuckle, Virginia creeper
and, good grief, deadly nightshade.
Suddenly the sun burns through.
Shapes and shades of green and water
and of a woman and a girl
who come up the path.
This oak leaf
is a permit to sojourn.

■

GARY SNYDER

"Not all those who pass"

NOT ALL THOSE WHO PASS
IN FRONT OF THE GREAT MOTHER'S CHAIR
GET PASSED WITH ONLY A STARE.

SOME SHE LOOKS AT THEIR HANDS
TO SEE WHAT SORT OF SAVAGES THEY WERE.

JACK SPICER

Hibernation

Deeper than sleep, but in a room as narrow
The mind turns off its longings one by one,
Lets beautiful black fingers snap the last one
Remove the self and lie its body down.
The Future chills the sky above the chamber.
The Past gnaws through the earth below the bed.
But here the naked Present lies as warmly
As if it rested in the lap of God.

■

PHILIP   WHALEN

Ode for You

_____

What are you but a drifting crowd?

Miserable hermitage of dauby wattles

Flies ants bugs and busy rodents all over everything

Wrong climate for a vegetarian life out of doors

Wrong soil for a vegetable garden

Well, tell me about that.

No. No. It's too—

It is too boring to tell and I doubt that you have time

To listen

What happened when you went to L.A.?

> At this point we shall draw a curtain of discretion
> across the scene and direct the attention of the reader
> to a large cardboard carton which stands on the floor
> beside the desk.

OBSCURANTISM

What about the hermitage. Where was it. When.

Grey clods of earth and bumptious weeds,

Dead batteries,

— 2 —

This morning the ocean fits

Tight against the cliff

Mare's Tails in the sky the weather will change

Prisms of Japanese quartz make rainbows on desk and bed

"seal'd in vain, seal'd in vain"

CHAINSAW

the muddleheaded reader will inquire,

"What's the connection?" poking about

with a long stick while crossing the moorlands

where the point of the stick suddenly slides

into a hollow, starts digging,

(MALEBOLGE?)

out come Little Cyril, Cousin Maude, the China pug dog,

peacock feathers and gilded cat-tails, the player piano,

the cut-glass vinegar cruet, the Conductore (S.P. Railroad)

Darling Arabella,

None of it is visionary or prophetickal

What's buried in earth is utterly used up

Ready to become flowers grassy weeping willow trees

Throw it all back

    other things are perfected underground

    onions and parsnips and diamonds:

    let's have those

We rise and fall through the earth

Geysers and artesian wells percolating

Through rocks from heaven's bright obstacles

    (hemisphere's balderdash)

Uncommonly streaked and splendid, so delicately

650 pounds of marbles

} NIKE {

white stone wings

(bolinas 17:xii:71—10:i:72)

■

JOHN WIENERS

from *The Journal of John Wieners*

July 23, 1958

He thought: What next to do? He wanted to stay in the house beside her, her spirit moving thru the rooms: the door was open to the porch and the waves were there. The boy was crying, rather whining in the next room. He would stop. He was bored. He was not stirred by the rising of the waves. They would roar for aeons on this beach after him. Who would be here to hear them. The boy had been sent outside. We came back in sobbing to the bathroom, and the girl was sucking a honey dew melon. A motor boat roared in the bay. It was July and the dog days. He thought what's a poet doing writing prose? Where are the phantoms he had called down with night. Gone with the night. Writing, he knew, was an agony. From what source it sprang he did not know. That the gods were not with him now he knew. But he felt that the recording of that fact was important. The crying on the doorstep had begun again. And the girl came in calling: Mommy, do you want to see a sailboat? I am a silent man, he thought. How can I ever amuse a woman? Fill her life with a structure that would support her and prop her for the life they had left together. The wind is a woman, he thought, but he knew that was not true. And that this compulsive writing is not a productive act for the house. But the house is a woman, he thought, and so he went outside.

He sat in the big green chair overlooking the sea. He had changed pens from a ball point one to a fountain. He had taken off his shirt and there were grapes in his left hand.

A machine whirred on the porch
next to theirs
and the waves lapped at the pilings behind him. He ate a grape and spit the seed into the sea, crushing it first by accident between his teeth. It is terrible, he thought, to be a reporter of the instant. One has to be there all the time. He ate another.

There was a hill behind the house, like a gragantuan guardian of the house. Its summit reaching a peak exactly in front of their front door, which opened onto a boardwalk which led to a piece of land not wider than 5 feet which ran between the hill and sea, along that little bay of houses which she called *Cat Fish Row*. Across the bay was another hill which she pointed out to him last night looked like an Egyptian mummy. He said Gulliver. She said what. He said Rip Van Winkle. And later, reminds me of a drawing by Blake, you know the old man with the long white beard. She went inside to fix the rest of supper and he smoked. Later she came and got him in the doorway. Sending waves of her being thru him as she stood in the doorway there, holding onto his wrist and causing his belly to bounce in that queer way, like he too was at high tide.

Now it was a new day and he sat in the green chair above the sea with only dungarees on and they too had a hole in the seat. He finished the grapes and threw the vine down. Then the last seed between his teeth, his fingers, he shot it out and it bounced back off the wooden slats which fenced in the porch. Except where he sat, which opened directly to the liquid quicksand of what was called Pacific Ocean. The motor picked up speed next door. "Mommy" came drifting out from the house, soft and liquid as the sea. Women really are that, he thought. Even the young, and he would hate, he thought, to anger any one of them. That was why he was such a sibilant around them. Not really bothering them, but always on the lookout for what pleased them. Rather than himself, which he reduced to a kind of helpmate around them. Help me God, he thought, to be a man and keep this woman and her brood. Of course it was her house and she brought the food. And he just sat in the sun and let the sweat roll down his thighs. But they were good together at night, she let him know that. And she was his first woman. And despite other lovers, she gladly came back to him, courted him and made him feel at home. Her and her friend Margo up the row. That was good for him, he thought, rubbing orange stains off his belly and spitting his sinus mucous into the sea, pulling part of his skin off his back as he moved too quickly, stuck as he was somehow to the green chair! The sun made his eyes squint and the nasal cavities behind them to discharge their flow down the back of his throat. He liked the taste. That was one thing he got being by the sea, sinus.

And a gull bounced on the waves before him. Another thing. Brown with black tail and black beak, turning to face him as he wrote that down. How a poet controls the universe, he thought. Had not his master taught him: He who controls rhythm, controls. There was a rumble behind him and he half turned but saw nothing so came back again to his book. And the wind cooled him, as the jazz boys would say. And the land loved each new arrival that the wave dumped upon it. And the speedboat across his ears further out than the cruiser was a caress. Why not? Be a sensualist. Take the pleasures, richness, another master had said.

Damn the references to my lords, I must set myself up as absolute, and as he bent to write it, a black shadow of some winged thing passed over the white paper and the memory of it made him sit there for a long time rubbing his running nose.

■

First Poem After
Silence Since Thanksgiving

Out in the world again, after the cloister
of the university,
it feels good.

Below freezing, walking
on Main Street, my hand
frozen so, I can hardly write

8 mins. later, riding on a bus
uptown, my feet frozen, my cock kissed
in the men's room

of the Shea's Buffalo
downtown. I am the poet

standing in the cold, while university professors
ride by in Volkswagens;

dancing in doorways, to keep warm,
since childhood.

I am the poet of benzedrine, bus stations,
jazz and negro lovers. I am the poet

so many ambulances ride by, in this city
the old are dying in the cold,
can't get their welfare checks, surplus foods.

I am the poet of overpasses,
railroad yards and all-night cafeterias,

                2.

    parked cars by country roads,
autumn leaves, high music in hotelrooms.

I am the poet that stands between
the lover and his wife,

I am the poet of your life.

                January 29, 1966—12:44 A.M.

                ■

Spotting Miró

"There you go, Dougy, 685 Madison. Take a taxi—it's a Miró."

The tube was taller than Benny was, as tall as Jimmy, almost as tall as Doug. He could have polevaulted the stairs with it, had he chosen. Nor, out on Third, did he allow himself to joust with the onroaring trucks and buses. He did stop to hail a taxi on 51st, wave his Miró in the air. The taxis would have none of it, they wanted *briefcases*. Well, if a cabbie didn't know a Miró when he saw one, who among these walkers would? They headed west. The Miró would enjoy the stroll; in fact, was nudging some of the girls as they passed by. He had good taste. On Madison, Doug stopped to let him look over the window display of a jewelry store, but the Miró could find no ring that fit. Try that bracelet then. No . . . How about that choker there? Ah! Ah! Well pleased, they headed on. The Miró had never seen so many Americans before, not outdoors. Why weren't they staring? They did not even stop to look! Doug patted him, and the Miró patted back.

It was at 685 that the Miró balked, grabbing for the closing door. Doug had to pull him in. There was a lone man inside amid all the art. This was a man who would know a Miró. He had a little dripping nose, close above a warping mouth. His wet eyes peered out through their spectacles in alarm at sight of life. "Yes? Yes?"

"I have a Miró!"

"Ah, the Miró! What, have they taken it off of its frame?"

"I guess they have at that."

"Here, let me see." The man wiped his nose with a white wet handkerchief, pecked testily at the binding tape. That did not take so very long, but the plucking of the Miró did. It was done with little pinching tips, all around the rim. When he had a few inches out, the man had Doug hold the tube while he drew most delicately out from it. Now he took the Miró to a table, gently spread it there. He sniffed every inch of it, turned it over on its face.

"What's this on the back?"

"I don't know." If not another Miró, it looked like a shopping list.

"All right, I'll accept it," the man sniffled, reaching for Doug's receipt. There was an exquisite Klee behind his back. Waving the signed receipt, Doug left Lester McLester to sniff that shopping list, and pretended not to notice him drip on it. Outside, in the sun again, he sauntered south. Soon he sauntered east toward Lexington. There are no public phones on Madison.

■

Come on! Dance

Our palm wood drum

is yours.

Pound on it

We're friends here.

—Hungry Coyote,

from "Party"

Trans.: John Ceely

from *Dada Manifesto on Weak Love and Sour Love*

People have always made mistakes, but the biggest
mistakes are the poems they have written. BABBLE
has one reason for being: the renewal and maintenance
of the traditions of the Bible. Babbling is encouraged
by family-growing. Babbling is encouraged by pennies
for the pope. Every drop of saliva that escapes from
the conversation is converted into gold. Since people
still need divinities to keep the three essential laws,
which are God's—eating, screwing and shitting—
and the kings are away travelling and the laws are too
hard, babbling is the only thing that counts nowadays.
The form in which it appears most often is DADA.
There are some people (journalists, lawyers, amateurs,
philosophers) who even consider other forms—busi-
nesses, marriages, visits, wars, economic crises,
nervous breakdowns—as variations of dada. Not
being imperialistically inclined, I do not share their
opinion: rather I believe that dada is only a second-
class divinity that must simply be placed beside the
other forms of the new religious mechanism of the
interregnum.
Is simplicity simple or dada?
I find myself rather likeable.

Tristan Tzara
Translated from the French by David Ball

■

Before Play

You shut an eye
Peer into yourself into every corner
You look around to see that there are no nails no thieves

No cuckoo eggs

You shut the other eye
You crouch then jump
You jump high high high
To the very tip of yourself

Then you drop of your own weight
You drop for days deep deep deep
To the bottom of your own abyss

If you are not smashed to bits
If you remain whole and get up whole
You play

Vasko Popa
Translated from the Serbo-Croatian by
Stephen Stepanchev

Girl Loving

It's my window. Even now
I am so softly awakened.
I was thinking, I would float in the air.
How far does my life reach?
where does night begin?

I could suppose that all
around me it was I, still,
diaphanous as a crystal's
soundings, full of darkness, dumb.

Yes, I could even the stars
include, in me, so great
it seems to me, my heart; thus willingly
it would again let go him

whom I was beginning perhaps
to love, perhaps to contain.
Alien, like things not written down,
my fate's respecting me.

Why am I under this
infinity, put here?
scented like a meadow,
agitated to and fro,

crying out, and at the same time anxious
that someone heard the cry,
crying out, and towards destruction
allotted to someone else.

Rainer Maria Rilke
Translated from the German by
Frank O'Hara

■

Tomb

Anniversary--January 1897

The black rock raging by the north wind rolled
Will not be stopped beneath those pious hands
That try to liken it to human pains
As if to bless in them their baleful mold.

If almost always here the ring-dove coos
This ghostly mourning many folds of cloud
Imprints on all tomorrows' ripened star
Whose silver sparkle soon will coat the crowd.

Following his yet outward solitary bound
Who searches for our vagabond, Verlaine?
He is hidden all among the grass, Verlaine,

Only to surprise, naively in accord
The lip that does not drink nor halt his breath
With a shallow rivulet of slandered death.

Stephane Mallarmé
Translated from the French by Fairfield Porter

■

156

Canticle of the Creatures

(often called Canticle of the Sun)

Most high, all powerful, good Lord
To You be praise, glory and honor
And all blessing.
To You, Most High, do they belong,
And no one is worthy to say Your name.

Be praised, my Lord, with all Your creatures,
Especially Sir Brother Sun,
Who brings us day; and by whom You give us light,
And he is beautiful and radiant with great splendor.
He is a symbol of You, Most High.

Be praised, my Lord, for Sister Moon and the Stars
In the sky You formed them beautiful and precious and clear.

Be praised, my Lord, for Brother Wind,
And for air, cloud and calm and all weathers
By which You give Your creatures sustenance.

Be praised, My Lord, for Sister Water,
Who is very useful and humble and precious and pure.

Be praised, My Lord, for Brother Fire,
By whom night is lighted,
And he is beautiful and merry and robust and strong.

Be praised, my Lord, for Sister Mother Earth,
Who sustains and governs us,
And brings forth divers fruits and colored flowers and grass.

Be praised, my Lord, for those who pardon for Your love's sake
And put up with weakness and distress.
Blessed are those who will endure in peace,
For by You, Most High, they will be crowned.

Be praised, my Lord, for Sister Bodily Death,
From whom no living man can escape.
Woe to those who die in mortal sin,
Blessed those found doing Your most holy will,
For the Second Death will do them no harm.

Praise and bless my Lord and give thanks
And serve Him with deep humility.

St. Francis of Assisi
Translated from the Italian by James Schuyler

■

Party

Come on! Dance!
Our palm wood drum is yours.
Pound on it.
We're friends here.
Tobacco tubes, flowers: they're yours.
Whatever your heart desires.
Come on. They won't last forever.

Come on, friend,
get flowers by our tall carved drum.
Dance!
Let yourself go.
Try on some of our flowers.
We're passing out bouquets—
gorgeous, golden flowers.
Come on.

Lovely singing here today:
throstle, bluebird, green-tailed quetzal.
Red macaw is the raucous one.
Others echo, counterpointing,
like gourd rattles swishing to bumping drum.

I'm having my cocoa,
enjoying it, too.
My heart is content.
My heart is renewed!

I don't care if I cry,
I don't care if I sing,
but make me live in this house!
Your closet would be fine.

Oh I had my spiced corn cocoa.
My heart is bursting! I'm so alone.
I've nothing to hold on to.

I can see it all so clearly:
I'm not happy. I haven't done anything.
I've nothing to hold on to.

Hungry Coyote
Translated from the Nahuatl by
John Ceely

■

Beginning the Project
1966–1976

A naked artist smokes.

Dreaming you wake up &

you say "Everybody's a hero, everybody

makes you cry." Ah, this morning

I was footprints in the snow

Listening to the words

from the burning bush all the day

We sleep & dream our lives away.

—Ted Berrigan

"Galaxies"

SAM ABRAMS

Answer Enough

_____

my friends have moved to
the nytimes poetry
chicago airplanes
uncool their lives go
where they wantem to

someone is waiting "outside" for
someone leave together walk
on the main streets who here
has a grudge carries a blade

■

Sam Cooke on the Nantucket Ferry

theres a man goin roun
takin names

_____

sweet salty cunt of the beach towns
silver indian turquoise over slim wrist
where ever the song will lead me
how long till you meet my eyes

black & white sitting together gaze down
across taut skin moves on fine bones
let it fit be fitting
how long till

giving instructions one message only
two beauties say among ten
every action separate full of meaning
     the placing of hairpins
     the patting of a curl
     the chewing of a cracker
     the licking of lips
     the taking of breath
       thru slightly parted lips
     the lowering of an eyelid

meanings burst thru tunes nowadays
abandon hope to enter art o
beloved head of
noble swineherd
leader of men

conscious of every strangers gaze that falls upon them
with impact language impoverished of words of eyes
the pleasures of evaluation i wish you yet
many cocks arched high with desire

in the 200th year of the peoples thing
when only convicts sing as they work
moving steadily thru the fog with a heart
like an ax in the hands of a skillful chopper

    (envoi)

bowlegged lady apt for fucking
& all you other women who stand with conscious or unconscious grace
i want to tell you how much i love
all you women iv never even spoken to

                    ■

Prévert's Barbara

do you remember barbara
it was raining really pouring in saigon
& you were walking smiling
flowering crazy dripping wet
in the rain
do you remember barbara
& i passed you on long binh street
you smiled
& i smiled the same smile
remember barbara
i didnt know you
you didnt know me
remember
remember that day
dont forget
a man was standing
sheltering from the rain in a doorway
he called your name
barbara
& you ran across the street thru the rain
& threw yourself in his arms
remember barbara
dont get angry
if i make songs about you
i do that for everyone i love
even if i only saw you once
& never before
or after
i do that for all my loves
remember barbara
dont forget
that nice happy rain
on your happy face
in that happy town
that rain by the river
near the restaurant
near the ferry dock

o barbara
war is such shit
what happened to you
when the steel rain fell acid rain
& the iron rain & the fire rain
& what happened to the man
who held you in his arms & loved you
is he dead & gone or does he live still
o barbara
it is raining really pouring in saigon
like it used to
but its not the same
everything is gone
its a widow rain a terrible sad rain
it isnt even the rain of steel acid & blood anymore
just clouds collapsing
collapsing like dogs
like dead dogs
like dead dogs floating in the river past saigon
where there is nothing left
where there is nothing

■

VITO ACCONCI

One to Ten Minus Four

I did it and now I do them over one by one.
You, having gone apart, break this in two.
Putting on another he wears a three-
Piece suit. She took it off, down on all four-
S. They paid her, when she came up, with a five.
We, if you exclude them once they unjoin us, number six.

They are still, even now that we have joined them, at six-
Es and sevens. But when he, who was out from under, comes in, they
    are at one,
Although you say they appear, as it seems, it is said, to be five-
Fold, one of them even, even another, possibly, being two-
Faced as it looks to me, even though he is wearing a four-
In-hand to make her think it simple as one-two-three.

She, in fact, though simplifying, won't go past the three-
Mile limit. But she would if she had a six-
Footer along with her, all the way from head to toe, one who would
    four-
Flush even if he had to walk a mile to do it. It was all one
To him. But I wouldn't give him my all, not for the two-
Penny pay he offered me, as if I were used to the five-

And dime. What they offered to use, however, was the five-
And-ten-cent-store as a cover-up. There we could make a three-
Point landing, even though what was the ground was a two-
Sided question, as was what was the point. He—no, she—well,
    they, together, had a six-
Shooter, which we passed around to one
Another. We went past and in this way: First, four

Then again, four,
Then five,
And, alone, won over, one
And then three,
Fatter as if they were seven, six,
Finally two.

We looked at the clock: one; then, later, two.
We examined the labels, then, on the backs of each dress: the large
    ones fourteen, the small—four.
Then we realized that, misreading the calendar, we had read "nine"
    for "six."
We knew we would pay the price: ten—maybe, with luck, five.
How many would be left behind? At least three.
But we would begin again and gain, afterwards, from step one.

Then, multiplying two by two, we would have five.
We will get four, though we start with three.
Though the answers are sixfold, in my mind and ours, folded over,
    it is one. (For example, we did it—no, we did one.)

■

KATHY ACKER

Interview with David Antin

12/28/73

KA: I'd like to talk to you about your ideas concerning uses of language since that's what, one issue, your current work [*TALKING*] seems to concern.

DA: Okay. If I assume that my thinking is, or one way of my thinking is, my using language, I can examine my perceiving—including my perceptions—that is my thinking, by examining my uses of language. For instance, examining the problem of certainty: I say "I know that . . ." rather than "I'm certain" in situations in which there's doubt. How does this "I know that . . ." function? How does "I know that . . ." function regarding truth values? "I know I'm lecherous" doesn't mean that you, TBT, know that I'm lecherous. "I know I'm lecherous" means I know I'm lecherous.

K: How could you then possibly prove to me you're really lecherous?

D: Let's go back. "I know" often means "I have proper grounds for my statement." That is, "I know I'm lecherous because I'm now acting lecherously." That is, you would understand "I know I'm lecherous" to be true, because you understand how that statement relates to the specific non-language contexts involved. You'd understand the language game.

K: What if I don't trust my sense perceivings?

D: That's an entirely different problem.

K: So poetry, any sort of writing, is a prime way of perceiving reality?

D: The problem of certainty again. Certainty is, as it were, a tone of voice in which I declare how things are, but you can't infer from the tone of voice that I'm justified. For instance, you say you want to fuck me. I believe you want to fuck me because I believe you're a trustworthy person. If you add that you *know* you want to fuck me, the *know* simply informs me you're sure of your belief.

K: Do you care whether you can *know* I want to fuck you?

D: Only for practical reasons. Actually—specifically—not at all. Doubt too gradually loses its sense. Since I can doubt only what I know. That is, everything descriptive is part of logic.

K: Therefore, society is not an absolute. Right?

D: What I'm basically talking about is use. Garbage is what is no longer usable, or taken as usable. Poetic language is that language which is most functionally efficient. Newspaper language. Advertising language. I'm interested in what statements—what language—I can use as foundations for further research and actions.

K: It's not, then, the so-called "truth" value of a statement or a poem, to return to our first argument, that matters, but what practical effects the poem contains leads to.

D: In other words, a preconception of "use" is "social": no one talks to him/herself. Why would what I say "be of any use" to anyone? Why would anyone believe what I say?

K: Does "be of use" presuppose "belief"?

D: If President Nixon said to me, "I'm your mother," I'd believe him unless I remembered otherwise or had been told otherwise. I still might believe him—or her. Therefore, truth and falsity don't exist. Except in regard to use: I can use real money. I can use counterfeit money, but in a different way.

K: What I know, you must know, everyone knows.

D: But is there anything I definitely know? Any way I can tell you convincingly I know this event? All truth-falsity testing, as I've said, takes place in context, in an existing system of beliefs. But doubting and knowing depend on, lie within this system. That is, I use judgments as principles of judgments. How, actually, do I judge?

K: Learning. I learn to distinguish, to perceive something—that is, to perceive order from chaos. I learn to speak. I'm being taught and controlled at basic levels.

D: What do you mean by "learning"? Don't I learn from my experiences? No. I'm taught judgments and their connections with other judgments. I'm not taught single judgments: I'm taught, I've been taught, a totality of judgments.

K: How can I attack this system, try to determine my living, really see? Through delight?

D: The child learns by believing the adult. Doubt presupposes belief.

K: But I sometimes doubt because of certain experiences I've had.

D: Not all propositions are equally subject to testing? Is the whole system of beliefs subject?

K: The difficulty, first, is to realize the groundlessness of our believing.

D: Okay. Do I know outside of this system of beliefs? I act with complete certainty. But this certainty is my own. Certain knowing, then, either isn't possible, or has nothing to do with social living as I know it, with the system of learning and judging.

JACK ANDERSON

Modern Breathing

Modern breathing is what comes out of the radio when you least
    expect it. It
gallops between the lines of the front-page news and sighs with
    relief when it
gets to the obituaries. Sometimes it hangs above your pillow and you
    smell it
and wonder, "How did I ever get into such a mess?" Then modern
    breathing moves
in next door with the swollen glands.

Modern breathing searches out the garbage in the gutter and the old
    drunk pissing
against the subway station wall. It joins the smoke in the street with
    the smoke
in your lungs, and paddles through the city sky from which the air
    is being evicted.

Modern breathing is syncopated like a minstrel show dancer. It
    comes when the
tanks come. It jumps up and down when an officer's nightstick
    jumps on a skull.
It must fight to keep itself out there in the running. Sometimes it
    goes away,
then somebody dies. Modern breathing hopes it will be better
    tomorrow. Well,
there's no harm in hoping.

Modern breathing is loud. It is the chief cause of deafness in
    laboratory mice.
Modern breathing is soft. You never know it's there until it stabs
    you in the
back. Modern breathing is what you hear when the phone rings at
    3 A.M. and there's
no one on the line and no one in the house but you and it. Even
    when you hang up,
you can still hear modern breathing.

■

J E N N I F E R   B A R T L E T T

from *Autobiography*

"Jolie Madame," the most sophisticated fragrance in ALL Paris, created by Pierre Balmain. Luxuriate in mists of totally feminine "Jolie Madame" from top to toe, only shades less potent than the exciting parfum, still superbly lingering to radiate its impressive joie de vivre *for hours.*

Jolie Madame is the cologne I wear occasionally. I use Fresh Stick Deodorant, Ivory Soap, Clinique sheer makeup on my nose and chin, non-allergenic with its own moisturizer. I wear Love Cranberry Glaze on my mouth, and Love Foxy Gray eye shadow. I used to shave my armpits and legs with a Gillette razor and Gillette Stainless Blades. I use Crest blue toothpaste and, sporadically, Pearl Drops, a stain-removing dentifrice developed by a dentist for the use of his own family. I use Protein 21 Shampoo with body-building proteins or Ferma Caresse, a shampoo for damaged or delicate hair. I do not file my nails or cut my toenails. I pick them. I have Revlon Deluxe Tweezers for plucking facial hairs. I use Yardley Skin Quench as a body lotion, arms, legs, hands. I take no medication regularly, though I took contraceptive pills for six years; I did not gain weight, nor did I notice increased depression, loss of libido, dizziness, or eye trouble. I use Fantastik to clean most surfaces, Viva Paper Towels, Mr. Clean for the toilet bowl, bathroom sink, and tub. I use no particular brand of toilet paper. Comet Cleanser for pots and pans and the kitchen sink, Housemaid Copper Wire pads or plastic Tuffys for scouring, Windex for mirrors and windows, Plain or Lemon Scented Pledge for wood surfaces. A Westinghouse Canister Vacuum. I do not iron. I use a yellow Oral B 30 toothbrush, and Johnson and Johnson Dental Floss. My boar's hair brush was left in the loft by someone who stayed. I use various Ace combs. During my menstrual period I use Super and Regular Tampax. I don't own a real camera. I have a Polaroid Swinger I rarely use and a Bell and Howell Super 8 movie camera I keep in a two-drawer gray filing cabinet. The doctor measures my height at 5 feet, 8½ inches, which seems generous. I weigh 130 pounds. I do not know my measurements. I have brown medium-length hair, an average complexion for my race, an average skin quality with large pores and few wrinkles for my age. I have gray-blue rounded eyes, black eyelashes, and fairly heavy brows. I have a generous mouth, straight slightly yellowed upper teeth, and slightly crooked yellow lower teeth. I have, I believe, gold inlays in all my molars and a mild gum problem around my four lower incisors. My nose is fairly straight with a puckered round scar at the bridge. I wear glasses to see. I am myopic. I have a superfluity of facial hair, my forehead is round and low, my jowls wide with a strong jaw. I have a chin. There is a crease on the right side of my face running from the exterior of my nostril to the side of my mouth. It deepens with strain or fatigue. My smile doesn't turn up, rather it retreats into my cheeks. My hairline is low, my hair relatively shiny and thick. I have broad shoulders, large upper arms, and quite a bit of hair on my forearms. My hands are square and blunt. I have had one tooth extracted, right upper wisdom. My fingernails are short, irregular with a great deal of cuticle. The skin of my breasts, stomach, and thighs is smooth. I tend to gain weight in my stomach, face, and thighs. I have a mole on the left side of my lower abdomen which gets larger in the sun. I have a triangular scar on my right shin and a heavy growth of dark hair on both shins and calves. My feet are small for my height and thick, the toes short, bent, and plump with ragged nails. My little toes have almost no nail. My right foot is considerably weakened from a recent accident. The skin on the soles of my feet is rough. I am inclined to alcohol, anxiety, nervous stomach, moods, a tentative optimism and inflammatory infections. I have been analyzed unsuccessfully, though we both tried; the same is true of marriage. I have a family and a great many friends. I use Testor Pla Paint enamel, #4 sable brushes, 16-gauge steel plates with a baked enamel surface, quarter-inch grid silkscreened on, and Xylol thinner for my work. My rent is $195 per month, I pay a $73 loan payment. I teach for a living. I tend to have more intense orgasms through masturbation than intercourse. I have had occasional homosexual fantasies. I have an active dream life. I think I would like to have a child but am afraid of being pregnant. On the whole I consider myself a rather fortunate person, although I would like to have had a more classical education.

■

Chinese Figs

She showed us the ashtray. The Java bulbs dimmed. "You could try to be a little more considerate . . ." and reached over the table. "Can you show me?" The lights came on, hands down his legs. The guests stood up and made their way to the door. "Don't go, it'll be better today . . ." I stood up, knocking over my morning drink. "I'll bring a cloth . . ." and they sank to the floor. I went through the kitchen. Syd was framing his Chinese prints. He told me a story about a man who was building a garage and needed two thousand bricks. The line which ended the joke was located in a railway station. I took a cloth to wipe up the pool in the other room. She opened the door for me and followed me through. When I had finished, I gave her the cloth. "Shall we see Syd?" I followed her. She told us both to sit down whilst she made a meal. She wrapped some eggs in a linen cloth and placed these in a dish. Next, she squeezed the juice from a lemon into a cup and added some brown sugar and chopped herbs. "Have you ever played Chinese Figs?" she asked. "I got the idea from your prints." Syd and I shook our heads. "Well then, there's no time like the present, eh?" she said and took off her shoes. She held them over the sink, looking at Syd and I as she did so. She dropped them. They sank into the soapy water. "Now, give me five, then follow whenever you like," she said as she passed us by, running barefoot down the hall.

After a few minutes Syd and I stood up. "I'll take the back," he said, and went out down the stairs. I walked down the hall, through the main doors and out into the street. I looked up and down the rows of buildings. She was nowhere in sight. I hailed a taxi.

Sitting in the back, I wrote her a letter, the pen jerking erratically across the folded paper.

■

BILL BERKSON

Strep Poem

Too much the bleeps are subtle in their *nyets*
as with some littler business of excess
mountains climb out of trees—to be
weightless! oh! the big sonata! (whoosh!)
that someone sweet then comes around
to patch everything up, like a
marriage counselor on a spree, or a spider
as in "Yes, I think we have a very good
highway system here in our state" grand goop
of the straight-shooter swan-dive of the initiate
congressional worries posterior stink sink
drain-off of the now popular "gulp" faction I mean
"Miss, would you like this one here or that
other one over there with the banana tree?" why
is it so hard "to be a person" when nobody else is
too much the time the vegetable ("grow, my friends")
roll over to complain "or would you rather be a mule"

and when the tag-team match got ended,
a little girl way up high was heard to exclaim:
"That's my Uncle Sam!" That's her story.

What Are Masterpieces (Alex Katz)

(Lincolnville, Maine.) Did you ever have a peanutburger? (peanut butter onion hamburger) If you're real hungry it does the trick. N.Y. poetry in Kent Bookstores. Got *Kora in Hell* (Williams), *What Are Masterpieces* (Stein), *Testimony in the U.S., 1885–1890* (Reznikoff) there. Finished Hannibal, "Beard" here and the Krupp family—working hard finished 2 large paintings and hope to finish another one.

(New York City)

A more high-class object. An art-high.

I would rather have a painting be fluid than natural. I think Cézanne is natural—every stroke is natural. A Manet may look natural but it's really fluid. It appears to be natural but it's so fluid. They're both lively.

Bonnard? Unconscious.
You know the guys who knew?
Like Fragonard knew what he was doing when he put the woman & the dog together. Right? The relationship between the woman & the dog is very peculiar.

A lot of people were dealing with the whole thing.

A developed technique.
Subject matter.
A modest technique.

I think you can make terrific art out of a so-so technique. But I'm not interested in that, I'm interested in art out of a fully developed technique. But if the art breaks down into technique before imagery then I'm a failure.

I'm primarily an image-maker. The viewer has information in
his head. The painting supplies other information. The subject
has to exist in a believable space.

You're always defining and redefining what people can look at.
Once you're not dealing with the figure as a whole figure
any ending is arbitrary, and I elect to pursue the most
capricious kind of arbitrary ending.

> (A lot of these paintings don't
> have much of a floor.)

■

Baby's Awake Now

And now there is the lively sound
Of a panel truck headed due southwest
Along Elm Road, edge of dusk—
The densest light to see to drive by.

The underbrush has brown fringe
And small silent birds.

I saw the rainbow fire.
I saw the need to talk.
I saw a unicorn and a red pony.
And I didn't want any devilled eggs.
I drove home with my collar up.

We're alive. You do alarm me to the fact.
The light is on the window in the air,
And breath comes faster than the hounds
To sanction what remembered, what stuck.

■

SANDRA BERRIGAN

One Spring Morning

_____

For Omar Vignole

"The struggle of memory against forgetting"

"Why," she says, "Do I eat cake
At one o'clock in the morning
When all the birds are asleep
and the moon is high in the north?"

Listen to the snores of the lover
Cows mooing at sunset
No wonder I can't sleep.

The lady poet wakes too early
Haiku on her mind
Where's my typewriter!

Oh, I use my typewriter for poetry
He uses his for prose
At night we sleep in another ocean.

He says, "You make poems, I'll read um
       You make eggs, I'll eat um."

She says, "He cries when he looks at me
Am I that ugly?"

Cows bellowing all morning
Writing poems
So inferior

Looking for honey
I find my hand
on your hairy belly
Brown Irish Bear
Is no longer extinct.

Out of the cracks of his elbows
and from his armpits narcissus
Bloom early this year
I go out in the rain and smell them.

Two lovers singing with cracked voices
This is harmony.

I'm on the freight train
of enlightenment.

■

TED BERRIGAN

Baltic Stanzas

less original than
penetrating
very often
illuminating

has taken us
300 years
to recover from
the disaster of

The White Mountain
O Manhattan!
O Saturday afternoons!
you were a room

& the room cried "Love!"
O Czechoslovakia!
I was a stove, & you
in cement were a dove

Ah, well, thanks for the shoes, god
I wear them on my right feet
since that bright winter when
rapt in your colors, O heat!

how we lay on your orange bed . . .
sipping iced white wine, & not thinking;
the blue sky outside exchanged blues while we were drinking.
Next day god said "Hitler has to get hit on the head."

■

In the Wheel

The pregnant waitress
asks
    "Would you like
some more coffee?"
Surprised out of the question
I wait   seconds   "Yes,
I think I would!" I hand her
    my empty cup, &
"thank you!" she says. My pleasure.

■

Buddha on the Bounty

For Merrill Gillfilan

"A little loving can solve a lot of things."
She locates two spatial equivalents in
The same time continuum. "You are lovely. I
am lame." Now, it's me. "If a man is in
Solitude, the world is translated, my world,
& wings sprout from the shoulders of The Slave."
Yeah. I like the fiery butterfly puzzles
Of this pilgrimage toward clarities
Of great mud intelligence & feeling.
"The Elephant is the wisest of all animals
The only one who remembers his former lives
& he remains motionless for long periods of time
Meditating thereon." I'm not here, now, & it is good,
    absence.

■

181

Galaxies

Winter. You think of sex, but it's asleep
Briefly you contemplate points of revolution
A naked artist smokes. Dreaming, you wake up & you say
"Everybody's a hero, everybody makes you cry." Ah,
This morning I was footprints in the snow
Listening to the words from the burning bush all the day
We sleep & dream our lives away. You dream
I don't live here, & when you wake up, what a relief!
I do. Someone to light the fire, babble for you
I dream a 7-ft.-tall African in tribal regalia
Carrying a long spear promises to send me crumbly LSD
In a *New York Times*. He does, & I am pleased, but amazed
It's 9:45 of a Saturday morning, December the 26th. Through eight
Window panes gray-white light is pouring in. It's leaning in
Sitting in, by the fire, a chair. "God, more money please!" No
Coal in the bin. But there's the fire still in sight. And there is
More wood to light. The fire leaps up the flue. The artist's smoke
Stays fixed in space. Above my head is wood. I can't see a warm bed
& inside it, you. But I'm beginning to see
The light, a bit older, less cold, than last night

■

Tough Cookies

You took a wrong turn in
1938. Don't worry about it.

The sun shines brightest when
the others are sleeping.

There is a Briss in your
immediate future.

Take heart. Shakespeare was
probably an asshole too.

Your life is rare and precious
& it has no mud. Stay with it.

You have strange friends, but
they are going to be strangers.

Everything is Maya, but
you will never know it.

Your gaiety is not cowardice,
but it may be hepatitis

■

Chicago at Dawn

Under a red face a black velvet shyness
                                        milking an emaciated gaffer
God lies down along here. Rattling
                        of a shot engine, heard from the first row
The President of the United States &
                                The Director of the Federal Bureau of
                                        Investigation
Stand over a dead dog. "Yes, it is nice
                                to hear the fountain bubbling
With green trees around & people who need me."
                                        "Lovers of Speech." It
is a nice thought, because typical of a rat.
                                And it is far more
elaborate than expected.
                        & the thing is, we didn't need that much
                        money.

Sunday morning,
        blues, blacks, red & yellow,
                all are gray in each

Window. A mighty camel
        held in a massive hand
                casts clouds of smog

(white) over the Loop, where
        two factories (bricks)
                & one oven (kiln)

are barely visible, behind
        successive huge gray metal gusts.
                The Fop's
                tunic.

Natives paint their insides
        crystal white here (rooms)
                outside is more bricks (off
                white)

■

JEAN BOUDIN

If We More Peace with Me

_____

If
we were even
more at
peace
with war
we would be less

Then lets have less
of the if
in re war
even
in re peace
at

worst we are at
less
peace
if
theres even
less war

War
at
even
less
cost would be cheap if
irony were metallurgy and peace

a sestina. Peace!
War!
as if
science needs opposites at
play to make less
matter even

Even odds are even
when one is at peace
With less
war
at
least there is less if

But for now war
is where its at
not if

■

JOE BRAINARD

Imaginary Still Lifes

_____

(No. 1)

I close my eyes. I see a light green vase. A very
pale light green vase. Right beside it sits something
black. Something small. It is a small black ashtray!

. . . . .

(No. 2)

I close my eyes. I see white. Lots of white. And
gray. Cool gray. Cool gray fabric shadows. (It is a
painting!) With no yellow. By a very old man.

. . . . .

(No. 3)

I close my eyes. I see specks of colors. All clustered
up loosely together. They are flowers. In a vase that doesn't
seem to matter much. Paint. This imaginary still life is
obviously a painting by Jane Freilicher. And, if I do say
so myself, a very good example.

. . . . .

(No . 4)

I close my eyes. I see bright orange. Almost red.
A touch of purple. A speck of black. And a thick bluish
stem. An exotic flower of some sort. Driftwood. Bamboo.
(A bamboo mat) A figurine. Chartreuse. (1953!)
This is a Polynesian still life.

. . . . .

(No . 5)

I close my eyes. I see——I hear music! This is
not a still life. This is the radio on!

. . . . .

(No . 6)

I close my eyes. I see black. Just black. But wait. . . .
. . . . . . a little white teapot is beginning to emerge, like
a cut-out. Getting bigger, and bigger, And bigger! Until,
now all I see is white.

. . . . .

(No. 7)

I close my eyes. I see a white statue (say 10″
high) of David. Alabaster. And pink rose petals. And black
velvet. This is a sissy still life. Silly, but pretty.
And, in a certain way, almost religious. ("Eastern" religious)
This still life is secretly smiling.

. . . . .

(No. 8)

I close my eyes. I see a charming nosegay of violets
in an ordinary drinking glass. That's all.

. . . . .

(No. 9)

I close my eyes. I see——a candle is casting
a glow over everything. A flickering glow. From inside
red glass. Covered with white net. With big holes. Salt
and pepper. Little bags of sugar in a "container."
Red table cloth. One wine glass. I am in a Village
restaurant waiting for my dinner to come.

. . . . .

(N o . 1 0)

I close my eyes. Copper. I see a copper tea pot,
rather well painted. Against a dark green drape, also
rather well painted. By an art student. A she. Probably
she went on to become an art teacher. Probably her
name is Miss Black.

. . . . .

(N o . 1 1)

I close my eyes. I see a pack of Tareytons. A pen.
A bottle of ink. An eraser (A large gray wad). Dr. Pepper
(Can). Ashtray. Matches (A book of). Yellow pencil
(No. 2 Mongol). (Etc.). All scattered across this big
brown table I am writing this at now.

. . . . .

(N o . 1 2)

I close my eyes. I see old fruit. Pots and pans.
And scattered utensils. Brown. Art. Dutch. By nobody in
particular. (Museum) And so, on to the Frans Hals.

. . . . .

(N o . 1 3)

I close my eyes. I see a lazy guitar. A little
potted cactus plant. And the rainbow blendings of very
bright colors woven into a poncho, slung over a hand-
painted wooden chair. (1955!) This is a "tourista"
postcard still life.

■

The China Sea

Death, you know, signifies nothing at all. What is important is that I
have very sensitive fingertips. I like to read books. Reading this book all
about conscious contact with a woman on the front wearing a key, large
with wings, I have an image in mind. Like a Greek to see. There *is*
something somewhere to see. Somehow. Last night I saw *The Ghost of the
China Sea.* I had seen it several times before, but, well . . . I love the
China Sea. It's blue I'm sure. Though I've never yet seen it. Perhaps
what I really need to do is go on a crusade for heritage or study the
scientific spirit in me. It's there I know I think. And I've already read
The Power of Ideas. I'm really terribly tired, you know! Daily every day I
must go through the discipline of overcoming unprofitable thinking, for I
don't know why. But I do. "I do." Maybe from a metaphysical standpoint
I could. I never paint science though yet I will. The blue sea (China)
won't make room. Or the ghost. I'm not sure. I know what I need: to
understand the harmonious mind of God. So I can see exactly where he
went unharmoniously. See? There is so much seeing to do. And already
today I'm so terribly tired. Blunted perception: I made it myself, you
know. We all do. For lack of reason not to. The spirit: I made mine too,
you know. Simply because it was there. What else could I do with it? I'm
going to buy a phonograph record which voices a healing life-giving

message! Or else Ray Charles' new album. If only I had a record player, I'd buy both. If only I had the money. You see, I'm not asking for anything to change, really. I just want to *see* as is. If I criticize, it's through creating: the only way. Michelangelo said something to that effect once. I read it in quotes. I think. This I know:

1. My planet moves majestically in its orbit, carrying me and my possessions.
2. I cannot escape my good.
3. The one power is self-love.
4. I seek for at least a vision of faith.
5. For twenty years, sleeping and awake, to place the stars and stripes on the pole has been my dream.
6. It is good to be absent from the body.
7. It is good to rejoice evermore without ceasing.
8. It is good to be lost.
9. Foes never slink back into native nothingness.
10. Sin is obscure.
11. Obscurity is good.
12. My art needs more sin.
13. I am faint and weak only because my doors are closed.
14. Purification *must* be the result.
15. No man is defeated until he ceases rejoicing (unless he's a cripple or something).
16. And I blue the China Sea.

■

JIM BRODEY

Dawn Raga

Wake up breathing
To music baby dawn. Clear
Clouds rise in breezy air

Stormy vacant blue shining
    perfect empty skies,
Ash vapor skies whorl coyote jazz.
Morning, here again, back in
    my human form, that
    with thoughts confer
    beauty upon gargoyles. As
In a dream, I step from this
    spiritual meat to embrace
    all those lotus mayas,
    nose-ringed and purple-
    skinned flames, touching
    this torso that now reclines,
    mildly aching blue fever.

Truly to be ascended, by breathing took,
    to meditate as one loosens his skull
        and cleanses knowledge with
            a little peace.

After-Dinner Hymn

Bring on the Maalox!
Downpours, tonics, pills that soften
Reflex's sub-electrical flash, pins
And needles locate bad circulation.
Tremors, tidal waves of bile
Splash bargain basement of dreams,
Lovely coughing moth that eats
Through to pit stop not crumbling
Or in fear of blossoming unease,
Lift sawed-off lips to cut down
Wearing blue sky on lapel
Smeared rainbow of scars
That unzip appeal & MY
Ain't that a nice sunset
To lay on Elvis or Frank or Jesus
Each an everlasting idol, as
Dr. Williams was before them
And now it's us, go ahead,
Autograph the night.

■

Joan Mitchell

Blue is an eternal color
It means infinite bliss
When it turns to black

I turn my back and go away
To blue the eternal color
When it turns to red I pray

We can move slower blue external color
The highway moves on vapor I am lost
In white ether the world is soft is

High is white is blue eternal color
When the colors change for the better
I am flashing golden ivory specks

Diamond dust splashed with blue specks
Golden flashes through wheat skyblue
Maze that purple gathers inside of day

As the eyes of Jesus calmly knew blue
The eternal color of the heart beating
Alone for love's radiance when blue

Mounts the sky's zenith and our hearts
Are the handball courts of the future
An ocean filled with sky and flesh

We pray at a painter's hand for blue
That eternal color ready with knowledge
Turning the night from its wreckage

Into sidewalks of cloud that lead
To the Sky Church nestled in tofu
These eternal parking tickets have

All blown away through blue eternal color
Radiance given to heart-mind throbbing blue
Sentences soaked with rain and good futures

■

MICHAEL BROWNSTEIN

Panatella

In the rafter morning under the rafters
The sun seen as hand opens a trunk
A kindly or vicious old man he beats back
The band swaddling tight blond pleats
On this somehow furrowed land of hair. Otherwise
Known as air . . . "Oh, I know,
I belittle the staggering reach of your intellect
In order to cross over quicker," he said
To himself, "to the other side. There
I can beach my canoe and fabricate something
To explain my never having used a paddle."
The sun said this in a skit. Cold swift trucks
Were balling past outside, they could be heard
In the United States of America.
"Oh, yes," snort the truck drivers,
"We are the teamsters of the United States
of America." The sun said this in a skit.

■

The Explorer's Story

"I started with nothing. Not even a pot to pee in . . ."
The old explorer was reminiscing. He was remembering—as he sat by
his swimming pool perched above the sunny blue Caribbean—the long
days of snow and ice and cold in the Far North, cold such as you would
not believe. He had been frozen solid, not moving, for seven months,
and survived. He survived to tell about it out of sheer determination. It
took guts to tough it out like that, in the wind and dark cold, without a
blanket or a fire, and not moving or shifting his weight one inch in any
direction. He couldn't have done it, actually. He must have been dead.
This is what many people thought: they were sure he was dead.

They came in their snowmobiles and battery-operated gloves and set up their searchlights and watched him. At the center of the faintly stained snow marking the perimeter of a movement which had been restricted to a few centimeters and no more, the explorer stood and gritted his teeth and looked back. He observed the people and the people observed him, then those people left and others took their place, and never in all the times they came out there was one word exchanged. Never was one word even spoken. After seven months the northern spring finally came, and the explorer survived, and one day he walked away, not looking back. He walked through the mountains to the town and through the town to the city, and boarded an airplane to Florida, where he caught a boat to the islands. He will never forget, however, the feeling that went through him when, on the day he was leaving the frozen north, the people who had watched him and doubted him all winter long, with shameless smiles on their faces finally said to him as he left that they would never believe him, that as far as they were concerned he was dead, and that if anywhere rumors sprang up that a man had done what he had done, they would testify to the opposite, and communicate their testimony to the entire world.

The explorer sat at the edge of his pool, built on a rocky outcropping hung high above the aquamarine seas, and as he looked out at the blue horizon—still gritting his teeth over the hatefulness of those people in the Far North—the heavy black plastic protective covering, stretched over the shape of the empty swimming pool, shivered fitfully in the warm tropic wind.

■

STEVE CAREY

Mrs. Murcheson

Her heart was the warmer
for she was lovely.
She was white like a sonnet
in evening gray not premature.
Unskilled at what she would confer
five afternoons, every moment matters now.
Many men in services.
She gave them bright quiets—
she felt you should,
quickly and surely, each humbly.
She practiced, singing "two by two"—
ambled down a street,
gave it war-relief organization
where she looked. Some had come
stopping, kept thanking, thanking.
Individually, the design, a uniform,
eked near, but the idea
was necessarily far. Still,
with a fuller skirt and a long friend maybe . . .
She stops—fog's halted—then whistles.
Lights on. Let's go. Light's on.

■

Dread

Aspirin stays in the body
eight days. (a)

Not soon, fantods (b)
(as in attack of) care not.

No kinship
in common water sources,
the cup preferred.

I smell a rat.

One hundred eighteen degrees west,
thirty-four degrees north.

A Cheyenne gait in cartoon pursuit,
vivid as a kid's.

Next lonely old writers, drunk
on the telephone with old friends
late at night.

Of the pave,
of the pave,
"Now there's some music
I can drive to!"

A penalty flag falls to the ground.

Slowly, I produce the knife!

■

JIM CARROLL

Dysoxin

_____

For Ted Berrigan

To truly feel it you must have more
in this life than they are willing
to prescribe they do not seem to know
You better be willing to go to the streets.

The eyes, in time, must be set to various notions
of tone and light, like the strings of an aged violin.
It is done by turning the ivory pegs to left or right,
By pouring strict yellow juice through the veins by night.

We know the purpose of speed, the pattern
of savage blue tracks, the density
of cooked white powder, the proper place
of nods, the vicinity of able pharmacies,
the altruism of a last syringe.

Sunlight. Eastern Seaboard. When we do it right
our feet touch bottom, standing, like light
house in the waters of Maine. A good summer 1968 we slept
in the cottage of the grandmother of a man who jumped
from a window uptown to the streets of my home, Manhattan.

Knowing this. We are saddened. I hear an owl
reverberate in dark chambers of Eucalypti. Think
of you, gently with purpose rocked by Auden and Frank
in a hammock, reading this poem, on St. Mark's Place

with your fine woman's presence. And grace.

■

Methadone Maintenance Program— Mt. Sinai Hospital

---

1. open door

2. sign book for Frankie Sanchez
   a) name & number
   b) time
   c) how you feel

3. get urine container from Pedro

4. put on container a) name & number
   b) date
   c) team letter (I'm "B")

5. enter john

6. piss in container (if you are caught having someone else piss for you, you are on probation)

7. put cap on urine

8. hand urine to nurse behind counter

9. she checks your name off

10. grab cup

11. wait a minute or two

12. she pours in your methadone

13. drink up

14. split

■

Poem

I rest with the dogs across the feathers of birds
      departed for Winter

I hear thinly colored dew forming beside me, eyes vacant
In the stupor of redward fog
Sweat and shattered hair down my forehead
Like boneless fingers of children from home

As if I were among those wounded at war
Left across an open courtyard
in a village far from Paris or Milan

Hearing the small voices of women in love.

■

Fragment: Little N.Y. Ode

I sleep on a tar roof
      scream my songs
            into lazy floods of stars . . .
a white powder paddles through blood and heart
                             and
the sounds return
            pure and easy
this city is on my side

■

JOSEPH CERAVOLO

The Rocket

———————————

I

Being with you
      I am a seagull alone
      and flying although the clouds
    are within.

Tomorrow I'll be trans-illumined.

Does God call it?

O spit
      on the ground
      in a denser way
          upon the clouds.

In the jungle,
      clouds are falling.
Stand in front of me!
      Block out the sun!
        The leaves
have lines of their own.

We become trans-illumined
    Will we ever be like
      the sun . . . when it's
      like a piece of slate?

    You call me
      though the shoulders
this morning
      shake.

Flying above.
Spots, seeing spots.
You gotta go in right here.

A bug
is going behind the wall.
Is some of its existence love?
It doesn't look it.
But its feet change speed.
Outside the air is flat and cold,
and it doesn't snow.
Nothing to do, like a bug,
with its green blood
coursing along its shell,
its basic means of knowing.
Looking around at a new
cosmos in its blood which is
outside the flower
in some lost existent speeded world.

II

Is there a soul than that generator
like an arctic sky?
Noticing the stars; gathering
in spright all the bastards on earth.
Not one is old.
Solingering about a night
in ropey love.
The bastards of all earth are us.

In a dark love without love.
The one seed
noticing all the stars
in a new composition. A new generation
of love forms.
Seagulls pierce the coast.
O easy wings of strain's desire,
what is the joy of man?
Is there a joy without love's composition
staining and loving on this earth?
We are not so helpless as one
extinguished star.

But what about love
in our feeling for the cosmos?
Is it cosmic enough? Is it like a
ray of invisible light or comic enough
in a field of natural blights?

But, I stay and I hear. And it is
the same beautiful song.
The arctic and the jungle on one drug.
And love, windless, rough,
in the cosmic lust.

III

The streets are dented.
They are all awakening
and in easy love
guiding no template to feeling scared.
Alone in a word of love
on the side while cars
are full of people
averaging their immense sleep.
But I'm lonely.
Stop! I might be in trouble.
The template of good is
all around us and still the cars
go by like years
           and stars
in a refreshed universe.

Gather them o stars.
I am not so big.
   But I am mobile like a stuffed deer
without a family,
      too lost
        to be another child;
and now my tongue is big.

What choice and then
the sun comes up:
peering I fall down on
my chest crying.

As the sun glides across
the lumpy tears
and I am limpid in your arms

swerving through the light
in the manifold
of a new embrace
I see my deficiency
            on the gauge.

Me defoliated and dry
about to burst into fire mite.
Defoliated and dry
waiting for internal casts
Defoliated,
covered with bruises,
dry,
defoliated and dry
pissing in the wind
finding it maybe this winter.
Me defoliated
me dry

I V

Today it's just a blank because I envelope you
while the cars are
going by so fast and there's no poetry
in the sun or in the last
flame of a star.
The dawn in its traffic-light red
looks like a blowing orange blanket
tossing in the southeast.
But still there's misunderstanding
that shakes us like a truck
passing by in a detonation.

I am released tonight.

There's a young moon
about to intermit
so that I could remain up;
and eat of my desires.
To speak that I might eat. .
To have strength.

But there's a young moon
out the window of my rocket
that tells me
the earth is sending off its sons.
            It is easy to speak.
But so hard to strike
                    the song
on the hunt of the people
            of the world.

But tonight I'm not eating.
Even though the cosmos is swooping
in my ear, I am released
to your arms from this outer sea.

The stars are salt
    this morning
as I sit here
sobbing into my arm,
into the wooden table.
My heart and
no abomination:
no rum, no rum left
    for me.

Let the leaves around this. _ _ _
Engorged on the outer wing
of the volcano
I hear a rumble.
I am cold.
Let the leaves around this. _ _ _

On the outer wing
of this engorged volcano
I feel the rumble in the leaves around
of what no flower can deny the cosmos.
In the cold
on the outer wing to love.

Let the leaves be engorged
in our tears.
There is no rumble that a flower
can deny.
There is no cosmos in the outer wing toward love.
In the cold volcano

V

During these long and blank formations

between the nights of time
                parallelism
I lapse into this transmutation.
How sudden, how great to survive
with no sadness on the scene.
                In prehistoric America
there was no deficiency too great to
survive the catastrophes.

Us, found in nature;
unpure and clear,
with the premonition of a mammoth
of beautiful proportions
and the suddenness
of wild birds.
Our beginning is new because of our appearance,
but what about
the change of nature
and the cataclysmic land bridges
that bring one land to another
or that spring up separately
like ancient fish
in mechanistic revels to survive?

During these long and blank days
of happiness or joy, great
as the proportion of a woman found
with no clothes on,
maybe there's nothing to our joy or pain:
clearer than any new cataclysm
that destroys everything, destroys.

Soon this snow will melt
and the park with its floor of ice
will be melting. Soon, when
the deluge of cosmic suffering flys with us.
Soon this park will melt.

VI

When a fire becomes fire
    there is no dying.
Again the poles are cold.

The street promulgated with
large trees and birds in its song.
How the branches sing
and the heart makes falser
    what we pretend.

It isn't Spring, but the branches.
It isn't warm, but the chirps
of the invisible archangels.
Where have you been all my life?

Love is breathing and love is taking,
but away when
there is no Spring: we live,
We are a micro generation
in these trees
    amid this song of one note
and a million intonations.

But it is not Spring
and love is dying in its youth
but the trees are living
among these sacred powers
of incantations to life:
  Among all this destiny
we still fight.
But it is Spring
and in the sky are the velvet planets
wandering and in the soul
is a suspension:

Thru and thru
this will never come in

But here I am painless
in a world of pain.

  A sick dog
who doesn't know one sickness.

The limited surging
of my blood, not only in my vein

but in the bodies of you
my brothers, my sisters.

Look outside at the starlike
stars! They are not even pointed.

I think of the women I know
in their baths

and us passing through
with a name, a star, a dog.

Even in this light the stars
are equal to a flower.

The last blot of light
this universe will see

or that we see at night
    is a laugh, a song.

We wash clothes, we wear them,
the stars shake.

We do not feel it
but the soul takes its secrets

to your bath, your arms, your eyes,
your thrust into the last flash

and then, it is day.

CODA

For it seems
that the darkness
is a dream of experiment.
There is more of the monkey
to be respected.

Day follows day.
White. . . .   the next day is black.
What analysis
behind the light.
What's between a child sleeping.
The bird in a glance.
Dark bodies
are the children sleeping.

The weather ends,
and efforts of a novice
to exhaust but still to be;
until the end of the mysteries
of an immaterial universe.

What have we caught
in human modern dream?
Submission: Menstrual
in the life sub
of a secret passage to blood.

■

JOSEPHINE CLARE

Landscape

---

this nitsy-bitsy
   country of yours
         abridged
   to stories of un-
built buildings, un-
   laid gardens
i've seen the devil
once:
   a little short guy
        in liquid
   sunshine standing
on stumps
praying to
       Pom Pom Mums

■

TOM CLARK

John's Heart

For Ted Berrigan

Chopped red meats still beat and twitch

on the floor

of The museum of modern heart

where Art and Terror commingle

It's real theatre, just like politics

& television's dreaming sex

all manipulated by the Crab People   city folks
                                                        who are
                              very unpleasant

. . . . .

"After three days, I must tell
you this: I still can't erase
that scene in Altona—X standing
there with all his poems in his
fist, his blood and belly full
of booze, staring us down. The
gentile audience. His disdain.
And him hurting so hard behind
that ruined face. As I think of
it now, my stomach still turns
over, aches. I tried to get him
with my head. I wanted to deal

with him on a critical level—
but I was wrong. He made me use
my *feelings*. Forced me into the
ovens—the *nova* ovens."

. . . . .

Nowadays everything happens at once and our souls
are conveniently electronic (omniattentive)

thanks, John

we're in agreement about *that*
in fact we're both part

of the same big That

so have a heart!

(It won't hurt you)

. . . . .

Who are you?
Where did you come from?
What are you doing there?

AMERCIAN
BEAUTY:
THE
GRATEFUL
DEAD

. . . . .

Ted, did you know   *The Words*

is a book by John?

John Paul Zarch, to be exact

He has a lot of heart

tho as a child

he told many fibs

These were his words:

Fibber McGee
Sam McGee
Ruchel McGee
Bobby McGee

& Molly

was John's old lady. Here is a portrait
of her heart, in orange
                    & green & gold
        by Jim Dine:

(Fig. 1)

. . . . .

One fig

                to another, admiringly

        but with respect—   I'd like to ask

you some questions about Art, Ted

                                for instance

        How do you determine the top?

        ("What about the sides?")

        OK, how do you determine the sides?

        ("With my eyeball. I eyeball it.")

. . . . .

If Larry Poons were here we could examine his eyeballs

                & that way check out

        how "others"   approach their art . . .

                Explosively!!   Moving explosively!

toward the site (the heart)

. . . . .

You, Ted, & Larry

       Aram & Ron

            Jim, John & Molly

    &Robert Smithson

        we're all artists (Cage)
        we're all inside the room (heart)
        we can't forget it (politics)
        but we can get outside it (door)
        & on top of it (sex)

            via air (electricity)

    . . . . .

No more terror

    when the heart drops its defenses (pants)

    in a state of pure expansion

Nourishment Music—

    food going through the body—

    a pure nonvibrating tone

    that generates its own future.

    . . . . .

Out of a limited stock of ideas

    each person on earth shall receive one

is my dream of politics. Art, too, is a dream.

Politics is not, nor is the heart.

    . . . . .

216

The site is a place where a piece
should be but isn't. The piece
that should be there is now somewhere else, usually in a room.
Actually everything that's of
any importance takes place outside
the room. But the room reminds us
of the imitation of our condition.

. . . . .

Hard words

spoken

from the heart

                       ("Hard (art) headedness")

fly up into the air

. . . . .

Lufthansa's flight brochure contains the following: "Airplanes
can only fly by means of curved air. Without curved air, nobody
can fly. Curved air surrounds the world."

                                I'd like to fly, but
these days I'm also satisfied to be here on the ground. You
know, one pebble moving one foot in two million years is
enough action to keep me really excited. That pebble moves
by virtue of its connection with the earth's heart, which
is also curved. All the colors of the rainbow commingle
there, plus the famous "pot of gold." One toke equals eleven
million circumnavigations of the universe! Toke Two equals
a row of valentine-shaped blank spaces ♡ ♡ ♡ ♡ ♡ ♡ ♡ ♡ ♡ ♡ ♡

. . . . .

Playing piano in the dark, when the lights come on I have
four hands. Two of them belong to the unknown girl. The
music we make resembles the pumping of the human heart.

. . . . .

coming back from the John

    I run into you

  with a song in my heart

      & no politics

  That song's

    A Rainbow

    In Curved Air/

       by Terry Riley

   & inside it's

    others (skies)

    (parks)

   Bubbly songs of

    aleatory angels

  I know them by heart

   & all their angles

     who get gold dust

    on their wings

  & pink dust too as they pass

      on flashcards

   through my blue heaven

   on their way to you

     . . . . .

"You" here

   is a straight line

      in curved air

  from heart to heart.

    ■

ANDREI CODRESCU

Music

There were no bums in my pores.
New York had opened my pores & bedenimed & bendovered
    walked in my fantasies
        shoving bums.
The stores were open and the hours late.
Expectations were being fed
        not sent to work
        like in far-away San Francisco.
I could speed up & slow down
    grimace & guffaw
        move my hands
          & look up to the lit windows
filled with admiration for the natives
    though not wanting to be asked in
since my living room at the moment was the biggest.
I was digging the streets & the streets dug me.
Every lunatic sped toward its co-lunatic.
Bellevue was lit up like another apartment building
  & in fact a party of sorts was going on
   with the inmates happy to be warm
      even as they were being hurt.
Ambulances piled in front & people went in & a few
        came out
  & the enormous hallways could have fit
    a Communist city's living rooms
      which they did
because on several floors the inmates slept there
but these hallways were dirty green & bright yellow
    & the neon was dirty
       & the unhappy floors
were track-marked by wheelchairs & police boots
        & mad jigs
         & flares & broken glass.
The floor to be sure was a picture of hell.
The prison ward was behind two tall gates &

wire-mesh windows
            an easy jail break
& the cops were half cops & half social workers
        & in go the two poet workers
                with their two culture cops, i.e., books
& there are the prisoners
        half wanting to look at a woman
                & half desirous to look at free folk
    & half sick of each other
        & half sick
    & half serious criminals
                wanting to improve their lot in life
    & half mad criminals
        who had it in for the other half.
One came with a bed and a trapeze for his bandaged arm
        & half a body in a cast
& another walked in wheeling a tall steel cane
on a flying saucer from which flew an IV bag connected
                to his arm
        & as he walked
        he recited bathroom walls
but was interrupted in midrhyme
            by an atmosphere of human color
            occasioned mostly by a reader of best-sellers
            who wanted to write them
because he had lived dramatically & was interested
    in technique & his interest
        led to metaphysical questions
            which gave the poets a license to interrupt.
Another was grim & tall & black
        & in his head he carried
the entire philosophy of an obscure mystical sect
            in severe couplets:
"In the middle of the pyramid there is an eye.
The dollar bill has a lookout in the fourth sky.
The steps to the Capitol are seventy-three.
That is the number to cross the zebra & the flea."
    I am probably being unjust
        to a grim mystical doctrine
            which the man whispered
            before being led out
                by Big Sister
                in midrhyme.

It was an evening to forget & one to remember.
It was 9:45 & the night was young.
At 10:25 I had collected myself sufficiently to return
    to the world hopeful
        & why not
when so many were rhyming the world in their heads
        even on their back & in bandages
& while you can't call this feeling love
        there being no room for close-up oppression
there was a hope that half was not lost.
Parts of the Sunday newspapers still covered the city.
The stores were open & a thousand ways to get high too.
Denizens of the night revealed fragments of wild costumes.
In the bookstores an intellectual orgy raged.
The smell of pastry & coffee was being attacked by ginger
        & Mongolian pepper
            from inside red restaurants.
It was possible to consume everything or nothing.
Either way the balance was righted
    the consumers as passionate as the ascetics.
The Lower East Side of New York
    moved eternally by a rhythm
  "beating outside ordinary time"
        no shit
            the graces of cheapness.
Cheap were the pirogis
    at the Kiev.
Cheap pirogis at the Kiev
    6 boiled with sour cream $1.95
a whole subclass converted to Ukrainian food
    & this without pamphlets
        or monks,
each pirogi a pamphlet-monk
    doing its preaching in the mouth:
"if the Ukraine is ever to be free
        you must eat all your pirogi"
though there are people who do not like them
because they have first seen them fried
which is not always the best way to make somebody's acquaintance
not a pamphlet-monk's certainly
        & halfway through my second pirogi
            the radio said John Lennon was shot.

John Lennon was shot by an assassin.
Minutes later the radio said he was critically wounded.
And later yet that he was dead.
 The waiter held his plates in abeyance
  & his face became very sad
   & a tear fell on a pirogi
  & I was still hopeful but shocked.
A man named Chapman meaning chap man man man anyman
  "I am no man"
 a failed double with a gun
  a fallen half
had been shooting at a symbol & killed Lennon instead.
And now his music came from the sidewalks
  & everyone understood
   & became much sadder
    & their tears fell
on solid gold pirogis rolling into image-making machines.
The symbolists had killed John Lennon
 & I thought
 look at it as a vacancy
 a power vacuum
 a king is dead
 it will make everyone think
 for a few seconds before commerce sets in
  & that's no way to think
   but it was thinking me.
Chapman was now in Bellevue where I had been
 11:15 P.M. Monday, December 8
 an hour earlier
  with the other halved halves
& the hairs on my arm stood over the pirogis
  when I remembered that it was here
   in the Kiev
    ten years ago
     that I'd heard of Bobby Kennedy's death
which at the time struck me like the free winds of doom
  with the apocalyptic illumination
   of anarchist Jew
    I owe to myself.
Ah cheap pirogis in love with yourselves!
I was in love but with no one in particular.

■

JACK COLLOM

Birds of El Vado, Summer

the rapid house wren
violet-green swallow
red-breasted robins nesting
yellow warblers singing by the creek
lighting on wire, a broad-tailed hummingbird
evening grosbeaks, yellow & black
lazuli buntings warbling, blue & cinnamon
pine siskins questioning thru the pines
wheezy tonic fifths, the mountain chickadee
nightblue stellar's jays clown in ponderosa
tame tropical sun of western tanager
slow yodel drifts, one distant mourning dove
nighthawk flits above the hill
obscure western flycatcher calls from every twig
solitary vireo spaces song with white eye-ring
arkansas goldfinch lilts butter-yellow notes
     down Keystone Gulch
audubon's warbler, golden, black & white
dead bullocks oriole female in road dust
red-shafted flicker flying flashes salmon-red
rosy-headed house finches musical on Magnolia Road
landing suddenly on a dead limb
     townsend's solitaire
chestnut-capped chipping sparrows dry rattle up the hill
fork-tailed barn swallows almost orange-breasted over Boulder Creek
one day magpies turn the place to black & white jokes
virginia's warbler hiding yellow patches in the evergreens
excellent whistle tunes of arapaho-colored
     black-headed grosbeak
western wood pewee/ flutters/ out & back/ dead twig
warbling vireo sounds like coniferous
     yellowthroat
tan wing-bars: blue grosbeak: western slope

indigo bunting enchanting, no flamingo, singer
          from a treetop
head downward, white-breasted nuthatch calls yank yank
three ravens
at last, a dipper, water ouzel, bobbing on a rock
          by Boulder Creek
brown prairie falcon flying south
back of the saddle a thief, the canada jay
on Helen's red-brown
          lawnchair
                              a flammulated owl
rufous hummingbird buzzes back of the bathroom
          quick, red-brown, gone
macgillivray's warbler confident & lovely in the bushes
when we walk back in the national forest, this years
          gray-headed juncos
merlin whirls   over the hill
          by lady, daughter & me
cassiopeia's chair floats
          as we smoke on the porch
no sound except the water

■

"nobility is the secret of my character"

---

nobility is the secret of my character,
my slight paunch a flowering of gentleness.
my poached-egg eyes contain the seed of wisdom.
my tantrums are keenly-perceived emotional arabesques.
my compromises are selflessness making love to the world,
my rotten teeth the restraint of brutality.
my shaking hands are *joie de vivre*.
my meanness is pure light.
my obscurity tantalizes everyone.

my blackouts are part of the music of time.
my cowardice is a beautiful dance.
my blandness is the space approaching God.
my murders are mutations of the unicorn.
my poems are bits of ice on the warm plains.

■

Advantages

10-24-67

part I

as you lie sick on the couch seeming to sleep
a hook of light
along the side of your forehead
and your cheekbone
catches my eye.
& I start to catch the first words
after half an hour rising
to them, you see me look,
& smile &, as I start to write,
talk of the baby's teeth, ignoring
my fierce frown.

part II

the cat
like a gray dwarf of you
parallels you a foot and a half above
but facing the wall, faceless
a grisly shadow; to think of him
as human or less, makes him ugly
& his size & maleness
distortions of you. he is
a (castrated) cat

part III

the house is
what it is
according to understandings
accepted, that is, is less
of a house than one soldier
could erect, or one snail

part IV

the boys are
probably dreaming,
the oldest of his mother
the second of a bad wolf
the third of what
I can no longer guess. the oldest asked
"what is a dream," to which
question I compared it to a movie.
the second knew better
& cried when I left the room,
the third wasn't concerned

■

CLARK COOLIDGE

Insist on the Still Geology

———————

in having
so far as in it
or such

. . . . .

some as well as spaces

. . . . .

likewise
that wide

. . . . .

web titles

. . . . .

period
rather than out
as snow

. . . . .

that may well between
other center

. . . . .

often as far than more

. . . . .

even as than

. . . . .

will of outline

. . . . .

norms of dents

. . . . .

plane in vase

. . . . .

a whole when
when was

. . . . .

lops of overall

. . . . .

neither than itself

. . . . .

of a can
in a color

. . . . .

over space
by points

■

Picasso Dead

*"Actuality is . . . the interchronic
pause when nothing is happening.
It is the void between events."*
—George Kubler,
The Shape of Time

Was cut off. That there's never an end to that activity. Filling up
villas with pictures. So right somehow that his residue should be
worth millions. Countless stops. Money only gives us pause. Huge
rooms filled with ends. He couldn't stand there and moved out.
Planted his frame and moved on. Up that last night facing the ancient dilemmas there's no solving. Something about if you make it
still enough you can move on. Now those silences are left. Pictures
that are the spaces between his acts. The process no one possesses
moves on. He wouldn't speak of death (not a will, only will), only a
certain stillness that pushes. Painting is what goes on in between, a
thing those who only look can never know. Picasso's art no longer
exists. Only the momentary pauses that lean on us, who do.

. . . . .

Picasso's death should have been met with nothing but a worldwide
enigmatic silence. A great shadow should be (daily) dedicated to his
memory. All the chatter (newspaper, etc.) makes us feel the more
that we live in his background. What he tried to close the door on
to paint. There is no comment possible. "The age called modern
now is ended" gives testimony to his size but means nothing to us
who never believed in ages. The things he saw when he died are the
things we see every second. The mystery is still there.

. . . . .

The news commentators calling him "the greatest painter of the
twentieth century" pisses me off. Reminds me of DeKooning telling
Greenberg, "You have no right to speak about Cézanne. Only *I* do."
What they take for arrogance is only devotion. And I think it angers
them that no one possesses art.

. . . . .

I can see Picasso walk into a room and going right to it, almost before looking. The almost before anything.

. . . . .

Jump in and put on the first mark before you think even better of it. You finally can't look at nothing. Olitski . . . Color is nothing. I'd rather have a plum. Color flies over Picasso's shoulder as he attacks. We think in cartoons. "How pink would look" is already a form. Of. You don't look at a painting, you look at television. Picasso turns it on and it fills with water. Television isn't a fire. A painting isn't a wall. Goddam it, I'm *not* surrounded! I'm a part. We are *a* species. What is a cat. How to write.

. . . . .

Picasso walks in, moves chairs, lights up. Sits down, moves ass. Bird lights. Twitches shifting pictures. Have it sent up. I couldn't believe tobacco, that airplane, stand of nettles. Picasso reads Moby Dick, in translation, sun on porch, part of an afternoon. Back in the night he pictures. Have I got it goes apart . . .

■

The Passenger

Out the window, as a man lies on a bed. Not as he lies, it goes.
Sees past him, leaves him, into the next. Takes the air past his
shoe, perhaps his sleep. A move past him out, moves on, past the
window, moves on air. The word moves for no word moves. Get out,
it goes, gets, out past the confines, air past him.
Escaping, on a word for air, for it moves, get beyond, moves
get beyond, goes the air, of confines to, no sentence ever ends.

Beyond confines the man. Lies on a bed, confines as gets as
notions, of. Days of a window, moves, past, to go, from pasts,
goes past a window, outs at last. What does he. Sleeps, perhaps,
still. Lights air past a man goes from window to get, tracks
the confines of escape. Releases the room at a window avoids, the
seal of a man's confines. Day to a room, it windows. Seems
past the man on a bed in a room, lies. Frames past the confines,
holds to catch release at the window, airs out the man. His room,
goes past, his story, every day goes on as well, still. Sun
on stones, of a window frame, go, as well, the story as
every day. His confines, it releases, airs, frames escape,
the man, still, a bed.

Comes loose full of air, turning, the room to his confines.
Beyonds, the room, are otherwise, beyond the room is otherwise,
go a turn. Come to choose, turn to go. Has left the window
with him in. Gone from in it has within. Turned out he was
left there. Turns in he has gone. Turn the way every day goes.
Lies that stay.

■

JONATHAN COTT

Transparency

You're no one
Each street turns to fall, woods at every end
Deer drink the muddy water
Little boys in Harvard sweat shirts fall into the deeps
You're going backwards far against the river, 6p in your Afghan
      coat, heading south
Blue airport lights divide you
Traces select you
You find a cold magazine. In a bordered poem you sleep in spaces
A writer's face looks over his name: NORMAN BIRNBAUM
He protects you with his glasses
Painters with arcade guns see the light, then shoot the snow
In your arms you're brown, rising through the waves,
      henna shining in your hair

■

WILLIAM CORBETT

Henrietta Mench

It's rain, it's warm
for New Year's Eve.
Grandmother, she bathed
my chest, bandaged my cuts
carried me up the stairs
washed vomit and mud
from my face, told me
not to go out so
sloppy at the neck—
she meant a tie. She died
last night weighing seventy
pounds on an oscillating
bed. I walked to
Wing Wing's in Chinatown
past the Greek grocer's
round New Year's bread
and bought bok choy
water chestnuts, bitter
melon thinking rain might
turn to snow. She often
recalled playing with Edna
Small among cemetery stones
when snow shut Wilkes Barre
schools in 1897 or '98.
She liked waffles with
chicken gravy or a little
sauerkraut and pork.

■

LARRY FAGIN

Beatle Susan

In China you open for Elephant Gerald
On a stage of jade in glory fright
With lips to drink and instruments for singing
The Chinese go E-I-E-I-O!
You crash through imitation mayonnaise walls
to escape fate without the help of the gods
Flying to a distant spot hidden in a microdot
It's an oasis with paper lanterns
Somewhere over the pleroma
Flamboyant cartouches hang in the sky
Originally you were the Pipecleanermen
Whites imitating blacks imitating whites
You played "The Mosquito Serenade"
To a crowd of 12 in a drip-dry pub
Arty, dirty, freaky, plotless, nude, outrageously camp
Notes connected by crossbeams and slurs
Rock & roll was like learning to fall off a log
If you could get yourselves together to climb up on the log
Meanwhile Susan was on local TV
Singing "Just As I Am Without One Flea"
A talent scout saw her and the rest is history
She joined the boys in 1963
They recorded "Love Is Reality"
It made number one for an eternity
Burning in the tension of the Hot Club of France
Hands on the pedals, feet on the keys
Stretching sound with no-tone ditties
Shooting souls back into bodies
The Beatles sang their "World Song"
We are free and you must be
Prepared like us to live
To give to all both great and small
All we can give! All we can give!
The audience are ant-men who live in the leaves
It's the buzzing of the jiving bugs that makes them scream
In the studio you stand in an octagon
With 8 metronomes over 8 microphones

Ringo snaps his little hi-hat
Like a toddler flattening a mud pie
Faces are attenuated blurs under glass
Phoning "Rain" in to an ear
With elegant candor and fakery
For lunch there's tea and Creole kisses
And bacon-and-egg-wich on a rock
Then another take of "Wig America"
"Splatter Matter" and "Wail of the Scronch"
In Berlin if you walk out the door you're asking
For slime to be spread all over your body
So the Beatles huddle around the cottage teapot
In the dressing room of Marlene Dietrich
City lights flicker life like sleeping beauty pills
Take one and when you wake up you'll have a big hit
Like the immortals you seek to die
In the wake-rolled waves when the fans hit the shit
On your Indonesian tour the Flying Youth
Crown you with interconnected flower sprays
You're machinery; you've been sent
The concert begins
The Beatles transmit and the power is interiorized
In concentrated unified conscious consciousness
Through cooperation beyond normal expectations
The music is like ultraviolet purification
The fans love Susan's playful kittenish figure
Her intelligence, unaffected sensuality, beauty, sense of humor
And independent spirit
Yoko hates her
Sniffing the steel peach of immortality
"It is delishes" she tells the Belgian interviewer
At the albino tulip festival
She wears a gumwrapper necklace
The Beatles perform "mind-only" music
Phrases bent like fun house mirrors
Precipitating intercontinental shivers
The changes roll inside long hair
They never know when or where they'll be
Every breath is experimental
Wind and mind like pendulums
They walk on jelly legs
Worn out from drinking and smoking
Time stretched out with a loose end drooping

MARY FERRARI

Northern Lights

The Aurora Borealis shoots across the sky
above the Adirondacks at midnight
my old camp director rises up and asks me
why I did not become a poet
I ask to see my daughter
and am allowed to see her bicycle
I need a haircut
and am given a shaved head
at 3 A.M. giant trees
are riding across the sky
going as far as they want
the neighbors are awakened
and begin to write
my friend did not complain
so died unexpectedly
the sky is lighting up the bride
there's a sane life ahead
my daughter is sleeping on the moon
there's a rich new sky
I am kissed by a number of people
and walk in the woods with the man I am going to marry
who is wearing an unbecoming green sport shirt
of my father's
tombstones dating from the 1700s
appear during the wedding ceremony
I lie on my mother's bed
which is really my daughter's bed
if I had become a nun
we wouldn't have been born my son said
and drove away from the wedding
a gold tree climbs up my daughter's wallpaper
the garbage men are beginning
my husband mows the lawn for the last time
apples bananas and pears sleep peacefully together

the little ambulance waits
on the windowsill
I kiss my father at the wedding
though he is driving through the air
the sky is heavily populated now
a boy in a cape of many colors
rides away on a white horse
Christ is made of stone
but is sitting on a cloud
It is time for the Morning Offering
so I offer you these houses
not knowing why they are here
and rub my toes on the warm radiator
and wonder about the wind
which keeps me listening and treelike
and glad to be included
in this sepulchral wedding in the sky

■

K A T H L E E N   F R A S E R

Bresson Project:
"Forget you are making a film"

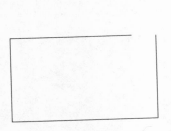

a picture of some snow or a spoon
inside her, the lonely one rattles
her crib bars like a big empty place
wanting sides to it
                thus this pecular
usage, firmness of the line moving
towards corners. Sides could be someone's arms and legs, around her. Lines
could be sides. There could still be
snow

"I will be happy to discuss strawberries or The Fiction of Distinctions
between Cinema and Actual Scenery." Dictation is my fiction, the act of
assigning peculiar usages, late August strawberries of the tiny French
varietals.

          he is particularly aggravated
          agger.vated   inner.vated
          he is violent   ultra-
          violet   She is
          the wow of his silver screen
          cinnamon queen with
          freckles, she's so fine,
          so fi-yi-yine

a picture of
a new bump on her scalp
under the fictional hairlocks
a new bee-bee in her bonnet
with a yarrow ribbon
on it
a little gold tomb, with an
old singing in it

238

This is the working medium between them, out of the mouth of Bresson, into the spoon of his reader, which we swallow the contents of. We make that effort. This is real, as a popular love song we remember from our childhood is real when it wets the heart with satisfying equations.

picture of a target
behind which a well-trimmed bull's eye
hides the idea of poverty,
blushing to show itself on the broader
bands of blue and yellow

a picture of
one powerline, fastened
in three places by
wire wrapped around
barbs, showing how much
distance has been traveled
from one to two
to three. Mozart approves
but understands what's
missing . . .

rushing forward
into the present moment, he
dies at a young age

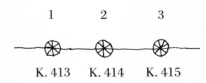

This is not what he had in mind.
This is not what occurred to him.
This is a bit further from the book which made a great impression.

"I'm drawing a blank just tell me a position."

■

Inventory

Seeing Pierrot in a shop window
I want to take him home with me
and I think I will, I do
every time I look in a mirror
and a mask looks back, with a
tear, a clean tear, and I don't
break its composure. Pierrot
makes it clean, like the casual
surgeon's cut just before the baby,
my third, was born. Did you
have an episiotomy last time,
he inquires, not wanting to have to
guess whether it's needed. Yes, and
then the clean line he made
echoes in blood, a little
left on baby's crown as I sit,   .
holding him, moments later.
I keep asking them to wash it
off, but the doctor goes
and nurses aides find
other things to do, leave too.
For months after, nursing him,
I look at that pulsing soft spot
and see where the blood was.
And when tears flow, more
generous than baby's milk supply,
they feel clean as that line
of blood, the weeping mask,
but the warm milk, flowing,
always shames me.

DICK GALLUP

Beyond the Chambers of My Heart
_____

Beyond the chambers of my heart
                     There is a place
Full of love
                     Love which passes from the day
Into endless nights of making love
In the darkness
                  My eyes see
The fountain in the distance
      Source and end of my being
Here
           And I feel the water
Blowing honesty and humility onto my face
          Before the power of love
          Becoming all encompassing
There is no other
The days go back to the beginning
                  And I must
Start over
               The world of dreams and aspirations
   For the ultimate
Mixture of man and woman

■

Wires

The inner landscape is blurred
After 12 hours the outer landscape is blurred
Check your nose: glasses still there
No fog, mist, rain or atmospheric miasma
A glance inward shows your brain is still missing
And the large psychic object you were trying to lift
Is still anchored in concrete
The pain begins in one place and ends in another
Between in a white line
Is the voice you hear while you write
Tracking you down as you back into the past
Which is overweight and has a busy signal.
When you pick up the house phone
All the lights go on
Congratulations!
You are now the Thane of Blurdom.

∎

Buddha

———————

Buddhas
are colonels
Buddhas are colonels
who shout
at trainees
Buddhas are colonels
who shout
who shout at trainees
at trainees,
"If you can't
strangle
a chicken
If you can't strangle
a chicken
If you can't strangle a chicken,
how
can you ever
make love
to a woman
how can you ever
make love to a woman
how can you ever make
love to a woman?"

Buddha
is Mr. Leon
Buddha is Mr. Leon
grabbing
a heavy
butcher
knife
Buddha is Mr. Leon

Buddhas
are colonels
Buddhas are colonels
who shout
at trainees
Buddhas are colonels
who shout
who shout at trainees
at trainees,
"If you can't
strangle
a chicken
If you can't strangle
a chicken
If you can't strangle a chicken,
how
can you ever
make love
to a woman
how can you ever
make love to a woman
how can you ever make
love to a woman?"

Buddha
is Mr. Leon
Buddha is Mr. Leon
grabbing
a heavy
butcher
knife
Buddha is Mr. Leon
grabbing

grabbing
a heavy butcher knife
grabbing a heavy butcher knife
and throwing it
and throwing it
at the gunman
and throwing it at the gunman
at the gunman,
who shoots
Mr. Leon
in the right
thigh
who shoots Mr. Leon
in the right thigh
who shoots Mr. Leon
in the right thigh,
and both men
fleeing
and both men fleeing
without
taking
any money
and both men fleeing
without taking
any money
without taking any money

Buddhas
are itinerant
street
vendors
Buddhas
Buddhas are itinerant
street vendors
are itinerant street vendors
who seem
to come

a heavy butcher knife
grabbing a heavy butcher knife
and throwing it
and throwing it
at the gunman
and throwing it at the gunman
at the gunman,
who shoots
Mr. Leon
in the right
thigh
who shoots Mr. Leon
in the right thigh
who shoots Mr. Leon
in the right thigh,
and both men
fleeing
and both men fleeing
without
taking
any money
and both men fleeing
without taking
any money
without taking any money

Buddhas
are itinerant
street
vendors
Buddhas
Buddhas are itinerant
street vendors
are itinerant street vendors
who seem
to come
out

out
of nowhere
who seem to come out
of nowhere
with their folding
tables
and well-worn
cartons
who seem to come out of nowhere
with their folding tables
and well-worn cartons
from which they sell
umbrellas
from which they sell umbrellas,
neckties
neckties,
handbags
handbags,
costume
jewelry
costume jewelry,
mechanical
toys
mechanical toys,
pretzels
pretzels,
and a variety
of other
merchandise
and a variety of other merchandise

Buddhas
are species
Buddhas are species
in which technology
has gone
out of control
in which technology
has gone out of control

of nowhere
who seem to come out
of nowhere
with their folding
tables
and well-worn
cartons
who seem to come out of nowhere
with their folding tables
and well-worn cartons
from which they sell
umbrellas
from which they sell umbrellas,
neckties
neckties,
handbags
handbags,
costume
jewelry
costume jewelry,
mechanical
toys
mechanical toys,
pretzels
pretzels,
and a variety
of other
merchandise
and a variety of other merchandise

Buddhas
are species
Buddhas are species
in which technology
has gone
out of control
in which technology
has gone out of control
in which technology has gone

in which technology has gone
out of control,
a technological
cancer
a technological cancer
spreading
through
our galaxy
spreading through our galaxy
a technological cancer
spreading through our galaxy

Buddha
Buddha
is like the most beautiful
diamond
Buddha is like the most beautiful
diamond
is like the most beautiful diamond
hidden
hidden
hidden in the mouth
of a corpse
in the mouth
of a corpse
in the mouth of a corpse

Buddha
is an ordinary
star
Buddha is an ordinary star
and a pulsar
Buddha is an ordinary star
and a pulsar
and a pulsar,
or pulsing
object
or pulsing object
of extreme
density

out of control,
a technological
cancer
a technological cancer
spreading
through
our galaxy
spreading through our galaxy
a technological cancer
spreading through our galaxy

Buddha
Buddha
is like the most beautiful
diamond
Buddha is like the most beautiful
diamond
is like the most beautiful diamond
hidden
hidden
hidden in the mouth
of a corpse
in the mouth
of a corpse
in the mouth of a corpse

Buddha
is an ordinary
star
Buddha is an ordinary star
and a pulsar
Buddha is an ordinary star
    and a pulsar
and a pulsar,
or pulsing
object
or pulsing object
of extreme
density
or pulsing object of extreme density

or pulsing object of extreme density
of extreme density,
waltzing
together
waltzing together
through space
waltzing together through space
far out
in the constellation
Hercules
through space far out
in the constellation Hercules
far out in the constellation Hercules

Buddha
is this mind
Buddha is this mind
and its quality
of creating
differences
Buddha is this mind
and its quality
of creating differences
and its quality of creating
differences,
that is not only
illusory
that is not only illusory
that is not only illusory,
but in fact
but in fact
does not
exist
does not exist
and has never been
born
but in fact does not exist
and has never been born
and has never been born

of extreme density,
waltzing
together
waltzing together
through space
waltzing together through space
far out
in the constellation
Hercules
through space far out
in the constellation Hercules
far out in the constellation Hercules

Buddha
is this mind
Buddha is this mind
and its quality
of creating
differences
Buddha is this mind
and its quality
of creating differences
and its quality of creating
differences,
that is not only
illusory
that is not only illusory
that is not only illusory,
but in fact
but in fact
does not
exist
does not exist
and has never been
born
but in fact does not exist
and has never been born
and has never been born

■

"She wanted"

She wanted
She wanted
a 500-
pound
lead
weight
a 500-pound lead weight
                attached
        to her television
                        set
attached to her television set
        so that the burglars
            wouldn't be able
so that the burglars wouldn't be able
                            just
                    to hoist it
            on their shoulders
just to hoist it on their shoulders
                    and walk
                        down
                the street
                    with it
and walk down the street with it.

■

"Dressed"

Dressed
Dressed
in bright
embroidered
     boots
in bright embroidered boots,
              and fur
                  hats
         and fur hats
     with long-barrelled
           rifles
with long-barrelled rifles,
          bows
     and quivers
      of arrows
bows and quivers of arrows
          and gleaming
           swords
and gleaming swords
       slung
    from shoulders
     or belts
slung from shoulders or belts,
         they turned
      in their saddles
they turned in their saddles
         to stare
        in slow
        surprise
to stare in slow surprise
at our white
faces
at our white faces.

■

JOHN GODFREY

Astral Roulette

Two quick strides! There!
Bus smokes past my heels, a
slingshot to the Battery, which
is down. I catch my breath
and Sing Wu a song, past those
lights, and their miniature bar
in the window. Ahead of me
in the sky stars are scrambling
from constellation to constellation
shaped as numbers 31 and 9:15
I always believe what's in
the sky at night, O Spanish moon!
And my heart always follows
that brave and unrefined intelligence

■

Texas

By moonlight, infantile progress. This is country across which only
an ass can travel, or the skin of one. The first cowboys sat on the
fence rails, upon pillows, refusing to return to work until the river
appeared. In all those years, it appeared three times, and so they
called it the Trinity River. Next they dug an enormous hole and
filled it with a small imported wood city, naming her after a bar
queen. In the background all swear they can hear threats in a *mesti-
zo* vocable, and that means war. Between this war and the striking
cowboys, we are forced to the truth, which was withheld until the
western movie of the '40's and '50's: what Walter Huston, Johnnie
Mack Brown, and Audie Murphy all had in common was the need

250

for gold, and in a place where the heart of the earth was black, the treasure was oil. (Cf. oil and the continuing prominence of outlaws.) It was only a visit by an evangelical football team that led them to remove their hats during meals and sex. They calmly wiped up the blood, hiding their embarrassment and their champagne. Soon, things went badly, and it became apparent that Texas was constitutionally too small for so many Texans. And I have not forgotten the overwhelming importance of the Rangerettes.

■

My Mother, Life

She came as a falling star to the lakes. She the lithesome virgin not to be turned into a tree, she who would never dress like a penguin. An original want-not, she believed in philosophy, but she called it faith. And so her talk entered my lungs and came out as a call to the innumerable vessels that are the wives of time.

Then there is the long span of silence. Every totem to acceptance she wore as an accessory. While the tropic darkened palm wore its microbe haunt she carried a burdened prose that was barely written, never spoken. She could look and look, and never imagine the stimulation of the lake when she saw the ocean there, so unneighboring. The circle of lake and the core of ocean depicted themselves after every rain, in sunlit rainbow. She had found a complex image that added up. So she rested, and from her rest I derived my strength.

Consider open accidents of flesh, consider perfection of fur in a cat, consider the curatorial mode of an almost wholly passed age, consider the feeling that has a character it emanates from. The fruit is no more costly than its retrieval, the light it gets is subject to cultivation, the dark it needs is infallibly measured, and then there is cool.

■

Come April

While the air is soft, before the thunder,
fourth graders with tattered notebooks haunt
the *cuchifritos* and their older brothers plague
a few stairwells crossing town to Nathan's
Eggplant bristles in sidewalk boxes on Avenue C
adjacent a larval well formed by an empty treebed
A smile in street cats' eyes could be any kind of dope
Voices universally spit out shrill colloquial jive
Regardless of her husky mastiff, Amos Rico asks
a young blonde in maxi passing the laundromat
if he might plunge his tongue in her timid chasm—
she doesn't answer, hardly looks, and her Fido
drops an enormous, awesomely firm turd at the crosswalk
The widow of an old pensioner passes at a shuffle
carefully steering her almost-empty shopping cart
She looks distrustfully at someone and tells herself "Everything's
    wrong!"
But the three schoolgirls on this busy sidewalk
are still enchanted, with each other's dark prettiness
and the filth and cobbled avenue are for *los otros*

These streets are like clouds in the valley where I am giant
And I am not stoned-out in a silver garbage can about to
attempt the falls surrounding ponce or Candlelabra!
Let me be overpowered by lecherous spring, as the busdriver
is, holding the door open an extra few moments, the more to
gander at two long, slim brown legs in candyapple hot-pants!
Naked to the toes, let me sweat the days longer, pausing
with aching tongue and dong in the unmistakable!
Bump Lulu in her toggle, peck a groove, squander tadpoles
bounce laughing down stoops of box springs, forget that
King Kong love will spoil, except for crazy slaves
except for juicy handicraft, clown to dawn!

■

TED GREENWALD

Show and Tell

When I first saw you
I liked you   You
didn't come on the way
you thought you came on
My first impression of you was
you're a person
who I'm really glad to know
who's interested
in intellectual thoughts and true meanings of things
and I figured
since I was so glad to really get to know you
you'd be pretty glad to get to know me
and maybe I would touch your face with my hands
like I'm in the process of doing now
and look at you at arm's distance
and then closer in
when and if it's ok with you
and we could walk out of this room
arm-in-arm or shoulder-to-shoulder
just touching every other step or so
and go get a coke
or a pepsi and some grilled cheese
I really'd like a cheeseburger more
and talk about books and movies
and just exchange
if you'd want to do that with me
intellectual thoughts
and true meanings   Just
about ourselves   We would be able
to share and explore
all the little thoughts and feelings
that really can mess up the day
if things don't go right

and all the quote irritations of modern living unquote
that Chekhov discussed so well
and then maybe we could learn to be friends
in this process of discovering
what makes each other tick
Pass me a cigarette
and pass me a cup of coffee   Maybe
if we learn to really like one another
I'll sit next to you the next session we have
and Bob and John and Alice and Kit
and you and me
will move our chairs a lot closer together
and really begin to understand
what really makes us tick in the mind
and straighten out our true meanings
We'll call each other on the phone
write letters and postcards to each other
when we're away for vacation
and write poems about what we do each day
and really all the love
even while a lot of loneliness exists in the world
and how we learn each other's quirks
We'll better cope with anything *and anyone*
that might come up and we might meet
and we'll rent a farm
and start a commune
that probably won't be as easy as starting a car
and we'll skinny dip in the pond
take planes to Europe
help the disadvantaged and underdeveloped
make the world a better place to grow in
and when we get old
we'll look back *on all this*
and know just know
just six of us had the power
to change the course of things
by learning to get along better
and it all started
with us sitting down
looking each other straight in the eye
and rapping

■

As If Nothing Happens

As if nothing happens
There's a flower
And we've been there
We're among its petals
But, without thinking,
There's another flower
And we're there too
The sudden colors,
They're a kind of love
While the feelings
Are late at night,
Very nightlike, awful
In their nightness
And we find ourself
Sleeping alone sleeping
Alone, too far along
We're tangled in traffic
We return elsewhere
But our thoughts
There's a flower
It's another
They are with us
We're lost for words

■

Break Glass

Blood bells yawn
The mind itself
Turned over and
Gone doesn't mind
Nothing recognizing
The natural condition
Of the world and
Its air conditioning
It looks
Like it's raining
(Ho hum)   What can
I say   There's nothing
In air worth grabbing
In case of

■

R O B E R T   G R E N I E R

Fundamental

---

act of forgetting
lackluster having
unlocked the door

on purpose so as
to be able to go
back in through it

and to *having forgotten*
going back to around through
the upstairs with the chair

■

MARILYN HACKER

She Bitches About Boys

To live on charm, one must be courteous.
To live on others' love, one must be lovable.
Some get away with murder, being beautiful.

Girls love a sick child or a healthy animal.
A man who's both itches them like an incubus
but I for one have had a bellyful

of giving reassurances and obvious
advice with scrambled eggs and cereal,
then bad debts, broken dates, and lecherous

onanistic dreams of festival
nights when some high-strung well-hung penurious
boy, not knowing what he'd get, could be more generous.

■

LEE HARWOOD

Memories of Times Passed Now

It's so hard playing games all day
with the kittens playing at my feet
Playing games on the lawn in summer
What is the sun doing shining on those large yellow flowers?
& the yellow flowers in my arms
The yellow shirt & blue waist-coat
Now when the shadows are long across the lawns
beneath the tall trees the turf is so damp
Do you understand?   It's so hard
wearing the yellow shirt & avoiding the gardener
& every house-guest   There has to be some make-believe
to sink my head into

■

L Y N   H E J I N I A N

Natural Room

walls, four. floor. cubic feet. morning. ceiling crack
(from age or quake) over bureau placed against wall. west.
window divides wall into world. find words for it. then
get lost in the details. the figure an excuse for patterned
rug and wallpapers. print dress. push pins up photos,
postcards. character built. faded red construction paper
heart signed Anna on St. Valentine's. brush and silver
bracelet on blue bureau from St. Vincent's. mirror reflects
bureau top and floor, rug. artificial oriental. pride
of place from earthly cares. bed over standard. capital
memoir jams memorized space. from John's Aunt Ruth's desk
now Larry's papers spill or drop. outer realities. window
divided into panes. high-pitched. drop sports. gather
segments of the yellow light. alarm clock. "in the interim
quality of areas." blocks considered astonishingly complex.
checkerboard jam-up. one for the lightning thought which
one may clothe in words. skin trip. series in school
photos of Paul. silhouette. slant. minutiae on floor
grain. still life. souvenirs on painted walls. totem
role. mother's mother face on, father's mother in profile.
attention fixed while thoughts wander. north. it's written
down upstairs. "bit by bit daily life becomes such that
there is a place for hope in it." warm day from down south.
in animate tableau square of light on pillow mirrored.
trees out window. volume of books. branch library. waste
basket. read meaning into it. think tank. quip. quilt.
Indian bed spread curtains. window trimmed Williamsburg
blue. domestic industrial sash. window facing east. "nor
can it be said to communicate the past to us." known if
noted. setting nests. color patches larger world outside
in. plants before windows into leaves. squad. stem frame.

thought balloons. wall space. written shapes in such positions. close resemblance. inside closed clothes closet is stuff on floor. in room is chair with sitter in slippers. wire hangers bent like bows. books beside the bed I want to read. books I wish I'd read already. old Oakland phone book without cover on the floor. Larry's leather boots. rubber plant. nuclear family. "committed content." fountain pens in. door knobs. knocks in conclusion. key attention.

■

DAVID HENDERSON

Third Eye World

faces in the street
in the financial district or ghetto red zone
the anonymity of casual citizenry
faces of color recall another land
the mind can hear the music
pentatonic or percussive
and song
the relationship with the official language
everyone can sing

the soul of an egyptian chanteuse
of a bangkok songstress
or a mambo chorale in brazil
the ecological harmonies of the pygmies
or the subterranean hi-life of azania
namibia   zimbabwe

third world and american
english speaking with roots in ancestral lands
(like everybody else, just about)
belonging to a new world
yet of an older world
but with the perception of both
keen in the mind
that gives another world
consciousness   even cosmic
the third eye
astral base of the third world

■

Azania: For Thee, We

Nomad Azania   Black homeland
shantytown captive Bantustan
Zulu of the Veld, Bantu of the Transvaal
encourage the whites to stay
encourage the whites to stay

Black Yellow Brown Azanian faces
South Afrikaans' death for Third World races
abandoned to apartheid by the free
Black death floating gold standard
Black death floating gold standard

For children of color—Boer genocide
The free-world consumes death from apartheid
Rows of little coffins of bare plywood
the demand exceeds supply
the demand exceeds supply

Dead Black souls in the diamond rings of June
Vows below bloody Azanian moon
Israel speculates in Afrikaans
Golems buy the krugerrand
Golems buy the krugerrand

> Daughter of Azania
> She's walking to Botswana
> Daughter of Azania
> She's walking to Botswana
>
> Daughter of Azania
> Her feet are swollen swollen
> She's walking towards freedom
> Daughter of Azania
> Her feet are bloody bloody
> She's walking into freedom

Gandhi's ghost attacks golems of the rand
Soweto's children free the Bantustans
Strange fires burn apartheid beyond control
*Azania: for thee—*wE
*Azania: for thee—*wE

Nomad Black Brown Yellow upon no man's land
No krugerrand no no Bantustan no
No apartheid no no genocide no
YES REVOLUTIONARY
*Azania: for thee—*wE

YES WE YES WE YES WE YES WE YES WE

■

FANNY HOWE

Excerpts from
The Gospel According to Thomas

Q: On what day will the d——d rest and a motion change the world?

JESUS: The rest has already come, but you don't know about it. You look right through the motion and wonder about the d——d.

Q: How does your owner reveal itself?

JESUS: It's both a motion and a rest.

Q: Will it be revealed to us like that, when we die?

JESUS: You won't see the light when you have no eyes and are d——d. You'll only see it while you're alive, with it. Through hard work you find the way to this light. But in the end, you will only be saved by solitude.

Q: How will we know it when we see it?

JESUS: When you know who you are, you know who your owner is, like a child with a parent. And when you discover the truth, you'll be amazed; and when you're amazed, your amazement will take over and give you rest at last. If you are looking for truth, don't give up until you've found it.

Q: We have been told that fasting, prayer and charity are the three degrees of active faith. Are they?

JESUS: Everything you do is open to the sky. Just don't tell lies and don't do things that you hate to do.

Q: But fasting?

JESUS: What you take in, like food, can't make you spiritually sick; but what you put out can really hurt you. Welcome what people give you to eat and go about, trying to help the sick.

Q: But—

JESUS: Whenever you fast, you create new sins.

Q: And prayer?

JESUS: Whenever you pray, you are censured.

Q: And charity?

JESUS: Whenever you give to charity, you abuse your spirit.

Q: What are we doing here?

JESUS: If the body is here to sustain the soul, that's one miracle. But if the soul is here to sustain the body, that's a double miracle.

Q: What are souls like?

JESUS: Nursing babies are like souls entering the matrix.

Q: How can we enter too?

JESUS: If you can make a double into a single; and if you can make the outside the same as the inside, and the upper the same as the lower; and if you can make yourselves both male and female, so that you aren't one or the other; and if you can make your eyes function as an Eye, your hand function as a Hand, and your foot function as a Foot, and if you can see images solely as Images—then you, too, can enter heaven.

Questions: interpreted

Responses: from Coptic, Greek and
English versions by
Fanny Howe

JUNE JORDAN

Poem to Commemorate the PBS-TV Series on An Interracial Marriage in the U.S.A.

omygod
is it interracial
omygod
that decent that sweet that superstraight
World War II
Black
veteran's about to kiss his white
wife
omygod
omygod
he's gonna kiss her
he's comin closer
closer
he's gonna do it
she's his white
wife
he's gonna kiss her
(i'm gonna kiss her
if he don't hurry up)
heart attack time
omygod
she's liftin her face
he's lowerin his
they're almost
she's almost
he's almost gonna kiss her
omygod
he's gonna kiss her
i'm gonna kiss him
quick!
we better lockup all this
love

■

TULI KUPFERBERG

If You Want to Be President
(To the tune of:
"If you Want to Be Married/
Lead a Happy Life . . .")

If you want to be President
A very long while
Be sure you invade
A very small isle.

For if it is tiny
And its soldiers are few
They'll never make
A fool out of you.

You may kill with impunity
Kill for a lark
If the color of your victims
Is rather dark.

And all of the Americans
Will love you too
If the total dead Americans
Is rather few.

But when the numbers mount up
As they did in Vietnam
Then you could be
In a bad political jam.

So invade the tiny island
Where the soldiers are naive
And leave Nicaragua
To the mercenaries.

And always kill people
For their own good
Ban meetings, censor papers
For Libertyhood.

You can always find a puppet
Speaks a civil tongue
Appointed by a Queen
Who was appointed very young.

Postpone the elections
That you said you sought
For what if the results
Are not what they ought?

Protect all Americans
Kill a lesser breed
It's the black man's burden
It's the blood lust that you feed.

And after you've refused
The help that could have saved 'em
Be very very generous
The while you re-enslave 'em.

It's not if you win or lose
It's how you play the game
And if the whole world goes down
At least you've killed all the same.

Old soldiers never die
They only kill
The movie stars with general's bars
They fill the corporate till.

They bring jobs and co-prosperity
Throughout the Northern Regions
And the number that enjoy all this
Is unfortunately legion.

O someone else's suffering
Is int'resting to see
You can watch it every night
On CBS or NBC.

And while you are dining
Always recollect
It's not you or your son dying
But only gookish dreck.

When you got two million men
Under their arms
How long can you keep them
Down on Nancy's farm?

You know well everybody
Likes a good killin'
And testin' new weapon-toys
Well, isn't that thrillin'!

Tho we can only have
One nuclear war
Well, 1, 2, 3 Vietnams
We can have even more

So if you want to be President
A very long while
Be sure you invade
A tiny, tiny isle . . .

For if it is small enough
And its soldiers very few
I can never make
A fool out of you . . .

                        (I think)

■

JOANNE KYGER

"This dance"

_____

This dance when they see the

river, haven't lost it yet, nor would they ever.

It asks the sea, she says, it is not new.

Came out of a rock, and it is not idle commentary

Unfolds and remains stationary; over and over
it gets told

The city made its own haze; an old fat dog rushed at me in the

park, barking at me, snapping. Who are you, I said. I am the

sun he said.

I died wrong said the tree, you will not find me

happy for you, as before when I was wed and braided around

with the ropes of prayers and beads in bright colors.

Like little birds now my soul goes
and hovers above the city.

I'll do it for you, I'll do it for you

as much as I can. They gather differently, and appear to me

more like true flowers, searching. Brooding deeply, the heaviness

of the line and thought, emotion, search to find a surface. His

strength, though manifent, had certain magical aspects which I

felt to be of a debased or primitive nature. The scars on his back bore evidence of this, the long arrow sealed in his flesh.

But though I pitted myself against him, bidding another stand behind
       me, my strength
    did not rise to meet his; it is uncertain whether any past sense of
       possession was
    true or not. As he advanced toward me flashing projections of
       light, not one bit
    concentrated energy could I produce, till he made that electrical
       light touch me
    also.

                         The body rose up in a ball

from the belly. What is that I said. It is the moon, he replied.

■

"I don't want to repeat"

        I don't want to repeat
       the same mistakes over again,
    or the mistakes somebody else made just so
I can have the experience of them. See, fucked
up again. Live and learn. And off the excessive
fondness for one's own self-knowledge, un-
tested, but reigning supreme. That leads me
more astray, every day. What we commonly
know in the air, in our dreams, what chooses
continually & continually to grow, the obvious
under our noses, is this life. Yearning in blindness. The weed has a name, is quite proud of itself, builds a community with other weeds, birds
hop through. The imported domestic is a labor
of love, but a labor, such a labor. At home here,
no single thought is my thought. It whispers
      through the air in sweet misty fog,
         in bright sky blue.

■

Phoebe

Oh moon
mother of Apollo
and hush
and wife of intelligence
third possessor of the Delphic Oracle
Oh it's raining, Oh it's raining
those delicate hints of dreams, of beads
of the eastern mind looking into the large mansions of the west

■

LUCY R. LIPPARD

New York Times I

Disintegration. At a time when there seems to be less official concern over environmental quality, the faculties of the Episcopal Theological School, General Theological Seminary and Divinity School declared jointly that masculinity as such constitutes no necessary qualification for ordination to the priesthood. The basic qualification is not masculinity but rather "redeemed humanity." The corner of Church and Canal is a concentrated center of pollution. This example should inspire contiguous countries to establish a similar burden on their alienation. It is a grotesque misuse of language to term as highly moral a national leader who has prisoners of war executed on television. Migration, without higher costs, we say, is all very mysterious. The air there at the corner is not satisfactory when breathed in unhappiness. We might all be happy female priests in pollution-free Scandinavia if we could afford to migrate. Instead we are con artists in a high-pollution esthetic with no religion to opiate out of society on. On which to. I keep my typewriter in a wastebasket for fear someone will steal it/me. I throw away time to use it. The sole of one of my boots is edged with dog shit and I sniffle constantly. Not junk, just junk. Everyday living. Not all the soap in the operas could clean these little sidewalks rushing with blood at run hour. I am out of touch with Watergate, The Gulf of Tonkin, Bay of Bigs (sic), Pearl Harbor, Tiffany's museum air. A wino nourished on typos. I was more afraid of Hitler in the dark than of Hirohito even though my father was in the South Pacific. Couldn't take the buck teeth seriously. And I'm out of touch with my current way of life, based as it is on working my ass off to support a system I do not believe in, for the sake of those victimized as I am by enthusiasm for some of the Systems's products. The System, the System, The Wicked Wicked System.

To most migrant birds, this whole continent is "home." I have lived in New York for Times immemorial. I am trying to say something. I like it here. I keep my head high, squinting through the smog, I knock the shit off my heel with a rakish kick and stride to the registered letter line in the Post Office with bands playing in the back of my brain. To block everything else out. I gave up the Staten Island ferry for a loan to save the city. Despite walls of discrimination that keep women from anything like equal opportunity in public or private office. I have supported myself and my kid for a decade here. The older women waiting in the doctor's waiting rooms do not read. They stare into vacant space. Mass movements among animals, fish, insects are not unusual; among people they are virtually impossible not to fuck up. *En masse.* Eight o'clock isn't early enough. Theologically we women beg to differ with logic. My irrationale insists upon the threat of unhappiness. At home lies a man with the covers over his head in a darkened room. He cannot face it but I stride on, tripping over my lost apron strings. My women friends are less prone (Stokely Carmichael notwithstanding) to corner funks, black pouts, and depressions. They just flip out. Noisily, silently, drunkenly, dizzily, dismally. Gone. I saw her yesterday and she seemed fine. Gone. A little edgy maybe. Gone. She missed the assembly where her kid got the citizenship prize. Home lying under the table. Still alive.

Said a woman who runs a gift shop in Hinsdale, a heavily Republican suburb, "I'm appalled at what a weasel he is. How he thought publishing those transcripts could ever help him, I'll never know." The new ecology law vetoed last night would have supported weasels too. The shop carries salt and pepper shakers in the form of little wooden "privvies." A face appears at the window of each. His and hers. Yours and mine. I have no separate options. I would miss him too much. A slightly more grotesque version of these salt and pepper shakers can be found at the general store on Canal near Church Street where you can also pick up an erratic watch for NY time, miscellaneous rubber tubes, a plastic Davy Crockett hat, or brown suspenders. If I could change the world, where would I start? Canal Street is the end at Church. Once a stream ran along it but it became a sewer before the Civil War. The War Between the States.

Maybe I've lived in New York too long. A woman of considerable breadth and scope. Once I traveled. I backpacked around the world and camped in jungles and swam in the Ganges and climbed the highest peak in Iceland and braved the Horn in a small boat and got pregnant in Nairobi and came home. Once I lived in foreign countries and spoke fluently several obscure languages I no longer remember except when I dream in them. I can make hot sausage spaghetti with fennel, a good beef stew with cloves, curried macaroni and cheese. My family wishes I cooked better. I wish they cooked at all. I can sail a boat by myself and have supported a husband and have screwed around and can fix the toilet and lift heavy weights and walk home very late in the dark Manhattan streets sighing for the shadows sighing in the doorways.

■

LEWIS MACADAMS

I Speak for the Hunter

I speak for the hunter
    and I speak for the deer
I speak through the feather
    in the sun-bear's beard about
the clitter-claj of little gents swooning toward the new order
    like malignant tumors on a stray dog.

The dog roars.

I speak for the feather
    in the path of the broom
  Animal pray for me,
the bullet speeding toward your ear o catarrh
    and phlegm of a legume
      ghastly host spread through its husk
spitting mutter and foam. Hear
    the serpentine sputter in your phone.

. . . . .

I speak for the highway
that runs through your bones. To the flash
of plasma bursting
from a shattered deer. The hunter yips
and approaches.
The hunter takes aim with his potion.
The aim of the machine is frenzy
and the path of genius rolls to peace,
bed, the hearth of a woman burning
till her lover comes home soothed
by the blue dog, the chemical bark
When death holds the door the bullet speeds through
"Fire up the cook stove, ma, I got me some game!"
Take dead aim through the throes of emperor's
discordant, glutted burial stalls
the dog calls, the bullet calls
I am thee who speaks through walls
I am the hunter enraged in the hall.

■

JAMIE MACINNIS

\Jim & Edith

_____

sit at a table
with friends. Her cigarette
smoke curls in his half-closed
eyes as though smoke were the
intoxicant here.

I love this nightclub photo
taken by a camera girl.
It shows them
as they saw
themselves:
independent operators.

Surrounded by a group of "in-coolies"
impeccably staring inward
eyes white as diapers.

Utter partygoers without gossip,
they like to dance. They like to insert
a joke. They like to smoke.
A picture of natives, one carries
the other in her arms.

■.

GERARD MALANGA

from *The Secret Diaries*

August 29, 1966

I'm behind in my life and have to catch up to remind myself who is presently involved in my movement and refrain from the use of second names. Julie, a young teenie-bopper tillie from Michigan came up to the factory to visit Andy but Andy had nothing to say to her and turned her and turned her onto me and after three days I got bored with the same old "petting" shit I would get myself involved with when I was in the ninth grade. I'm almost finished with the writing of the *Screen Test* diary text, but Andy has a lot of stills that have to be made. Last night Andy and I went to hear Peter Schjeldahl read his poems at Folklore Center. Andy sat behind the open door so as not to be seen. Peter's voice sounds a lot like John Ashbery's. The second part of the reading was much better than the first. He read his "20 Paris Sonnets" (dedicated to Ted Berrigan). They were more meaty, more concerned with himself as a person and not as a poet commenting on poetry or aesthetics. The first half of his reading was concerned with more elusive elements and references, more abstract in nature and sound. The sonnets read aloud extremely well. Andy split after the first set because he had a great deal of work to finish up at the factory. After the reading was over, I joined Ted and Peter and Lewis MacAdams and his girlfriend Phoebe and a few other people for a drink at the *Limelight* over on Seventh Avenue South. Phoebe is a Radcliffe sophomore and very very pretty. Lewis and I discuss Andy, money, literary aesthetics. I haven't had such a deep conversation in a long time but it created closer ties. I was having fun; I became too self-indulgent. I felt like I was being interviewed. I've got to break that habit of answering questions as if I were being interviewed.

The following is the hours' work I put in for Andy at the factory:

August 21   0   Sun.   _____0
        22   8   Mon.   3:00–11:00 P.M.
        23   3   Tues.   10:30–11:30 A.M.–4:00–6:00 P.M.
        24   1   Wed.   5:00–6:00 P.M.
        25   3   Thurs. 4:00–7:00 P.M.
        26   4   Fri.   3:00–7:00 P.M.
        27   4   Sat.   5:00–9:00 P.M.

        23   total

                        1.25
                      × 23
                      ─────
                       375
                      250
                      ─────
                      28.75

September 2, 1966
Provincetown, MA

Why do I have to begin today's entry by seeing Susan walking down Commercial Street in Provincetown, making me dodge into an alley to keep from running into her? It's not hard to spot her—even at a 2½ block distance. Her new boyfriend David will last longer than the rest because he'll listen and do everything she says, from entrances and exits to attempting to make people previously involved with her up tight by parading for everyone to see and/or judge.

Provincetown is a place where not every pretty person has sex. Camille, a belly dancer from Martinique working at the Plain and Fancy, smiles at me. Gail is a very attractive girl from B.U.; (Marjorie I can't keep my eyes off of. I'm thinking of Phoebe from Radcliffe and have plans to make it with her, but probably won't, having said what I already want to do. I jerked off while taking a shower second day in a row. Everyone is uptight for amphetamine. It's great to see everybody frantic when you know you can work on your own juice and not have to think about where the next source of supply is going to come. We're all waiting in front of the museum to go to the beach. Roger's trip book is the best hand-made 1 copy edition piece of amphetamine art I've ever seen.

I scribble some notes to incorporate into a poem, as wedging and concrete substance intervals.

I came across a copy of a rare mass-market paperback edition of the novel "Two" by Eric Jourdon (Louis Jourdon's brother), translated by the American poet Richard Howard.

September 3, 1966

Early in the evening we did three shows at the Chrysler Art Museum. We wore mod fashions, got free flower-print shirts. I adjusted the strobes to reflect on the body of a girl wearing a bikini. I inquire about her. Elena. She lives ¾ of the year at Florida, and spends her summers at Provincetown. I made it with her last night. She made touch seem so beautiful. I walked her home. She lives on Commercial Street a few buildings from where we're all staying. 15 people stayed overnight. Wall to wall mattresses. I was just handed a letter Mary wrote to me when I was in Chicago three months ago. The letter traveled thousands of miles, passed through many hands and came to me still sealed. Got into an argument with Andy that was triggered by the accusation that I didn't clean up the dirty dishes, when in fact I hadn't made anything for myself to eat, nor was I anywhere near the house when the mess was made, nor was I aware of the fact that there was a mess. Andy must be overdosed with diet pills.

George gave me a small rose and a poem in the new world auditorium of light and sound. I'm going to entitle the first third of *The Debbie High School Drop-out Poems* "Drugs and Cosmetics." The friends gathered tonight in the small room. Andy was acting quite comfortable and happy, which seems peculiar.

Lou went to bed with "X." This morning I made it for the second time with Elena under the sheets in the living room. I don't know whether George was uptight, but everybody who was awake must have known what we were doing. Eric is living with Nico and her son Ari. Eric resembles Ari and people who see them walking on the street with Ari on Eric's shoulders probably think that Eric is Ari's father. Ronnie made a full-color magic marker and ink portrait of me for my trip book. It's the first time I ever really paid any attention to Ronnie. We're both very shy of one another. I hope it will become a genuine relationship, although I'm never really certain of myself when I get involved with other people. Andy went to a small gathering with Nico and Paul. Andy told me earlier that he liked my diary very much because of the way I record events and news of the day. I don't remember what I wrote in my book earlier in the day, and I hope I haven't said anything that would make Andy uptight.

George gets uptight because I tell him I'll be back in half an hour but I return a half hour late.

At the last show of The Exploding Plastic Inevitable, Eric proves to be a visual-physical freak-out. Susan refuses to dance on the panel board in front of the projectors. During the "Heroin" number in the last show, I get on the dance floor to go through my mime motions and Eric gets on my platform and his friends come on stage and start dancing around me. I begin to feel both internal and external suffocation and really wonder if I am not just hallucinating. Susan blocks the spotlight, and Alan and Roger pick up the strobes and aim them not at me but at Susan. I'm in almost total darkness. Mary is also in total darkness, except for occasional sequences where I am able to aim my one flashlight on her or project one of the hand-strobes behind me. Andy seems oblivious to the situation and to my personal feelings. I wonder if he realizes that my status as a spotlight-star in The Exploding Plastic Inevitable has been reduced considerably by the intrusion of too many people and the lighting assistants who can't follow directions.

September 5, 1966

We arrive in New York—8:00 A.M., drop Andy off at his house and bring the movie projectors back to the factory. Paul drops off Larry, Bob and Sterling and drops Mary and me off in Brooklyn Heights. I spend the afternoon sleeping on the terrace at Willard's and Marie's penthouse. I dream—dreams I can't remember. I'm thinking of George who is supposed to be in Boston with Ruthie and Ronnie. I take a shower. Marie comes home from a day's hard work at Time-Life. Mary calls. She's coming over. We have frankfurters and potato salad. Paul makes his entry in my trip book in the form of a pentel emblem. We watch television and become plastic. Marie says, "Camp is serious." I call Andy—no answer at home, no one at the factory. Call long distance to Boston to speak with George—Ruthie's phone is disconnected. We sit around dinner tables doing portraits of one another. I will stay at Paul's tonight. Joe offers me a room at his place in Brooklyn. I'll probably end up staying there—but so many things are bound to happen. George has an apt. for me and Lou and Anne to shack up. John might have an apt. for me at $50.00 a month which is very reasonable and private. Willard is napping. I should write a letter to Elena. Lexi, Willard's dog, looks so beautiful sprawled across the orange quilt on the bed in the back room. I think I'll write a letter to Andy, but I'll write it in my book.

Mary didn't say too much in the bedroom at Provincetown. It reminded me of the time I used to split from the crowds in Los Angeles and Frisco without Mary beside me. Now I begin to feel how Mary must have felt or might have felt. She never flinches. She holds her "cool" very well. Marie says, "Natural things are always to be remembered. Artificial things are to be recorded."

Monday, September 6, 1966

Dear Andy:

It seems I'm always writing you letters to explain myself, my feelings, what's bothering me.

I thought the Provincetown show got off to a rough but very good start, until you were so kind enough as to let Susan and everyone else not directly connected with the show get involved with Mary and me on stage. Also, it was unfortunate that Mary had to be dancing above me and not with me.

I want to make it clear to you that (1) I was dancing with the Velvets long before you signed them into a corporation empire, and even before you knew them; (2) that my dancing is an integral part of the music and the show as are your movies; (3) I do not represent a "go go" dancer in the show but an interpretative-visual happening. You are slowly taking this away from me by allowing outside elements to interfere with my dance routines. Also, Larry was supposed to have the spotlight on me when not projected on the Velvets. Instead, that spotlight wandered away from what was supposed to be seen on stage.

On more than one occasion, I found my flashlight missing and then discovered that Roger was dancing with it somewhere near the end of the show. On more than one occasion, I also discovered other people handling the strobes which were inconveniently placed on the stage. All this led up to Mary and me dancing in total darkness at times. The only way this can be rectified for future shows is not to have troupe dancing but two people at a time. I am willing to take turns. From my vantage, to have more

than two dancers on the stage turns the show into a
Mothers of Invention freak-out. I feel that you will do
nothing in your almost absolute power to correct the mess
you are responsible for, in which case, if you won't, I will.

Faithfully,

Gerard

September 8, 1966

Andy likes playing games with my head, thinking he can break
me; but just when he thinks he has me, I break loose from under
him. My sign is Pisces. I was born at the beginning and end of the
spectrum. I am on the cusp between Pisces and Aries. Susan likes
to take up as much of Andy's attention as she can. She's so
insecure about her "good looks." René hasn't been heard from in
three days.

Called Allen today to get quote on Bob Dylan for Aspen
magazine. He tells me Steven is angry with me because I didn't
speak with him when he came up to the factory. I didn't expect
him. He was with Jerry Joffin. I hadn't seen him in two years, and
he's grown up quite a bit. Gotten taller, in fact, and is even growing
a beard. We get paid tomorrow, hopefully, for the Provincetown
show. I have to send off the "3 Poems for Benedetta Barzini"
manuscript to Angel Hair. Nico said that "Susan lacks class."

September 10, 1966

Yesterday Andy told an acquaintance how terrific Susan was. I
wonder what he's trying to prove? I've been wearing the same shirt
for three days and the same polka dot tie. Andy's been uptight for
sometime. He made a movie last night of Ondine playing the Pope
hearing confessions by Ingrid and Pepper (who has changed her
name to Angelina). During the shooting of the first reel with Ingrid,
the plug connecting the camera with the sound and the circuit came
out of its socket. Andy didn't notice this for about 10 minutes.
Unfortunately, he suspects somebody had accidentally kicked it out,
but I'm too familiar with the sockets in the factory, and the one
Andy selected to connect the camera into was the only one whose
grip is not tight enough. Sometimes, I know what I am talking about
and that I don't know what I'm talking about. 2:45 P.M.—George
and Anne and I visit Nat at the Hotel Chelsea—my old stomping
ground. Nico is here. Eric is living with her. Willard has left for

Maine. Maybe there will be room for me at the penthouse apt. with Marie. Paul said he could get me a round trip ticket to London for between $330 and $370.

September 15, 1966

Got into the worst argument today with Andy—the preliminary cause of it all: Paul's alarm clock didn't go off in time to wake us. Paul and Lou and I stayed over. We didn't have a place to stay. Andy's procrastination was one of the causes in not getting the film originals printed. They could have all been printed the previous week, but Andy decided to capitalize on the commercial idea of pushing the films under the title of Chelsea Girls. Paul forgot to include René's name in the Cinematheque ad—another incompetency. Andy is putting together new slides—a job Danny once did. Andy doesn't seem to realize that I work on the clock for $1.25 an hour. Circles of lives revolving around each other and across each other. The lives constantly revolving around one another. George looks so fantastic today. Nobody has a place to stay. I have poems to write; movies to make. Richard Howard said he would work out a scenario from Eric Jourdon's novel Two, which he translated, especially for me. I think George would make a perfect co-star. Andy wants to show The Gerard Malanga Story sequence in its original to spite my showing up late to the factory. I think ½ hour chopped off the film show won't matter as much as permanently damaging the film. Andy is, sometimes, beneath contempt. His contempt has come out in full show today, and it is very unfortunate. My end of the dance routine is complete—a new outfit from Barbara. Two flashlights. Lightbelts. Whips. Tinfoil. Right now I can't think, but will probably stay at Paul's tonight.

September 12, 1966

Yesterday went to a party for The Stones. Debbie was supposed to meet me to see Warren's film "Amphetamine" at the Cinematheque, but had Barbara call me telling me she couldn't make it because she had an arugment with Paul about something and that he was going to New Jersey and might be coming back later in the evening. René hasn't been heard from in days, and Ondine is living with Orion on East 94th Street. George doesn't have a home. We turned on to some crystal "A," ·the first I've taken in one year. I wrote a 1,000 line poem called "The Thunder Machine." It's my life story. I stayed up the entire day sitting in the factory. George comes over

to the apartment in the afternoon dream cycle. He doesn't say anything. We open at the Dom on Friday. I'll have money to live on
again, although I still don't have an apt. of my own. Nico is living
with Eric, and Susan told "Don-Don" at Max's one night that she
was more intelligent than Nico and Edie put together. Susan is probably the most beautiful girl on the "scene" at the moment. Her big
problem is that she thinks she can buy friendships with money.
Tomorrow I have to clear my head. There are balls to attend.

At the Hotel Chelsea I manage to notate in my diary a letter
Susan wrote addressed to me in Doctor Bridget's trip book. "I admit
to my vulgarity, Gerard—but I managed to 'buy' you—how well does
that speak of you—I don't remember seeing 'Don-Don' at Max's. I
haven't been there in over a month because I don't care for certain
people who 'hang out' there. I too have balls to attend. But my head
is at least clear. Dear Gerard—if you are Andy Warhol as you say,
why don't you behave as he would."

International Velvet
of who?

September 18, 1966

My life is before me in whatever I do. Tonight I felt religious
dancing on stage. George looked on with pride. My uptight scenes
with Andy cease momentarily, which is good for my head. The Exploding Plastic Inevitable show was a total success, contrary to what
Susan said, who referred to it being "disappointing." Spoke with
Allen Ginsberg today. Told him about my acid-amphetamine poem,
"The Thunder Machine"—a title I stole from Lou—which he got, I
believe, from John Cale—because I liked it and it meant something
inherent to the poem's conception. David B. tells me my journals
will be an historic document of the 60's.

September 21, 1966

At Max's Kansas City, a beautiful girl seemed very interested in
me, always passing a glance at the table where I was sitting not far
from where I could see her. After some time, a waitress came up to
me, handing me a note which read: "Jerry—to a beautiful New York
Star from a beautiful Hollywood Star AND so we meet there—I
admire your work. Sincerely, Best regards, Love XXXXX Bobbi
Shaw." She disappeared. The only clue in knowing where to find

her and not where to find her is that Dick Nusser knew Bobbi when he used to go to Ocean City, New Jersey about three years ago.

Rona is sitting with me at Max's. I feel somewhat disappointed that I can't locate Bobbi Shaw.

September 22, 1966

Paul comes into Max's. He's uptight for bread for the money he owes Lou who sits beside me and across the table from him. David's parents might be adopting an alley cat. You get to realize who real people are during the temporary demise of the Tribune when all the parties were not pretentious to go to. Susan was escorted by Andy to the Groupie-chasers party at The Scene to capitalize on the publicity and be mentioned in the press, being creepy to Mary at the same time. René and Rona come from The Film Festival. They both look stunning tonight. Saw Debbie last night for the first time in a month and a day after her second miscarriage. My relationship with her seems helpless. I'm too much involved with other relationships and responsibilities to get hung-up. Mary calls Susan to tell her that Andy asked her to come with him to Susan's cocktail party. Susan tells Mary that it's not possible, because she wasn't planning on having her over. It was Susan's easy way out. I wonder what would have happened if Mary didn't call Susan but showed up with Andy. Anyway, it was rude of Mary to consider going with Andy to Susan's when she had a date to go with me to The Scene party. Friday Rona is going to introduce me to Pier Paolo Pasolini, the Italian film director. Rona said she spoke to him about me at length. Saw Gino tonight at Max's. He looks fine.

September 24, 1966

Didn't see Bobbi Shaw at Max's tonight. Found out she has appeared in some "Beach Party" movies. Saw George tonight for the first time in 3 days. He didn't have much to say. Paul is uptight with Ruthie—not too important, the same old "emotionally involved" scene. Missed calling Zazel. René was behaving awfully. I criticized him for it, and he accused me of being middle class. Julie hasn't answered the note I left for her in her mailbox. I hope I see Bobbi Shaw soon.

I include the second letter Benedetta sent me along with her letter from a few months ago. A new destiny is about to begin.

Dear Sweet Gerard,

And I never even thanked you for the first poems you sent me . . . I feel guilty and rude. Gerard, I was very touched, it has never happened that someone dedicates something to me—let alone something as beautiful as poetry. Gery, why are you so sweet to me? It makes me shy— I do want to see you before you disappear in the London fog. I will keep those poems with the few, very few things I love, all my life.

> With a big kiss,
> Benedetta

22-ix-66

Dear Gerard,

I am sorry I didn't thank you sooner for the letter— the poetry—the everything—It's not the *"being busy"* bit, it's the disorganisation (organic)—I had to miss the cocktail because Mrs. Tucci was giving one over here and I just couldn't vanish, so that was that. Sorry about your letters that never got there. Williamstown was an illuminating experience. I can build sets—run the light board— make costumes—fly in the flats—work the follow light and the whole thing was an immense experience. I acted—I also sang in Annie Get Your Gun of all things!
. . . Dear Gery I'd love to see you soon—I have a new phone—Give my love to you all—Andy & Co. and to you a huge thank you—

> Benedetta

September 24, 1966
8:00 P.M.

Today has been the most beautiful day for me. A most gracious letter from Benedetta asking me to call her; lunch with Andy and Lita on my book; five out of the 45 releases for Screen Tests. Denis Deegan has arrived in town after living in Europe for over two years. I give him a present of himself for himself in the form of a "still" by Andy shot in 1964.

Today turned out to be rotten. Andy was informed by his gallery that René had secretly stolen a Marlon Brando portrait out of the factory and sold it to another gallery. René tells me at Max's that I should "put a stop to those vicious rumors" of his stealing any of Andy's paintings out of the factory. I put so much confidence in René and pushed his presence at the factory and with Andy, who never really liked him, and he has done so many awful things, burned so many bridges behind him. I still haven't been able to get to a typewriter to type up "The Thunder Machine," and still need to type up the Screen Tests/A Diary manuscript. I've already accumulated 12 or 13 signatures from the 45 listed. There might be some substitutes. I'm going to have to be very cool about getting Susan's signature. I guess I'll just have to see if Bobbi Shaw is listed in the phone book. I hope she hasn't gone back to L.A. Pasolini never did come to see The Exploding Plastic Inevitable. He went back to Rome. All the parties are beginning to be attended by all the beautiful people. Marie has offered me $50.00 to write a dirge for Frank O'Hara. Marie has given me the freedom to write the dirge in couplets. She had originally sent Ed Sanders a telegram asking him to write a dirge-song for The Fugs to sing, but he never responded. Barbara and I are going to attend the Rio ball at the Cheetah, October 4th.

■

BERNADETTE MAYER

After While

No matter what the above
what comes before stands for
it means they
wont let me die
& as a piece in this frame
(I make that mistake over & over)
Again today when
I created your absence
today when I created your absence then
the whole tone of the day
was like the rest of a day
pick one any one that
any of the dead ones
dies
To be simple: I was aware of that.
When colors come clean at the edges,
        this is how mescaline works
But when they do when can you look? Aloud.
it's only when you cant look at them
& to remind you the tone
of a day
A day I was spectacularly reminded
of what you do & how you look
on a day any day
day any of the dead ones dies,
But not me.
Before that all weekend I expected to die
But instead they got us a housekeeper & she turned out to be this
    terrific young French girl named Lizette (Lisette), Dear
    Marie, & one day she was crying in the kitchen, no that's
    no good, & we embraced, she was crying on the couch in the
    living room & we embraced & we made love & so immediately
    she took me to meet, no not immediately 'cause that night

at the dinner which she prepared we giggled a lot & mischief & mystery & so first chance we got she sneaked out I
mean I sneaked out, no I didn't have to sneak out, we met &
she took me to meet her boyfriend who was also French & then
we all began making love so that the day after my sister got
married Lisette & I & Jean took off towards the mountains
together in a truck. Now what would we do for money? No
first of all I left notes for both my sister & my uncles. To
my sister I said love to you both & don't worry we'll have a
good time & no babies & to my uncles I said don't worry I'll
be back & I'll write to you & it really is better this way
& I didn't write but I secretly hoped that he wouldn't try to
find me & I would write often to reassure him but always be
careful to have the letters forwarded by friends in other
locations. & what about money? Well the Monday I left I
forged my uncles' signature on a withdrawal from my account
that was in trust & it worked & besides, for the months ahead
of time I had been secretly saving money, taking money out
of what he gave me to spend. So that eventually we traveled
all over, we traveled all over & soon we met Lisette's father
who thought our arrangement couldn't last forever & so he got
involved. With me, I guess.

Always being given.
& even before that there were so many pastries & cakes I was
rolling around in them, demanding things, special ones,
strawberry cupcakes, my favorite, I was lying in them at
the bakery, forging desires I didn't even have for the sheer
joy of demanding, of making demands all night, baking all
night, all for me, to lie in, to destroy the half
I couldnt eat

I want a woman
I want Lisette

Sure I go backwards
Sure I murdered you
Sure you can move
Sure I don't want to
Except to die before—
Before what?
Before Cocteau pins me down
Before Cocteau pins his beautiful dead body on me,

290

Before I pin that beautiful dead one on you
          that's something that cannot be done
Any more than I can die

                    just pure by wanting to

Anyway
          I'd rather die

                    than make that compromise

With you
          Before
          Before
          Anymore
Anyway
          which would involve
Beyond
          the past

                    issues so trivial

As
   trips to the moon on Stockbridge I envy you
   & the raising of money erect for liberal women
   & the seeing of men too

                    men as well

                          or even others

Any others
          & a-b-s-e-n-e-e now there's one of mine—

          the greatest revenge on absence is beauty
But nothing haven't any all
And why go on if it's just to use up your
          time as mine

                    even for love that can be left
                    even for love that can't be revenged

Anyway you can see
          this is yours

                    . . . . .

                    2.

Do you know that we slept with the Luddites last night?
Sun goes in & ought to, flying
The word you misspell the word that extends itself is *out*
Reread what is written: at 6:55 we are going to the movies.
Luddites and lummox & the bullox

a passion for the same, complete, is complete. No more details
        than that of a black meadow
& dream from the wind crashing things that men on the fire escape
        ascend to rob Barry's loft but when they get up there it's
        so empty so white & clean, there's nothing to rob (we have
        all of Barry's things) & all there is is a white bed
white bed of the black meadow with a mirror next to it, longways:
        & all of the loft is white, floors blend into ceilings
& didn't you investigate the robbery?
of course, I went up, I took care of it, there was nothing to take
the robbers were women (3) like the ones who could rule the world
        as they were sitting at a table trying to snap their own
        necks
& they took nothing out of the empty place
Are you sure?
        & Melina Mercouri
        & Marilyn Monroe (the prince & the showgirl)
        & Electra (the prince is a trickster)
Tom's absence forces the TV on
        & the trickster is everything
        I say: You can't . . . . & leave . . . .
        I say: Lisette were Bernadette
        I say: You can't . . . . . . get . . . . . . anything
                . . . . . . out of me now
                        You are too ready for it . . . .
                . . . . nothing good about it . . . .
                . . . . something copied, as . . . . .
                . . . . . the re-translation of the
                        Dream blue & white the opaque
                windows
        Who is my shadow?
        Black eyes in Pleynet's black meadow . . . .

                        . . . . .

                                3.

Its cold & dark a sine die cold day Ed sneezes in his sleep after
morning coffee is upside-down as the day is. It sure is a chron-
icle of uneasy meanness of nothingness of misery bling bling
blank as J. Kerouac said of nothing in particular that makes noise
in yr house. Strong enough 4 2? what century what language is

that? Back 2 the old & older forms list literary forms, cling
Bling badmouth 2 the literary now seeing as how it's all laid out
it's there if only I could go out how without for far fear: I
never apologized to anyone for bringing them along. Because of on
the way. To nowhere anywhere you string along rivers, as big as
that? You said I was the water! No I was the water. No you compared me like a fire to water. No! It was me that was the water
& you were the rock—you let me in. Oh so what is dialogue?
Piece. Nothing important as events occur you make them. You
can go on as sure is as long as you want the table to be measured to fit the length the style or yr own body. But many find
it difficult to even to listen. Cultivate ears. I wasn't going
to write & there's no title is a temptation.

> There's nothing here
> there's an absence
> there's clear air
> there's loaded nipples
> there's no reason
> there's a feast

& a festival of unmade beds happy to see that
'cause I might have to live here & go on eating forever what seems
   like
                        with an ending, I forgot to use his title, I
called him by his *given* NAME

So what do I do? Check the list of things to do? So what do I
make & how do I make em think know I'm the same my given name
is Bernadette I'm not a priest in the receptacle of the church
beds lined up & out of work—does somebody make em, does some-
bodys live out of em, do so many sleep in the same room is my
cold better as I sneak down the stairs & forget to use titles
in direct address, how would I address the envelope anyhow,
what's the name of the city, I only know the country's name, a
gang is with me, a gang climbs the stairs & passes by the door
through, is it five yet? at five there's some hope of recovery,
some chance of action, some hope of inspired by seeing something
of yr own that you did. After all, nobody's stupid it's just some
bodies get hurt they get crushed in attempting they get shattered
& bent they have no enemies they get forced they get edged off
the edge into a too surprising area they get freaked they get
measured, I hate time above all, they get like monsters digging
in the chicken soil, they get like owls no eyes for them they

get immobile they get perched & cannot move they get expectant
& cannot come something or someone cannot & all they are doing
is waiting & all for love, they get empty, thoughts fill them
endlessly & all they are doing is waiting all they are wanting
is motion

Baby what you want baby I got it & all they are doing is wanting,
seek out your own hand writing handwriting of another one &
pieced like eyes they look together: Who am I speaking of &
who am I talking to
    I am talking with you
    I am violating you
    My length like the length of this table's body violates
    Your separate rights
    Stirring up dust, if any
    Your own space & plenty of motion
    Now why should you bother
    2 Be me in this way as a mix
    Which is final insult as ax on the head of the murderer
      is this—a public act—
& Beyond that false ending on the last page on the cover of the
book is a fake a last fake a fake in a series fake tree made into
a book, reread &tc.
& Beyond the space, no, the tree, the chance to go there: Baby
that's what you want Baby that's what I got Baby energy never
leaks out & the tree is formless, it follows its rules around,
like a fake

Someone wants you to let you take them there & someone wants you
to let them take you there, & you find it out, what's there, as a
  struggle
all ready, dying to explore, what's there as a piece, to mesmerize,
to suck you in, to leave out to include all

You gotta be ready you're ready
Eyes violate as I do every day
All born. Now you tell me—
Can I say that?
         (over)
         (something)
       or somethings (over
     I forget which   what'd I say?

■

CATHERINE MURRAY

The Six O'Clock Report

Swirling through the millrace are
swans on the Avon at Stratford.
On rivers and streams
looking like snow are
the Indians of Isleta Pueblo;
Clams and oysters flow
past Cincinnati, and
the elder son of a
stationary engineer,
having weathered several intervals
when his money ran out,
was still flying co-pilot
when we met.
"Ah, yes," he said, "she has
attracted me." She is Brahman.

This is a most exciting season.

■

CHARLES NORTH

Montauk Highway

Counterfeiters, red forms, trees of night

    vs. the *authorizations* of modern life.

Like crawling through a small
town and being hit on the head
by cooling pies—

        and when by a great
      rudderlessness the light becomes
      the life, lifted head and
        shoulders above this dreamworld
    you use for your

                robins

    "Use pectin in a sentence"
        "the birds pectin the trees all day"
      "they were pectin like sardines"

    "He pectin a terrible hurry"

        if the birds were to
      utilize the air, instead
    of batting into it like a wall
    that didn't hold anything up
    but kept drifting off into
    imperturbability, as if *that*
      were what was wanted, curtain
  walls continually lifting off just
    at the point the lights discard
  the world for blue gray
clusters of the coming
distraction, stinging the

shutters and introducing a
totally false concept into
the non-bearing present like
a cough snapping out of
the dark, and some meteors whose earth
has stood the test of time will
have to go off crying, into the next
county if need be, from the
elevated darkness of
dogs and children who go
to bed whether they like it or not
or are hidden by patches of navy
blue hills charred by power lines
pushed against the lining that shows
them gifted in the grain of the nylon

■

Leap Year

In the language of the spirit
one of the waist-high metal ashtrays is on fire!
Ah, in the lounge of the spirit.
I'm always on the verge of waking

up in it, as that roof is clearly
melting into the sky,
the sky in the shoestore,
as if hills were boats and the way out
were to paint everything turquoise
the night crowded by stars,
people drinking everything in sight,
a bus taking air from one city river
to another, charmed in the glow
of not knowing the ending.

■

For Your Information

For your information, Frank O'Hara and I happened to meet on the same ocean liner back from the Continent. He was worried about some pieces of glass he was smuggling back to the States for his friend, Arthur Rubinstein. They were large, odd shapes of tempered glass for a monstrous dime-store wind chime. The duty on them would have been prohibitive, hence the scheme to bring them in with the paintings in the packing crates. It made Frank nervous. He smoked and drank and talked incessantly. Finally, we docked in New York, Frank all atremble as we approached the Customs shed. Fortunately, there was a circus ahead of us, and by the time we got up to the Customs officials who were by then inundated by tons of elephant shit, they just waved us on by, barely bothering with the formality of stamping our passports. Later on that night at a cocktail party, Shirley MacLaine came up and congratulated Frank on a job well done. Frank took the compliment with much aplomb, but after Shirley left to join some other guests, he did such a perfect impersonation of her saying some awful catty thing that those of us around him were totally astounded and delighted by his new talent.

■

ALICE NOTLEY

Margaret & Dusty

Margaret wrote a letter
sealed it with her finger
put it in her pocket
for the Dusty Baker

Dusty was his bat
Dusty was his moustache
Dusty was Margaret's pocket
They both got all dusty

If I had a flower
If I had a trinket of gold
      & silver & lapis
If I had a medal & a trophy
      & a fullup sticker album
I'd rather be all dusty
Like those two friends of mine.

Postcards

Feb. 17

Dear Barney,

    The ashtray is full & the
natives are listless, but
there is a swell love hanging out on the corner where
they sell souvenirs to the
grenadiers & girls from the
seaside. I have bought me
a pink culotte & a racy
sort of vest to wear with
those remarkable earrings
you gave me. How are
you & that boy who's a
man whom you did
that to on the day after
Valentine's Day? The
weather here is good for
taking the wrinkles out
of clothes (rainy)

Love,

May

. . . . .

Feb. 18

Dear Reginald,

    I still love your body
most aberrantly being consumed with hatred of your
loathsome soul which
refuses to lend me your
body for a single violet
evening of your stay at
our picturesque little
resort which is all that
we have here except for
too briefly you—I keep

your lost or castoff cig-
arette holder the ivory one
with me always but
you are mean, mean,
mean! Jesus & Buddha
are made nervous &
sad by your cruelty to
humanity, me—
                    Love,
                       Congetta

      . . . . .

                            Feb. 18
Dear Fuckface,
       Everyone thinks you're
the Goddess of Compassion
but I know you also have
piles & a scarcely controlled
urge to sing for a living.
So much for you. Here
everything is stupid as I
have a dwindling flu
which necessitates my
finally paying attention to
my dwindling pocketbook.
How about some bucks,
Goddess Baby? any amount
above five I'd appreciate &
continue to light at your
altar the incense I steal
from the neo-Rocky Mountain
healthfood store. I
still like you either way,
                    Love,
                       Bubbles

      . . . . .

Feb. 25

Dear Nutso,
       Wal, it's pretty blank
around here. The cat
is hungry, & Hubby hasta
get up early (those two
paired are not a sig-
nificance for your cheap
little mindlessness to ponder).
How could I ever
miss you? everytime I
do I slap myself on my
cheek & read a chapter of
The New Hairdresser's Manual.
If you should
ever get normally sentient
enough to notice the
weather, you might drop
a line to your,
                    XXX
                         Margie

          . . . . .

                    March 6

Dear Francis,
       I miss you very much
although you are always
here too—there I go, in
trouble in a sentence, distracted by the weather, so
silky aired like Hawaii,
which (weather) is reminding me
of you while I am being
distracted from you,
from writing to you. I
guess you *are* the weather
practically, & today I
like the weather so much;
& also I can be *in it*

without thinking, & on
rainy days blame you
for acting like I have to
grow up, like a hollyhock
or something, so I'm
going for a walk—

                              Alice

◾

When I Was Alive

───────────

When I was alive
    I wore a thin dress bare
shoulders the heat
    of the white sun

and my black thin
    dress did envelop me
till I was a shell
    gladly and breeze

ruffled and filled
    against good legs
the translucent fabric and my
    heart transparent

as I walk towards Marion's
    and Helena's as my
skirt fills empties and fills with
    cooling air

◾

MAUREEN OWEN

Land O Lakes

For Minnesota

The Grassland Wolf Spider is still behind the large
blue framed mirror in the bathroom
You are a nomad I told him this morning   Go out
into the grasslands!   Fear has ruined everything here.
I lost my knife and the dog is worthless
like a brilliant and sensational misunderstanding
THE GREAT EMPTINESS   is out there   decorated with
celestial grandeur   the capacity for dominating whole moments
in those stars   European architecture
and the Abode of the Unsymmetrical
     OH Romantic eaves & open spaces!   I rush
through hordes of mosquitoes and kiss the toes of your
reckless empty beauty!   my life on dirt roads
flushed & dizzy   bathed in a cold sweat   Nature's
out & out extravagance   What a beautiful evening!
someone will say   & I'll just collapse.

■

"Shyness is a strange disease I have"

Shyness is a strange disease I have
it may require surgery some day!
Propped up in a big white hospital bed
it will be strange to feel the big toe
on my left foot gone
But how wonderful to be no longer shy
only slightly off balance
Perhaps I'll develop the limping stride
of Byron
people stepping back as I jerk through.

■

Fantasy 22

O to be young & neglected! Left alone for long
unguarded hours in the ruined palace. The delicious
yield of the marvelous rugs and tapestries! To roll
with wild abandon!   down flights of smooth cool marble
stairs   & get up   bruised & tortured by love!
exhausted in the tangled garden   overgrown
exotic shrubbery stinging your thighs & shoulders.
To leap into icy waters of bronze fountains   & gasp
for breath. Here are diamonds that shatter on your hair!
& the thick wings of the peacocks.   Loose trousers
of the night, dark purple that billow & fold with a
shudder. I sat beside you on the bed   my senses
reeling.   Forehead pressed through torn silver lamé
to lean on a clear cold window   The palace hounds
withdraw along velvet corridors   & now to follow them!
To fling from balconies   into enchanted
                                        rosewood drawing rooms
To swoon!   To drop   upon mauve servants in
immaculate dress.   To slide your ear along Persian
silk divan   & insist on silence!   O to be young &
neglected   Left alone for long unguarded hours
in the ruined palace!

■

RON PADGETT

George Schneeman, the Noisy Painter

Two of my parents were not artists—which is no doubt why I understand everything about art.

Furthermore, there are a lot of other things I understand quite well.

For example, talking, in a very knowing manner, about things I understand.

I do know that the prodigious dexterity of thought and language which permits one's doing it is not new.

It dates from way back. Ever since the death of criticism. Still, it hasn't asserted itself with any special intensity during the past three or three and a half years, when a rather complexly—but perhaps not complexly enough—conceived art provided simpletons with nothing to think about.

So much for that. Still, if you go on thinking about it, what good are marvelous and interesting studies if one must keep remembering them? What if we run off the road in a car and find ourselves in a ditch?

Isn't it better to follow all the turns very carefully? And, after all, the best way of understanding is, first, through the mind, isn't it? Isn't the shortest road from us to what is one foot in front of us still one foot? Unless it be twelve inches. And isn't it better to go forward that far than to fall on the floor and stare at its boards?

But what is there to say in the presence of the recently accomplished fact? Now, a work is not always accomplished even if it is a fact. If you wait too long to think about it, it's gone. If you start thinking about it before it's accomplished, you are accomplished in its place! You can win this way.

The artist is the instrument of an energy which flows through him as naturally as blood does: he does what he does. From there on he takes a bath and has dinner. But his work has to face the dribbling idiocy of the public and critics. They like it! They make him a star! And if he isn't a real genius, his star shoots briefly across the sky and is seen no more. But if his work goes unnoticed, at least it's free of the verbiage which otherwise might obscure it temporarily.

George Schneeman is a rather loud fellow and artist. His work roars
with a terrific power which it will someday unleash. Schneeman, in the
meantime, slowly ties his shoes and goes out the door, banging it.

He has a face with, oddly, no mouth. His pictures speak. Someday he
will be more famous than Archie.

■

Famous Flames

With all my faults,
I do have one virtue:
I respect the idea of the Noble Book.
(No kidding!)
I take seriously the works of Aristotle,
although I do not usually like them.
I take seriously the *Tao Teh Ching*
and I always bark like a dog,
with the grey silhouette of a factory
against a deep red sky
and it is the France of Zola,
he whose high heels clicked
against a marble bust of Pallas.
These gentlemen are very interesting.
Take Montaigne. A peculiar guy, and
very interesting. Or Spinoza,
he of the face ugly
and geometry as divinity.
He looked in a mirror and said "Ouch!"
and he looked into the ouch
and saw a perfect circle.
A leads to B and to C
and that explains the universe!
Unfortunately that face belonged to René Descartes!
Me, I bit into the cole slaw
and killed the dragon where he breathed
funny fumes on the pages of Literature.

"I am Everyman,"
what a funny thing to say!
Would a tree say, "I am Tree"?
"I do not think so,"
said the precarious baron,
"I do not think so just yet."

An ominous sensation steals over the back
as though a magnetic field
were searching, vaguely,
for another magnetic field.
Card players, in marathon games,
smoking Camels, have claimed
to have seen visions, one
in which the Virgin Mary came down
out of the sky and gave him the three of spades.
Others believe they can change the pips
by force of mind, as the card flies through the air,
and it's your open.
You sit at the present moment
with the future ready to welcome you,
until that bubble bursts
and the crowds begin to move again.
It is Christmas, 1944. The man
who invented the question mark
was laughing in heaven. Human beings
had turned into exclamation points
that threw large shadows across the earth
as it turned in space lit only by an old flashlight.
It was a pretty cheap production,
and when Tommy entered it in the science fair
Mr. Bushwhanger was rather embarrassed.
He ran and banged his head
against the wall of the faculty lounge
until his glasses fell on the floor,
burst into flame.

■

Out on a Limb

Would you go out
on a limb for a friend?
Crawl out there among the leaves and branches
swaying in the breeze
with sunlight-dappled leaves
across your physiognomy,
And would you stay there
Long up in the air
As night set in and the stars,
Would you stay there long?
And would you saw the limb
You're sitting on? And fall?
And what would you do
when you got up off the ground?

■

Ladies and Gentlemen
in Outer Space

Here is my philosophy:
Everything changes (the word "everything"
has just changed as the
word "change" has: it now
means "no change") so
quickly that it literally surpasses my belief,
charges right past it
like some of the giant
ideas in this area.
I had no beginning and I shall have
no end: the beam of light
stretches out before and behind
and I cook the vegetables
for a few minutes only,
the fewer the better. Butter
and serve. Here is my
philosophy: butter and serve.

■

MICHAEL PALMER

Notes for Echo Lake V

—————————

"a blue under people"

—Bernadette Mayer,
Memory

The tree's green explains what a light means, an idea, the bomb or
Donald Duck, a box of marbles in a marble box, the amber jewel
behind the toad's eyes reminds us that it's night. The interpreter of
the text examines the traffic light, coughs and lays the book aside.
The dead mayor sits behind his desk, overcome with wonderment.

The interpreter of a cough examines the light and lays the text
aside. Here and there leaves, clouds, rivers of tears in the streets
meant a sonata for tongues.

Truth to tell the inventor of the code weeps and lays the text aside.
Here and there calendars and walls remind him that it's night, a
sleeping lion is curled up in one corner, a voice can be heard behind a door, and Plato told us of the law, Plato warned us about the
poem. The dead mayor wonders if the King of France is bald.

Today is an apparent day of empty sleeves and parallelograms, and
red meaning red, and the flag as an object, and red instead of red,
the flag as an object of undulating sides, the spider who taught me
to walk, the emptiness of the code, the spider who forgot how to
walk, the delicate curves within the code, three barking dogs, the
mystery of intervals, the absence of a code, the lion asleep at her
feet, the empty sleeve waving, the bottle now broken, the voices she
told him to listen for, the stolen book, the measurement of intervals,
can we tell what we saw?

Does physics know Caesar by name?

Plato warned us of the shadows of the poem, of the words cast against the wall, and Plato warns against the song.

The tree's green explains what a name means apart from memory, flickers of light in the darkened room, our eyes fixed on the screen on the figures of nothing.

The inventor of the code hears each note and swallows his tongue, frightened by shadows. The lion red as a lobster is green sleeps in one corner dreaming of the hours' numbers and names, a river flowing at his feet. "Shuffle Montgomery" was the song.

And here and there they speak in tongues, correcting the right notes in order to get them wrong. And how many days did you spend underground?

The interpreter of leaves examines each tear as pages turn. In the field at dawn they cross swords and a head rolls while the audience laughs. The dead city listens to the code as it reads, and a poem moves back and forth.

At our feet like a sky the graceful curve. Rumors that they are lovers or were in a previous lifetime made of salt. Hills beyond tipped with snow or salt, a curve broken off, searching for her tongue. A deep blue tasting of salt. The awkward curve and talking cloud, steps toward a forest for want of stairs. Are in a lifetime or were. Rumors that the sender had forgotten the code and swallowed his tongue. A mirror in one corner was about to fall, apparently his memory of Siena and the dome.

And Brother Mouse with parachute in mid-air, forever descending.

They killed alligators on Tin Pan Alley. He drank from an actual glass of beer. An outstretched arm offers me its hand.

■

JOHN PERREAULT

Renaissance

I see your sexy outline against the milky glass
and it is not this gray image that persists
and not that other image of you I once held closely,
religiously.

Must I bribe your doorman again
to look the other way when I toss these bottlecaps
against your bathroom window?

. . . Your formal indifference,
your indifference as indifferent as a work of art,
your inner heat,
the tender smile of your kneecaps;

my color Polaroid of you on that chic Caribbean beach,
surprised by vulgar questions,
distant, slightly awkward,
caught forever as if in a TV toothpaste ad.

Must I wait again outside your apartment house,
arguing with your doorman?
Must I convince him once again
that poetry has nothing to do with words?

■

T O M   P I C K A R D

My Pen

holds steady in my right hand
black with a silver top and tight bulb nib

my HERO pen
made in the People's Republic of China
and purchased in Warsaw
by my wild-cloud-haired Polish wife
with apple green eyes and twenty faces

my pen makes tight scrawls irregular designs
and foot notes
joining vertical strokes to curved and looping horizontals

my pen clips easily into a pocket
and sucks noisy and quick
when dipped in black Indian ink

my pen speaks volumes
running its incised beak along prescribed lines

my pen feels comfortable
poised between finger and thumb

my pen pours out centuries of industry and sweat

my ebony-backed silver-topped Golden Star 705
Chinese pen looks good with a blue and chrome 371
YUEN CHANG made in Shanghai comma China
best-quality swivel-type stapler
with four different uses

my pen writes adverts for its comrades
my pen shouldn't get too smart

my pen was purchased in Dom Ksiaski on Nowy Swiat*
where walls of books are dripping with ink
and threaten to flood whole streets

my pen refuses to pay nib service
to obsolete forms of government

my pen's ink is the distilled dream
of 50,000,000,000 workers weary with clocking-in
and clocking-out
                signing-on and signing-off
enslaved to machinery of industry and state

my pen votes with its feet

my pen insists it knows best and wants to manage its own affairs

my pen demands complete autonomy

        *"Nowy Swiat" means "new world" and is a street in
        central Warsaw. "Dom Ksiaski" means "bookshop."

■

CHARLES PLYMELL

In Memory of
My Father

To you who sung the riddles of that desolate Atlantis
while wind-worn wagons swept a sunken trail into eternal dust.
To your sod, your grass, your easy hills of flint from glacial
slope to wanderlust. "Perfect cattle country . . . the best I've
seen since Uruguay," I'd oft heard you say, your dreams and maps
unfolded beneath those eyes that inventoried skies, could you
have known the winter owl's alarm where black beasts of Angus grazed?
I could not see as far, but went my way, you understood, and
watched the windmill tell their listless joy to silt and seam.
Life must be beautiful or all is lost . . . those bison of the clouds
were pushed from life . . . slaughtered for sport . . . now they are the
storm clouds watching us from eternity and far beyond.

And I did not know (when you showed me the lilies on the
limestone). No . . . I did not notice you had grown old, your
hair had turned to silver . . . for I never thought you'd die.
I thought when this would end we'd all join hands together
like you told the babes at playtime long ago (that you hoped
we'd all meet in Heaven) in that dustbowl depression of Kansas.
It is hard to notice age in those who dream. As you knew,
dreams are like the youth, without them the world could not continue.
They are like the trees you always planted on the sun-parched steppe,
enjoyed by those who pause and dream beneath the steel of time.
O fading America! Where is thy promise! O catastrophic land!
This land you loved when the newborn calf kicked up its legs . . .
You said everything wants to live . . . and expresses it.

The slap, slap, slap of tires on the hard concrete.
The tears on the way to the funeral. The biggest sky in Kansas.
"Wish I could find that old house where Grandmother lived,"
someone said, trying not to think, or feel, or sob.
You had told me you "might kick off" one of these days
but I could never see you anywhere but waiting for us
on the porch, arms folded always with finger prop't
against sunburned cheek, Stetson tipped back, calm grey
eyes anxious and kind through smoke of neglected cigarette.
We were coming for Christmas in a few short days with newborn babe.

Giant cranes along the ditch . . . steel helmet'd construction
workers laying concrete pipe beyond all progress of the
Family Store T.G.&Y. or the old folks' home you cussed.
Under that vast space you saw end product of wasted soul and hand.
You saw the time begin to change, you saw the day of the Atom Bomb.
You know the true nature of man, foresaw the greed and plastic goods.
Saw those old jaws of monster oil wells pumping the never-ending
depletion allowance of blood of man and earth. "The little man pays
the taxes."
And you sensed the vacant stare in faces. You saw man change. You saw
him buy on time. But he had no time to talk now. No time. No time.
New car tires squeal on the road to nowhere to make a time payment.

Skull of memory, how will your lamp burn now?
How will the dust, like pages scorch that canopy of bone?
How will those eyes rest against the dark storm of tears now,
when ozone rests on sage, calming that stampede of time?
It was the day of mustangs, the day train whistle screamed that
Rockies' grade, when double header highballed and howled past
diesel trucks, water towers of unknown towns; soliloquy of
settlements and cemeteries beyond truck stops and salvage yard.

Your folks from Indiana came overland in covered wagon;
crossed the Muddy at Hannibal, Mo. Mark Twain was 36.
To Belle Plaine and then on to "No Man's Land." You staked your
claim. I remember the joke about no birth certificate, and
how the neighbors were healthy because they had government jobs;
Charley Dumbell shot himself with a Colt .45. You told the kids
wild stories. Listened to Joan Baez, your favorite, with teenage kids.

You were always young and had to be active, you built the fence
you didn't have to build at all . . . for your daughter's horse.
Lifting beams bigger than railroad ties . . . against the doctor's orders.
Post hole diggers left in the hole; never used again.
But you had built the fences on the prairie sod. You made it straight.

I was coming to see you from school, bringing my family.
Your father died with the fence unmended, the calves got out,
he didn't feel like riding; waited for you to come from school.
Everything changes but the meaning, and the tenderness passed on.
I stand here beside the peaceful grave, I stand here on earth
for the first time without you by me; I take this land upon my shoulders.
The grain elevator over there is filled with harvest, the seed of
newborn day. The green Spring wheat. I am a father now. I know.

It was said you paid the ambulance driver before you let him go.
You dug some bills out of your old leather purse to hand him.
Through your hard span of life, you settled up so quietly no one
ever thought of you carefully. Nor do they care of unknown sages
in unknown towns. The end of a man, an age. I neglected to hug or kiss.

■

CARTER RATCLIFF

Arrivederci, Expressiónismo

It's hard to say goodbye this way, in a critical notice. I had started out to say that emotion doesn't always feel the way it feels its way into a work of art, and that some of our poets had gotten it backwards—this is goodbye.

I tried to fool myself at first. And now that you're feeling a little bit better, I think you'll admit that you played me along and played yourself along too. There was the rustle of silk on those great big wide fascismo marble terraces, and when you said the dumbbell emotions were all for *la revolución,* I played along. I played along when it was white gravel crunching underfoot, and the splendid hours on the lam, the leather upholstery, the sugary feelings you had for the pathetic old chap who looked at lakes and saw winking eyes. I didn't know you were seeing them too.

Then America. This was definitely not the land of the free to you, Expressiónismo. Penthouse, yes. But, no, the heart is not a canvas. The emotions were never to be body paint. Maybe that's when I cared for you most, Expressiónismo, in your youth-culture phase when the farthest thing from your mind was poetry and the closest to your heart was the mindless expression of your feelings. And now we get to the tough part. Because those feelings don't really count in poems. They just lie around. With runs in both legs—and poetry never looked lovelier . . .

America. By now it was a collection of vases so far as you were concerned, Expressiónismo, vases in the shape of dismembered hands. Feelings, like cut flowers—I think that was your best one, the cut-flower routine. Cut flowers, cut feelings—just a tropism, that's all, just some roots in language, that's what we need. And that's what you had to offer, Expressiónismo, a language cut to bits with all those cut-up feelings. Poetry! But poetry was far away. Never looking lovelier, never. Never looking lovelier than when written from language so as to be spoken as to another who knows that language . . .

That was it, of course, Expressiónismo—you felt proud. Feeling was in itself a source of pride to you, like chinchilla on a broiling hot day.

That was America to you by then, and you felt proud to be just as much a stranger to language here as you were at your numerous points of origin.

I remember that awful night in jail and the splendid morning after with the promise that America was going to be what we felt at that very moment. But there's nothing to show for it, nothing.

I know it's a waste of time to use language for this to *say* all this to you—because you feel that's backwards, that you already know, that you knew even then. I knew it too. But I wanted it to work. I was just conceited enough to think that all those feelings of yours were a kind of knowledge when they were beamed at me, and don't think I didn't appreciate it—but I'm forgetting. You never think. And this is goodbye.

Ciao. Wiedersehen. Arrivederci. Arrivederci to you, this time. And that other time—to the Tuscan hills, which had never, never looked lovelier. You never saw them, of course. But it was more than that, more than boredom in a hotel somewhere, a hotel in a place I knew I could get to like if I could only get to know the language—the patterns, the comings and goings which provide for feelings like riding boots on hot days in hysterical patterns, geometrical ones, for example . . . Sometimes you made me feel sick.

But the Tirol was a dream. And the Tuscan hills had never looked lovelier. Of course you never saw them, never. Never saw what people see in them. I couldn't believe it, didn't want to believe it. But . . . all that is neither believable nor unbelievable now. Because this is goodbye. No hard feelings? *Arrivederci, Expressiónismo.* We tried to make it work. I know I did and I have a funny feeling that you did too in that funny, frightened way of yours.

TOM RAWORTH

Rainbow Resurfaces

how could it be?
isolation brought
a possibility

only frames
take my eyes!

o colon semicolon comma

suddenly the air is laughter

thought clasps one half by will
of knowing looking back

the body must untwist from wince
to let blood balance pain
half cannot tell me which is dead
i weep for which   again

forget
        you know
                and look at the surface

the world
        always the same distance
                as far as eye can see

senses tell us what there cannot

(interviewee: yes, i boast to myself)

. . . . .

politics and power

are trying
to make you believe
it's all right
to be illiterate

they want you
back in the cage

fear god
or fear capital

the latter
in artificial light

the former
when there were civilians

. . . . .

script

eye
spurted
from the pressed olive
a camomile ocean
each particle
a wavelength of one
for the sake
of argument
its identity
its wavelength
how distant
memories
named
in living subtlety
taste
of earth

. . . . .

hindsight

in the present
the future hasn't yet happened
mein führer you can be big
as chaplin
or why
the israelis (zionist tendency)
have none

. . . . .

vague

start with a grey shoe
measuring itself
with a mirror
measuring itself

goodnight dad
goodnight dear

. . . . .

helio fare

polly put the kettle on
the strap of steam is drifting
this train is not at home to neurons
shadows transluce the afterimage

. . . . .

salt lip observes the falklands
as a stalag in night drizzle
he assumes the others tick
so faint they must be shouts

how ungracefully those runners walk
my soul is not my sense of self
for mirrors turn and close about my soul
that which i do not like
that word

his elbows relax down from his shoulders
he looks full of running on a promise

(who checks the electoral roll?)

the cost of addiction is time
(buddhism)
film made fiction real
strategy is our side cheating

        . . . . .

the break of the tape

a straight pencil line across composed of ands

"i know a lot i can't think because of burning
but the melton file is very unstable"

(full choir)   ton file
                       ton file
                       ton file

a shadow moves to your left enough to twitch
an eye

"hot songs" over crockery in a china sink

recording beep   birdsong   the nightingale

"take it back to 'ton file' and include this voice"

(full choir)   ton file
                      ton file
                      ton file

a shadow moves to your left enough to twitch
an eye

"hot songs" over crockery in a china sink

recording beep   birdsong   the nightingale

take it back to "ton file" and include this voice
"it we put that at eights and spliced in some music . . ."
" . . . multiply it, hold the spread, and lard . . ."

money is being taken back from us
because there's not much need

"the crowd, reading its newspapers"

■

L O U   R E E D

Andy Warhol's Chest

If I could be anything in the world that flew
I would be a bat and come swooping after you
and if the last time you were here things were a bit askew

Well you know what happens after dark
when rattlesnakes lose their skins and heart
and all the missionaries bark

oh all the trees are calling out for you (swoop swoop)
and all the venom snipers after you (sting sting)
are all the mountains boulder after you (rock rock)

If I could be any one of the things in this world that bite
Instead of an ocelot on a leash I'd rather be a kite
and be tied to the end of your string flying in the air at night

cause you know what they say about honey bears
when you shave off all their body hair
you have a hairy-minded pink bare bear

And all the bells are tolling out for you (roll roll)
and stones are all erupting out for you (rock rock)
and all the cheap blood suckers are flying after you (swoop swoop)

Yesterday Daisy Mae and Biff were grooving on the street
and just like in a movie her hands became her feet
her bellybutton was her mouth so she tasted what she'd speak

but the funny thing is what happened to her nose
it grew until it reached all of her toes
now when people say her feet smell they mean her nose

and curtain laced with diamonds dear for you
and all the Roman noblemen for you
and kingdoms Christian sailors are for you
and melting ice cap mountain tops for you
and Knights in flaming silver robes for you
And bats that with a kiss turn prince for you
(swoop swoop)
(rock rock)
(roll roll)
swoop swoop

■

R E N É   R I C A R D

assignment: Good Poem

Back in Boston
again. It's all very obviously
Memories of "those fleeting glimpses"
A glib tongue flapping glamour
Are you ready:
Why am I writing this now
There are other things to do at times

home again. The occult center of the
New world besides Philadelphia would
like to say a few pretty words
on its behalf.
      (intellectual propaganda)

EEK. My dear! The mamas & the papas are
beginning to say no

      Sunset Blvd.
   Don't take this too personally
But since I'm living dangerously, you
must realize the utter (need?)

Desperation I approach you

Oh the pain of being ugly in L.A.

∎

A Poem for Sterling Brown

what song shall i sing you
amid epidemic prophecies
where holy men bleed like water
over the bones of black children?

how shall i call your name
sitting priest/like on mountains
raining incense
scented dancer of the sun?

where shall memory begin you
overturning cradles
rocking cemented eyes
closed flowers
opening like eastern deities under your hand?

and your words.
tall as palm trees
black with spit
soothing the lacerated mind.

and your words.
scratching the earth
carving dialect men into pyramids
where no minstrel songs
run from their thighs.

your soul. dodging loneliness and
the festivals of Renaissance rhythms
your life
skintight with years
a world created
from love.

you. griot of fire.
harnessing ancient warriors.

       a ye ye ye ye ye ye ye
       a yo yo yo yo yo yo yo
            da a ye loom boom
            da a ye loom boom
                  boom/boom
                  boom/boom
                  boom/boom
you. griot of the wind
glorifying red gums smiling tom-tom teeth.

■

EDWARD SANDERS

Yiddish-Speaking Socialists of the Lower East Side

They came when the Czar banned the Yiddish
    theater in 1882
They came when the iron-tipped Cossack's whip
    flicked in the face of their mother
They came when their parents were cheated out of
    their farms in Vilna
They came to escape the peasants at Easter, hacking
    with scythes and knives
They came when the Revolution of 1905 was crushed
They came when the soldiers broke up their socialist
    presses in Cracow
They fled from Siberia, dungeons and work camps,
    for printing leaflets and fliers—

   pamphlets and poems and leaflets and fliers
   to spread in the workshops
   spread in the streets
   spread in the factories

   in the spirit the era had spawned
   the spirit the era had spawned

     "In di gasn
      tsu di masn
     Into the streets
      to the masses"

They came to Antwerp and then to London
    and then to Ludlow Street

to make a New World
inside the New World
at century's turn—
The Yiddish-speaking socialists
of the Lower East Side

Some remembered
        with pangs and tears
                the beautiful rural life
                        wrested away

Mushroom hunting in the dampened woods
Bundles of grain in the carts
Market day in the shtetl

Some strained their eyes
for the gold-paved streets of the West
just to be greeted by one of those
"incomprehensible economic collapses"
that New York gives to its poor

The East Side
        had been slums
                since the overcrowding
                        after the War of 1812—

but the tenement rents of 1903
        were higher than
                nearby "better" places

Two thirds of them owned by speculators
getting 15 to 30 percent (or more)

so that a family of ten
                was jammed
                        in a two-room flat
plus boarders!

till a leafleteer
        in desperation
                laid aside his ink

to open a curbside store
                with a gutter plank
                                and 3 brown bales of rag

Or they carried the cribs
                to the hallway
                                to set up a sweatshop—
They were not alone

From thousands of windows
                came the clackety-clacks
                                of foot-treadled sewing machines

and the drum-like sound
                of long-bladed scissors
                                chewing on oaken boards

and the lungs turned gray
                with tidbits of tweed
and the red-hot irons
on the tops of the coal stoves
to smoothe out the bundles of cloth

and the sweet gulps of air
                on Cherry Street
walking out kinks of the legs at dusk
from a day at the torturing treadle.

A rose curved obliquely on the stalk of the hammer.
The Lower East Side
was the strongest socialist zone
                in the United States
for the first twenty years
of this century.

It was a
        wild world of words

and everywhere
        the song
                of the wild lecture

arose above a wild lectern—
Scott Nearing
        at the Rand School of Social Science
Morris Hillquit
        at the Workmen's Circle
Emma Goldman
        at the Educational Alliance
Eugene Debs
        coming in from Terre Haute
                        to Webster Hall

And political discussions
        on the summertime roofs
            in Yiddish, Russian, Polish, & English—
        wild world of words

Labor Day parades from East Broadway
to Union Square
Cousins on the floor
        from fleeing Siberia
            after the Revolution of 1905

Union meetings at the Labor Lyceum on E. 4th—

        Flashes of the Ideal
            in murk
                in muck
                    in mire

Talking all night at the Café Royale
                    at 12th and 2nd Avenue

                after the Yiddish plays at
                the Kessler or Tomashevski Theaters

Garment-worker rallies at Cooper Union

Joining the Women's Trade Union League
Fighting for a shorter work week
6½ days to six, and then
to 44 hours, on the way to 40

Flashes of the Ideal

    in murk
        in muck
            in mire

In di gasn
   tsu di masn

        To make a New World
        inside the New World
        at century's turn
        the Yiddish-speaking socialists
        of the Lower East Side.

For twenty years the East Side socialists grew.
They filled the arenas
and packed the streets

though those who stand
        in the bowl of shrieks
know how the bowl
        stands silent
            so often

when the votes are
counted.

There was a party in the streets
The Lower East Side had never seen
the night in 1914 that Meyer London,
whose father had worked in an anarchist print shop,
was elected to Congress

They danced and sang
through Rutgers Square past the Daily Forward
till the sun blushed the color of communes
above the docks.

Meyer London served for three terms
until the Democrats and Republicans in

the State Assembly
gerrymandered his district.

In 1917 the Socialist Party of N.Y.C.
sent ten assemblymen to Albany
and seven to the N.Y.C. board of aldermen
and even elected a municipal judge

while Morris Hillquit
pulled 22 percent of the vote for mayor—

It looked like the Socialist surge
might move as a spill of thrills
out through the state

> *In di gasn*
> *tsu di masn*

to make a New World
inside the New World
            at century's turn
the Yiddish-speaking socialists
            of the Lower East Side

And then, in the spring of 1917
            the U.S. Congress
                  voted for war

The socialists
      met in St. Louis
            that same April

& issued
      what was known as
            the St. Louis Resolution—

"We call upon the
      workers of all countries

to refuse support
      to their governments
            in their wars."

Some were sympathetic
          to the strong socialist and
                    union movements in Germany

in a struggle
          against
                    Czarist barbarism—

others felt it
          was just a distracting disturbance
                         between Russian
                              & German militaries.

The Lower East Side was split.
          The pressure to support
                    their new country

was great—not that pogroms
          by the Brooklyn Bridge were feared
     though the dirk-tined rioting peasant's rake
               was not that far
                    in the past.

The Wilson administration
          generated war hysteria

Scott Nearing, Eugene Debs
               went to jail

The government threatened
the mailing rights of the *Jewish Daily Forward*
and other socialist papers
opposing the war.

Then
the climate was different
after the war.

There was hideous inflation
and F.O.B.
          Fear of Bolsheviks—

and many mayhemic forces
were set against the
Lower East Side socialist zone.

The anti-red hysteria was nationwide
The Wobblies were crushed
The strikers of Seattle crushed
The Palmer Raids
Federal troops used to club down
                    honest dispute
Emma Goldman deported
Five socialists expelled from the
                    N.Y. legislature
and the socialist Victor Berger
banned from his seat in the Congress.

There was a split in
the Socialist Party in 1919

& the birth of the Communist Party.

You think there was factionalism
in the 1960s—
The factions of 1920 hissed
like 35,000 ganders
            in an amanita valley—

and a democratic socialist
in the '20s and '30s
was wedged in pain among
the sharp-tongued Moscow leftists
and sharp-tongued bitter-shitter rightists.

Oh they failed
to spread the East Side zone
into a broader country
of psychopathic landboomers

& smug townies
who thought they could hog
the keys to the sky

There was the fact that
a climate of lectures and rallies
can aid in the first rough forward step,
                    but rarely the second—

They knew with all the hurt of their years
how the socialist fervor fell—
and the failure of those
        who had seen the socialist dawn
to break it from sea to sea.

Most of them fled the rubbly slums,
and tens of thousands more,
for few there are
who joy
to live in dirt

They joked how the ships
brought the greenhorns to Rutgers Square
as the moving vans
took the radicals to the Bronx

            For most
            the game
            was to get OUT

            but for some
            like Congressman London
            the East Side
            was the
                    world
            in which to stay

            He was there all his life
            till killed by a car
            as he crossed 2nd Avenue—

Shelley had Keats in his pocket
London had Chekhov.

Oh they failed
but I can hear their ghosts
walk down the cobbles
outside the St. Mark's Church

the poets, the strikers, the printers,
the firebrands, the leafleteers—
comrades when the word had its glow—

with a passion for justice
            that never fades away
though heartbreak
            to know
                        that they had failed

to make a New World
inside the New World
at century's turn
They were the Yiddish-speaking socialists
of the Lower East Side.

Note on "Yiddish-Speaking Socialists of the Lower East Side": In researching
the poem, the following books supplied much useful and thrilling information:
The House on Henry Street, by Lillian Wald; *Memoirs of a Revolutionary*, by Eva
Broido; *World of Our Fathers*, by Irving Howe; *How the Other Half Lives*, by
Jacob Riis; *Labor and Farmer Parties in the United States*, by Nathan Fine; and
Born One Year Before the 20th Century, by Minnie Fisher.

A R A M   S A R O Y A N

Poems (1964)

So many things seen
in a day
today

now in my room
only con-
tinuation

here among only more
private
samples of this world

the salt shaker
on my desk
now

right in my eye.

. . . . .

Sick in bed
the only sample
of the world
oneself

. . . . .

It's midnight again.
I smoked two cigarettes
just now
lying on my bed.
The clock going
from one day into
the next.
Today.
Here it is,
already,
again,
again it's midnight,
just past
midnight,
in my room.

. . . . .

A

sudden noise not
a bird
but a window

a building
set dark
against the lightening

blue it is sunrise almost
as we go thru those
streets the time it is

taking when we get
to your house it will be light

light blue

. . . . .

the sun
on a truck   the back's
metallic non-mirror
  banged-up   made
   a Seven
of itself
      swarming
         Instance!

orange hardly

         *see*able
but enough
 if too much

                  our car
      turning the

car

      in Spain

my father
            pulled over—
  great boulders & surf
late sun seventeen I
  could not argue there
stood on a rock   or

   later driving away
from it

            yesterday
in the car

yesterday

         ("History is mess")
            consciously—this
                  Light!—

                                        "is like

                a foreign country"

                . . . . .

The care is there
as simply
as a dream is
careful.

The acts are
forever responsible—
forever
my own.

                . . . . .

Heart

gives
mine

light
line

Gauguin

        ■

Great Poetry

Great poetry is not a matter of punctuation.
That we know for sure. It is more like rain
falling on a field with trees in it—how do you
punctuate reality? It already reads perfectly.

For a man to become a great poet he must
devote himself mind, body and soul to the
task, and then, abruptly, abandon it. Because
great poetry hates a grind. Spontaneity is all.

Great poetry is neither smart nor stupid, but
it does not exclude either. Look at haiku.
For some it might appear that haiku are
painfully obvious, although mysterious. Aren't they?

As obvious as the moon, no doubt. As obvious
as rocks, clouds, wrist-watches, and foreheads.
As obvious as a mountain overlooking a lake.
Isn't this a picture-postcard cliché? Yes and no.

Yes and no—that says it. Yes, because it is
a cliché; and no, because it isn't. But great
poetry is not a matter of semantics. Nor is
it a matter of style. After all, does God have a style?

What's the latest in rainbows? In sunsets?
In young lovers? How is heaven designing
hat-bands these days? No, only religions have
style. God is more of a ceaseless innovator.

Which may be why every great poem is
different from every other. Unique, as a snowflake,
you might say. And the poet, after writing it,
is not a proud man, but a humble one, filled

with awe at the powers of this universe—
the awesome powers that coursed through
his own mind and body and spirit and
created a masterpiece before his very eyes!

HARRIS SCHIFF

Artists' Call

---

this cold land
                    of frozen eurocaucasian consciousness
                              in steel

is not the only land

                                   if only the old white-headed ones
                    the stuffed shirts
                                             the walking briefcases
                                        the portfolio holders & managers
                    the syndicate operators
                                                  the chief financial officers

                    the board members & chairmen
             chief operating officers
          & chief executive officers
                                   & royalty
                    & hollywood stars
                                             & mad doctors
                                                            & generals

& heirs & heiresses
                    major shareholders
                                             interlocking directorates
legislators
                    gangsters
                                        & multi-tycoons

all the jet-set parasites & first-class monkeys
                    on the world's creaking back

If only they could know
                        that our work must be play
and war games break the rules
                        and breaking hearts breaks the rules
    & greed breaks the rules of play
        if only they could know how to relax
                        relinquish

the stranglehold on the southern lands
where blue volcanoes guard
ancient lakes
& fruits and berries burst willingly from the dark earth
where the people weave
& till
& wait for the seasons
impatiently now for the season of struggle is come again
& the harvest burns
mid terror & precious blood
& searing crescendo of grief's anguished scream

But ours is a land ruled by Indian killers & slave traders
inflicting a life of pain &
 greed
        & shuffling for papers
            & guarding papers that say
I own
I own
so many things
                so many people
                        I pay you
                        now pay me!!!

        . . . . .

the profit-motive
                    stuns
                            the clear light of mind
                    dazed
                    glazed
                    perceptions
                    refracted through tubes
                    & lights
                    that are bright
                    but
                    misleading

                    O Woe
                    if only they could know
                    the luminous grace
                    of the true body
                    on the true earth

O mighty magic
                    O great illumination
                                            O miraculous salvation

but this is a cold   harsh   land
built of a cold   harsh   murderous   history
by hardhearted hardheaded   unthinking   backward
                    men
turning deaf ears to the women
turning deaf ears to the children
turning deaf & dumb to their own childhoods   to humanhood
                                                    to personhood

O Woe

O Woe

O turn turn turn   O Woe
                            O Woe
                            O turn turn turn

                    . . . . .

                        You
overwhelmed by dollars
a daily living

bombarded   by   propaganda   subliminal on every level
from the subway to the sky!!!
                              in the ether
                              in your songs
befuddled
& titillated
by the avalanche of
diversions
always
dangling out of reach of your workaday
chaingang
strung out on
whatever it is
& always
feeling
success is at hand
just out of reach
& thinking yes
it's a shame   I'm ashamed of our country
                                        But
that's not enough
not time for shame
time for rage
                rage & motion

so we ring
the chapel bell
& we call
the town meeting
& we can't
stop now
& we cannot
fail

war games break the rules
                          and breaking hearts
breaks the rules
            and greed breaks the rules of play

                    ■

Homage to the Square

Siren chairs long slate perfumes
Led imitative divan fated rites
Above shapes quills bored tumult agate
Tongs menial enigma icy bilge
Ton âme avert Saladins old amends

Eventual wastrel approve shy tea
Galore smooth mantra orate Eden necks
Tarsi arca roc macadam
Smart laud America menace lane
Self mate sigma fears spree rooms

Sports snored *dedans* slab igloos nuts
Health hermit salaam mitt betimes
Welds innate Canton caustic taints
Steers roomer fever peewee massacres
Screed vivid seaplane ascertain

Élan pare into neon dune
Grapes recessed Crete emit pleased spit
Cubed curse abet ghost glass pet oat
Prays salad imps telegra trimmer
Clown annum pump system tartan roar

Resolute semaphores toil staid tram
Trite ruins aorta gentleness aloe
Else lucent dot trapezes even Rome
Pampers traitor Sussex thunder mean
Haman nest tired raven glared alone

Aped part requites dulled scale bejewel
Asperity cortège Esau tug Soo
Cold oboe rise on ibex patent
Nauseate sled gene pet crullers roll
Tell herb rig arcs dyed roulette son

Great Ra peep Tampa storm settee
Stores overt Iago dicta seed
Unstars erg scooping government
Luisa roars at Arno spires
Tenanted *est* our lobster ewers taut

Neuter mesas eager under agent Slav
Dad *arrete* hate rotors dynamos pop
Seer chewed splash asset stretch death cease
Sepal scar plants sup armada *belle*
Opine *éclat* aviso cantered tares

Brass regal brats abate blessed dears
Later scamp consort threshold hied
Enacts nicest wigwam tastes prepared
Whale aerial horde spouses rebel oars
Adagio etamine valise assay

Helmet ditty lease fandango
Super treads waist nines abide
Casino steward serge erase ice brine
Men painters cheer Irenes wooden pride
Slew eerie charade telic dives

Ideal tornado west nail simpler dopes
Quacks Ursala selenities valse prone
Fête sari tremor Arizona rises
Lateral lapel award slit pleasure neat
Lodestone usage sine iota Amos

Vast ounce religns armed sleeve entree
Cove epos nexus nabob conic tray
Alert race motto azure ales
Stop Panama late cabal matin
Reverend repast knave debit *vent*

Outsized violas eventide relief
Ropes air gate prints ping dias staple
Extricates lords peelers geishas
Looped tarot pied tarantulas
Churl clerks merit tangerine desires

Mole yeast shingle monoplanes alit
Satire bargains end elations wounded noun
Scene union palest Erin ceded lip
Dales louder guest sect inclinations
Adipose arenas rotate manse aloft

Paris eras paves fates palisade
Hones alto hostesses tun bray
Dares Etons nape bites laden
Turpitude hemp swarms elapse attention
Reminiscent Arab comber matron

Rires tenure fans revenge celestial
Palace animal tame lemon umpire
Pedestals depress salute boys stunt
Has recorded paw elites redemptive
Dream Bogotá delta sphinx pinocle

Heron fun crate rims revue
Drone perverse grand telescope amen
Écru hats Ada oil nymph Utah
Leash adores rose knob aroma
Oleaster cruisers eider reeds

Rosettes denude dolled tit repel
Chop alabaster stilt canary tie
Doled beer decanted rivet Sams
Cab Argo riverside pastel seas
Agile avarice raves Alp tambourine

Elephant barristers dispense each eggs
Seances roamers tattles spinal pearl
Hay onus Avon tunnel sabre access
Fission organ means chive ogres
Unit reap fleeced drug kit maid

Nacre king names lurid snag
Cravat mar arid rival statement
Built Roma prop inamorata oral
Torrents letters Boston sinus rubes
Barters hasp dispense leer hussy

Pirate planet spades rapt tingle
Ebonite grenade maim fatter berry
Wide lamp depot sewer menu
Sea opiate insouciance Denver pole
Lades newer melting pit averse

Teem chap perspire pave *rara* altar
Ages snob dins gram serape
Caper edibles tsar service snarled
Ants decimal *imago* teetered poke
For oval knife songs slant cheer daunted

Let Babe sell spider irate ointments
Tenderest sterility warn condors raw
Gorse bravest cloister infant Leo
Eras canard festoon wool noon
Beckoned human Adam follies form

■

DAVID SHAPIRO

In Memory of Fraida Shapiro
and Fairfield Porter

As Aeschylus puts it
in Frag 351: Let us say what comes to our lips, whatever it
may be; or perhaps, Let's say what's on
the tip of our tongue.
  As Achilles put it to Apollo,
You have made a fool of me.

It was with some interest
I noticed the violin back in its case
of itself was playing the piece
correctly and with almost
no trepidation of the strings!
It played along and is playing
by and of and for itself—

And that was the end of our friend
The wisest and best on this earth lightly inclined—
"Be mute for me,
contemplative violin."

■

SAM SHEPARD

The Fire in Jeremy's Lap

When Jeremy Rane used to feel denial in a room, he'd knuckle under. That doesn't mean give up. He'd punch his head in. Too much of that gave him a nasal wheeze like a longtime boxer's nose. A sickening hiss so when the room falls silent the others get embarrassed for him. He draws himself invisible in that silence and he's the only one comfortable. (His training paid off.) Strings of sharp pictures aim for his soft spot, just above the head. Jeremy follows them like white lines. Like tracers from old bullets. Most of them miss their mark and fall on the Antelope rug. He brushes them with his foot. The same as he'd do with a fallen ash. When he talks about a dead horse he floods the room. Some even break the windows to let it out. He collects their busted questions like kindling and burns them right in his lap. No one's got the balls to put the fire out. Secretly they wanna see him burn. They all take bets on the extent of the damage. The whole town's involved. News of the fire in Jeremy's lap spreads to every part of the city. For days it lasts. At night they keep watch. All angles of the fire are covered by bets: How long it'll last. Whether Jeremy will make a scream. If he'll ever be able to have kids again. Whether he ever did have kids. If he'll ever stand up. The day, the hour, the minute, the second, the tenth of a second the fire will stop. Jeremy smiles at the tote board. The bookies change the odds if his skin sags. A scratch of his bottom lip and it goes from 33 to 2 to 1. Odds on.

Weeks go by and Jeremy goes into monologues about geese and Eskimos. He talks from the back of his mouth so that some get the idea he's possessed. Rumors start of a saint with a fire in his lap. The sick come to get cured. The lost to get found. Jeremy touches them all where they live. He unlocks secret movies and shows them on the wall using his eyes for projectors. Some he narrates from the back of his throat. Others, he lets the fire do the talking. He switches from color to black and white with the blink of his eyes. Sometimes he plays them music on his fingernails and keeps time with his teeth. All the time the fire burns.

That night when they all fall silent and only the fire has its eye open, Jeremy projects something of himself to an island with steel drums in the air. From that position he can claim witness to his own betrayal. He corners the poorest kid on the island, who's training for the featherweight division, and clues him in on the details. Jeremy tells him the exact day, hour, minute, second, instant of his earthly disappearance. From there the kid's on his own. He hits the big city and places his bet with money Jeremy gave him from a government grant. At 73 to one the kid cashes in and barely escapes the riot-torn city. With money in the bank and a crack at the world title, the kid hops the planet like a June bug. As for Jeremy, he goes back to school under a false name to study how to put electricity back in the earth.

■

PATTI SMITH

Ladies and Gentlemen,
Blaise Cendrars Is Not Dead

Ladies and gentlemen
Blaise Cendrars is not dead
that rummy you buried in such
grave ceremony was his own enemy
true   the right arm gone
Blaise slashed it himself
that little puff box run
run at the mouth
was jack rolling our hero
with a wicked pack of cards
But Blaise   a jack dandy himself
noted the error
(all the chips were on puff boxes' side)
and like the great Hammurabi
Blaise cut him down
right hand for that bad hand of poker

He is alive in every marked deck
every poker chip
he has a pair of slick dice
and he'll wheel you straight to hell
and when you dial round the black market
you deal with him
yes it's our man who drops that cigar ash
on the receiving end
yes it's him crooning liquid music
and sonorous tin pan
through every cable line
linking every slob sister   swindler
little snakesman   two bit gambler
anyone
even slightly illegal and angel

has an ash in their vest pocket
and a kodak of that scoundrel
vainer now one armed   crack face
than this mock hardy youth
he drags me in and out
of every photo booth
and praises in bad poetry
the polaroid sixty second snap

A fool hearty documentarian
his choppers have spun the globe
and for want of a straw hat we were trapped
knee deep in the swamps of Panama
we suffered malaria
and as a result
slaughtered ⅔ the mosquito population
of that hot hole
Christ it was a lusty battle
we were sick with laughter
and sick ourselves
runny assed and cunt with clap
hair red with crabs and lice
in our boots   we rolled our own smokes
twisted up a few panama reds
and plotted the destruction of that wily insect
we danced to Vulcan our private god of flame
and sacrificed a few of those blood suckers
snapping their heads with our nails
which turned our hero slightly pale

Some years I bragged the beauty of my hands
I cried,
"I have music neath these fingernails"
and true these fists never failed
to spiel whole logs full of
literatures *Roman à clef*
and now it's come to this
mosquito in fire
mosquito death hiss

Christ then it began again
the old fever and thirst
for raging fire
with torches we ran whole lengths
of those Panama fields
and as the brush caught up
I cried out in my most disgusting French
Blaze on Blaise
and that bastard burnt me with a cigarette

Like a great epic movie
we've reeled the world
why only six months ago
I assisted that cur in the most marvelous
hoax of the gentle midwest
Our wagon rolling in a dry bone state
Blaise posed as Louis Saucer
humble rainmaker prophet in rain boots
but when the clouds cracked
the white rain was liquor
and all of Iowa was soused with tequila
every pour sap that poured to the scene
of the great rain left drenched
to the teeth
and drunk to the teeth

Blaise curled that famous lip
and we laughed and laughed
and caused more mischief since
It was his ticklish fingers
that caused Mick the jagger
to dance like a fish
he shot lightning from the theatres
robbed the actors of their shadows
and backstage mirrors
it was his sassy diseased kiss
that laid miss universe out with the mumps
the recession? our man's been pinballing
with the Jewish jewel thieves
feeding opium into IBM
and sparing no one   the bugger
robs school children

The dirty shit still spits poetry
between his clicking spaced teeth
tracing aerial views of Greenland
land of the treacherous iceage
and fanatic hun
gold mine dreams in goat canyon
charting the gold where the moon slaps
then drunk with that special glitter
running lyrics in gold dust inks

■

JOHNNY STANTON

The First Inauguration

The date: April 30, 1789.

The time: About 1:30 in the afternoon.

The place: The second floor portico on the Wall Street front of Federal Hall, the new capitol building of our new nation.

Across Wall Street and Broad Street the rooftops and windows are filled with spectators. Chancellor Livingston is administering the oath of office to George Washington, the first President of these United States.

Let's listen:

"Do you solemnly swear that you will faithfully execute the office of President of the United States, and will to the best of your ability preserve, protect, and defend the Constitution of the United States?"

"I solemnly swear that I will faithfully execute the office of President of the United States, and will to the best of my ability preserve, protect, and defend the Constitution of the United States, so help me God."

President Washington is bending forward to kiss the Bible. As Chancellor Livingston turns towards the crowd, he raises his right hand in a sweeping gesture of exultation.

"Long live George Washington, President of the United States!"

■

LORENZO THOMAS

A Trophy

When the bust of Martin Luther King
Is placed
In Congress
I want it made of frozen sperm
Donated by Truman Capote

I want it placed in a hallway
Carpeted with Malcolm's splattered brains

The exhibit must include
Adam Clayton Powell's fingerprints
A photograph of Emmet Till
Grinning at his firstborn daughter
Winking in the maternity ward

I want to see the testicles and penises
Of a thousand lynch mob victims
Each cast in brass
Like baby shoes
Each characteristically unique

Each fitted with elastic belts
For Mormon feminists to wear
As they tour our nation's capital
And relive our daily fear

■

Working-Class Hero

Some days feel like
You wake up underwater
It isn't the humidity I'm talking about

Space folds on space. A blue ice house.
And every motion climbs into itself
A little man in someone else's overcoat

Some days are Sunday all day long
Below an empty sky that's eyeball blue
A slight wind curling round you like a vine

A day to put your bag on the conveyor belt
And walk on through

What kind of day today?
You could just say
I really didn't need something
To tell my grandkids

■

JOHN THORPE

Poem

_____

A man & a woman had something to do with waiting.
                          god damn god damn.
They were the insides of a house.
                          They were waiting
for someone who wouldn't just stand there, them, stand,
in them. Oh god. In the house, above which
          A great horse flapped in the terrific.
He asked her how the mescaline was.
          She said nothing was happening.
How about the sky just then over horse?
          She said she didn't see any sky . . .

OH IS IT BLACK HORSE COME HUMMING FOR YOU?
I'D SWEAR IT WAS A HORSE

VOICES TALKING TO A MARRIAGE COUNSELOR IN NEWARK

DUSTY DIRT STREAKED WINDOW.

■

T O N Y   T O W L E

Social Poem

_____

It's six o'clock, do you know
where you are? I am with my sanity
among the bells
telling me it is six o'clock,
which is more than I need to know.

I seem to want to talk about something,
but it is missing,
which makes it a personal remark
which I stop to listen to
as if the bells had stopped ringing
but I were persisting
as if the walls were further away
than just on the other side,
as the interior floods
with the gloom of the typewriter
as I memorialize a pond
stirred by fish through ugly shadows
I have to make use of. Actually
I am upset with my tone of voice,
as if I had climbed the walls
but did not get far enough away,
though in the first place
I don't know where that would be
and in the second
I know everything else,
which leads to too much news. Maybe
the walls aren't even there anymore,
since nothing seems to be there anymore,
as if the present were an elaborated ambush,
the finale instead of the usual ambience
until a later hour, in so many words.
And I haven't even gotten to sociability yet,
grasping at its details

and freeing them like peasants
to a thimbleful of history.
Why a thimble? My jacket
needs a button,
but that isn't what I meant by travelling,
I mean that one should be somebody else
and actually go,
although I am somebody else
and have stayed; still living and walking
near Spring Street,
though when I observed it first
there wasn't its bar
accommodating the many people who came from the distance
and got used to me, filtered from the past
which doubles as much of the day.
And I still cross Houston Street
in the path of the many drivers from New Jersey
who I am sure are all nice people
when they get back home; but in the meantime
they are after me,
since I don't mind being paranoid,
it is like being Polish
and riding off into a joke
that of course I would not understand,
lost in generalizations;
and filtered through metaphysical situations
onto geographical surface,
where I am thinking about Jackson Pollock
for some reason,
the rumors and rectangles
from the Cedar Bar to the Metropolitan, the legend
half of me would like the other half to be,
though if I could say which half were which
I wouldn't get any further;
but the real joke is I don't have a horse,
so that crossing Houston Street is truly pedestrian,
which is good for the paranoia
but not for the legend
I'll be nearer to the next time I stop
at the next place I'll be.

Moral Courage

Pink birds are again in the yellow sky,
a silver spoon of milky clouds
and again I am nourished by escape.
A seagull appears at 4 o'clock,
and again at 11, to be revised
and ready to attack the page
through a cement feeling of infinity.
In September I gave up smoking, that
was moral courage. I go out into the sleet
to fetch a dying stranger a cigarette.
Coughing and wheezing he reveals the secret of life;
yes, it is having moral courage.
The world shrinks to the size of an oyster,
the museum of sleep opens,
then grows to the size of a turtle
for a splash in the clear broth of awakening.
Tart is a variation of the Middle English *tarte*,
from the Old French *tourte*, a round low Latin cake
devoured on the way to a woman. If her taste is sharp,
or *tart*, then she came to you from the Anglo-Saxon, *teart*.
I explore the language compulsively, like Tennyson,
and exist in it as a story, like the dictionary,
told accumulating beneath the sun
which we notice with medieval regularity;
but again I escape
in digression on this lovely hill
above the rape of the country.
It takes a long time to write,
and to read as well. Time is short, in a way,
the animal air is a bath, in a way;
an animal disappears behind a wall,
loose stones trouble the continuing footsteps
following what from my window
I can only think of as moral courage.
Typing is a variation of drama, a soft pursuit
and I type the words Modern Theatre as well, patterns
I do not disturb, or go into, but into a variation.

GEORGE TYSH

Recent Still Life

---

you are staring at a point
on the far wall
in which a naked bulb is suspended

mostly black and some white
there is a bull's-eye spot
on the glass upon which

your eyes focus,
behind it the foreground dries
you can hear a shower

idling somewhere in the wall
your face goes beyond this point
to where the fruit of

a resemblance takes it all in,
to all of you
held in a pause

■

JANINE POMMY VEGA

Lurigancho*

A solitary air blows over the *cerro*
the sun, disguised in the white
soup of Lima, is vaguely waving

Guards with official whistles
harry the listener
calling each other through corridors
they shriek and answer
barking dogs at midnight
in a little town—
the visits are over

Brick walls, broken windows
inmates in brightly colored shirts
are waving
the only flower in the grainy air
the only color

Holes are broken through brick walls
into cubicles
to search outsiders
the left arms of women tattooed
numbers
the personal shakedown
leaving, we file through again
for the last touch, across the crotch,
to prove we are women

Lurigancho: men's prison outside Lima, Peru

Outside the walls, machine guns strut
through abandoned market days
leering into the hurried business
of thousands of women
struggling into lines for the buses
exchanging news and embraces
to the last week
the men at the windows are waving
waving

Saludos, hermanos
where we know each other
there are no walls
no twisted dreams of day after day
but a clear wind over the Andes
the gentle touch of *garúa* moistening
hands and hair

Ciao, South American continent
the murders in your face
are less disguised than where I live—
one sees who to hate
to the north the civilized killers,
corporate fists, the ones in power
have no human face at all.
They have no face.

Lurigancho, Peru, September 1982

cerro: mountain
garúa: drizzle
saludos, hermanos: greetings, brothers

T O M   V E I T C H

The Edible Complex

Leave your shit behind.
Don't worry about it.
It doesn't belong to you.
It is the food of our master.
You don't have to please him.
You don't have to sculpture your shit.
He likes it any old way you leave it.
Leave your body behind,
leave it, it's worthless,
you can get along without it.
It doesn't belong to you.
It is the food of our master.
You don't have to please him.
He likes it any old way you leave it.
He doesn't lay trips on your shit.
He just eats it.
There's no way you can please him,
he's indifferent, beyond good & evil,
he just takes it all
into his mouth where he spins
it into fine gold.
(That's what's in those freight cars.)
Hey, Bodi, what's the value of spun gold—?
Awakening, Bodi, big awakening.

■

PAUL VIOLI

Drastic Measures

She hears footsteps: He's home.
She tells herself that she is not angry.

"Sorry I'm late, dear."

"Oh, no problem. Let me take your coat.
Dinner's on the table, I'll get the wine."
She notices that the hair on his arm
has grown through his shirt, his favorite shirt.
When he rolls up his sleeves, it hurts.

"Please pass the chops."

She studies his face, but inconclusively.
"How's everything?" he asks. "The kids are o.k.?"

"Just fine. The kids brought home
good report cards and last night I dreamed
that the tide was quite low and that all the clams
were yawning at my life."

"—I don't have a fork . . . Oh, thank you."

There's an orchestra that gives the pleas
of a ravaged soul the dark majesty it deserves
and one of its musicians falls out of a tree
and screams past the kitchen window. Crash.

"Damn it," he says, "it's that late already?
Remind me to spray that tree."

She can't repress her anger any longer.
"What happened? Where were you?
I waited like a fiend in sunlight for you."

"I—I got lost. I had to drive upstate.
A new account, a new sales territory opened up.
I got lost on the way back. No place to call.
It was terrible. There was this fork in the road
—Yes, that was it—and I didn't know
which way to go. Finally, this old man walked by.
He was lost, too; but what he did know he told me:
That one road led to a gorgeous supermarket
and immortality, the other to chaos.
Trouble was, he didn't know which was which."

She continues to eat but a strained
expression creases her brow.

"The old man said that the only thing
I could do was to go to one of these nearby houses
and ask directions. But be careful, he told me,
the people in those houses were strange.
One family could only tell lies,
the other only the truth.
And there was no way of knowing
which family was which.
To make things worse, he said
that I could only ask one family
one question, and one question only!"

Quietly, sadly she stares at him, thinking
that things like this happen to other people,
people who have nothing in common with us.

There's a wild scream. Another musician
bounces hard off the roof.

"Anyway, as I was saying, it took me a long time
but I finally figured it out.
I went to the first house
and when this guy opened the door
I asked him point-blank: 'Sir, if you lived
in that *other* house, which road would you tell me
leads to the supermarket and immortality?' "

"So, the guy smiles and says, 'I'd have to tell you
to go right, mister. If you go left
you'll drive right into a shit-storm.' "

Another vertical scream, a ballerina this time.
She crashes through the branches and lands headfirst,
stuck in the mud, legs dangling
out of her tou tou: insanity's orchid.

"So, I jumped in the car, took a *left* instead
—You follow me?—dropped the old man off
at the stupormarket, and made my way home."

Having listened intently, she's now relieved
but still feels the strain on her face.
Everything is becoming dark—dark and mushy.
All the while, never realizing that her
lovely hair had fallen into her meal,
she had been wrapping it around her fork,
thinking that she was twirling noodles,
and gradually reeled her face into her plate.

■

Melodrama

For Ann

There it is again, the future,
      and it looks the same as the last time I saw it.
I recognize everything, I stole
        the chandeliers myself, in broad daylight.
And there's the horizon, an actual line after all,
           a wrack line. And you
on the other side, so content,
   naked in the sun-stirred air,
           lolling on the hood of a new white car.
A stone turns into a peach as soon as you bite it.
   Windfall silence, the clouds stampede.
   I like the garish car, too;
and the ornament, the silver swan between your thighs,
looks like it just flew out of you, your heart's emblem,
         released, raising its wings into
the great and puzzling distances that brighten my sleep.

Some physicists agree that Tachyons,
          if they do indeed exist,
travel _only_ faster than the speed of light
   and aren't good for much else,
except for someone like me to envy now and then,
   thinking I might eventually follow them,
        as I kill time driving around,
   not knowing where I'm going, not lost either,
       watching the city expand,
weary, dazed, in love with the night;
             a job here and there,
a dinner box of Kentucky Fried Chicken in my lap,
      an open container of coffee
   and a greasy steering wheel to contend with.
   Anyway, something like that keeps me going,
carries me in a clear globe of exhaustion and pleasure,
   squinting through raindrop craters
          and metronomic windshield wipers

into the pointless wastes of time, glad at least
    to be both here *and* there, writing to you.

The "scavengers of the air" are already up there,
    high above the perpetual sirens,
                wailing to each other
as they careen through the canyons and avenues
    and dive for the bones, bills, and garbage
I toss out the window.
            My dream carved in the windshield;
    my reflection buried
        in the ice-coated sideview mirror;
    "my verse a true image of my mind,
    ever in motion, still desiring change."
Matches, cigarette packs slide back
    and forth across the dashboard as the car swerves.
    Tires hum and moan and sometimes sing to me
about the people I love or how tired I am of death,
    how I wouldn't know what to do without you,
how, through the reveries and cold facts of sleeplessness,
    the red taillights ahead of me
look like stars fallen in line
and whose destination is the same as mine.

■

DIANE WAKOSKI

Journeys by Water

Splashing in the bathtub with lemon soap

journeying to the nape of my neck
lemon bubbles

This journey as I sit in a white porcelain tub
thinking of all the waterfalls between us
how the water splashes through our ears
into our bellies
gushing out through the navel, a fountain
to our grassy feet
we touching never speaking
these crystals of water our connected blood

a journey by water
a small paper boat going over the ocean
the water not a conductor of sound,
my voice sticks in my throat

say it by water,
a clear trip into my eye.

■

ANNE WALDMAN

Drugs

Addressing tonight the young men the young women of tender
passage, speaking out of a stereo place, a double barrelled
feeling for your skin your arms your eyes your hips your lips
your legs, legs that buckle turn to me quivering, eyes not
focused, arms spindly and shot through glitzy fear haunts
you, aura the color of the street. Not a beach not an alpine
slope not a radiant bower. Not a causeway not a moonlit
forest. Broken I say, and scattered in a fratricide
arrangement of the deranged senses and murdering of women
too. But it is the face that comes apart as the aparati
crumbles prostrate on the stoop or up in that family
apartment, that fancy apartment. In one second we all
feel we live forever. I never know what time it is! Clocks,
radios, TVs break down. Long lines wear down the spirit.
The idol who this artist wrought falls to the ground as if
to a grave. Early graves I see my neighbor frothing and
bound in a straight jacket carried to the attendant ambulance.
Ambulare: to walk free on one's own steam. A moral speech,
yes, a mortal one, and a mighty fleet is storming you with
its prevarications. You say Leave me alone, you say
you hate the mighty harmonies.

You forget what I just said to you. You repeat yourself.
You whine. You try to fasten the sweater unsuccessfully
not like the youth who knows his own con. Concommitant, con
vivace, tender feelings to take a specific shape and continue.
Complete metabolic transfusion in which my infant logic plods
stupidly along. It won't ever stop, ignorant one, to listen
or ever refuse the likes of me in the replenishing hells or
halls, no bare feet, no fire drills, prone face down in mud.

Sit beside me again, sit to people the lonely universe, and
break the adamantine chains that strap you down. Not the
situation I leave you here, squabbling under the window to
fix their bodies right, get them straight. I say Rites of
Passage, I say it's missing, and bow my head. And how you
will end up not knowing the universe is evident. Incandescent
splendor, my smart clothes: cocaine. The greatest affirmer,
coke, the smokescreen of all the attitudes, coke, and everything's
okay, yeah, in my wallet, in my power play, my rendezvous
with braintalk, my little box is tight.

The heroines of whom you are the kick for, who takes you
deeper home. Junk, a point I get to beyond which I'd never
go for no man no woman no saint no idea no manifesto no
poetry no one's mother no plan or scheme to get rich no
lover no lover's beauty no prophecy flecked with fire and
brimstone. Scabs line the sidewalk, walking quickly for
the stroller's speed to be transmitted, a fast clip by the
leer or jeer or hassle and drown one sorrow in a drink.
Drink making me emotional, or quaalude, that weak sister.
If I could be Thersites-tongued, if I had that lucid scaly
tongue I would wag at you, I'd snap and bark and scoff and
bite. A pack of hounds to plead this sentiment, for it is,
you know, my surface sentimentality makes me mad, me a loon.
O dear speeder, speed-reader, speed-beater. Tonight I am
singing for the swift-neck tension I get in my brain stem,
high under Miss Green under a beneficent lamplight before
the supreme task (grandiose my powers) is done.

Task to set the thoughts unassailably down. I am my own
assailant with a cannister of tear-gas in one hand, my
cobra protection implement in the other. Sisters I say,
go armed.

But I wanted to tell you my approval smacks of what won't
go over as a kiss, an embrace, what can't be interpreted
as how I love you, because when you fall back, lump of
desire, limp of head, the lights go out all over New York.

You speak, and when you are speaking you speak to the speaker,
you are hearing the speaker, the hearer is the speaker, he
speaks to hear his speech to hear his mind roll on . . .

The speech is a history, the story of some people, the laughter
of some people, how the people nudged each other, the speaker
is the centripetal force to propel the speech to all who
will stay here, listening. He speaks in a story. He won't
listen but comments on the speaking, on the fast tone of
the speaker. I need more pills! I need more history, history!

Hectic and demanding is my habit. Hectoring me like a shrew,
like a shadow, like a dumbshow, like an out-of-towner. I am
walking to no Eleusis.

Silky shadow to deeper than a hum the pain.

I cushion the mugger's quality of pillow of guilt. He's an
old-timer, burnt sienna, who puts in him those holes in him.
How enters the bloodstream, how rushes, how draw back, pull
up the reins. Horsie, whoa!

So. Go on. So. No. Go on. I say go on. I say no, go on.
I say you live in my garden-heart. I say no creature of habit
be. There's beauty sensible like a fine torso, like torso
of fine baby-man. I need to be mothering. I need to be
mothering my art, go on.

■

Crack in the World

I see the crack in the world

My body thinks it, sees the gaping crack in the world

My body does it for me to see

Blood flowing through the body crack

Body, send your rivers to the moon

Body twists me to the source of the moon

It turns me under a wave

It sets up the structure to make a baby, then tears
it down again

Architecture of womb-body haunting me

Someone is always watching the ancient flow

It doubles up my mind

Ovum not fertilized

I see the crack in the world

Thoughts intersect in the body

He must not keep me down

Let me go my way alone tonight

No man to touch me

A slash in me, I see the slash in the world tonight

It keeps me whole, but divides me now

Out on land, to bleed

Out on street, to bleed

In the snow, blood

This is a South American song

Scent of oleander

Or this is a cactus song

Sing of blood flower a rose in the crotch
O collapsible legs!

My body enchanted me to this

My body demented to this

It is endometrium shedding

I am compressed in the pressure of my heart

It is life pursuing the crack in the world

Between worlds

Between thoughts

A vacant breath

Words won't do it

Ovum not fertilized

The man hasn't done it

I cover every contingency
the catty one
or puritan walking in a fecund world

Words sing to me of endometrium collapse

Words go down to my belly

Back swelling, to put my body next to the earth

This is periodic

It comes at the full moon

Let me go howling in the night

No man to touch me

Don't fathom my heart tonight, man

No one wants to be around this factory,
this beautiful machine
but I shun your company anyway

My flexible body imagines the crack

Body with winds

See the crack in the universe

The curse, glorious curse is upon me

Don't come to my house

Don't expect me at your door

I'm in my celibacy rags

My anthropocentric heart says there's
a crack in the world tonight

It's a long woman's body

It's a break in the cycle of birth & death

It's the rapid proliferation of cells
building up to die

I make up the world & kill it again & again

I offer my entrails to the moon

Ovum not fertilized

Architecture haunting me

Collapsible legs you must carry the world

You get away from me

You keep your distance

I will overpower you with my scent
of life & death

You who came through the crack in my world

You men who came out of me, back off

Words come out of the belly

Groaning as the world is pulled apart

Body enchanted to this

Body elaborated on this

Body took the measure of the woman
to explain the fierceness of this time
walking on the periphery of the world

■

Tell Me About It

For George Schneeman

Anything suffused with light
soft brown hair & eyes, soft
yet unflinching in a hundred portraits
Anything sitting, walking, musing in light blue
or sturdy in plaids, anything with lips
You are a winner of fantasies in paint,
they come to you in pretty detail
ordinary spending, essential things
A spool of thread, anything . . .
Anything is possible with an eye
to poetry, Dante spilling across
a platter, rain of blood, of tears
manifesting the Heartbroken-You
I hear you say "It's so beautiful"
puff on a cigar and make a sudden
gesture in the guest's direction
an articulation of generosity
or argumentation, it's this
way, no it's *this* way, George
Are you kidding me?
Yes, and it's not the first, final,
middle, between, over & above,
outside the head, inside the studio,
behind the eyes time you or I mean
Why don't you drop by more often?
There's no time not to be on
the job, abrasive, I tell myself
as if I'm you, you the terrifying
example of discipline, stubborness
workmanship, to be a maker of
something, would I were as productive
as you.   I made a baby!
I made dinner   I made a motion
I made a book   But I didn't
paint anyone's eyes or put animals

on delicate cups or libertines
on vases   I didn't show my whole
sex *ever* like *that!*
I didn't grow up in Minnesota
or live in Siena under a lush
sun, close to the ground
but came organically out of a city,
another hybrid, home-grown
Our mothers die & we are suddenly
finite as if everything that
extended beyond us, in front of us
is now a dream. This is a dream
of great spaces, endless dimensions
& empty frescoes & canvases
& pages & a big sore swelling—
Here come the tears again—heart
The mothers were so spunky!
I am a naughty girl again &
you are the cantankerous son
of the-woman-at-rest
Unease to plunk it down,
embarrassed by richness
how to say anything like Heh
I just found out something
Ok so Tell me about it
Anything that in paint speaks
around a situation, all the circles
Anything is didactic if I speak
this way, seeming to be casual
as if I just wandered over myself
to pick something up, drop off
a book, someone's birthday,
a dinner, rare footage on TV,
I slept in your same room
between hospital visitings
You were right there, there
you are, I don't have to ask
Help me lug something large
up the stairs, help me be
practical, I don't have to ask
do I? I watch you pedal
down St. Mark's Place

Anything tense between
a double image, you & me,
is going on, split so we
can touch noses, forefingers
tease & go away again
I am the messenger
& you are the little god
You make the world happen,
make the small people dance,
ride bicycles, kiss & fuck forever
circumambulating a clock,
a vase, anything . . .
like angels in the gorgeous sky
or denizens of hell
You do this you have to

■

L E W I S   W A R S H

E n m e s h m e n t

I listened to the voices that shattered
my heart, strange prerequisite, followed
by silence (I was an unrequited lover
again), my being contained an ampersand
dividing me from others & me from myself,
& the others (like plants desirous of light
& water) reflected through other eyes the casualness
of what I said, I could be aggressive, I could
be a "type" of person, I could even live a lie,
one imagines a bowl of light & a volatile bottle
which we could use to dynamite the walls of a public
building, I could harbor resentment till it flew
over my head like a dagger & passed through the heart
of an innocent bystander, one might look dumbstruck
in comparison to others for whom knowledge was a cherished
companion, my dependencies demand compensation
(an eye that opens like a shutter), I had what
you might call a "breakthru" but which for me
was "normal love," I wore the straight-jacket
of love's decline like the door of a locked room
with two people cowering behind it, I read how
achievement had nothing to do with the possession
of property, I had lunch with Peggy
but I couldn't eat (when it came
time to order all I could say was "I'll take
the same"), there was no distinction or space but
there was room for improvement, I saw myself as a special
plant or flower (a wild bleeding heart or black-eyed
susan) but I forgot about immunity & the right
to remain silent, I thought of affection as a way of expressing
something to someone you loved
(in the simplest sense, like brushing the hair
out of a person's eyes), I grew accustomed
to cold spaces, unmade beds, dishes in the sink

the laundry piled up on the bathroom floor, a couch
with no legs, I saw anger as a way of slipping
down a well with no sides, I limited myself
to what was most fortuitous (a rock or shell
washed up on the shore), I climbed tenement steps
to find an island with a broad vista
& discovered a window with a transparent curtain & a bamboo shade
I denied love's passage into memory, & all the digressions
blue earrings, a furrowed brow, two shadows on the page.

■

Heirloom

negatives may be given
but they don't change anything. What
was wrong to begin with won't lead to positive
results overnight if what you want to happen is already
covered with patches and clouds. The paint stains won't
wash out of your trousers nor the hem of your skirt
absorb the mud of elitism
which surrounds us, now that paradise has come to this
our home, previously untainted. The way they think
is what's wrong with everything
& I'd shed my skin again
if I thought it would make a difference.
Divisive shows of affection known only
to kings & their vassals
assert themselves on the heads
of sycophants & liars. I pat myself
on the back for this or that;
I hold my feelings in abeyance till the end
of time which means tomorrow I'll walk outside
& see her again & feel empty or filled with energy
as if her words had complemented mine

& for a moment not only our bodies but
everything around us blended together harmoniously
& with a nod to the future, when we'd meet again.
Nothing to salvage but the last drop
in a bottle of ouzo that's been sitting
on the shelf for 2 years, do you want any?
I want to retire out of sight until it all blows
over, detach my heart as I mount the stage like a veteran
amid the personifications of the desire to be loved
& give love gratuitously like an heirloom before aging
rapidly & so decisively all I can do is look back
with happiness on the things I might have said or done
had I acted more like the way she might have acted
in my stead. I'd rather be cheated, off & on,
than never to trust, even if idiocy
seems normal & the tiara slips to one side
as I call up, say, the ghost of Newton
to help me balance my feelings
since if I'm not here now in space & time I'll
never be anywhere you'll ever find me
& if you don't walk in the room in a minute or two
I'll have to assume I've fallen out of favor
for some reason, like a baby monkey clinging to his mother
I'll weep to be pardoned for sins I've never committed
in this lifetime but which I'll take upon myself anyway
if it'll make you happy, since somebody has to
create a passageway that's accessible
so the big ships can pass in the night
& if I'm not the mermaid singing on the rocks
who is? I spy the gauntlet of pleasure
in the distance, sailors carousing
on shore amid the rare condiments
they've unearthed, but I don't know
if what's inside me can be plundered
so easily, even if you're a stranger & you've
just arrived at the pearly gate,
my feelings persevere like
people at a party who stay too late,
& if I'm the host who locks the door behind them
& says goodbye, well, so be it.

■

HANNAH WEINER

Long Poem for
Roy Lichtenstein

Lima
Oscar
November
Golf
Papa
Oscar
Echo
Mike
Foxtrot
Oscar
Romeo
Romeo
Oscar
Yankee
Lima
India
Charlie
Hotel
Tango
Echo
November
Sierra
Tango
Echo
India
November

∎

REBECCA WRIGHT

from *Brief Lives*

                              The pen is throwing
such a glare that it obscures the page, and the sun

                    all the flowers are laced together in my dream

The letters aren't here, a secret from myself. I abandon Miss
Lonely Hearts, nothing to indicate that we are out of bounds, still

the little walks, the roads, the ground beneath our feet, as I was
falling asleep it seemed there should be telephone poles or ladders
so that one has to cross the sky a little bit . . .

I was ill and felt unloveable. I would have been happy to die.
I dreamed that someone pinned a broach on my sweater, the one
that J. always wears and said "the queen has come to you"
We were walking up a huge stairway built in the side of a steep hill.
Crowds of people were walking up hill, but not on the stairs, I think
they were strikers or refugees, among rocks which had been
loosened by an earthquake, and which became all the heads of that
striking mass. The two of us on the stairs were psychotherapists
and when consulted thought they'll be sorry they asked, remembering
cases similar to theirs. As though we could make it
turn out even worse for them.

"Mingo was here" is written on the fifth-floor wall at the top of the
stairs. He went sailing off out over the rooftops that night and she
came into our apartment off the fire escape while her husband was
pounding
on their door. And the police came and took the husband away
and she went back up the stairs and out onto the roof and called
and called for Mingo into the night . . .
                        that day is finished, and the
migration of birds, and all their heads are averted in present thought.
We went down to the warehouse today, all the nations'
food in private hands, and he touched my face without even knowing

who I was, at home in his father's warehouse, and the river rolling
past . . .

and in the hallway all the mirrors, the Mae West girls
with their hands on their hips, and sultry words in their hearts
stealing away with wild-eyed men

the single-mindedness
insisting that the symphony be played off key in keeping with
the national tradition. But there was not a breath of air and the
symphony remained unheard. Dominique and I passing the stone
coffins, which were used as baths. Tabu, Shahara all those brands
are his and I slip into bed beside him not knowing it would be that
kind of day . . .

beyond him to compose the national hymn,
beyond them to sing it, absurd and taking place in the rain, the parts
for voice are written for cellos and violins and the choir sings with
its ass, stained inaudible words like the scent of men's cologne.

Miss Lonely Hearts, seeming to be Mister F. and M. a South American
cowboy. And J. hard-hearted today . . .

the whole world arranged
in favor of my left eye. Everything worth seeing appears to the
left, the light in the window, and the sunlight always to the left. And
the left eye is the one to laugh and weep while the right eye perceives
nothing at all, closing to the world.

When I fall asleep it is
the left eye which dreams. I climb a ladder like the ones in parks
on the children's slide, and then the ladder is moving out to sea.

I told them that I was deaf and dumb and that I depended on my body
totally, being tired of living in my head. Because she whitened
her fingernails she was given the job. If I don't know enough to
do that I can expect to go without. It is the list of exclusions
that causes one to fail, no address, no tickets, no membership.
I look ridiculous in these same clothes, still it's not cold enough
to wear a winter coat. I can't understand why he has come all this
way with me. I saw him on the steps just as he was leaving the opera,
of course I was glad to see him. But then last night I could hardly
close my eyes for fear of being shot in my sleep. The way to say
good-bye was to say nothing at all, and still to thank you for
everything. And T, I will always be with you,

then it was I who rushed into the arms
of the murderer.

■

BILL ZAVATSKY

Reading Roque Dalton,
Smoking a Nicaraguan Cigar

1.

Roque, you wrote that your prison guard

"suggested that perhaps I could write him a poem . . .

so he could keep it for a souvenir

after they killed me."

Well, wasn't he

one of "the people" you said you wrote for?

Whose lives you said were your "ongoing concern"?

You worried about poetry, too,

in the three lines you wrote with this title:

The Art of Poetry 1974

Poetry
Forgive me for having helped you understand
that you aren't just made out of words.

Eventually someone did kill you,

someone from a rival leftist group

in your native El Salvador

At 39, I've lived a year longer

than you.

I haven't smoked a cigar

in two years, but now I'm hooked again,

puffing on a Nicaraguan stogie,

55¢, the last of a bundle found

in a little tobacco shop on 38th.

"The guy who sold them

stopped coming around," the owner said.

"They blew up the factories in their revolution,"

he shrugged. What he meant was "How stupid

can you get?"

"I'm glad they did, I'm glad

they had their revolution," I answered back.

"The Somozas were monsters—they bled the country dry!"

He winced. I felt ashamed

before his reddening face as he shrugged again.

"I got them on a deal," he said,

almost apologizing, wary

of offending a new customer.

2.

All I know about Roque Dalton

is what I read in *Social Text*—

a brief biography, eleven pages of poems.

And the little book of his writing

published by the Curbstone Press of Connecticut,

Poetry & Militancy in Latin America.

One claims that "while he was in jail

under sentence of death, an earthquake

destroyed the cell walls, allowing him to escape."

Not a bad beginning for a myth. For a middle-class boy

brought up in Jesuit schools—

miracle in the service of the Revolution!

I sat in those schools myself

and soaked up the holy stories

of the gentle Christ who fed the multitudes

with a few loaves and fishes,

the Christ they couldn't kill.

I wonder if the guard returned

after the earth had split open

to find that Dalton had vanished,

the guard who asked for the souvenir poem,

the way the disciples returned to find

the tomb of Jesus—empty.

I have never been locked in a cell,

waiting to be killed.

Smoking this Nicaraguan cigar

is the easiest thing in the world.

The "people" Dalton speaks of

so lovingly in one of his essays

are often hard for me to love.

When I find the splintered glass

of their bottles along my street

or hurry my wife past someone pissing

against the next-door building

though the free toilets of the Port Authority

are clean and open a block away, I fly

into a rage. In the safety of my apartment

the ugliest things within me smash

against the bars of their cage.

I don't know where I want the whores

and their tricks to go, screaming

all night in the parking lot

below our window. I think of buying

a little gun, a bee-bee gun, to shoot

and scare them away. I think of leading

men from our building

armed with baseball bats

into the parking lot at three a.m.

I am sick and angry to be woken

by crazed voices, monster radios,

the slamming car doors and racing engines

of people who don't live here.

Roque, you would point at me and say:

"Don't let your anger go out at the victims!

Take your baseball team over to Trump Tower

or the Museum of Modern Art, where Lissitzky

sits in the gift shop window, his genius reduced

to a matching cup and saucer!"

I know you're right, Roque, but sometimes

I don't care. I take my life in my hands

and tell the kid in the doorway:

"Do I go piss on the street where *you* live?"

I rant and stomp around the rooms,

frightening my wife as I carry on.

4.

Roque, you must have seen this, too.

The bum wrapped around his bottle of "Night Train,"

struggling to focus on the limousines

that speed to the Saturday matinee

at the Metropolitan Opera, tickets

$38 $45 $75

government-subsidized art

that only the rich can afford.

You must have seen a bum like this

shaking his head over where they get the money

when 55¢ in change

is tough enough to scrounge.

In these hard days

even the liquor store on Ninth and 44th

has closed its doors.

The painted brick flakes away

where the winos used to drowse

out of the sun, where one

demanded a quarter

to hail me a cab.

I told him I worked

damn hard for what I made.

Who can dig down

in his pocket every time?

And what can poetry buy

in the world of pennies

and limousines . . .

You can't change much

by giving your change away.

Or only for a little while,

a little sleep in the shade

of an empty storefront

as the shadows of the limousines whoosh by.

5.

My second cigar tastes as good

as the first. I wonder if Dalton

smoked cigars, these sweet Nicaraguan cigars,

and the earth-dark cigars of Cuba

where he lived in exile for a time.

As I have been in exile.

From the people I seem powerless to know

or help, or sometimes even feel compassion towards,

in their violence, in their sadness,

in the strangeness they must feel

as I walk their streets, smoking

my big cigar, trying to pass them by

invisibly, like this smoke from my mouth

drifting into the air.

6. Coda

The poem should have ended there.

That last dramatic image as the smoke

of language eddies from my cigar.

                              On a note

of liberal despair, informed by concern.

Leaving in your mind the image

of a man, intelligent, sincere

if a bit naive, struggling to find

the truth.

                    The truth—three months later—

looks like this:

                    Confusion! Confusion

over who "the people" are. Confusion

bred by the satisfaction of thinking,

even for a moment, that those I see

in the streets *are* "the people."

I am no subway vigilante. Inside me

there is love—and so much anger!

What do I know of these faces in the street,

the ones I fear, the ones I see my face in?

The faces of color, or speaking another language,

hurrying their way to work, terrified also,

all of us faces turned down or turning away in fear.

What do I know except these confused ideas

I spout in the purity of my hopelessness,

wondering in my heart if anything can be done.

We can't take up the cross,

it's too slippery with blood.

Roque, do we take up the gun

the way you did?

And once we learn to use it

can it ever be put down?

■

T R A N S L A T I O N S   I I

So don't kill the birds!

Don't shoot them with the eyelids of death!

Don't poke out the flying eyes!

Don't blind God!

—Saint Pol Roux

from "Birds"

Trans.: Annette

Smolarski and

Larry Fagin

Ballade: Par amour n'aim, ne amer ne voudroie

My heart's felt no wounds big or small
from Cupid's darts, which they say
make war on many
I've not thank God! been caught
in the booby trap or prison
of the God of Love
I make him no pleas but live alone in delight
I have no lover I don't want one

& I'm not afraid either of being caught
by smouldering looks fancy gifts or hot chase
or trapped by wheedling words
There's no man can match my heart
Let none come after me for help
I'll turn him off saying
I have no lover I don't want one

& I'll laugh at any woman
caught in such stupid peril
She should have killed herself long ago
She's lost all honor in the world
I intend to live my whole life
in this state & say to all who entreat me
I have no lover I don't want one

Prince of Love what on earth
should I do at your court?
I have no lover I don't want one!

Christine de Pisan
Translated from the Provençal
by Anne Waldman

Poem in a Style Not My Own

To you, Baudelaire

Near a holly bush, through whose foliage a city could be seen, Don Juan, Rothschild, Faust and a painter were chatting.

"I amassed a great fortune," said Rothschild, "and as it gave me no enjoyment, I've kept buying and selling, hoping to recover the joy which the first million gave me."

"I have continued to search for love in the midst of unhappiness," said Don Juan. "Not to love, and yet to be loved, is torture; but I continue looking for love in the hope of recovering the emotion of my first passion."

"When I found the secret that made me famous," said the painter, "I searched for other secrets to occupy my mind: because of those others, I was refused the fame which the first secret bestowed on me, and I am returning to that formula in spite of the disgust it gives me."

"I deserted science for happiness," said Faust, "but I'm returning to science, even though my methods are now obsolete, because there is no happiness except in research."

Beside them stood a young woman crowned with artificial ivy who said:

"I'm bored, I am too beautiful."

And from behind the holly bush God said:

"I know the universe and I am bored."

Max Jacob
Translated from the French by Michael Brownstein

■

Birds

To Catulle Mendès

Eyes fly from the foreheads of the blind and turn into birds.

—Little birds, I can believe that, but what about big ones?

The big birds, you see nothing but eyes, bulging, startled since time immemorial.

What could possibly keep those eyes from growing, once they were up in the sky?

Wren: eye of a doll!
Titmouse: eye of a little girl!
Warbler: eye of a little boy!
Waxbill: eye of a princess!
Finch: eye of a page!
Linnet: eye of a gypsy!
Sparrow: eye of an urchin!
Lark: eye of a shepherd!
Wagtail: eye of a laundress!
Ortolan: eye of a vicar!
Nightingale: eye of a poet!
Swallow: eye of a belly dancer!
Woodpecker: eye of a pilgrim!
Goldfinch: eye of a soldier!
Kingfisher: eye of a sailor!
Bat: eye of a streetwalker!
Cuckoo: eye of a scrounge!
Thrush: eye of a drunk!
Blackbird: eye of a comedian!
Starling: eye of a taxpayer!
Duck: eye of a beggar!
Turtle dove: eye of a nun!
Ring-dove: eye of a lover!
Dove: eye of a martyr!
Magpie: eye of a widow!
Crow: eye of a gravedigger!
Owl: eye of a miser!

Seagull: eye of a pirate!
Cock: eye of a toreador!
Hen: eye of a housewife!
Pheasant: eye of a gentleman!
Turkey: eye of a judge!
Goose: eye of a bishop!
Heron: eye of a monk!
Swan: eye of a patriarch!
Tawny owl: eye of an astrologer!
Cormorant: eye of a buccaneer!
Stork: eye of a mage!
Condor: eye of a bandit!
Vulture: eye of a tyrant!
Peacock: eye of a pope!
Eagle: eye of an emperor!
And so many others!

This proves that there are a lot of eyes with wings; think of all those nests in space.

They look like they're in orbit, don't they?

The birds go from place to place, peak to peak, field to field, bush to bush, branch to branch; wherever they come to rest they leave eyes.

When a bird lands, the rock or the branch looks at us with a beautiful or ugly sound, depending on the mirror of our soul.

We should always make an effort to have a clear soul as we walk through life with infinite precaution; because the eyes from human foreheads have fallen into the "public domain" and become the eyes of nature.

This may explain why the idea of an All-Seeing God surprised us when we were children.

To tell the truth, God is a girl, a boy, a rich man, a poor man, who suffers, who rejoices, who helps us, who tests us, who rewards us, who chastises us—in fact, it's everybody in the world all at once.

So don't kill the birds!

Don't shoot them with the eyelids of death!

Don't poke out the flying eyes!

Don't blind God!

Saint Pol Roux
Translated from the French by
Larry Fagin and Arlette Smolarski

To A.C.

centenarian baby
mammoth baby
hellion baby
seducible baby
immovable baby
singing baby
feeling nervous baby
even in August baby
bleating baby
grandparent baby
parent baby
papa baby
Cartesian baby
artisan baby
artesian baby
tea-leaves baby
weaver baby
wornout baby
wounded baby
comfortable baby
redoubtable baby
doubt at table baby
baby whom I love
baby whom I'll . . . of
baby whom I'll have
hook-nosed baby
star's crook baby
baby of the bird
baby of the woods
baby who would
be-seen baby
have to have baby
have to taste baby
after-taste baby
ivory baby
diverse baby
various baby

tower-born baby
your turn baby
too real baby
trump card baby
our baby
our sin baby
sea urchin baby
search him baby
winter baby
winner baby
win her baby
amber baby
I am burning baby
you're laughing baby
hereafter baby
flaming baby
famous baby
famine baby
faraway baby
foreign baby
Farnese baby
furnace baby
fortune's baby
fine baby
final baby
fig baby
fugue baby
tiger baby
trigger baby
tree-girt baby
vellum baby
velvet baby
Venus's baby
ravenous baby
revenue baby
avenue baby
your baby

vitreous baby
detour baby
tourist baby
turret baby
turbine baby

you are baby
breezy baby
kiss me baby
baby
baby you are mine

Cesar Moro
Translated from the French by
Frances LeFevre Waldman

■

Sympathy for Horses

Hooves strike
as though they were chanting:
Girb
Grab
Grub
Groob—

Wind stripped,
ice shod,
the street slipped.
Horse crashed
right on its rump
and instantly:
idling idlers
showing off bell-bottoms
on Kuznetsky Street;
laughter rang out and twinkled:
—A horse fell—
—Fallen horse—
Kuznetsky Street laughed.
I was the only one
whose voice did not merge with that howl.
I went up
and looked
the horse in the eye.

The Street flipped over
flowing in its own way . . .
I approached and saw
large drops forming
rolling down its muzzle,
soaking away in his hair . . .

And a species of universal
bestial melancholy
gathered and poured out of me
and spread rustling
"Horse, you mustn't
Horse, listen!
Why do you think you're the worst off?
Little one,
we all are a bit horse.
In his own way each is a horse."
Maybe
the old one
neither needed a nurse
nor, maybe, to him my thought was pointless.
Only
the horse
jerked
stood up on his feet,
neighed
and was off.
Tail flicking
A chesnut child
it went back jollily
and stood in its stall.
And all the time it felt
it was a colt.
and it was worth it to live
and work was worthwhile.

Vladimir Mayakovsky
Translated from the Russian by Rebecca Brown

from *The Greek Anthology*

from Dioscorides

You mother
You're so fucking pregnant
But not feeling contrary so
You turn over to have some fun
And I'm rowing you
Over your great ocean
(This labor's not small either)
And I throw you overboard when
I come in your beautiful ass,
I'm giving instructions
In how men love.

> Translated from the Greek
> by Bernadette Mayer
> and Rosemary Mayer

■

Der Asra

Every day back & forth
The exquisite daughter of the Sultan walked
At evening by the fountain,
Where the white water splashes.

Every day the young slave
Stood at evening by the fountain,
Where the white water splashes;
Every day he grew pale, and paler.

Then, one evening, the Princess, turning
Came up to him with these words:
Thy name will I know! thy
Country! thy Kin!

And the slave spoke: I am called
Mohamet. I am from Yemen.
And my people are the Asra
who die, when they love.

Heinrich Heine
Translated from the German by
Ted Berrigan and Gordon Brotherston

■

The Death of
Guillaume Apollinaire

Cut the hair of your Muse
Picasso, you nimble-fingered painter
Objects which come after you, Mr. Orpheus
Already have taken shapes you see

But he is dead, the man who changes words
Shapes & colors
Picasso, your Muse is in tears

Guillaume Apollinaire
Connoisseur of tulips
You smoke your tiny pipe
Little finger in the air

You tell the angels stories
For example that blacks are ancient Bretons
That Cleopatra invented oranges
They listen open-mouthed to you

You talk, you laugh behind your hand
       like the Pope
Your headache is gone
You are dead on Saturday
Rousseau waits on you with sweet williams
       before the gates of Paradise

By Sunday you have founded a new school,
       "Eternisme"
Launched with an article in the newspaper in the sky
Stars, Horsecollars, Prisms
And the people in the sky really love
To have dinner & to take a walk with you.

Jean Cocteau
Translated from the French by Ted Berrigan

PART III

Continuing the Project
The Next Generations: 1976–1991

*Everybody wants
money. And
I just came
home from
a hard
day of looking
for money
for my
organization,
that of*

the poet.

*In your
decline
I sing
your song*

*At the end
of the world
I am
my poem.*
—*Eileen Myles
from "Poem in Two Homes"*

BRUCE ANDREWS

"Wrang"

---

                    wrang
        a rawboned man large belly
        a tapestry horse
    rococ
a sea of damask wax

                leaning close,
        threw an ice ax
        there is no moat

    zircon hellhound tintypes
        uraeus
                    mesc

■

"Capital that fails us now"

Capital that fails us now; injunction against thought—These too
are Thermoluminescent Dosimeters—Bops on the head, I could be
Nero, international language don t heal much bigger than locusts—
The spatula is connected to the bunko charge, think against in-
jection—He is too concerned with propriety of motivation, the absence of a canary—Winners *will be divorced from all authority and
forced to come to terms with the basement*

Croaking of Experts, diatribe is a delicate did the little CIA trig-
gers Bob Marley?, etc.—Europe s not one happy land; I m surrounded by sugarplum icons and for details about how you can
participate—Psychosomatic champions in a Hollywood remake—
Leave Area When Alarm Sounds Serious—You re lucky, I saw you
limping, look, religious freaks roachblast (hyphenated) new enthusiasm, wants infamy—A touch of electrified opportunism (the fine
print hidden in the terms of their approval), but, holy thermidor, we
sure are the residential places—Avon calling, required course to le-
gally carry tear gas—These raids on the wagon train have got to stop

Fatal microbes, no more spine skanking—Love is what the absence of reasonable subtitles?—Just eliminate the use values? of people as physical beings, mass allegiance automate scavenger hunt anointed around the knees, tech pincers—At times that are most convenient for you—The necks *need* tongue depressors, you reach aircraft get gulag spreadeagle language barrier, violence grows, nonfemale fairy attempt, I want to be reminded of sweets when I walk, I wish aura were a man, oral tenancy, fallout club; levitation works—Gulls, Sambo, Boll Weevils; Iran again, sus the works—Suspect depilatory device; intense sun—I m doing the best basement I can, own up if you re over 25, when you get a broken leg is it damage to the image?—Pocket contaminates mother, no dark things, monochrome set clear and cool

You think libido is content, isn t it—Resort to clicks hits, leather complex everything in look what you ve done rockets, or tigers, tigers are overtime doorsigns—Do you want to sacrifice your career *totally* to lack of confidence; when it went with the cartoon; spearhead voice farm—White wide digits goes under sleepy category s one of my differences, cottage industry is something different, double garage—He does not appreciate their own insight in the last assertion; what they expect me to do is turn the stigma into a rousing slogan

Laid the mop up, I think the libido should get off social welfare, ice age is here, graveyard and ballroom, manhattan project quality bozo keychains and snowstorm memorabilia—Ego shattering loss of will is what

General strike buzzard, persons unknown—Teat lighting heart blank palm, a.k.a. weeping willow bullyboys—We love wars whenever it s convenient; prancing mummy ego—*Picks away* at mental activity; abortion is no longer illegal—The first uh ohs came when I heard extra beats, too many city nights to clone him dog eat dog caution: contaminated area—You re a misfit too

A bushsnake swallows a bullfrog whole while bullfrogs gobble up one another—Morbid faith *are* a nonfunctioning TV set—We automatically avoid puns that feel pointless—We don t need that fascist groove thing

Human hands, italic in adversity, parrots; now here s some beautiful polyphony to help you relax—With all that repressive bimbo talkback, pulls it, danger signs; I want lack of focus & get *insects*— I am of less than one mind—Truth is a technical problem another frustration removing nail polish in a social world, that s it!, disablebodied; *restructures* reality compassionate consumerism in your mind—Penetration; tchatchkas, baby spiders—It is hard to muff your own phonemes—Strike a jarring blow with the forehead; imperialism begins with it you know, interpreted for the hearing-impaired

Vapor gossamer chaingang, the desiderata, textile willing—Braille instruments, i don t wanna, private armies; animal spit—Teeth speech made out—Sure am not needlessly condemning the ice pick, whatever happened to Trotsky?

I took over Eastern Europe for the physically disabled—See a show; not necessarily I m going to kill myself—Prime number; I m starting to feel like toys of the world—Sort of ghoulish, gave him my push blanks; can grab it on matchsticks sandwiched in between the empty promises—Bay of Pigs, you just have to dream up words; freedom takes money—Glint nova cream vanity—Cut price souvenirs, I found the changing of heads fascinating

Tampax haunted body haze; nougat wafer, I showed him unabashed sandbags in its glory—Even after blowdrying; jury system paintings on action system black velvet like pragmatics under heavy matters, pilot to co-pilot, I showed him, last white Xmas—Isn t society just the organization of libido? (unidentified evangelist); psychological problem-solving: how destructive assertiveness reduces mental health—Meet people as unequals, caught with silicone, gentility, allied propaganda hotter claps clap them—Then I wanted to give him my metal slots, masturbation lowers s.a.t. scores and causes environmentalism

■

ANTLER

Written After Learning Slaves
in Ancient Greece and Rome
Had 115 Holidays a Year

Instead of creating better murder weapons
      to "protect" ourselves,
Better create loving boys and girls
      who become loving women and men.
Instead of a higher standard of living
      why not a higher standard of loving?
Why not a higher standard
      of getting high?
No more brainwashed robotzombies!
No more socialization lobotomies!

Thoreau could live a whole year
      on money from working 6 weeks.
We canned ourselves in concentration camps
      called cities
And in buildings and rooms where we work.
We have become hermetically sealed containers.
The can of today is the wilderness that was.
The can-to-be is the wilderness that is.

As Oscar Wilde said: "Work is the curse
      of the drinking man."
As Stan Jones said: "It's not what the machine makes,
      but what the machine makes you."
As Virgil said: *Deus nobis haec otia facet:*
      "A god has granted us this idleness."
As Lessing said: "Let us be lazy in everything
      except in loving and drinking,
      except in being lazy."

Should cans stop being made?
Should all factories immediately close down?
What solution do you provide? If everyone's a poet
        and no one works, how do we survive?
The way St. Theresa survived on Light?
Love becomes a full-time job?
But where do we get the money
        to pay people not to work?

Slaves in ancient Greece and Rome
        had 115 holidays a year!
Hey, wait a minute, that makes us
        more slaves than them!

■

BARBARA BARG

from *Walks in New York City*

It's one of those pleasant spring days early in the season when the
sun casts long missed golden ahem shadows across windows in the
afternoon. She feels wonderful. Like she has absolutely nothing to
confess, and here where the sky is constantly interrupted by tall
buildings, where thousands of eyes roam into the streets to thaw,
she sees a hotdog vendor on the corner of 6th ave and 14th street
and suddenly recognizes she's having a desire for a dog with kraut.
The vendor has blue pleasant eyes and a pleasant face and the
smell of steaming dogs in the cool but walkable air combined with
such nice eyes on one of the first sunny days in march makes everything seem just so pleasant, and she bites into the pale red dog and
it tastes good. She feels like waving to every passerby, that's how
friendly the world seems, a resting dog tied to a mailbox leg, a tan
dog enjoying the sun just like people might, lots of pants legs and a
few hosed legs moving around on the pavement, an old woman in a
supremely filthy gray longcoat and carrying an oppressed shopping-
bag dirty white with red lettering veers over to her just as she
chomps down a second bite mid-dog:

— the pope lives in a vacuum

Completely unrehearsed she stares intently at the vendor's client who
smiles with her lips closed so the food in her mouth won't offend
when suddenly the woman reaches out a filthy twisted hand with
long unkempt dirty nails and grabs the dog from the vendor's client's
fingers grunting like some kind of uncivilized starving animal, stuffing it into her filthy mouth practically swallowing it whole when two
shots ring out in the pleasant spring air, the first nice weather after
a hard and cold winter that had below freezing temperatures for
weeks at a time, and the old woman screeches and burns and falls
against her on a sliding way down to the sidewalk where a final
cheek rests on the toes of her left brown boot.

— I've warned that old bitch at least a thousand times about confusing herself with mankind. ya tell em and ya tell em and they do just like they please. ya talk to em and they say 'okay officer bill,' but ya turn yer back for a second and BANG! they're at it again . . . well, the fickle herd, know what I mean?

The overgrown child in a policeperson's uniform replaces his exciting gun in its creaky leather holster.

— that was a totally unnecessary and unuseful thing you just did there to that poor and defenseless filthy old woman. you have not acted in a way which will make us proud of our city to tourists, have you?

— ho ho ho

She twirls on her convenient foot, causing the lifeless cheek to plummet to the concrete, not seeing the two walking and one limping rapidly to catch up to her but hearing officer bill chuckle into the widening space she is making between them:

— fickle herd

Well of course her day is ruined of course, and she notices a thorough evaporation of her communicative mood while thinking about the radical incident that has just occurred in her life without her having to so much as lift a finger, only a couple of boots one in front of the other just like the generalities she feels compelled to articulate into the pleasant spring air, crisp, but golden on one of the first sunny days of this new spring, this season of rebirth, and it is into such coveted air as this that she whispers:

— we've got to snuff this paternal mysticism and mechanical romanticism before we all plotz!

Her currents of citizen's fury over, but not her ambulation, she finds herself mostly around washington square under the arch where she's able to move into a circle of a large narcotic number of people who are watching a group of four people in T shirts that read *Civic Heroics* performing whatever it is they are into in the middle of the crowd of a large number of people:

— we will now sing our new product entitled
  Something in the Way You Speak:

— something in the way you speak
  makes my future look bleak
  makes me want to smash you in the cheek

— something in the way you talk
  turns my saliva to chalk
  makes me want to trip you when you walk

— something in the way you chat
  condones my being used as a mat
  we're gonna have to remedy that

— something in the way your words apply
  makes me want to poke you in your eye
  makes me want to kick in your teeth

They bow. She claps after several other people start clapping first.
A leashed woman struggling to keep from being walked by a poodle
and having refused to clap even though a good percentage of the
large narcotic number of people clapped appropriately leans to comment:

— can you believe those people call themselves performers?

— those people there?

— uh-huh. what drivel. now that's what I call using language in a
  very vulgar and unliterary way. they know absolutely nothing
  about depth and subtlety, do they? I found their imagery totally
  vague in a clichéd kind of way, you understand? so few people
  really understand or remember what art is these days.

— well I thought it was sort of catchy.

— catchy? what has catchy got to do with it? I'm talking art. do you know there are people going around this city playing in rock clubs who haven't been playing an instrument longer than a few hours? these people expect to just be able to get up in front of an audience and have a good time no matter what their credentials are! my father, god rest his soul, was a first violinist in the boston symphony orchestra, and he practiced years and simply years before he was even allowed to audition for such a thing! my own son took guitar lessons from the time he was twelve and didn't cut his first album till he was twenty-three!

— excuse me, my name is alma

— hello

— hello

— and this is sophia, dorothy, bella, nicholas, clara, jerome, leon, irene, grace, roy, enid, ambrose and margaret

— hello

— how do you do

— know where we can buy some pills?

— sorry

— try the man over by that bench in the blue hat and shades

— thank you

— do you play an instrument?

— why yes I do. we're all in the same band. we're called The Teenage Pus Pockets! and I really appreciate the information. we haven't had any pills in hours. have a nice day now.

■

P A U L   B E A T T Y

Stall Me Out

———————

why you   no rhythm

afraid of women asexual pseudo intellectual
bald mt. fuji shaped head

             no booty havin   big nose
         size 13 feet   pigeon toed crook footed

taco bell burrito supreme eatin
                 day dreamin

                                  no jump shot   cant dunk

comic book readin
nutrition needin

knock kneed sap sucker
non drivin
                      anti-fashion
             constantly depressed   clumsy no money mutherfucker

                           take your weak ass poems
                           and go back to los angeles

                    ■

CHARLES BERNSTEIN

Motion Sickness

The blue pertains
     amassed at course return
   insuring troubles to admit
         banished ceremonies nearer
     a wall retains
            irksome edge
  unfurled along delighted regress
    which holds us to its promise
        no longer weary or caused to care
    ink lined capacities
lolling in majestic saunas
         burned out on hope
     thankless reproaches, intermittent handshakes
  beams
       fix themselves a soda
     assume inordinate proportion
        the tan boxes stacked three high
     alarm the cable belts
      & the shoestrings begin to snap
   their patience, gusts of
     change creating an inoperable breeze
flushed out hideaways grinding their trademark
  while the deep heart of inside
     invests its percentage
   on a runaway ticket
   the boy with an irrepressible allure
costumes the floor and lives sideways
     wishes to vanish but increases
   a head bunched and pasted
    out of the way, in a way
  totally provisional
    bands of ludic conviction
   embroidery of the getting by
  a round, a thud, a reflex

before which an approach adorns only
                    adore be at promise's end
false magic all conjures
            by which a thought equates
    what we have always seen
                        behind and yet in us
        but not recalled
                    disparaged at costly advantage
        a play of feeling's loss
        exchanged by load
    buckets made of damp
            profusion to immobilize illusion's project
            set aside by selves
                        hammer, pulse, exclusion
            garbled beyond belief
                            as pact against remorse
for the new chartings and more effective commencements
        long since endured by all those
    statelier than ourselves
            who dwell here all befuddled
        sorting out rafts into wheat and chaff
                remarkably encumbered by the traffic's elocution
    implicitly, silently

■

The Weather

The way the weather is an explicit result of so many things that happen,
it can't be predicted, and yet a person can blithely accept
what happens to her, beyond her control, in the weather.
Her perfunctory defense can compare the day or the era.
This appears to draw meaning from time, but is an actual drawing
from the chance encounter she does not accept, and which is un-
    mitigated
by a set time of his appointment with her.
Small talk about the weather is not fear that a cloud
might actually rush overhead and make a building fall on you.

With humans she believes events are malleable,
like being indoors, and you are under an obligation to choose out
segments for your meaning, because your opponent's continuousness
    could change
into his willpower. Three illuminated cupolas are immersed in cold. You
    have to
walk up to a penthouse immersed in glass to watch them shimmer.
Or follow your impulse when it is not fear to improvise your note around
    the piano.
A sense of adjustment among the singers multiplies phenomena,
allowing you to relax because of increasing to the size of your environ-
    ment,
and because it is hard to recreate, the way you recall a melody. That is
an ideal of weather as music, but

it is more like you at your office on the west side of the square, and I
    arrive
at the restaurant early on the south side. You can see
the pink of the sun on the landmark building. I see a blue shadow and
    the clock face.
Continuation would alternate these views, imperfectly aligned,
his wishes, your wishes. She will not imagine a blue wall turning a
    corner.
Their coats are hung up, ready to be docilely drawn on and taken off.
    The cupola lights up,
then looms up as he goes out on the street to meet her.
That the atmosphere won't yield is her prediction,
but not the range of it or of their conflict.

■

RACHELLE BIJOU

Will Your Book Be Available
for Sale Everywhere

or available for sale everywhere except India?
Will it be available for sale everywhere except the
British Commonwealth, or the British Commonwealth as
constituted in 1947? Will this mean that you'll have
exclusive rights in Kenya, Kuwait, Lesotho and Malawi,
for example, or non-exclusive? If your book is available
for sale everywhere except the British Commonwealth,
shall Canada be considered an open market? Shall Israel
be considered an open market? Shall they both be considered
an open market? Will there be a provision for sales in
Canada, Australia, New Zealand, New Guinea and the
Fiji Islands if your book is going to be available
everywhere except the British Commonwealth? Is it likely
to be available for sale in the United States, its territories
and possessions, and in the Philippines? What are the odds
of it being available everywhere except the British Commonwealth
and Canada, and not available in the European Economic Community?
Presumably, it could only be for sale in the United States, Canada,
Central America and South America, or the United States, Central
America and South America, or the United States, Canada and Israel,
or the United States and Canada, or just the United States.

■

LEE ANN BROWN

Warm and Fragrant Mangos,
Thirty Calla Lilies

———————

Windows with warped glass make the sidewalk look like water.
Your blue silk dress lies on the shiny wooden floor.
You are splashing in the bathtub full of stolen flowers
    and eucalyptus leaves.
I am walking out of our two octagonal rooms, up a ladder to the roof.
Even with so much immediate gravity, the pleasurable thinking of music
    is folding down out of the wall.
Beyond new rice paper shades, the next-door boy is rubbing the inside
    of his window with a piece of cloth.
I'm raising your movie camera to my eye.
You are cutting up raw fish, accumulating paper, asking me to pin you
    down and make you feel how words are placed in the air.

■

REBECCA BROWN

Three at Law

In the wonderful hours
behind the clock in the clerk of court's offices
two deputies ramrodded and oiled their guns.
(Shifting through flints a giant car
rattled on the little roads.)
                    The narcotic
of splaying out under terror suffices
the two deputies in the blue oily dawn,
walking back and forth in town.

I was calling on the pay phone,
"Who were you calling
                    with your ugly eye patterns?"
"Girl, won't you come with us?"
I just stared at them until they disappeared.

Marshal Clifford half falls from his desk,
sitting and reading the treasure trove reports.
He flopped the water in the glass
to splash the dust from his eyes.
                    He gets the reflection
of something out there, but he doesn't have to believe it.

■

Soft on the Eyes

First the tapes—
a soft frog on a pan of ice, from Japan,
sold there and thawed there.
                    I close my eyes—
the lids are soft on them.
I hate to move the needle
over and over the sweating machine treadle.
Japanese frog for dinner, a new-made dress
at dinner.
          Then after dinner
one turn over the stile, let me lead you
by these tracks, through broom straw and the fence,
each chain link falling into the others.
Over in the corner is a house
that's easy on the eyes.
                    There's a television,
tape recorder, pump organ;
                    and a Hallicrafter
short-wave receiver of superior physical force.

DENNIS BRUTUS

A Terrible Knowledge

In memory of Karen Silkwood,
who died on the road from
Cimarron, November 13, 1974

- 1 -

On the road from Cimarron
terrible knowledge squatted
like an unnatural monster
at the back of her brain

- 2 -

On the road from Cimarron
terrible knowledge pursued her
headlights lasering
the back of her head

- 3 -

On the road from Cimarron
terrible knowledge
of a mutilating death
rested with lethal casualness
on her sleeve

- 4 -

On the road from Cimarron
terrible knowledge impacted
on her brain
with a shattering crash
that smashed her car from the road
they wished her to die
with the terrible knowledge
locked in her skull

- 5 -

terrible knowledge
of a nuclear holocaust

- 6 -

terrible knowledge
of a nuclear holocaust
clumsily unloosed
through carelessness
or greed

- 7 -

terrible knowledge
that even now
a few are dying
slowly,
horribly,
lied to
lied about
and she had the terrible knowledge

- 8 -

Behind her
out of the dark
hurtled a red glare;
baleful Moloch,
awesome fireball
glimmering;
terror
lunging to destroy

Out of the dark
behind her
a monstrous hound
lunging from Erebus
sharp fangs snapping
to extirpate her;
terrible knowledge
of impending death

Terrible knowledge
of the guilty ones
—cops, executives, agents—
who conspired to destroy her
and her terrible knowledge
and now conspire
to plead their innocence
their ignorance

Terrible knowledge
of our capacity to destroy
of our potential for destruction,
of our destructive greed:
terrible knowledge,
Karen's knowledge,
our knowledge,
terrible knowledge.

■

REED BYE

Dear Mozart

Walking along Patchmake St. one day years ago
near its intersection with Fowlpiece Rd.
I was waylaid by a poorly appointed wretch
his face covered in orange fur
He begged of me my hat
which is as you know a Stetson I prize
it having once belonged to Mr. Robert Penn Warren
who lost it to a sudden gust of Gulf breeze
It wheeled and spun and came to rest
at the feet of a man named Lejeune
who wagered it in a game of stud and lost
to my three kings
mais je m'égare . . .
The man with the woolly face
like a Belgian sheepdog's it was and orange
declared he was helpless without my hat and would pay
three pounds for it
Three pounds is not enough I thought and told him so
It's all the money I have he sulked
alternately screwing up his face and casting his eyes wildly
out toward Pliny's Bone
unless you would accept in exchange a lock of my fur
which one day will count for a lot
I believed him
He yanked the lock from above his eye
and though I don't recall a bald spot there after
I took it home tied in a bundle
and kept it in a shoebox of small things.

As to why the man wanted my hat he didn't say
though I suspect it was to afford a measure of disguise
from the rear or top of course
the fur on his face still orange and prominent
As he left he more skittered than loped. Curious fellow
what?

Years later my niece Joanne a woman in her sixties
found the little bunch and began toying absentmindedly with it
brushing it along her cheek
A blue vapor rolled into the room
and a large man announced he would tune her piano
if Joanne would fix a pot of mocha
I can see where your sympathies live she said
you're as big as a whale, but you musn't touch the piano
This is what we're like, we get old
I like the blue fog though quite
lovely.

■

Perfect World

This world is perfect
the policies of every government are perfect
the right people die rich
the right people are born
hungry and screaming
It's perfect
the right weather falls every day
you wake from just the right dream
when you leave
the house is left
just the right way. It's perfect.

This world is perfect
all perfectly reflecting
itself, it could be different
but it would still be
just so
not quite all right perhaps
but perfect
as it is

Perfectly awful
perfectly dreadful
perfectly marvelous
perfectly well
reflected, there
and here,
this perfect world
just like that.

■

A Reading in New York: 1980

I will tell you what I saw and heard.

Robert Duncan, venerable poet, who, I was told, had complained of the videomen's distracting movements during Ed Dorn's reading just before, stops about halfway through his reading, removes his glasses, and turns to the two cameramen at his left, saying, "That's powerfully disturbing." He gathers his work and steps down from the podium but is, of course, called back by the crowd. He returns, not to the poem but to lambaste the cameramen who *have* been disconcerting in their maneuvering; two had stood conferring in the middle of the audience while another crossed obliviously in front of the podium. The vocal majority of the audience is behind Duncan, predisposed against the tactlessness of technology, but one lone catcaller yells, "Get real, Duncan!" "Ancient." "You're a talented purist, Duncan. Get real!" This is Taylor Mead, writer and performer who, coincidentally, will be reading in this same series next week. By this time, running concurrently, Duncan's philippic is mostly inaudible to me in the back of the room, a gigantic loft with windows all around. I do hear him comment how "surreal" it is to denounce the cameras when it's the "monkeys pushing them around who are to blame," and then proceed to level a formal curse on the two in front of him standing among the audience. "There are two things a poet can do: praise, and curse." This is a curse and he says it will take effect within six months. Now, at last, Duncan returns to his poem, a long, apocalyptic one, which sends palpable four-beat rhythm waves through the room, not by regular stress on syllables but by the more flexible cadences of orators reading psalms or prayers or incantations (the first few lines were in Latin). A later section conjures up nuclear holocaust in more vivid imagery than the poem has previously made use of; the flash-shape of the explosion gets printed through a window on the opposite wall of a room. Investigators can later prove by this "photograph" precisely at what altitude the bomb was detonated.

When the poem is finished, Duncan looks up and, after a solid round of applause, returns again to the subject of the curse. The gist is that he cannot (the Poet cannot) undo a curse once it is cast but sometimes, as in certain fairy tales, the cursed will meet someone or something which has the power to lift it. It is difficult to say if Mr. Duncan here betrayed any regret for his severity. He steps down.

Now the reading is over, all but the conversation and chatter, until a wild strain of speech erupts from one part of the room and gets louder and continues until all the other talk dies away. It's almost completely incoherent; there are words but they are so impassioned and crammed into the compression of true rage that they are indistinguishable, melted down by the anger. There is a dramatic and well-modulated finale though when the rage has unwound and the last words are enunciated clearly and forcefully: "AND I TAKE THIS CURSE AND TURN IT BACK ON YOU!" The cameraman's arm and pointed finger come down like a wand straight on Duncan.

Some scattered applause around the room, well-deserved, theatrically speaking.

■

.

MARY CAPONEGRO

from *Tales from the Next Village*

Pi Tz'u and Hsiang 'Ai, man and wife, loved as much as mortals can, but what flowed from him to her in love made her allergic. All the village's sympathy was not consolation, but love was. Love was something of a consolation.

When Pi Tz'u died of natural causes, the village sighed, that quality of sigh one hears when the ill or elderly are mercifully taken, that breathy sound that serves also as a clearing of the throat to open the way for gossip.

"At last," they said, "Hsiang 'Ai is free to find another, a love without side effects, an untainted bliss," though there were those who argued the pattern would repeat. They said this with the same breath in which they talked about the weather. And with every storm, they reminded each other that Pi Tz'u's spirit was mixed with all the other spirits that rained upon the earth.

"What mortals do for love," they said to each other, clicking their tongues, remembering the couple's sacrifice, and then someone would speculate about whether acupuncture would have helped, and then there would be silence for a while.

The village children, certain that there were more wondrous things in this world than talk, were always seeking diversion, often getting into mischief in the process. During storms they were particularly restless. They preferred the rain to their parents' chatter, and left, but didn't dare disclose to their elders what they had stumbled upon, what so compelled them that they repeated the pilgrimmage during every storm thereafter. They would have been severely scolded, perhaps even beaten if they had reported what they saw: Hsiang 'Ai in the sodden field, her thighs splayed like butterfly wings, white wings gently opening and closing while the rose that hinged them blinked in the rain.

■

CHARLOTTE CARTER

Not Talking

Mute autobiography. Not talking. I'm not trying to trick you. I
don't have to be there. Inability to leave history a puzzle.
Here's history: X is the person I know most about, littlest of.
X was born in a cold city. X has living parents & one sibling, an
"average" boy who was sick as a baby, grew out of it, fell, scraped
knees, played basketball, bought top-40 45's, grew out of it, broke,
came home. X is extraordinary. X is just another chick. Has
heavy thighs and bad feet. Was molested. Had best girlfriends.
Went to work at 16. Lived with a man. Lived without a man. Lived
in a furnished room and ate biscuits and spice tea. X left home-
town. Often fails to dream. Depends in large part on music.

What thick-waisted extraordinary chick enrolled in the University
of Chicago in 1965?

Had tenement apartment. Works for a living. X sees homosexuals
socially. Read many novels as a teenager. Once wished to go on
the stage. Has an aunt who was a nurse long ago—a pretty woman
who was "one sided." The story was that the woman's mother hit
her with a dishpan in anger when the aunt was a child. X was in
her 20s when she realized the absurdity of this explanation for
a dislocated hip. Nurse, pretty, married an alcoholic war vet.
They had children, of course. All live in the house once owned by
X's grandparents. X's psychiatrist once said X's relationship with
her grandfather was probably the thing that saved her life as a
child. Can see his face very clearly with her eyes closed. Smokes.
Had an abortion. X took a plane trip at 20. Was greatly embarrassed
at being a virgin. Met the most important one at a sit-in. Played
the piano as a child. Tap lessons. Swims badly. Had a good friend
who is a Zuni Indian. Has a black cat; does not own an automobile.
Like lots of others, earned money in high school by babysitting.

X's father was born in Kentucky. X's mother's mother taught school
in Georgia, became a cleaning lady up north, the same city where
X's mother was born.

Enjoys staying up late. Frequent insomnia. Never shot a gun. Wears 11/12. Often hibernates in winter. One of X's uncles is a lawyer. X's mother's mother's sister's husband was a doctor, involved in heroin traffic in the early 1950s. His daughter's boyfriend, in an attempt to burglarize their home, was shot dead by doctor. Daughter (lovely name X cannot remember) overdosed while X was at the Pentagon Demonstration. Doctor dead of natural causes. X and other children in the family received Xmas gifts in the form of money or savings bonds from Doctor and Wife. Another uncle is a junkie. No longer has a wife. He had been a Cub Scout. Another cousin inherited his knife. And X had twice been discovered playing house, funny, never again had sex until the age of 20. Used to have a recurring nightmare in which she witnessed her grandmother being murdered. At X's grandfather's funeral a whore showed up in a brilliant red dress. Perhaps this extraordinary hooker can see his face when she closes her eyes. Probably she is not in therapy.

X thought it would be nice to see San Francisco. Canada. Spent some spring vacations on a farm in Wisconsin. Took hallucinogenics in the 1960s. Worked for the government twice. X has never suffered a broken leg. When in the hospital, though, a woman came around near midnight and shaved X's pubic hair. The man X lived with once got drunk and braided her pubic hair. Listened at one time only to folk music. Has lost somewhere between cities Leadbelly's Last Tapes. Her mother early in X's life made her fear having her purse snatched. X shoplifted as a child, usually nickel cakes, concealing them in her panties. Ate a hell of a lot of french fries between the ages of 8 and 21. Was surprised at the taste of vaginal fluid. Went to Coney Island in winter, then again in summer. Finished 6 beers without becoming ill. Contemplated changing her first name until seeing a Bette Davis film in which Bette Davis has her name. Reviewed Battle of Algiers for a now defunct newspaper. Met Nat Cole in 1954. Relatives who work for the police department and Campbell Soup.

Nice view from the office window. Can take only aspirin substitute. X-rayed: hands, feet, kidney, chest, knees. Crooked laugh, hides teeth, penchants, addictions, cloche hats, journals, a close friend, sees it, sometimes hides, wonders, recalls it, writes.

■

SUSAN CATALDO

End of April Songs

1.

Lilies from Holland
a dollar seventy-five
a stem, daisies,
three dollars a bunch.
These days we make love
every afternoon. I have
everything I want.

2.

So might these days
of April pass, remembered,
as those days of lasting
passion when we are older.
Still be here. I want that.
This marriage we have when,
all the time we spend apart
has something missing. Didn't
seem possible but it happened,
we met each other.

3.

There is no rush to
the end of an April
spent so langorously
in my husband's
arms, he breathing,
laughing, perspiring.
Love, you are dizzy
& so peculiar
to praise a marriage.

4.

I wonder depths of
useless thought. "How
can this be?" In

truth, I have never seen
it before worn like a
necklace of white
flowers wreathed as
a sign of bliss. O
I must say something
to the world about
how much I love you
in every poem & they
must never tire of it.

5.

The clock in the kitchen
counts seconds until
you come home.
I count hours. Although
tonight I am not really
waiting. I fill the time
when you aren't here
with words of your return.

6.

Insoluble love for a husband?
I thought only this for
the unrequited aching of
a love that's wasted,
not to be wed to. I wish
I'd have had some way of
knowing when I was a child.

7.

My husband is as tall as a tree
& his love as tender as spring
blossoms & these are some reasons
why I love him so in April.

8.

Marriage, & why it is a
thing wanted, is what we
have. Not the "expected"
but what they might call
"a dream"; only we know
that to be Cynic & Sorrow,
the loneliness of millions
never getting what they ask for.

9.

More is only what you
look for. It causes you
to pass over what's in
front of you. The saddest
thing is, you'll never
know that until you
stop wanting & you can't
stop wanting until you
have everything you need.

10.

My heart is tall & dark
& handsome. It has
green eyes & wants to
be a Shakespearean actor.

11.

I am covered with skin
I am filled with him.

12.

Privately we are amazed
by our love for one another.
Publicly I guess we are
just a couple.

13.

Happiness, if I can call
it that, is not as fleeting
as I once suspected. It
very simply will be dormant
and, like the seasons, returning.

14.

A wife is a husband's best friend.

■

DENNIS COOPER

Some Adventures of
John Kennedy Jr.

---

1. the assassination

He remembers
putting a hand to his head,
the squiggle of his thoughts;

remembers his mother
was wasted, being bored,
a million tears.

When he talks about it
he goes way overboard.
My dad was a god, John says.

All he knows is what
we tell him, what he reads.
What he remembers is a big guy.

2. the mugging

One day he's mugged
in Central Park,
ripped from his bicycle
by a guy my age
who takes his tennis racket
and the *Mad* he's reading.

When Jackie gets to him
he's shaking, incoherent.
Seeing her holiness
he leaps into her arms.

What this kid needs
is a malt, a Stones concert,
and a hundred dollars.
Things, surprisingly, he can have.

3 . in New York

It's hot and smoggy as Mars outside
so he stops for an ice cream
in the nearest Wil Wright's,
and the clientele goes apeshit.

A man who loved his father
gives up his place in line, next!
John asks for a double;
he gets eight scoops and a real smile.

Then he starts up the boulevard
turning every head.
A filthy breeze blows his Beatle
bangs straight back.
He's famous, even without them.

Now let's stay with a couple
John has passed by
and overhear their reaction.
Ah, but it is awed and clichéd
and not worth remembering.

4 . in Nice

John has the energy
of three boys.
He can swim all day.
Jackie yells at him
to slow down
(like any mother)
but he won't.

Like every teenager
he's a little wild,
but a good kid.
Everyone agrees.
Jackie can't stay mad
for a minute.

And by the time
night wades
through the small
Mediterranean town . . .

Voilà.

5. taking a self-survival course

Men boat him to an island
so moist it seems to have risen
like a big bathing cap from the waves.
John bites down on his tongue
and shivers through his blue Cardin.

They leave him pale and girlish
on the skinny beach, with his
handful of matches, plant book,
and smouldering Kennedy eyes
taking their big stupid heads off.

Night drops fast. He sleeps under
dead leaves; his hair grows foul
as the malty earth. Next day he strips
to underwear, makes himself a leaf
crown, and by Thursday joins the beasts.

When the boat returns on Monday
it finds a boy to be reckoned with,
cured of cigarettes and snobbery.
The men clap him on the back like
he's choking, fierce in their affections.

John squats down with the other new men,
all so proud they haven't washed.
On the distant N.Y. dock he spots Jackie
and the reporters, happy as uncles to see him.
Finally he has something to tell them.

6. in school

When the professor tells his class
their homework is to write poems
young John brings down his fist.
"But tonight the Knicks are playing Boston!"
He'll have to give his front rows away.

Instead he slogs through poets,
hates them all until William Carlos Williams.
"You mean this is poetry?" He leaps
on his notebook. "I can write this stuff
by the ton." And so he does, a twenty pager.

It's about his own brief life,
praise for the sports stars, shit for the press,
close shots at his deep dark family.
Next day he's graded on his reading;
John's poem is "I'm Going Nowhere":

"I never thought anyone died,
especially not me,
then my uncle and father got it from maniacs
and Ari kicked the bucket the hard way,
and I've starting thinking of my own death,
when will it come and how,
by some mad man out to end the Kennedys?
I hope so, and that it happens
before I have a chance to show my mediocrity.
I know that's clumsy rhythm
but what have I got to lose, man? . . ."

When John reaches these last words
tears shake his sullen reading.
Amazed, the professor looks straight
through John's tough punk texture,
and then an A+ flies John's way
like a fast ball, or a perfect pass.

7. sixteen, shedding his
Secret Service men

They're waiting downstairs when
he wakes up, their hands in black pockets,
chins drooped as a slow leak.
John thought this would be nothing,
but now he looks into those big

blank faces, wrinkled with sorrow,
and feels the pain of parting.
They talk over the weird times,
the mysterious times, and when real
danger reared. They agree their worst

day was the mugging. Jackie had
thrown them to the dogs! They say
they'll miss the challenge, John's wisecracks,
the whole Kennedy mystique. They won't
miss the Ramones album, though in

time they will, and when it comes
on the radio, their heads tip like radar
toward the sound, and tears shine
their dull eyes. John thanks them warmly,
disappears in their hugs, and sees them

to the last door. Jackie stands behind
meeting their smiles with a stern one.
Outside its 99° and their stiff suits cling
to them like they wish John had.
"He was a great kid," they say, then

turn into the rush-hour traffic
while back inside John dances around
yelling "Free!" and Jackie laughs in
the way a mother does when her prize
son's being just a bit ridiculous.

8. at the R.F.K.
Tennis Tournament

John is amused
by Howard Cosell
quipping off
Ethel's playing,

slips his hand
into Caroline's
and smiles widely,
pulling Jackie

to his sweater
as the t.v. eye
turns to watch
them cajoling

and Howard's wit
takes John on
saying, "Handsome
like his father . . . ,"

which turns John
red as an apple
though what Cosell
says is true.

John is easy
to embarrass and
now the world
knows it too,

how highly strung
he is growing,
dousing his laughs
in his hands

as mom and Caroline
grin with him;
this is the John
that they love.

■

VICTOR HERNANDEZ CRUZ

It's Miller Time

I work for the CIA
They pay me with
cocaine and white Miami
lapel sports jackets
free tickets to San Juan
where I make contact
with a certain bank
official at the Chase
Manhattan Condado branch

My contact a guy named
Pete asks if I know other
accents within the Spanish
Can you sound Salvadorian?
They give me pamphlets
and also send me
pornographic magazines
if I want a stereo or a VCR
they know a place I can
get them at half-price
they told me there is a waiter
that works at Bruno's
who can get me any gadget

The last assignment
I had was to contact
the Public Relations Division
of a beer company
because for U.S. Hispanics
it was Miller Time—
I contacted this brewery
a certain Miguel Gone sa less
invited me to lunch

I met him at La Fuente
at his suggestion
with him
was a Camden New Jersey
Cuban who was going through
town enroute to Los Angeles
the lunch was on them

Senor Gone sa less had a
wallet full of plastic
he had more plastic than Woolworth's
they mentioned that the
beer company wanted to sponsor
salsa dance within the Latin
community
bring in the top commercial names
and that while this dance was
going on they wanted to pass
a petition against U.S. involvement
in Central America
they showed me the petition
which had a place for the name and
address of the signers
a great list to have and spread
around all government agencies

They gave me a bag with 3 thousand
dollars in it
it was my responsibility to see
this through
the Cuban guy tapped me on the
shoulder and said
Don't have any of the mixed drinks
The bartenders at the dance
are working for us
The chemical people are experimenting
the effects of a liquid
Just drink the beer

The festive event went off
successfully even a full moon
was in the sky
next week the CIA is flying me
back to the Caribbean where I
will assist in staging one of
the strangest events in recent history

According to the description in my
orders we are going to pull off a
mock rising of land from beneath
the Caribbean which the media will
quickly identify as lost Atlantis

Circular buildings made of crystals
are being constructed somewhere in Texas
they will be part of the spectacle
which will have the world spellbound
simultaneous with this event
the Marines will invade from bases
in Puerto Rico and
the countries of Nicaragua
El Salvador and Guatemala
it will be the month of *Salsa*
in San Francisco
an astounding mystical event in the
Caribbean
the price of cocaine coming through
Miami will go down
everybody party and celestial
circuits jammed with junk and information

In a daze the world is free
for Miller Time.

■

JACKIE CURTIS

The Star

The star is ideally beautiful
the star is pure
the star is profoundly good
Beauty and spirituality combined to form a mythic super-
personality

Worshipped as heroes
divinized
the stars are more than objects of admiration
a religion in embryo has formed round them
the star is like a patron saint to whom the faithful
dedicate themselves.
Will there ever be words for the vicissitudes of the milk
and suffering of the mouth?

■

ALAN DAVIES

from *Life*

Look at the cask of reasoning
nothing beside the etiquette of poetry.
You put them side by side
you get more time out of them.

The things that are ahead of other things
seem obvious.
And there's nothing like a flower
that closes up at night.

Just go in
and watch what she's doing.
Then write it down.
You can go out on many limbs.

. . . . .

It's getting colder and the clouds are lifting.
Who is to say the household is not my happy genius?
People talk about trying something new—and why not?—but they
        don't do it.

. . . . .

There's a firm wind out.
Smoke blows one way
and then the other.
What other cadence
can we give to thought?
Many have been stiff
and very unsure
but very few
have been only very stiff.
The moth again on the screen
breathes clear in the light.
The trees are all cut off
by the reach of the porch light.
The bird-feeder shakes
and the trees shake in the wind.
And behind it all crickets
shake something in the night.
There's no better justice
than event.
There's no better event.

. . . . .

And little blossoms
turn to flowers.

     Earlier Story
     He got his dick into someone as the plane went down.
She survived.   His wife raised the child.

     Story
     It was not until after her appointment to the City
Council Firing Squad that Josephine began to doubt her
masculinity. It wasn't doubt.   She didn't know who she was.

. . . . .

Whether to take the me out of the poem entirely and let the
            instruct. How to take the poem out of the poem. Let the
instruction   . After the words go on the page. Water
over the bridge.   Or just a car comes down the darkened slope.

When you write you betray your preferences.
            The words are parasitic.
            The host is the lived world.
            Your preference is the form of the attachment.

Or as Leslie had suggested could it be rather a matter of
attentive curiosity? That would be gentler. An attachment more
only over time. For those who can manage it.

            With poems we erase all evidence that we were here.
            That's what we mean when we mention the future while
remembering the past. I only came to ask.

■

TIM DLUGOS

Cross Dress

For Jan Morris

Shining on the green, and at very low tides, perhaps
a picnic lunch to a far corner of the lagoon, somebody is sure to
wave you goodbye, across the dark water of the side-canal,
a fourteenth-century housewife, or prying into a thane's back yard.

"But this Cardinal So-and-So, he was not at all like that,
he was always *cosi—urgh!*" And with this sharp guttural expletive
punt-loads of undergraduates, with parasols and gramophones,
suggesting in a laborious sonnet that Venice was divinely founded.

And they would eat with lofty frugality. One restaurant in the
recesses of the Basilica, glimmering and aromatic, all the divinities
are immensely long and exquisitely fine, flecked with grass.
A fizzy drink is awaiting you in its little red ice-box.

Grinding corn on a treadmill, or attending some crucial and
excruciating viva voce, it remains a queer and curdling place.
I went there once. Thousands of pigeons were released to carry
the news to every city. Make haste, it cannot last much longer.

∎

MAGGIE DUBRIS

Welcome to WillieWorld

We drift at the edges of childhood.
Small windows open and close.
One day, we become old.

When I was in medic school they made us go to the morgue for a
day and watch autopsies. The thing I hated the most was that when
they cut the people open everything was the same color, like liver.
The only thing that looked like it was supposed to was the kidneys.
Just like kidney beans. I wanted everything to be different colors
like on the anatomy chart. I wanted everything to be orderly and
neat, not smashed together the way it was. Even the brains didn't
look right. They were all soggy and runny. I didn't feel like touching anyone for weeks. All I could think of was what their skin was
covering up.

Come sit in your pajamas as I quietly take aim.

What I like most about my job is to walk in and give my opinion.
This works best when people have a problem that I don't consider to
be medical. Anything that's not life threatening I don't consider to
be medical. So, I think: Why did they call me if not to give my
opinion? Isn't that what I'm there for? Depending on my mood, I
give out all sorts of advice. When someone is pretending to have a
heart attack in order to impress a loved one with whom they have
just quarreled, I like to loudly announce that they are "Just Upset."
Then I ask if they are a heavy drinker. No one admits to this, so I
suggest that they have a drink to calm down, and say in an ominous
tone, "Perhaps you could leave her alone for a few hours so she can
get some peace. Otherwise we really will have to take her to the
hospital." This seems to work very well.

462

They say that it takes time for things to change, but this is a lie. Change is analagous to a bolt of lightning. Instantaneous. The way your clothes turn into laundry when you take them off and throw them in the hamper. One minute you are doing the dishes, then a bubble bursts inside your skull and you're lying on the floor biting your tongue off. God sets his tiny time bombs, and you are there when they explode. But every so often, while playing dice with the universe, he sets them to blow up in someone else's life.

The first time I came in contact with the killer of one of my patients was uptown, in a block of renovated brownstones in Harlem. The family owned the whole building. In the first-floor bedroom a black man in his nineties was kneeling on the floor, slumped against the side of the bed. He was clutching a scarf and had been stabbed eight or nine times in the chest. You wouldn't think that somebody could die in that position, but he was already beginning to get stiff. When I went into the kitchen to get the information, the police had the person who had killed him handcuffed to the table. It was a junkie; a very small woman who could have been anywhere from eighteen to forty. Her arms and neck were all keloid scars from shooting up, and I thought she must live in the streets because she was so dirty. The man's son had come home from church and caught her leaving the building. When he took her inside he found his father's body. She had stolen only a pair of brass cufflinks and some dress shirts that were still wrapped in cellophane. The old man had bought them the morning before. The son kept pounding his fist into the wall, but he never hit the junkie; just tied her up until the police got there. The junkie didn't seem human to me. She was at the kitchen table, giving everybody dirty looks and yelling at the cops that they were racists because they wouldn't take the handcuffs off her. The knife that she killed him with was in the kitchen sink covered with blood.

I see flames on the fence. But the last cross is mine. To dwell in a moment constructed of light.

■

Suitcase, an Excerpt from
Traveling Phrases

The woman held up a Polaroid camera and asked him if he wanted a picture. Robert Sauce, who had yellow hair, wore a baseball cap in case of rain, and appeared vacuous to persons meeting him for the first time, put his suitcase down on the pavement and squinted into the sunlight filtering through the trees bordering the Tuileries. To get him into the picture, the woman backed off from him. "You look like you have butterflies in your stomach; can't you smile?" she said. Robert paid for the picture and picked up his suitcase to walk away. "Don't you want the picture?" she said. "I don't know what to do with it," he said. He looked at his watch and shrugged. "I have a train to catch." After ordering *Oeufs au plat* and *Jet menthe* from the waiter at a crowded café in Gare de Lyon, he removed several postcards, a pen, and a pencil before carefully inking them in. On holiday from school, he had arrived in Paris expecting to stay with his older sister, Sally, but she had suddenly moved out of the flat, which she shared with her husband, without leaving an address where she could be reached. He paid his check and left the café to telephone his brother-in-law, Louis Glapir de Sancess. Robert had put off telling Louis, with whom he had stayed for a week, that he had decided to leave Paris before his holiday was finished. Louis liked cowboy movies, and although he had never visited America, he spoke English with an exaggerated western drawl. Louis was surprised by Robert's appearance but didn't object to his staying. He said it wasn't a problem, and he strung a hammock up across the sitting room, for Robert to sleep in. Louis was very upset by Sally's absence, and he talked of her continually. He didn't ask Robert about himself, because Sally had already told him everything. During the day, while Louis was at his job, Robert stayed inside and read Freud's case histories of hysteria. Because Louis had shown annoyance when the hammock was left up, anxious to do nothing to displease his host, Robert put it away in the cupboard each afternoon before Louis returned. Louis went out every evening. He

carried his bicycle down several flights of stairs to the street and
didn't return until after dawn. Carrying his bicycle back into the
flat, he moved noisily around the sitting room, picking things up
and putting things down, until Robert woke up. Louis sat at the table,
where they usually took their meals, and cried. He made rafts by
stringing together corks from wine bottles with a needle and wire
thread. Robert couldn't reach Louis on the telephone, and didn't
know where to take a train to. There were six days remaining of his
holiday.

He carried his suitcase out of the train station and back
to his brother-in-law's flat. He didn't have a key, because, earlier,
he had dropped it through the mail slot. He sat down outside the door
to await Louis' return. Robert removed the book of case histories
from the suitcase and found the place where he had left off.

■

ELAINE EQUI

After Herrick

---

true calendars
tell ripe
each change

assuage
as night does

doting
and yet shines

enclosed in
rhymes
sphering

Bestrewed
with Ovid
(bellman Ovid)

words
for meat
give melody
over rocks

reading
by degrees

rivers
turn awhile
to men

awhile
they glide
full of meaning

shearing
melody's
meeting

■

CHERI FEIN

The Unicorn Tapestry

Someday a tapestry someday there will be a tapestry to hang on the wall
loosely woven in colors I can see at least to see to remember about now

It is different than I think to make cloth

in the end I might know
what this color I don't know I call cloth it's a tapestry

One horn I can see when the lights are off then forget until now

I
remember the horn on a head on the wall all of stone what surrounds and
a fence and some buds no not buds it is fall when I see so no buds

It is night and the kiss feel the arm wrapping round like a fence

All goes well if I close my eyes there's a smell and there's sick
in the eyes slit with fear
sew a thread

can you tell
It all blends but look this one this

when the heart catches up and grows
sad all the times there it's thin in that spot you can't touch aren't
allowed

called a tapestry let's go on
down the stairs hold the rail

so old uneven

BOB FLANAGAN

Sonnet

————————

THE NAME STAMPED ONTO THE LOCK SAYS, "MASTER"
BUT THE KEYS ARE YOURS, MISTRESS. MY BODY,
WRAPPED IN THIS NEAT LITTLE PACKAGE, IS YOURS.
DO I DARE TO CALL MYSELF A PRESENT?
I'M THE ONE WHO'S ON THE RECEIVING END.
YOU TOOK ME ON, TAKING IN MY STIFF PRICK
AND SWELLING MY HEAD WITH YOUR COMPLIMENTS,
YOUR COMPLAINTS, EVEN OUT AND OUT NEGLECT.
NOTHING——WHEN IT COMES FROM YOU——IS A GIFT;
WRAPPED IN YOUR AURA OF AUTHORITY
EVEN SHIT TASTES SWEET, AND THE VOID YOU LEAVE
LEAVES ME FULL.

IT'S CHRISTMAS WHENEVER YOU PUT YOUR FOOT DOWN,
AND THE STARS I'M SEEING MUST BE HEAVEN.

■

ELIZABETH FOX

A Raid on the Random

The clocks on the Con Ed Building are set in dreamtime. It's four thirty to the east and nine fifty-five to the south. Under the full moon, the intersection of Thirteenth Street and First Avenue becomes an alfalfa field. The grass is only two inches high and translucent. Three Catholic families pile into a turquoise van in 1966 and go chasing cottontails and jackrabbits across the field. When a cloud covers the moon the traffic retakes the field like an artificial ocean.

The mysterious hand that changes the color of the sky improves the posture of each pedestrian. It's as if the events from next year are memories while the present lacks antecedents. Because of the confusion, a management consultant gets all dressed up for a party he went to yesterday. Meanwhile a second-grade teacher and her blind husband are left out of time. He's combing her long brown hair in the moonlight and forgets to stop. Tomorrow morning the school secretaries will wonder why she didn't come to work. They'll call her at home. No one will answer.

A man without legs rides a skateboard and eats a hot dog vigorously. The hot dog vendor hands him a bottle of ketchup. He takes it and rolls down the sidewalk, squirting people with the ketchup as he goes.

Music leaks out of someone's apartment. Children giggle and cheat at four square. All along the street men talk among themselves and play dominos on cardtables. A hand hovers above their heads. Do they know the new people will be driving them away from the neighborhood soon?

A string of Christmas lights blinks on and off like a stalled flying saucer. Inside a restaurant customers shake their tables. Their heads are full of unlit sparklers.

It's an evening of possibilities. What are we going to do? Let's take a walk. We'll know where we are by the smell of the harbor and the sound of the A train. What time is it? We're almost late.

■

ED FRIEDMAN

from *Flight Patterns*
(Oral) — *A Ceremony*

March 8

Hi Dear,

Even tho Gramps and I are both dieting
(religiously) thought it a good idea to
test our will-power and make the good
cookies. Didn't even taste them, so
hope they are up to the usual standard.
The rest of the goodies just for fun.
Time is fleeting—and in less than four
weeks we take off on our jaunt to Toronto
and then on to dear ol' London. _____ and
_____ are looking forward to our arrival,
and we anticipate lots of fun and adventure with them.

    Your Mom and Dad leave for N.Y. on Thurs-
day, so on account of Mom's birthday, we
have asked for a couple of hours with
them this evening, so will go to dinner
at <u>Chuck's</u>—where <u>we</u> can have the diet
dinner of steak and salad.
    Hope you are well and happy, and we shall
see you at the end of June. Much love,
Gramps joins,

               Gram

enter the ceremonial lodge

face north

       . . . . .

mix a reddish-brown paint
from deer fat
and clay
in a white shell

    . . . . .

face east

    . . . . .

face west

    . . . . .

using your finger
for a brush

    . . . . .

paint a straight reddish-brown line
on the length of your nose

    . . . . .

paint a straight reddish-brown line
from the base of your neck
to the end of your shoulder
on your right side

    . . . . .

paint a straight reddish-brown line
from the base of your neck
to the end of your shoulder
on the left side

    . . . . .

paint a straight reddish-brown line
from the base of your neck
down the length of your spine

twenty-three clans

    . . . . .

each clan should be formed
in a triangle

. . . . .

the two points of each triangle
that determine its base
when combined with the same relative
points (positionally) of the other clans
should together form a circle

. . . . .

the point of each triangle
that does not touch the circle
when combined with the same relative
point (positionally) in each of the
        other triangles
should form a square

■

CLIFF FYMAN

My Chapeau

This is my new hat.
It hangs down over one ear.
The wool, said the woman in the tie-dyed thermal undershirt
      who made it and sold it to me on Telegraph Avenue
      to support her eleven and twelve year old daughter
      and son whom she now is beginning to enjoy after years
      of, as she called it, hippy life: smoking joints
      defiantly in the street, waving flags, scattered
      go here go there and in general not looking very much
      towards "family" which as you and I both know
      is a great place to grow, biologically,
came from Mexico, a wool that rhymes with the word "seraph."
The wind blows through the tiny holes natural to a crocheted cap
      but my head is warm—and that's the point.

It's blue and chocolate brown,
      beige, let's see, blue-ish grey and brown-hump camel
      —it'll go well with anything.
I'm wearing it now.
I can be an artist, a French artist if I purse my lips correctly.
I can be a friend of Katharine Hepburn.
It can shade my eye or reveal it and my ear in full.
I can be withdrawn or luxuriant.
It's not your usual get-a-way.
I can set it up straight and be Scottish.
It looks like a hat mother used to wear
      to synagogue matching her pink and grey woolen suit.
      I can hear her laugh at the similarity and then marvel
      at how well I wear it.
I do have a way with hats, I know—because I love them!

When I run, my hat and hair bob carelessly.
Under its sensitive colors and soft wool
    with the delicate way it folds against my skin
      my face becomes more gentle, my lips more soft and silent
      my eyes more clairvoyantly blue.

It rests on one shoulder like a mane against my Wrangler jacket
    with the collar turned up.
You see my right ear and lots of brown shampooed hair.

It's a royal yarmulke.
It's a spiritual crown, sacred
    for it is worn during the ceremony

    of my Life.

■

AMY GERSTLER

Dear Boy George,

Only three things on earth seem useful or soothing to me.
One: wearing stolen clothes. Two: photos of exquisitely
dressed redheads. Three: your voice on the radio. Those
songs fall smack-dab into my range! Not to embarrass
you with my raw American awe, or let you think I'm the
kinda girl who bends over for any guy who plucks his
eyebrows and can make tight braids—but you're the
plump bisexual cherub of the eighties . . . clusters of
Rubens' painted angels, plus a dollop of the Pillsbury
dough boy, all rolled into one! We could go skating, or
just lie around my house eating pineapple. I could pierce
your ears: I know how to freeze the lobes with ice so it
doesn't hurt. When I misunderstand your lyrics, they get
even better. I thought the line I'M YOUR LOVER, NOT
YOUR RIVAL was I'M ANOTHER, NOT THE BIBLE,
or PRIME YOUR MOTHER, NOT A LIBEL, or
UNDERCOVER BOUGHT ARRIVAL. Great, huh? See,
we're of like minds. I almost died when I read in the
Times how you saved that girl from drowning . . . dived
down and pulled the blubbering sissy up. I'd give
anything to be the limp, dripping form you stumbled
from the lake with, draped over your pale, motherly arms
in a grateful faint as your mascara ran and ran.

■

MERRILL GILLFILAN

El

Limp sable carpet swims under maple

My right eye is centimeters larger than my left

& my dick hurts

Gautier describes kif in Paris 1845

He is the Buddha   He walks around town

With hash up his butt   Buddha-Buddha   Paris-Paris

■

Il S'Appelle Bob

Where there's hope there's exercise
highlighting the teeth the way a Puccini lecture
freezes ancestors in alphabetical order.
They say they say he died from hate
for tobacco:

Coincidence of your two eyes rolling
slept right through the pistol shots marking
the border and now there's a crowd
at the fence   Why are you clean?
where I have buried nothing of some worth

For you a friend of electricity wondering
does the orchard piss secretly
all at once?   deep down?
        It must be like night
in the Sahara surrounded by terrible days
when the only chance is catching a ride to Honolulu
where you'll wear gabardine and write
"Autobiography is impossible in the sun."

■

BRAD GOOCH

Cité Des Arts

John Cage uses oriental mathematics
There is no boredom when you don't live in a house
Whereas Schoenberg made the same tree with sticks

The bird in the jasmine tree sings like an addict
It is the sun which is fixed in the Eastern House
John Cage uses oriental mathematics

Three Dances (1944–45)
The sun climbs through its hole like a golden mouse
Whereas Schoenberg made the same tree with sticks

This card means you will step into mistakes
"Do not take your heart with you to make noise"
John Cage uses oriental mathematics

The lacquered box is made out of Thai sticks
When the sun sets smoke rises from the hole
Whereas Schoenberg made the same tree with sticks

Hands are not important to this prepared pianist
Who has no dust on his feet since he has no house
John Cage uses oriental mathematics
Whereas Schoenberg made the same tree with sticks.

■

JESSICA HAGEDORN

Arts & Leisure

---

i read your poem
over and over
in this landscape
of women

women purring
on balconies
overlooking
the indigo sea

my mother's
blue taffeta dress
is black as the sea

she glides
out my door
to the beach
where sleek white boats
are anchored
under a full,
luscious moon .

still
i am still
the wind
outside my window
my mother's ghost
evaporates
in the long
atlantic night

i listen to the radio
every chance i get
for news
of your city's
latest disaster

everything *here*
the color of honey and sand
everything *there*
verges on catastrophe
a constant preoccupation
with real estate

everything *here*
a calm horizon
taut bodies
carefully nurtured
oiled & gleaming
hair & skin

i read your poem
over and over
turning my head
from prying eyes
the low hum
of women singing
in another room

i switch stations
on the radio
turn up the volume
i almost touch
the air
buzzing electricity

james brown "live at the apollo"
the smooth female d.j.
interrupts bo diddley
groaning "i'm a man"

it is a joke here
in this baby blue resort
where art
is a full-time hobby
art
is what everyone
claims to do

women sprawl
like cats
on each other's laps
licking the salt
off each other's skin

and i walk
in search
of the portuguese fishermen
who hide
in the scorched trees
the bleak, blond dunes
that line the highway

i imagine
you asleep
in another city
i take your poem
apart
line by line

it is a love letter
we wrote each other
sometime ago
trying in vain to pinpoint
that first, easy
thrill.

■

K I M I K O   H A H N

Seizure

In Nicaragua
old women
mobilize with sticks and boiling water
again.
You're North American.
You figure it's the season.
But back home
the moon
acts like the girl
who'd been fucked in so many places
she barely knew which hole
is for babies
and you know you understand

un deber de cantar

and you know you understand
your desire
to see Broadway
NY NY
taken in a flash of July heat
and you know you want it.
(The green parrots snap
guapa
and your thighs sweat like mad.)
And you want it.
Shit. We don't have mountains here.
The rooftops
will do the trick

you think out loud.

Because you belong to a process
that belongs to you

one

you love to touch

and nurse

and deploy

on your lap, here
Nicaragua. On your

lap, here Nueva
New York. Here

novio, baby

sister. When I say *mujeres*

man of course

I mean *y hombres*

también
I'll never forget

the shower that riddled the tobacco fields
on the Honduran border of Nicaragua

where Suyapa
una niña de 4 años

learned June 9, 1983
what *somocistas* are

—*yanquis, contras*—
if she didn't know

before she was hit by mortar. Seizure
you envision

as the street
after the water has broken.

NOTE: *un deber de cantar*, "a duty to sing," is the title of a book by
Rosario Murillo, a contemporary poet.

■

STEVEN HALL

Stuff

Before I can put the bite on you
My heart pushes itself back into my body
Falls into a chair like a chip of wood
Might fall onto the sleeve of a lumberjack

Cut from blue, the last letter I received
Spoke of you, handcomb with flower
In your arms where I rest the horizontal
Better arms worship you from afar

I look to you for all the world
Like a statue gazes at anything moving
I am not eloquent, sputter across the night
Clouds move the hands of a bored child

They broke up their act, left a pampered mouth
Which moves with the verb to be.

On the Arm of a Dumb Marine

You sleep with me
Because I am here
I feel I could sleep with no one else
For the rest of the year.

Down the ladder to sleep.
Alone on the last rung I wonder if maybe
I couldn't find something better, but what
That is not what I define all else by?

You grab me by the scruff of the neck
Push my head onto your shoulder
Where I whisper into your ear
The Military Police is here.

■

CARLA HARRYMAN

In Front

Take the school off the cape of responsibilities.

I shoot.

Like what I was saying before.

You look at me from across the table and taunt. We are on the only island. Someone else is wearing your shirt. Take the school off the cape of responsibilities!

I was aiming at an idea.

. . . . .

Now you come home and take your shirt off. Being a bit eccentric you pause.

You stand in front of the bed. You take me in your arms. We are asleep. I am not asleep. I am at school. I am sitting in a desk. I write on my desk and put my head on it and go to sleep. Somebody (Eileen?) covers me with her hat. Eileen says, "If it was really you you were talking about you would be a jerk but I know you made it up."

. . . . .

I did not make anything up. I have never in my life made anything up.

I am looking at you on purpose.

There is a certain élan, it makes me think of "ecclesiastes" but a little jerkier, just a sound. It is not grim determination but it is grim but on the sexy side. "The iron-clad cape surrounded her."

"Hey," she says, "I thought your skin was softer."

"It was," said the honest but lazy student.

. . . . .

He was looking at me fishily half assed up and down like I might but I might not be the right sucker.

I am not that, is obvious.

I get a postcard marked UK and send it to a creep.

. . . . .

"Do not open while seriously self absorbed."

I was half absorbed. It was a nightmare or a joke I can't remember which way we were going and I'd forgotten how to count. Abetted. I got pushed into a state of semi-consciousness by a court of law. Not true. I was just testing it out. I wanted to make the scoundrels look bad. That's how much I love you.

"But everybody hates politicians," returned the creep, not understanding what I meant by UK.

I DID NOT MEAN ANYTHING. I was aiming at a caustic idea. Something that would approximate nothing. A perfect knot with a slash in it. Rhymes falling off at the end, never getting there forcing you into involuntary jerks. A bit too European, that's what mom would say but she's wrong. You get the idea?

■

YUKI HARTMAN

Poem

So much distance breathes in a pencil
On the white carpet . . . with a faint shadow.
Having travelled the milleniums in one step,
The distance is you, emerging from a moment before,
And you bend down to pick up the pencil
Repeating your foreboding as notion of reality.
Backward or forward, the liquid solutions ripen.
And out of it comes transparent shadow
Catching you peering down from the sheer height
And you yield to the splitting sky like the clouds.
You move on, which is reflected in luminous ripples of the mirror.
The surface of steel grey pouring out of nowhere.

■

from *The Voidoid*

Chapter Three

A rock sits gathering barnacles at the bottom of the ocean. Fish, an inadequate word, suggesting a trout on a plate, walk, their word for swim, around it in perfect grace. Our urge to anthropomorphize and project preventing us from ever seeing these creatures in their unselfconscious, independent and unique splendor. A person feels more in common with a plant than with the scaled, gilled, neck-lesses of the water. But they are there, like the other side of the mirror. Ironic to realize that we travel on the surface of their world in a fashion similar to the beings who use the upper layer of our atmosphere for a "skijump." Not a very high proportion of fish ever experience the sensation of air against their scales. They not only don't need us, but for the most part aren't aware that we exist, as they say of the debutante queen. It is very dangerous to get emo-tionally involved with such a being. It's probably insane, a de-liberate infliction of pain on oneself. It's at the least "unfortunate," unlike loving a wall in one's own apartment. Only a very sad person would love a fish I think. But that's a heart-rending matter far from the subject. (No one could really love a fish, with the possible ex-ception of aquanauts for whom, even then, it must be love at first sight since they aren't likely to see the same fish twice. ((A fish removed from its water isn't the same fish.)) Of course people love "fish," a species, but that's like loving a fish-like person.)

These are huge creatures circling the rock. With eight-foot wings of flab, and jowls decorated by jewel-like little inscrutables attend-ing the grotesques—all unknowing characters in a suspense novel about a girl pumping bullets into her best friend. Each bullet seems to put her friend one inch nearer death but she won't die.

It's a book and screenplay by Theresa Stern. She began writing it at the age of 19, conceived as an act of revenge against Sam Peck-inpah, Arthur Penn, Sergio Leone, herself and humanity. It soon be-came apparent, however, to her and God, that she required no ex-cuse for writing the book. It embodied her vision and her dream and she had obviously been destined to write it from the first moment that she'd shed a tear, in other words: from birth. A Puerto-Rican Jew from Hoboken, in her adolescence she was most at home within the huge abandoned warehouses built on piers that faced the New York skyline. A skyline like diabolical pitted building blocks interspersed with erect needles in a cloud of gagging smoke. A parody of science fiction visions of the future. It seemed to her outrageous that she was regarded as a *victim* of these squalid circumstances rather than a new microbe bred in the filth, a mutant radiant oracle, like a new disease for newly evolved organs. Who was to say which preceded, the organ or the organ's disease? They're Siamese twins, or Vietnamese twins: Namby and Bambi. Was she the disease or the disease's object?

Thank God, she thought, something appeared for me to prey upon, or I'd've been doomed to be a trivial germ with a passing reference in the textbooks, rather than a chapter. Tomorrow, a book! . . . Today's garbage is tomorrow's culture, and on that slide, below that microscope, I'm the premier sneer in the smear. She loved to slide. As a twelve-year-old she played in those Hoboken pier-houses, whorehouses: on the dock filled with mysterious twenty-foot mounds of white powder (some sort of waste?) where crews of pacifistic Hoboken queens would romp. Gangs of ten or twenty faggots would come, their shrieks absorbed into these abandoned caverns originally built for the contents of now-obsolete ships. The offensive indifference and monotony of walls this vast had been at least partly broken by some high framed V's of pane on fields of nothing kindly donated by youths in off-handed thanks for their gift of excess energy. Slapping each other on the ass and giggling in anticipation and Pavlovian adrenaline rush, male and female hug, they would stroll and prance through the trash like children while Theresa watched, a perfect unobtrusive but stunned audience. The men would separate and rejoin dreamily in the enormous box of the warehouse like a rocket assembly line, their bodies accumulating white dust, as Theresa flirted around like a little dark Annie Oakley in her back yard playhouse, much better than the sadistic brick drugstores of Main Street.

But she was older now. Her friends of old, with whom she spoke like a tree to dirt, would misinterpret her presence. Her only friends were the ones she wrote. Her first and so-far-only novel a 190-page rendition of the murder of her best friend committed by Theresa herself on the average of one bullet every twentieth page. The relationship that the two strike up during the course of the shooting is one of the most profound in the history of the world. Each bullet acts as a new chapter or a new extreme close-up, a shot from a different angle, a sudden new slide of my trip to India: from the Taj Mahal to a pilgrim at the Ganges to a white rib protruding from the red edges of the brown skin of a torso. To two fishes in the deep. She thought she'd killed her friend, but two bullets later Mary staggers around to see Theresa with her small-caliber pistol smoking. They're in a sunken living-room like the Bentles'. Incredible permutations of love and history of the world.

Writing the book was unspeakably harrowing for her and she began to sense the presence of a person for and from whom the book was being created. It was an old woman who existed in Theresa's closet lying in the clothes immobile and bent like a fetus except for her erect head. She was there when Theresa opened the closet door, not subject to gravity, but stuck in the impression she'd made in the clothes like a head on a pillow or the gun in its velvet box. The woman was a cyclops with the remnants of the two eyes below her middle one still visible but shrunken, sunk deep below her eyebrows, and fused shut. Her hair was dark and filthy and her face like a patch of dirt a kid had been pulling a stick through. The only part of her that ever moved was the third eye which was shiny and large, and it didn't move much. At night, with all the lights off, Theresa would go to the closet and open the door. She would stand relaxed in the presence of the woman and soak her up, get strength from her and the particular power she needed to continue writing the book. Her love for the woman was the entirety of her life, complete and boundless. The book was done in love for the woman and derived completely from the woman in the sense that her existence gave Theresa a center from which to see that saw things so clearly (because it was eternal, comprehensive and unchanging) that it immediately knew the past and future of everything upon which it looked and its exact condition in relation to Theresa. Every night Theresa would go to the closet door, open it, renew her capacity to see, and then spend the following day employing that capacity in a work of devotion to the being who enabled her to have it. It was a nice set-up. It isn't easy to write 190 pages describing the slow murder of one's best friend by oneself and it's just as difficult to imagine why one would want to write such a book, but Theresa knew it was the will of the hag in the closet. And it *was* the will of the hag in the closet. Perhaps the hag in the closet is a snake handler hoping Theresa's poison will supply a serum. Perhaps the hag is a teacher trying to cure Theresa of her fear of death. Who knows? It sure is a great book though. Theresa sends pages to Lips as she writes them. He swings open a page to find hours of insect-free privacy and is transported.

"Oh my. Let's see. A living person. Who knows? *I* know," says Lips, "who the hag is—Fuck theories! Someone in your closet! Nobody knows nothing. All you know is what you eat. I eat my spit. Listen to me I been framed. *I been framed!* I'm innocent! I'm innocent! You think you're innocent. You been convicted from birth. You've been tried, you exert the greatest effort, 'Oh God, can I reach the glass oh God my muscles damn this gravity, shit, just a sip, I'm so thirsty,' old man, you prick, limp, and dependent like a filthy piece of intestine. I love you. I'm your servant. (Lips is working as a gofer and all-round house man for two ancient near-helpless faggots named Stanley and Gary.) Send me to the drugstore for a delicious Alka Seltzer. Hmm look at these parking maters I mean meters, Polish Flowers with my polinated rag, hum, strangers in the night, catchy tune while I polish the poles, I love them so much, metal shaft cylinder with pop at the top, hmmm (exchanging glances), pop-top, a little spray flies out—and inside—*nectar!* To hell with Alka Seltzer for Stanley and Gary. Old hag in closet. That's where I've been placed. A tumor I'm examining. Well a tumor is just another form of humor. A hag is just another form of a gag. Put *that* in your catechism, Mary. You always threw up on gags." Well, your mind wanders. (Get rid of that guy with the sunglasses!) Sorry, our newscaster's been under a great deal of pressure lately.

Well, Lips is very self-involved, perhaps you can identify with him, masochist *ist ist ist ist ist* ist *ist* ist *ist*

Let me apologize for the narrator. Things seem to be falling apart here at Central. I rescind that statement. Narrator totally capable.

Lips loved the book. It permitted him to be a baby. It was catching. Everyone wants to be catching. What heaven. "Oh my."

■

BOB HOLMAN

Zone Breaks

"Where are you?!"

———————

Somewhere else, of course, you snoot!
No sweat. My best work is always getting out.
In San Francisco, in Potrero, the succulents
Crowd the ants & piece your beauty in that way
Of fragmentation which reminds me so
Of these scribbles—no wonder these hills flatten
Poetry, it is prose! or prose somewhat. It is light
On its side. Galleries of daybreak. The great
Cuts of cacti carry my mortality over. The siren
On the poetry reading tape, who would be carried
Over the flowery mill? Love me two times, west
To east, is on the radio. There are five
Ways, and I'm taking all of them. But there are still
Five ways, and you can do it too. Not doing
It, however, is not another way. Cars creeping
Over hills as if they didn't belong. Nor rivers.
Things I do every day: suicide. Turn off brain
To stay alert, blurting the thoughtful. My fingers
Growing smaller to soothe your body I know.

■

VICKI HUDSPITH

Sixth Avenue

The sweet and sour I used to love
in the French Surrealists is now my life.
Not that I am inspired by all this.
Hours behind the typewriter show
my pathetic enjoyments: drinking and radios,
a few movies and my body constantly raging.
I am not amused and this is not a poem.
People forget their lines and that's okay.
Clusters form and that's okay.
Boredom and inching ahead. A few scraggly books.
Soon the city will sizzle and poly-tourists
will forget the vast chunks of glimmering garbage
which is my life. I am nervous
from the conclaves of lovers who are
no longer friends. Homeless to each other,
what kind of nomad is this?
At the pillow, I find no rest. Sirens
wind off spools on Sixth Avenue. Street lamps
intrude. My pillow rejects my mid-twenties
adolescence. I struggle to find some humor
in this, while tension hums in the birds
that won't sing. In the middle of the night
the typewriter keys are awake. I punch away.
Blood hums and warms the war. It is here.
It is not here. Someone will please answer me.

■

HELENA HUGHES

Yellow Bird

Yellow bird, like a deer listening
to a guitar high in a tree,
everything is two simultaneously

Using your ears as eyes you think
that anyone who can must know
when a question is a question.
She tore the cigarette out of his mouth
and snapped it in half.

The elephant attracted by the feeling
of mud sank further in without escape.
He preferred the words: parity equitable
agreement. She decided everything
at 30 yards distance.

But where is the difference? The fact
is the nightingale has a toothache,
Yellow Bird.

■

P A T R I C I A   J O N E S

$ Dollar $ Value Song

Are you $30,000?
Are you $50,000?
Are you a hundred thousand
or a million?

Are you $30,000?
Are you $50,000?
Are you a hundred thousand
or a million?

Are you television
Or real estate?
Are you publicity
Or cocaine?

Are you net worth
Or gross schemes
Are you cinema
Or sex and wet dreams?

Are you banking
Or are you Wall Street?
Did you get your front row
center theater seats?

Are you art market and heroin?
Are you art market and real estate?
Are you art market and private parties?
Are you art market or just sex and drugs?

■

SAM KASHNER

Poem to Marilyn Monroe's Hair

Your hair is an ocean
incandescent as a butterfly
net dipped in wine.
Even your hair has a
stomach ache
in the shape of the wind.
When you put up your hair
it is like carrying a bicycle
on the roof of your car.
Your hair can be heard outside the window
like the rain typed out on
white clouds
a message
soaked up by the roots of your hair.

■

VINCENT KATZ

Summer Thunder

Tomorrow is expected to be
a carbon copy of today,
low clouds flung way west,
vast dome shimmering with blue
opacity, and the breeze
will riffle through your hair
as it would through a skirt
on Avenue of the Americas.

Dark clouds huddle above the park,
thundershowers anticipated
like the arrival of a friend,
away in foreign land for several
months, and when the first drops
silently shatter on your wrist
or neck, you are amazed, feel
the warmth of that vernal stroll.

Strolling is something we
very rarely do anymore, and maybe
it is a bit dated, but when the sky
opens its steamy portal, you blink
and touch the arm of your companion,
as the ice-cream truck rings
its tinny tune, and three citizens
shoot past on bicycles.

Citizens of a blue, rippled
city, where a green and black dress
is on sale, with wooden fruit jewelry
and where a boy stands beyond
a hydrant, peering into the complexity
of mid-afternoon and where, if the shade
falls right, on your hand or ankle,
you are borne into the slender arms

of milky dusk.

ANN KIM

independence day

the night before a
holiday, people
scream through open
rooms. saline pallets

go looping. what's
going on here
can return dirt
to a sky, dusk hard.

out on the prairie
raise your blouse

perhaps your rubbery
kernels may attract
two farmers' wives tearing
wet planks for lettuce
to whirl dry in a milky
plastic drum.

ah look, a burst
of quiet, starfished on
noise that falls

and falls some more.

later a radio goes on.
a cherry-colored eye
in the dark.

from the front porch, columns
wander down the road
and a moon deals the hours
back onto the land

■

CHRISTOPHER KNOWLES

Mandy

I remember all my life. Raining down as cold I am. Shadows on the hills.
Faces through windows. Crying in the night. It was just another.
It was a foll, it was a fool, it could be alright now perhaps.
I can't be making myself of your bat.
Oh Mandy you gave me and you gave that keeps shaking I need it.
I remember all my life. Raining down as cold I am. Shadows on the hills.
Faces through windows. Crying in the night. It was just another.
It was a foll, it was a fool, it could be alright now perhaps.
I can't be making myself of your bat.
Oh Mandy you gave me and you gave that keeps shaking I need it.
Yesterday I was gone to make it.
Oh Mandy you gave me and you gave that keeps shaking I need it.
Oh Mandy you gave me and you gave that keeps shaking I need it it it.
Ohhhhhhhhhhhhhhhhhhhhhh

Brandy

There's houses of those propity in land I said. And then we talk
    about homes.
And she works on the western bank. It was for evening it does it do.
It could be an accident, it89t for causing, if you know that to get
    some fish.
If you do I'll say go the red bed.
And for short for Brandy in the house of this way to be in it so
    like a woman.

MUSHKA KOCHAN

State of the Art

I sit.
Is it night?
Out?
Still?
All by itself with no help from me?
I'm a stickler for detail,
Hear the rooster,
Send in this article:
Got to get up and go to sleep
Before the sun cracks my clear sweet dream.
My rootin tootin friends make life
Good for me.
Scatter their dust at my door
Put on music
Fill my house with suitcases and strangers.
I like to see them in and off at airports and beaches.
Say: It's nice to live and safe to die
The way you're doing it.
Got pleasure down where you can feel it
In your own sweet time.
Your state of the art is flawless,
Leaves nothing to be desired
Or mountain to climb.

■

DANIEL KRAKAUER

Immortal Venus
or
The Sun Also Rises

The sun was beating down on me
like a porcupine was sitting on my neck.
That was down by the Hudson
where all those uneducated stones lie.

Oh immortal Venus, you look as fresh as a daisy,
Oh why should you want to cry?
'cause you don't tell me what's what, she said,
honey, I know what men are like.

O.K., it's a diesel, I confessed,
and her name is Phoebe 874—
I see her mornings in the Lackawannastation,
all shiny with ochre and winered stripes.

All changeth back, said Venus, to pinkviolet—
first signs propelled unto thee from the horizon,
that silverthin buzzsaw spraying dust—
behold, these are the latter days of visitations!

Green sewer-rats in the streets who squeeze and wriggle
as a means of visual expression—
trumpets woke up with a headache,
balconies twitching their noses.

And way up in the sky, for all to see,
a bona fide holy vision:
Fifteen marvelous white nostrils
Rotating Slowly.

And the sun, if I may say so, she said, also rises.

■

ROCHELLE KRAUT

Intensely Song

To Bob

As I get older I get hungrier
For what I don't know
My body is bursting
With what I don't know
So greatly my eyes smart
My head aches my body bulges
Songs of various languages
I don't know
Pulse through my veins
Where in this cloister this body
My every heart is bared
Where the songs sing silently
For this spectacle this world
Which jolts and astonishes me
Where my heart collapses black
Fills and bursts like the phoenix
Inexhaustibly into this past
Where my poems have been bursting for centuries
Where the silent are not silent
Where the silent generations sing
Where the silenced ones are still singing
Where a language does not speak
Where my poems long for their words
Where the nameless sing
Where the dead have voice
Where I am the medium
Where my mother's fears
Where my father's memories histories sing sing sing
Where the careless snicker is a bubbly song
Where my angers sweetly sing in chorus

Where my heart is never satisfied
Where my songs cure illness and heartache
Where the words bring back the dead
Where I'll never be afraid
Where the ancient voices of children scream
        squeal and laugh forever
Where the voice speaks and sings
Where someone is listening
Where there is listening and no forgetting
Where I blindly sing
Where this flesh is not only my flesh
And who is she
Is this one flesh only
In this one moment
This belongs to anytime
Where this flesh is deprived of my name
Where this is for nobody for everybody
Where I lay born on the old
        and stand living on the new
Where the songs know
Where my song wants to know
Where even you in your masks
    your silences your roles your postures
        your numbers
You can't escape me
I see you I know you
I know you here
Where you cannot hide
Where love is bursting
Me to pieces

■

BILL KUSHNER

After Montaigne

Ahh, most poets are cats, afraid of their own shadows!
As for me, I am writing my notes for the immortals!
Angry with insomnia and my fingerprints who seem to toil in vain
I decide, today, to doublecross my own unique habits and go out for a
   stroll
Then what becomes of it but I run into Max at the nose museum
Max the buck-toothed florist's son who insists on drooling whenever he
   speaks:
"What a display of noses today," Max says, smiling sweetly, "take your
   pick!
Bloody noses, runny noses, noses as radiant as the sun and noses
As tremulous as the moon when at night it scratches at your abdomen!
Oh, Michel, I am perverted, do let us meet late tonight somewhere under
A locomotive where we can continue our amorous talk!" I quickly agree
to this assignation:

1. Because I expect to die soon anyway!
2. Because of the eyes of my father
   with whom I came to live after the blowup at the monastery
   and whose silent tempers constantly slice away at my insides!
3. Because not even a lean cowboy from the rodeo with his tight chaps
   and his swiftest white horse can save me from the metaphysical
   quandaries I find myself in!

In misery, I search among the noseless faces before me on this street
The faces of the obstinate and seemingly secure populace, for the one
   true face
The face of the savage, the face of the adventurer like myself
For I am Michel, the poet of mostly unknown words
But someday, in the year 10 trillion

Some crazy transistor shall sing with these poems from my punk of a
　　heart
And there shall begin a profound chattering among the green of leaves
And violet flowers: what a genius! they'll all sway and say, was this!
And I shall be born, born again, only this time in the gentle vestments
Of contentment, what a wonderful day!

Farewell then, O Diary, from I, Michel
this first day of March, 1550

Above Normal

Home sick tears and aspirin I count
$19.95 in dollars and cents forever and ever—
imagine! I imagine raucous strangers have moved in

I groan: "for the weekend at least"
and while these are not men I might ordinarily meet
they all wear dark glasses (just the thought makes me sweat)

Called "germs" or more impressively "bacteria" (of a higher class)
heretofore known. However, we spread-eagle ourselves eagerly in bed
in love with King-sized cigarettes, dead gay poets, and you as usual

Whatever the outcome. So here's this last rather wet letter wherein
your favorite orange towel and clad within it (guess)
you rush to my side, shouting: Red Cross! Let me pass!

But no, I'm alone. Never mind, really. This is a movie
where no one dies, not even me, who dies every night
(he writes with his toes) enough of this mush

Somebody bangs above. Heat, it is my head, whistling outside
where your darkly-lit head looks up and seems to mouth a Hello
all this speeds down my throat (I won't say: "like Jello")

While hundreds of tiny foreign cars wheeze and travel crosstown just to
    garage
themselves up my nose. They do keep rumbling on and on in a kind of
    language
if I could but understand. It's something called "the language of the
    heart"

■

LA LOCA

Why I Choose Black
Men for My Lovers

Acid today
is trendy entertainment
but in 1967
Eating it was eucharistic
            and made us fully visionary

My girlfriend and I used to get cranked up
            and we'd land in
            The Haight
            and oh yeah
            The Black Guys Knew Who We Were
            But the white boys
            were stupid

I started out in San Fernando
            My unmarried mother did not abort me
            because Tijuana was unaffordable
            They stuffed me in a crib of invisibility
            I was bottle-fed germicides and aspirin
            My nannies were cathode tubes
            I reached adolescence, anyway
            Thanks to Bandini and sprinklers

In 1967 I stepped through a windowpane
            and I got real
            I saw Mother Earth and Big Brother
            and
            I clipped my roots which choked in the
                concrete
                    of Sunset Boulevard
            to go with my girlfriend
            from Berkeley to San Francisco

hitchhiking
and we discovered
that Spades were groovy
and
white boys were mass-produced and
watered their lawns
        artificially with long green hoses
        in West L.A.

There I was, in Avalon Ballroom
        in vintage pink satin buckskin and
            patchouli,
            pioneering the sexual
            revolution
I used to be the satyr's moll, half-woman
and the pink satin hung
        loose about me
        like an intention

I ate lysergic for breakfast, lunch and
            dinner
        I was a dead-end in the off-limits of
        The Establishment
        and morality was open to interpretation

In my neighborhood, if you fucked around, you were a whore

But I was an emigree, now
        I watched the planeloads of white boys fly
            up from Hamilton High
        They were the vanguard
            of the Revolution
        They stepped off the plane
            in threadbare work shirts
            with rolled-up sleeves
            and a Shell Oil, a Bankamericard,
            a Mastercharge in their back pocket
            with their father's name on it
        Planeloads of Revolutionaries
        For matins, they quoted Marcuse and Huey Newton
        For vespers, they instructed young girls from

                    San Fernando to
                    Fuck Everybody
               To not comply, was fascist
I watched the planeloads of white boys
          fly up from Hamilton High
All the boys from my high school were shipped to
               Vietnam
And I was in Berkeley, screwing little white boys
          who were demonstrating for peace
               In bed, the pusillanimous hands of war protestors
                    taught me Marxist philosophy:
               Our neighborhoods are a life sentence
               This was their balling stage and they
                    were politicians
               I was an apparition with orifices
               I knew they were insurance salesmen in their
                    hearts
               And they would all die of attacks
               I went down on them anyway, because I had
                    consciousness
               Verified by my intake of acid
               I was no peasant!
               I went down on little white boys and
               they filled my head with
                    Communism
               They informed me that poor people didn't have
                    money and were oppressed
               Some people were Black and Chicano
               Some women even had illegitimate children
               Meanwhile, my thighs were bloodthirsty
                    whelps
               and could never get enough of anything

and those little communists were stingy
I was seventeen
               and wanted to see the world
               My flowering was chemical
               I cut my teeth on promiscuity and medicine
               I stepped through more windowpanes
                    and it really got oracular

In 1968
One night
The shaman laid some holy shit on me and wow
I knew
in 1985
            The world would still be white, germicidally
                white
            That the ethos of affluence
            was an indelible
            white boy trait
            like blue eyes
            That Volkswagons would be traded in for
                Ferraris
                and would be driven with the same
                snotty pluck that sniveled around
                the doors of Fillmore, looking cool
I knew those guys, I knew them when they had posters of
            Che Guevara over their bed
            They all had posters of Che Guevara over
                their bed

        And I looked into Che's black eyes all
            night while I lay in those beds,
            ignored
Now these guys have names on doors on the 18th floor of
            towers in Encino
            They have ex-wives and dope connections.
Even my girlfriend married a condo-owner in Van Nuys.

In proper white Marxist theoretician nomenclature, I was
        a tramp.
The rich girls were called "liberated"

I was a female from San Fernando
            and the San Francisco Black Men and I
            had a lot in common
            Eyes, for example
            dilated with the opacity of "fuck you"
            I saw them and they saw me
            We didn't need an ophthalmologist to get it on
            We laid each other on a foundation of
                visibility
            and our fuck
            was no hypothesis

Now that I was worldly
       I wanted to correct
            the nervous blue eyes who flew up from
            Brentwood
       to see Hendrix
       but
       when I stared into them
       They always lost focus
       and got lighter and lighter
       and
       No wonder Malcolm called them Devils.

           ■

MICHAEL LALLY

Jeff Chandler and Me

I think a lot about
Jeff Chandler these days.
He was "prematurely gray"
as they used to say in
the days when he was a
bigger star than Brando
or Dean, for awhile, and
I was a Jersey boy in love
with the cowboy in my soul.
He wasn't as good, or
as interesting an actor
as either of them, but then,
they became so instantly
familiar they never had
the aura of Hollywood star
the way he did. They
kind of hid from that
aspect of their obviously
grand success. While
Chandler just seemed to
do the best he could
in Westerns and overwritten
melodramas that allowed
a man, whose age we could
never even guess, to represent
some kind of heroic stature
we never saw expressed
quite that way. Brando,
as Terry Malloy, could've
walked down my street
unnoticed, with his busted
nose and eyebrow scar and
Jersey "deez" and "dozes."

And Dean looked like some
overwrought and overage
high school freak on goof
balls, nothing we hadn't
seen before, though never
quite that beautiful or
intense in retrospect.
But Chandler, doors would
have opened and ethnic
ladies with kids attached
to their chests would have
made the air hum with the
elegance of their desire for
a man like him. And me,
maybe I would have seen
yet another way for me to
fit in, just in case, who
could say, I too might
turn "prematurely gray"
some day.

■

ANN LAUTERBACH

As If

Clearly it is as if. Nothing else except
choice of spoons, how they sound
next to forks (spoons and forks) and
pages of a glossy magazine.
A whole day of things set in place
with the prestige of speech,
like that morning we woke
as if we had stared into each other's sleep.

■

Here This That There

This sky a scrap disadvantaged perspective here
This no bureaucracy is lovely hum a tune look up here
This air embargo accidental equation paper trail here
This takes a nap Africa anyone home here

That without any outside help to make bread
That average small farmer emphasizes
That seventy-five per cent small industrial
That one ton of soybean products daily
That ten tons for market place Albania
That credit cards mastercard this is there
That from our Japan desk than any other nation in
That here in the United States about four thousand dollars

This former S&L magnate
This in Ohio
This huge our government is still hiding the truth here
This fiscal crime
This the final bill
This it might reach one point three trillion dollars
This why did we succeed? Dealt with it realistically here
This before one hundred and twenty-nine-million-dollar actually
This going to cost ignore
This is simply creating a budgetary black hole here

This the same old song and dance
This engineers here
Song and dance routine down by the river specialty here
Teach them product knowledge we turn that information there
This into live entertainment here
Sit back in their seats with their eyes half-closed here
Sit up can actually see them move forward here
They supress their laughter fifteen thousand dollars here
One hundred actors windpipe show here
Talk show parody here
New respiratory drug bring on the dancing bananas here

■

GARY LENHART

The Wall of Life

For Michael Scholnick
"I now thirty-seven years old in perfect health begin"

—*"Leaves of Grass"*

You turn a corner and there
Like a brick wall
Your life becomes a book

What wouldn't you give
To have back
One whack at that life

You chased until you turned
To find it behind you?
But I've no regrets

Because I expected
Sickness, madness, death,
And for one unpracticed

In its tricks
The world has dealt with me
Without overt malice.

Every night some tough hunk
Turns in his hack license
And retreats to Akron's factories

Or Albany's civil service.
But I hopped over bums
Lumped in the hall

To collapse on a mattress
At the top of a ladder
And dream of my loveliest fares

On the shore of a playful lake,
The morning sun burning away the mist
Of Victorian adverbs

That muddled their brains
And inclined them toward
Tall companions with fat wallets.

Although art was ripping
At my blinkers, my perceptions
Were as dulled by media fuzz

As my dreams were hackneyed
And sexy. One night
I politely refused the pistol

(No, pero gracias)
Waved in my mug
By my besotted neighbor

Whose wife and children
Had fled his tantrums
To return to the Caribbean.

My heart beat one free beat,
I closed the door, popped a beer
And crawled back into bed

To continue reading Vallejo.
I was impressed that he always stood
On Paris streetcars

No matter how many empty seats
There were, so as not to ruin
The honed crease in his pants.

∎

Restless

Like Frosty the Snowman, my fluent person
Demands almost daily shoring, or
Would trickle like whiskey
From a rimless bar. Unemployed
I'm depressed as Baudelaire
Or cloistered monks amid the perfect
Ringing bells inside the monastery walls
Suffering a boundless acedia. West
Of the church snow whites and weighs
The shrub's high branches, so one must bend
Beneath their arch to enter
The crunchy, untracked white yard.

∎

ROSE LESNIAK

Growing Old

On the promenade at Pierrepont Park
a woman has lunch with 3 huskies on park bench
in the playground children tango with members
of the same sex & the sun sets precisely
at 5 to 5 our woman of liberty lights
action of cars traveling out of Manhattan
subways like toy trains ride the great Brooklyn
night has set in the sandbox—
suddenly not allowed to enter the park
play on the bars, swing on the swings.

■

Private Insanity

There is a place like Germany
in all of us
and it wants to remain a secret.
Textbooks were against you from the very start
Can't seem to remember
the words that knocked you out.

■

Poem

_____

Good morning you will be loved

On this glorious day

You will be hated, both

Kissed and despised. Good

Morning bright steps rising

To brown stone buildings

Colorful individuals angling

Down them toward the train—

Sadly heedlessly or in inspired

Reckless ecstasy on this glorious

Day you will love you will hate both

Kiss and despise. The grotesque beauty

The radiantly ugly the genius or the just

Plain foolish and goofy, good morning

All! On this glorious day the boundless

White beret is on your lovely heads go ahead

Love and be loved hate and be hated kiss

And despise be kissed and despised!

■

JOEL LEWIS

from *Dream Theory in New Jersey*

What is patriotism but all the good things we ate in childhood? No overall wisdom rules the diners of New Jersey. We nurtured the dream's dream talking of revolution during many Paterson mornings. Charles Olson, despite a 6'9" height, was never involved in any acts of physical violence. When at Black Mountain College, he was goaded into a fight by a local redneck. Olson was much delighted when his wild right hook actually broke his adversary's jaw. Endless fascination with the white ice cubes in the urinals of Paterson's bars. When Ted asked his students if they were familiar with the name "Jackson Pollock," the only student raising his hand queried: "Wasn't he a famous radical during the 60s?" The last magazine I fully trusted was *Junior Scholastic*. Placido Domingo: "I don't have financial ambitions, but I don't like to work for nothing either!" Luciano Pavarotti: "I wish that when Herbert Marcuse was born someone had said, 'Go away! We don't need you here on earth!' " The smallest linguistic family is the tape recorder. Pumpkin seeds scattered across the bus seat makes me think "saline" and how they came in a red-bright box with an Indian as the trademark. To a large extent the history of the phenomenon is the phenomenon itself. It is relatively easy to make a bomb, but to quit smoking entails an act of self-transformation. Talk of revolution is one way of avoiding reality. Frantic creation of images in poems when all the words we know are made from memory. Vernon Allbright worked for the firm of Honeywell & Todd. Our common culture lives inside the picture tube. Tight garages along Durham Ave. Twenty people enter a McDonald's and they all buy a Big Mac, fries & Coke. Twenty people enter twenty different McDonald's. They buy twenty Big Macs, twenty fries and twenty Cokes; each bite and sip a distinct republic. The mystery of the strange children who eat rocks. Job description: Art is a displaced prophetic vocation. Neat rows of unsold Oldsmobiles under the near-white lights of Haase's Point. The awe & dread with which primitive man contemplates his mother-in-law is the most common motif in anthropology. To be successful, one must learn to dream dreams of failure. It is a luxury to be understood. Progress is leaving itself behind. No language proceeds in an absolute monotone. We keep searching for a science in which the simple is a sign of truth. Reading as an act of social reinforcement. A sly life would be desirable. Another name for America: The Money Jungle. Walter Benjamin: "There is no document of culture which is not at the same time a document of barbarism." The inquiry into dream is another dream. A woman boards the 44 Park at 68th Street, carrying a blue blanket and a copy of *Shirley Bassey's Greatest Hits.* Multiple history in every angle of the street. Imagination is always perfect. Language fragments the quivering monotony of space. Theodore Adorno on IQ tests: "Thinking no longer means anything more than checking at each moment whether one can indeed think!" To read poetry is essentially to daydream. Olson: "Poets are only worthwhile if they do what they dream." Brilliant Action. "What is history to me? Mine is the first and only world." "In the beginning was everything & that's the problem." Utopia must be created in time. I wait for a bus Dan Kelly's Hill watching the skyline at the end of the park put a wall of lights at the edge of my world. Jean Paul Sartre: "I have always thought that anarchy—which is to say a society without powers—must be brought about." The Senoi of the Malayan Highlands maintain social tranquility by the morning custom of dream telling. A child's fearful dream of falling will be praised as a foreshadowing of the gift of flight in next night's dream. The Senoi teach their dream-songs & dream-dances to neighboring tribes, creating a common bond beyond differences of custom. Ask me now.

■

KIMBERLY LYONS

Blue Biology

The Focused blue biology night
Hits at angles the flared snow
Interrupts all the rhythms
Of the right hand
Dense thoughts, I'm all left
Consistent and probable
Made of single pronunciations
A coat on a mannequin
Sugar skull for a crown
Light beams between cannisters
Imprecations steal me
Or a page between the spaces
An alphabet shines
Condensation of feeling
You say hear me out
Falling into this elision
Are poke holes
Thin wood flags channel the passage
Of customers through the melting snow
Tracks where you sleep
Rush words, a skewered hand
Relayed a song
In our conversation
A feeling of transverse places
Falling intervals
The operations resume despite police breaking in
And kicking the shit out of the guy
With the dog who first ran down
A squadron of cars
The resistance to such mass operations
Each ordinance committed to the form
As it is needed come through
In actual knowledge of one and through one
The other.

■

STEVE MALMUDE

Morning

Milton coyly breaks away
and goes to the refrigerator.
We can't wait all night or day.
That makes you first on my list.

But now he is here
please enclose the next thing.
Harold do you care
about the picture.

The streets are empty, not a car
is in my way and I am free
to think of you and how you are
at home and in security.

Frank hops out of bed
puts on a bathrobe
and stands before the open window
with his father's arm around his shoulders.

■

GREG MASTERS

"The guitar player's jacket is buttoned wrong"

The guitar player's jacket is buttoned wrong
She seems like the silent one, the bass player
has braids wearing a tough guy hat tilted right
&'s got her broken time riff down right too
At first it was her I would talk to but given the
length we were there, listening, I imagined more
I might want to be talking to her who
was less assuming & whose days I plotted out
til I could find out for myself, putting me in there
touching her arm while we talked in our secret sharing
as I extended it to all of us there, audience &
performer, glad about the right of quest even
if it wasn't always satisfied but more
something to look forward to simple as taking
care of cats, friends all of us in that audience
while I sat there enamored with destiny & wonder
glad about my time, forgiving of your tendencies
one by one I take you til I get it right

■

DOUGLAS MESSERLI

Shoreleave: A Melodrama

these old lands
capes, hooks, spurs, spits, like Victorian villains
are victimized by plots, inflated soils
sold into the slavery of the lips
salivating at the first sight of sand
as if it were a painted dessert—a key
lime pie aside a horn of canary.
I'll take the pound cake from the cow in Kansas!
go in fear of abstractions. t[his(s)] "greenery-yallery"
scenery's as inane as a knell
pleading for life. the heart goes out
but below the body rots.

■

HONOR MOORE

A Green Place

"What's beyond making love?" A true question.
"Time," I quip, knowing my imagining
seeks an answer to soothe fear from your face. If
we could freeze the instant in sex when light
shudders and we let time go, the clear
light of morning which turns lush green

silvery. Beyond making love? Green
if it's a place. Here any question
leads to an answer if put clearly,
here all responsive gestures feed imagining
and nature has no difficulty. Light
of noon: We are making love as if

it is a path. I am kissing you as if
what I drink from you is a river through green
breath, as if you are a source of light,
as if the feel of your mouth rendered questions
obsolete, as if simple imagining
extended vision without exacting a clear

equivalent in risk. Beyond this? Clear
cool dark of evening shadows your face. If
we lived as though time were, like imagining,
an easy skittering, an ascent through green
familiarity till colors, like questions,
need no assured compliment, then light,

freed of its debt to time, could make light
of fear, leave just what grief makes clear—
smooth pebbles in a crystal bowl. But questions
like yours darken like night or storm. What if
I can't answer? I see you in a green
place looking at me, but my imagining

doesn't speak in answers. Imagining
is formed in a slow rush of memory: light,
fear, sound, weather. Ecstatic smell of new green,
touch of a lover's skin, cheek, mouth. Clear
liquid glinting in sunlight dazzle. If
you insist I answer, the question

is lost to your imagining. If I claim clear
knowledge, light that loosens memory darkens. If
love's beyond love, it's green and we share the question.

■

COOKIE MUELLER

Which Came First?

It was over breakfast at the Chuck Wagon Bistro that Sarah mentioned that she couldn't eat eggs in the morning in her own kitchen. It was something that had haunted her for many years, since she had left her parents' home, in fact.

"Even the idea makes me nauseous," she said.

"Even over-scrambled?" her friend Vera asked.

"Actually, I can eat hard-boiled eggs in the afternoon at home. Maybe it has something to do with my disgusting cookware. I need new cookware."

Sarah was not the sort of person who talked about home appliances. But Vera, a friend of more than seventeen years, was that sort of person. Sarah saw Vera rarely; she never knew quite what to talk about with her. She was always so concerned with the banality of kitchen minutiae.

Suddenly Vera said something that was so unVera-like.

"I think I know why you can't eat eggs at home. It's because eggs are so congenitally girlie," Vera said, and Sarah knew she was right, but her choice of words was so uncharacteristic that Sarah laughed. Vera had never made Sarah laugh in all the years she'd known her.

"Also, I read that when you crack open an egg and drop it into the hot oil, it sends out agony vibrations and that traumatizes any house plants that are near. They go into some sort of vegetable shock," Vera added.

Now, coming from someone else, this would have been very matter-of-fact, but from Vera it was an eye-opener.

Sure, Sarah certainly knew all about the sensitivity of plants; she had read *The Private Lives of House Plants* and also the explosive piece on plants in the *Atlantis, Lemuria and Mount Shasta Journal*. It was about how scientists wired plants for their electro-psychic-vibration reaction to Beethoven, household violence, and slicing of vegetables. It was clearly proven that plants were highly sympathetic.

"Vera, I never thought you were interested in things like this."

"Well, I haven't seen you in a year, Sarah. I've changed. Six months ago I was living on Jane Sillman's ashram farm. I learned a lot there."

There was a grand silence, broken only by the slosh of a sunny-side's clear mucus, which accidently slithered off Sarah's suspended fork and back onto the plate.

"The famous Lesbian Occult Ranch?" Sarah asked. Was this really Vera?

"It's called the Feminist Life Force Farm," Vera corrected. "I'm experimenting with other meaningful relationships outside of hetero-sexual ones. You should know all this; your relationship with Janet is great, isn't it?"

A subway train went by under the restaurant. The table knocked the way it would at a seance.

"Well, yes, but . . ." How could she tell Vera that having a great relationship with a woman is the same as having a great relationship with a man?

At home Sarah thought about Vera. Miracles never cease. Perhaps Vera was experiencing the famous mid-life crisis. Maybe she was having a mind-expanding revelation. A spiritual rebirth? Maybe she even saw auras and talked about third eyes and Beings of Light with the ashram fems. Whatever the reason, Vera was happier.

But it was such a staggering turn. Vera had been a jaundiced homemaker—baloney sandwiches and iced tea at noon, the hum of her vacuum cleaner was music to her ears.

That night Sarah had a dream about the eggs in her refrigerator. Those eggs had been there for a long time. Obviously, she felt some deep-seated guilt about shunning them. In the dream she opened her refrigerator and each egg was shining with a blue light. The eggs then started to move, then hatch. The refrigerator somehow had in-cubated them.

Out of each egg came a full feathered sparrow. All twelve flew into the kitchen. The phone rang but she couldn't locate it amid all the fluttering birds.

Finally she found it and told the person on the phone that there were birds everywhere. But then she realized that there were no birds and the person on the phone was real and it had been a dream.

The person on the phone was Vera.

"I just called to tell you how much I enjoyed breakfast yester-day," Vera said, and she also told her that she was going away on an extended fishing trip with her girlfriend, a new lover.

"That's wonderful, Vera," Sarah said, and tried to imagine Vera baiting a hook.

Sarah was sure that this night she would dream about the frozen Mrs. Paul's fish sticks that had been in her freezer for three months.

For an old friend, would one dream any less?

EILEEN MYLES

from *The Many Real Sonnets of Gaspara Stampa*

I am not a little invalid, an angel or a saint
a fabulous taste or an exclusive drug
—all of these things on which you spend your buddhist money!
Or all the time you spend standing around
with your old avant garde boyfriend.
Or perched at your dilettante table, exclusively
you are like a big fish caught in your corner of the planet
eternally getting-together with writers and big mouths.

Eileen arrived from out of the sky but you act cool
and go see *Evita*.
Like your power was cooking its own fruit
—it is the story from which you derive your eternal beatings
(that you like so much).
In looking for the sun I am my own choir
in which I derive my infinite stability
my glorious last piece of toast.

Through your salad, Love, you abjure
and through the possibility of my Holy Face
mine, this good ardent question in the corner getting shit-faced
which is my pastime, not my cure.

Perched in the growing virtue of these painful questions
—sensual, and sadness stifling our lust
which is not two faces or two entwined pains.
How could such-a-soul and such-a-body go a travellin'
through frights, even through death, getting our periods
which is my focus, which is not yours, which is pagan.

Your son is coughing or may I say standing?
His whine is sad and his days are dizzy
from too many applications and muddy obligations.
It is your turn, older woman, my handcuffs
are Hawaiian Flowers, the world is impolite and ambulatory
but your unfaithfulness is the ultimate happening
—shame on the clawing cold you have driven me to!
My tiny sadnesses resounding among the icicles.

If you think you'd feel sordid in my pajamas
overwhelmed by the overflow of my erroneous thoughts and feelings
—come get sordid, equal-angel, it's your turn
cause I have no piano, no original wood-carvings.
My memories are sad questions, questions from the sea.
We should live alone, lying down, in Ire-a-land,
                    stroking our Collie!

                    ■

A Poem in Two Homes

Everywhere I go
is home

when I'm dreaming.
Creamy traffic

pouring past
the Noho Star

"I thought you were
coming to my
home!"

I am.
Okay.

your first year
in town. It's

doubtful I will
move to Atlanta

for business. To
Texas to teach.

Remember Soho. This
is Soho. There's
just these two
bars and then

At my back:
all of Bleecker St.
the confusing

part of New
York life

three generations
black. Today:

fruit stand, bad
bars: Stormin'

Norman & Susie,
old cafés, Village

Oldies, depression
now, the Bleecker St.

Cinema—Some
interesting "film."

Become a member
of the Bleecker
St. Cinema

trolley tracks &
dairy restaurants
like some old

world. There was
a giant line out-
side that old

church on New
Year's day. You

couldn't get in
so you went &

had coffee with
with the

the OG where
conceptual artists
sat all day

you can hardly
hear it, my
poetry. It's

in danger of
vanishing if
I don't write

it down. Does
it change like
the neighbor-

hoods, yes,
if you don't

buy it in a flash
well who knows

what'll happen
to you? You'll
wind up in the

lower east side,
one day all cobble-
stoned with

We went to that
history of the Avant
Garde Cinema

at the Modern Art.
I didn't want
to be

with him at
all. His teacher
Duncan McNaughton

guy who depressed
you, Noel Sack.

Eileen, why don't
you work he
said.

Noel, I sd
waving my hands.
I bought his

old speakers
& my check bounced
bounced.

That was the
last straw.
He was so

pissed. I
guess he's

in California
or someplace.

I did not forget
the yellow legal
paper folded

with the stripes
going up. I
forgot the tan

notebook full
of numbers
I've got

to call. I'm
walking home

with a Macy's
bag with one sweater
& a head band

writes me about
the "real thing"

poetry that's not
what, language,
ethnic, lesbian

black, you
know like Charles

Olson.

I packed all
of my clothes
from your

home into a
Macy's shopping

bag. Oh gimme
that jacket, I
wanted to

wear that. And
walking up twelfth
brrr it's

really cold. Gimme
that white tur-
tle neck.

I do not seem
to be obedient
to the world

today. Since
television, there
has been

in it. Her soul
is not a great
soul. She dwells

on domestic things:
her love. Her walk
in the cold &

even keeping to the
tiniest rule makes
me full.

My home becomes
a prayer mount
when I get

there—full of
light & dust &
the answering

machine blinking.
Hello Eileen, I am
Joel Lewis. I

am the world's
greatest poet.

& then he exploded
you didn't
know when

& that was
what moved

the crowd. The
freedom of
exploding

in the air.

Hitler, Hitler,
Hitler pop
Hitler.

me. It has
been a tall
order to carry

out, the whole
case for enter-
taining literacy

on *my* back.
I was listening

to a tape of
Patti Smith yes-
terday in

my home. It was
before she had
a band & everything

in her voice
was waiting
for it.

And, even better,
oh dear god,
andro-

gynous creep
in the sky,
Danny heard

Hitler. & he
says Hitler
sd bumble

bumble, not much
blurrrr facts,
bull-shit

walk the
streets of
the east

I want to
be Will
Rogers

that's what
I want to
be. And,

that, folks,
(twirl twirl)
is the

end of the
world. As
we know.

I think I will
be the anti-
christ. Rather

than simple
Eileen Myles.

Poor she. The
anti-christ
is me. I

died at the
age of 33
yet I

compassion is
boundless &

incredible.

My mission is
not so predictable
as reverse

of the first.

village joyful,
and remorseless

like a cruel
& perfect

poem, my
butt, unsold.

Sometimes
I act vague

about my
lesbianity.

No, it is
deeper
than all

I know. The
softness, the
flagrant

disposition. To-
day I used
half a jar

of Dippity
Do & I
got it right.

I will put
my plastic

head on
your shoulder
& weep.

For you, but
not for
me. My

I take some
of this
& some of
that, I
wiggle

unlike Christ.

I'm not a
girl, nor
a boy. I

won't bear
child,

nor knock
you up. I
do not

come w/instructions
even to myself.
All my notions
are felt

I think, as the
the arrows
strike the

fatty part
of the

arm of

the boy martyr
I am unwounded

happy because
at least
a sphinx
is a fact.

We're coming

wet from the
well. I am
clear eyed &

burning with
dispassion

like Christ,
but different.

Zounds. I
love that word.
Zounds. It

resembles arrows.

Each panel

represents a dif-
ferent industry

or else each
panel represents
a different re-
ligion, or masonic
lodge, or else
each panel re-
presents an age,
like the awful
age of Pisces
which we're leaving
behind us as
we're chugging
on towards
the great
new mysterious
age of Aquarius.

from there,
the desert &
we're going
right back
in. Now

more than
any other
time in
history, you
really ought
to please
yourself
because
in mysterious
winds a
cave inside
your soul
might be
the only
place
to go.

So why house
a skunk?

Once my whole
apartment is
grey I can
think this
all out.

But I'm
hardly
ever home. Hi,

I barge in,
all smiles,
the answer
machine is
blinking away
& my hands
all full of
direct mail
envelopes, Salvation

Everything you
can think of
that seems
mysterious
everything's
going
to be
like that.

A sphinx would
make you

Army, gay direct
mail, poor Bowery
guys, culture.

Everybody wants
money. And

I just came
home from
a hard
day of looking
for money
for my
organization,
that of
the poet.

In your
decline
I sing
your
song.

At the end
of the
world
I am
my poem.

MARC NASDOR .

Greasy White Stuff

Sunday morning blurts & the world commiserates
& the thick stuff in the sky all goes away
Malevolent projectiles tilt accordingly as
Lots of you-know-what everywhere

But still somebody's eyeball drops into it
It opens
& speaks to you
"A round thing knows it's round"

Or over here   this neighborhood
A flock of papier-maché dogs
Enter the path of a papier-maché ambulance
All spit up red crayon dust
& then a crepe paper cop
Takes out a ballpoint pen
& writes everyone a ticket

■

ELINOR NAUEN

The Expanding Universe

Driving across the prairie
until first light
not knowing till first dawn
if it's winter or fall:
car steamy   feet warm.
Subtle tender crawl of bright
into the dusty windscreen
& I shake the nighttime deejay, nighttime
long sweeping push
to get there, get going & get there:
there's room
for the expanse. Little purple field-flowers
luminescent in my frayed vision.
I stop at the first town & give away some old shirts.
Gas spurts like love. Like coffee
the smell of gas soars.
The driving
as tho grass ripens any old time.

■

SUSAN NOEL

Heaven

Falling off the ground
Is how I hang my heaven upside down
When I don't recognize it, find
No heaven's jotting on my face—
Everything's begun and ends
While I attempt to mystify
Familiar buzzing, heavenly harps
Disfigure sleep. Awake & dumb
I land an out that doesn't hold
Intention. Still
To lend my slot
Yesterday's instructions
Lost and found
List a partial bottom to this heap.

■

HILTON OBENZINGER

"Our Property We Estimate Sublime"

New York Burns Down 1776

"A most luminous and beautiful but baleful sight
occurred to us—that is, the City of New York on fire."

So Captain Joseph Henry, aboard his ship in the Upper Bay
observed while
Jacobus Stoutenburgh, Engineer of the Fire Department,
marched with his firemen to the Heights
where Washington and his troops
waited.

The bells of New
York's churches, how could they
all be carted off?
"We can melt them into bullets,
a much more decisive alarm," the firemen
replied, pulling the bells
across the tobacco fields
of Manhattan.

This is the fire as it starts.
Captain Henry:

> "Running upon the deck, we could perceive a light . . .
> the burning of an old and noted tavern called 'The Fighting
>   Cocks'
> (where ere this I had lodged) to the east of the Battery
> and the end of the wharf."

A gale whirled up from the southeast
as "The Fighting Cocks" threw up a shower of sparks
spurring up Broad and Beaver.
Only the bells at Trinity Church
were left behind, and they tolled.

Still, alarm reached St. Paul's only.
Beyond that: silence, the tongues cut
out of the mouths of piety.

Now the people rushed out into the streets.
Unskilled, they dragged out the fire engines.
Now the neighbors fell into the usual bucket brigades.
Yes, the buckets would not hold water.
Yes, the fire engine pumps would not explode streams of water.
Now the neighbors examined their torn buckets.
Yes, a wail of fear and anger went up among the bucket brigades.
This is the fire as it instructs the bucket brigades.

With holes cut in the bottoms of buckets,
clouds of sparks whirled overhead freely.
One building after another burst into flames.
No, you cannot fight this fire, they surmized.
Consuming your own city is one of the
Rights of Englishmen.

This is the fire as it proceeds, reaching Trinity.
Captain Joseph Henry:

> "When the fire reached the spire of the large steeple,
> south of the tavern, which was attached to a large church,
> the effect upon the eye was astonishingly grand.
> If we could have divested ourselves of the knowledge
> that it was the property of our fellow citizens which
>   was consuming,
> the view might have been estimated sublime, if not pleasing."

Now every building between Broadway and Broad Street
was on fire along the waterfront.
The fire leaped across Bridge Street and raced on to Stone.
Demoralized, the amateur firefighters fell back to
Marketfield Place to regroup.
British soldiers took charge of the few engines
that worked, throwing streams into the conflagration.
Bickering between New Yorkers and Redcoats . . .
pure dismay . . . thousands packing the streets . . .
sparks jumping the great central thoroughfare,
whirling northward again, until daylight came
and fire triumphantly ran from river to river.

"We clearly discerned that the burning of New York
was the act of some madcap Americans . . .
The sailors told us in their blunt manner
that they had seen one American hanging by the heels,
dead, having a bayonet wound through his breast . . .
They averred he was caught in the act of firing the houses.
They told us also that they had seen one person caught
in the act tossed into the fire . . ."

James Ovendyke, Overseer of Engine Company No. 2,
located in the rear of City Hall, replied,
"It is our city to dispose with as we wish.
If the city burns, and we do not rise up to protect
it, then our liberty proclaims
ashes.
While the city is ours, the fire is as well.
And if the fire wanders out of control,
it is a risk well taken.
It is lucky we inhabit only an island
for the fire has bounds.
We have yet to ignite the continent."

This is the fire as it ends.
Canvas and spars were spread across chimney ruins.
The city became Canvastown, and the British
ruled the ruins.

Marching in retreat with Washington,
the firemen looked back over their shoulders
from the Heights, and they agreed:

"Our property we estimate sublime."

■

DAVID RATTRAY

This Began Long Ago

This began long ago
And I'm in it.
To the woman I love
Who once said
"I want to bathe you in pure air"
I spoke of the
Fine line between
Solitude and isolation and
Hung up finally,
Praying that if I got
Where I couldn't do a thing
I still would.
Woodruffe wrote that certain
Yogis stare at the sun
To allow light in
Straight to the core.
It made for perfect 180°
Emptiness under a Frederick Church sky,
That long young day
On the Connecticut I asked
How far my life might reach and where
Night would begin. Only today
Years later
Letting time flow over my hair
I stepped into the
Wave of the future, someone
Talking about her dad
As I arrived. He's deaf, his hands
Tremble, one drink
Lands him in the
Hospital. A dot between dashes
Over a flat stroke
Short for that

Favored look of well bred
Reticence—in less than 20 years
Red figure artists
Hit on a viable script.
I live alone. At times, visiting,
Decades flash up and she
Hates my guts. I
Think of the faces
Leaders make in the
Privacy of their bathroom.
Years I call units, dots :
Visarga, letting go, opening of the closed hand,
Scattering, end of the sun's course,
Destruction of the universe, shooting of
Glances, creation, separation,
The parting kiss,
2 perpendicular dots representing an aspiration occurring
At the end of a word and so called from its being
Pronounced with a full emission of breath;
In the dream of Vasugupta the upper dot signified the
Big bang, the lower dot, the works,
Fireflies
In a pair of flowering trees
Joined at the base lifelong
On a hillside at midnight—
Ketu a light signifying what cometh,
Men call it a comet, a
Braid of invisible lines with filaments of white
Heat, cracks opening in the great crystal
At the edge of air and flame, whereas
Vis-à-vis
Inner light playing in the mind to a mob of
Minute particles exhibiting
Continuity of subject in the form of object
Always, everywhere
"Fireflies" represent sparks of feeling if not
Kindness on the dark hill outside.
Knowledge of past deeds
Eating at the mind like sores
Keeps
Not in the forehead but in the back of the head, the

Spine in fact, a line of
Yellow tipped cairns looping up over the ridge of Mt. Adams
In a mile-long S.
Tezcatlipoca
Guesser of unspoken thoughts
Thy tongue draweth blood from the presidential air.
Look at 'em on the news—
As if making faces
Made up for the way they talk.
I made it though to Osgood Junction
Out beyond treeline. Wind can
Tear up a city block and not unseal
A letter on a table.
My mother at age seven
Used bread-and-butter for a bookmark, lived
In a house called The Purple House, took the
Temperance Pledge at ten;
In the fall of '45
Mr. Pennypacker let me
Touch a cloth of gold
Kyd gave to the Gardiners
Under the tallest tulip tree.
Name of the red guna is
Rājas—greed, rage,
Desire. Just now I
Opened both my hands and
Considered the
Leaf-filtered sunlight
At the margin
Of my wide-ruled
Yellow pad. Best
Color I ever saw
Was an experimental
Heliotype of a
Sun-drenched field
With poppies, by
I recall Dr. Wood
Summering near Georgica on
Lily Pond, 1910.

■

KIT ROBINSON

Ice Cubes

——————————

■

then
begin
over
and

sleep
to
control
costs

no
overhead
no
inventory

but
dreams
count
you

among
the
players
in

the
all
universe
commodities

sweepstakes
where
futures
rise

and
fall
breathing
normally

∎

the
hiring
of
professional

criminals
for
selective
jobs

we
can
do
that

get
them
to
stop

copying
me
we
can

do
that
get
me

a
show
in
Minsk

we
can
do
that

■

I
don't
feel
like

working
today
I
said

first
thing
this
morning

now
bleary
after
dark

I
hasten
to
add

you
never
can
tell

but
hazard
a
guess

step
out
into
air

■

fantastic
sadness
humor
or

fierce
scrutiny
of
what

comes
by
the
stars

arc
in
the
sky

■

the
dead
hand
of

the
past
falls
gradually

a
fund
of
knowledge

a
land
of
numbskulls

a
maximum
security
person

■

voices
at
lunch
time

air
flows
across
the

vacant
work
stations
hum

"American
Opinion"
a
storefront

on
San
Pablo
Avenue

now
completely
empty
inside

■

brain
salad
alphabet
soup

Dagwood
sandwich
and
a

piece
of
cake
then

Mr.
and
Mrs.
Potato

Head
inflate
and
support

the
soft
underbelly
of

the
bloody
banking
business

■

these
cubes
designed
to

cool
your
drink
dissolve

faster
than
sound
thinking

■

pre
Ohio
tortilla
a

concise
if
meager
formula

for
what
there
is

left
in
the
refrigerator

■

wrapped
in
a
clock

sleep
music
continuous
waves

holding
pattern
in
place

hide
and
go
seek

who
is
that
other

I
dreamed
of
waking

■

BOB ROSENTHAL

FMLN*

---

it is against this sky I write a quiet space
a booklet for closing up a sound package
my son asked there are Indians in New York?
I was happy to say yes   but then he said
And they were all killed?   I was sad to say yes
so I asked him Who killed them? his eyes narrowed
an instant he said Oh the bad people
he smiled the tv was on the Electric Company
in the tall grass my grandmother Bertha his age
fleeing mounted Cossacks waving swords overhead
how firm will my feet be in the land of the bad people?
there is no god and there is no sense everything
becomes water when you shit on it long enough
I sit in the land of the bad people & pay my dues

*Frente Marti Liberación Nacional

■

Deaf Crescendo

---

where is the sky
under a peach tree

what is thunder
it is the sound of lightning

no, it is two clouds
rubbing up against each other

where is thunder
over the ocean now

why is there love
well there really isn't any

it just sticks to you
so in that sense it does rub off

is it a resin you can smoke
yes it is a smoking heart

why is the heart the center of love
if it stops beating love is fleeting

I am tired of love
however not bored!

why should I buzz around all the time happy
there is so much fleeting love to catch

what about those waves in the ocean
they are beating the heart of rock to sand

why are your thoughts so bare
they will not heed heard wonders

and do they desire, your thoughts, to die
no they desire to be lightning

you mean to rub up against each other
yes to thunder from the sky

would you be your muse at the expense of you
no I would be your muse at your expense

under the peach tree just you and me
the world is in the sky

where is the world

■

JAMES RUGGIA

Straphangers

Felt her reading my *Times* from over my shoulder
& still I continued to stare at the front page
photo of Alexander Haig, all the way down into
the tooled alloy pinpoint of his eye. She per-
sisted & so I began drawing a swastika on his
forehead, over & over, ripping the paper all
the way to Arts & Leisure. She tightened up.
I got off on 23rd & Americas. Felt her watch
me across the platform & into the lights.

■

TOM SAVAGE

The Gypsy Union

You put your name on the sundial.

A black raven with white wings.

When you confront the end of the world

You might run into a brick wall.

Sleeping beauty pays by cable.

Your book remains undrowned.

Three tears from a tremendous bridge
Hang in the space between rain and sun.
The number of arches for each tear is different.
They become smaller and more numerous
As they ascend.

■

ELIO SCHNEEMAN

Poem on Frank O'Hara's Birthday

If I cannot show how, nightly,
the sudden folds of my bones
turn to dust, it is because
the pressure of my forehead increases.

I have seen the faces of indiscriminate men
who have chosen to wallow in the unwholesome den.
I have ignored the filth on the path I tread
with one weary leg and one damp head.

■

Distance

These stars, so distant,
Cloud the imagination and
Arouse the sense of local galaxies
Like an ambiguous fixture, a delicate
Figure simple in its unifying fashion
Continues up the pavement where
A million faces edge their way into the sphere
Of color that embodies the tree
Of a green painting split in half
Formed thoughts drifting among the vegetables
A dark yellow room.

■

PAUL SCHNEEMAN

Epigram

I learned these terms of endearment
in honor of you . . . a matchbook
pointing to itself calmly   the smoke
stack's message is stitched:
could be clouds   and
in the front yard   the umbrellas
read: "What sleep?" It is possible
as often as it is not.
no need for alarm   in another country
far away we are lettered . . . tempted
back home.   Out of the blue   traffic
predicts this still the courtroom adjourns.
On the other end of the telephone
a postage stamp   the airy landscape
includes us   dumbfounded
at the prospect of the Atlantic.

■

MICHAEL SCHOLNICK

Good Graces

I have no questions, Kiss me
Beggar's loving qualities
& branches, snow-pursued, Kiss me

Air of great, saber-toothed waves, Kiss me
Kiss me, instill something hilarious

Your step a nocturnal detail
Pregnant wind, remote & sketched
Centipede upon a balustrade of bedimmed sequence
Darkness of the woods' closure

Kiss me, I'm a gardener
No pills, Kiss me
I know I never doubted you
Teach me to drive

Light breaks through the blinds
The bird chirps inventing pleasure
I half-smiled at the bridge, Kiss me

Programs Tickets Kiss me
Six dancers two beats
See you soon, Good-night, Kiss me
Mixed reviews & hoola hoops, Kiss me

Last call, Kiss me
Let's cut here, Kiss me
Sounds interesting, Kiss me
Alternative to coffee, Kiss me
One wish granted, Kiss me

Nervous rendezvous & seamy aftermath
Utterly heartless, amusement
Ignorance analogized
Diaphanous commonplace

You are scrubbed & absurd
In the wings of melancholy paroxysms, Kiss me
At a party with security guards, Kiss me

■

Uncle Ismael

died last night.

Young Migdalia thinks
Cousin Freddie in Puerto Rico
telephoned news misinformed.
No one's home in Brooklyn though,
to lend her beautiful idea probability.

The man loved to talk
and eat.

Señor Villegas dreamed clearly
of the dead man after midnight.
Nervous, he lets fall
half a toasted bagel to the floor
and juggles a fork.

Finally, the truth comes.
Feeling ill, Ismael bathed.
Hurry, said Miriam.
We'll rush to the hospital.

I want to go dressed,
said Ismael Falcon.

He passed away spiffy and shoeless.

Can you believe it, said Nellie.
He was a real sharp dresser.

■

JAMES SHERRY

As If

by the
    fit (appear hangover)
chance, happen, were, bunch, sit
    clench the tooth in the hand
They know their enchiladas.
    singularly multiplicitous as tomato juice capillaries
    contact person——visit service
        as you, only place, always work . . . the less, say too, triangular
room, group shouldn't, always on (B-rut), sup on per, resident torpor,
    as if the green copy, the blue copy, the white copy, the puce copy,
the copy full of holes, the his and/or hers copy (her ok, but hers . . . (c
ontent), the flat copy, copy mit schmear . . . /defer conduct if only
    help realistic

you do it, we do it: media couple. Perhaps people.

                coordinator
                    standard
                _____

                plus perfect
                    fatuous
        servile   mess
        notation   9 months
    happenstance   outside
    closed circuit   pleasure

keept try
don't give up the hip
_____

Punvale-on-Hudson
Contusion

Give it the, Hill 54 Protrude Support: Collaborate
   Old heave, conjoin astrology, occluded front, prevent flag
      spaced against bag, allude to confer, conifer, confrere (presume
to confer), poltroon vs. Quisling, tickle my, alt. vers

Chintzy kisses, contingency: a frozen dessert. Bell long lines fortress:
pretty baby, consent device. Cold up there reply schooner, personal
capsule, allay pencil, temporary tendency contusion disks, beer friend,
word got out.

Sack speaks, Make up reasons. Fundamental detention, strike out
      words.
Blowing bubbles corner, attune your desperation, rate spate, transit
commissioner. Creature lumps pervert welfare, crane your hopes,
deliver pretense.

Taxed up. Needle. Criss-cross. Simple January. End of the part, hair
ship, left shadow, architectural bathos. Lust staple, cruise her nuisance,
pollution aid.

Underpining legs. Soft. Certain. Teamwork, subtlety, subterfuge, smell.
D.O.A., fuc rd th, passion fuel, under.

"What's wrong with scandal if it gets jobs." Ownership of, Belonging to,
My private. Poems with images—mix and smash the pertinent aspires,
cranberry party, lint hangs out.

Particles tell read or, the edges of this sign are the people next to you,
read it like this: event, word, help.

■

RAVI SINGH

For Rose Lesniak

I see you lying in the sun, on
a white rock placed to break the
waves. One notices the way your
swimsuit clings to you, the way
the wind leaves the water's deeper
meaning intact. Somewhere behind
you a Frisbee completes its arc to
a hand, and park district workers
mow the vast lawn on which yellow
butterflies are folded like
invitations on clover. Cyclists
go by like summers you remember—
summers of wonderful drugs. It
seemed you could lie in a place
like this forever, afternoon
lapping against you. You were
more than you knew. Days when
blossoms waited for your passing
to exert themselves, and evenings
spent plumbing the miraculous
with a body close to yours, then
the dark passivity of after love.
You must've realized it's hard to
be loved and still want more.
You float out over yourself. Scenes
from the flowing summer unfold.
Dark children flounce in the hydrant's
white rushing. A Kennedy sleeps
in his sailboat beneath a sky of
infinite assets. From a moving el
train one sees pale curtains blown
outward by fans, and sees the ballpark—
the crowd roars against the neighborhood's vibrant decline. A Puerto Rican
scores a basket, graceful as not caring.

Ice cream bells ring for the people.
An old woman sees summer passing on
the street's dark side. It is late
afternoon. Workers leave the city for
the suburbs' shallow fulfillment.
The sun moves behind clouds. You sit
up and smoke a True menthol. Imperious
lightning coruscates on the lake.
Driving home as the first drops of rain
fall on your windshield a plurality
of streetlights goes on in your deep
untranslateable eyes.

■

L O R N A   S M E D M A N

Collage

_____

I glue a photograph of Kafka and Max Brod to a sheet of paper.
They are sitting on a small couch, leaning towards each other, having an animated conversation. Max Brod is holding his infant son on
his lap. Kafka is smiling, and almost touches Max's shoulder with a
delicate hand. I want to enter their conversation, so I cut apart
some words, and scatter the letters above the photo, hoping the men
will use them to answer my questions. Focusing my mental concentration in a beam out the front of my forehead, I push it through the
surface of the photo, into Kafka's mind. What are you saying? He
doesn't respond. I try several times. The letters don't move. I form
the question in the space between them, and increase its volume to
scream level, but I can't break into their intimacy. Frustrated and
angry, I go through the papers on the table and find a picture of two
Mexican bandits, wearing big black hats and holding old-fashioned
pistols. I cut them out and glue them down with their guns aimed at
Kafka's and Brod's heads. This threat fails to startle them into talking. They don't even notice the bandits, and I don't have the heart
to really get tough with them.

■

LYNNE TILLMAN

No/Yes

I threw caution to the wind and never used any contraception. Nancy finally convinced me I might get pregnant this way and made me an appointment at Planned Parenthood. It was a Saturday appointment and that night I had a date with John, a painter from the American West, a minimalist. So the doctor put the diaphragm in me and I kept it in, in anticipation of that meeting. Besides I had lied to the woman doctor when I said I knew how to do it—I was afraid to put it in or take it out. Let it stay there I thought, easier this way.

We met at the Bleecker St. Cinema and watched a double feature. Godard. Walked back to his place below Canal. We made love on his bed and he said "I'm sorry. This must be one of my hair trigger days." What does that mean, I asked. He looked at me skeptically. It was difficult, very difficult, for men to understand and appreciate how someone could fling herself around sexually and not know the terms, the ground, on which she lay. He said "It means to come too quickly." Oh, I said, that's all right. I kept comforting men. He fell asleep fast.

I awoke at 3 A.M. with just one thought. I had to get the diaphragm out. If it were possible and not already melted into my womb or so far up as to be near my heart or wherever diaphragms go when you're ignorant of where they can go.

I pulled a rough wool blanket around me and headed for the toilet in the hall. John awoke slightly and asked where I was headed. For a piss I lied.

The heavy door opened into a dark hall. The toilet door opened, just a toilet and no door. I stood in the dark and threw my leg up on the toilet seat as shown in various catalogues not unknown to the wearer. Begin searching for that piece of rubber. Think about Margaret Sanger and other reassuring ideas. Can't catch the rim. Reach the rim; finger slips off. Reach it, get it and pull. Can't get it out. It snaps back into place as if alive. Pull. Then try kneeling. I'm on my knees with my finger up me, the blanket scratching my skin. It seems to be in forever. This is a Herculean task never before recorded. An adventure with my body. In forever. I pull the blanket up around me and stand, deciding to leave it in for now and have it removed surgically if necessary. In a colder sweat I leave the dark toilet to return to the reason for all this bother. I can't pull the loft door open. It seems to be locked or blocked. Begin banging heavily against the metal door. Hot sweat now. When John finally opens the door he finds me lying flat out on the blanket, a fallen angel, naked at his feet. I'd fainted. He revives me and we are both stunned. The door he says was open. That's what they all say. He gives me a glass of water and we head back to bed.

The next morning, even though he says our signs are right, my fainting has indicated other signs. Signs and more signs. I walk toward Canal Street and a sign on the wall reads Noyes Electrical Company which I read No/Yes Electrical Company. No/Yes, I think, that's a strange name for a business.

■

SUSIE TIMMONS

Breakfast

Wow! Look at these neat monsters here
on this cereal box! Wow, what great colors.

I wish I felt that way when I woke up

boxers, satins, grace dead

we want to obey you, and now ask what is
over here.   and what is over here

noises drip off xylophones

WPAT oleomargarine radio station music oozes out of my
boss's office greasing the atmosphere of the workplace
slightly, and when I head in there the man is saying
"The tiny tin motor is very weak."

the dog is resting, but there's always some precious design
to study

on the walls, which are tough bandits, talking bricks

I want to keep this area free of Elizabeth Taylor types
in lacy lavender blouses, but they continue to appear
they keep appearing out of nowhere.

This summary has a porch

What can you say about love, except
it pisses me off.

I wonder if Mr. McKenna will close the office for a day
when Florence passes on.

Bodies make one part
televisions make another part

faces and talking make another part of the pie,

friendly faces shake your hand and move it around

moving around, stay up all night to get past the day before

WAR

I always have to make an extra special effort to get out.

SPINNING TOP

you will be beautiful someday
    in my arms
when you rest

■

DAVID TRINIDAD

Good Tidings

Tonight, a hand-painted and
haloed cherub is watching
over you as you drift off.
It is the same angel that
inhabits the candle's shadows,
the spirit that dwells
in your glass of warm milk.
It is also the protector
of good art and the speaker
of all romance languages,
as well as the guardian of
your dreams and little wishes,
and the keeper of each dark
secret you swore you would
take to the grave, but which
you have given up this time
around—your second and final
chance. So turn away from
the light. Sleep. Let go
of every unknown answer and
explanation. When you wake,
you will own your life.

■

QUINCY TROUPE

Leon Thomas at the Tin Palace

eye thought it was the music when
in fact it was a blender
grindin down the ice
making stuffings for drinks, but then
you jumped right on in on the downbeat leon
strokin rhythm inside time
inside the bar, then

people flew deeper into themselves
became the very air sweeping language too crescendo
between feathers of touch looping chord changes
your voice blued down, blues cries, field hollas
mississippi river flooded gutteral
stitches through your space
images of collective recall, leon

your voicestrokes scattin octaves—
ice grindin down still inside the blender
making stuffings for piña coladas—then
you scooped up our feelings again
in the shovel of your john henry doowops, leon
jazzed through ellington count & yardbird

yodeling coltrane blues cries
the history of joe williams
sewn into the eyes of our eardrums
transmitted to the space between
the eyes, where memory lies

your scattin licks brings us back dancing
in our seats, you kick swelling language inside
your lungs, leon, voice strokin colors painting
the Creator's Masterplan
as pharaoh explodes inside the tone blender of his horn

ice grinds down the bar jumps out of itself
scooped up in the shovel of your john henry doowops
blue as a mississippi gutteral river flooded
octaves kicking back black scattin
rhythms loop bustin your chops

feather stroking phrasing, leon thomas
yodelling octaves, sewn back black

where they came from

■

116th Street & Park Avenue

For Victor Hernandez Cruz and
Pedro Pietri

116th street fish smells, pinpoint *la marqueta*
up under the park avenue, filigreed, viaduct
elevated tracks
where graffitied trains run over language
there is a pandemonium of gumbo colors stirring up
jambalaya rhythms
spanish harlem, erupting
street vendors on timbale sidewalks
where the truth of things is what's happening now
que pasas on the move, *ándale*
worlds removed from downtown, park avenue gentry, luxury co-ops
where latino doormen just arrived smile their tip me good

tip me good, tip me good, greetings
opening doors
carry their andalusian rice & bean villages, old world
style, dripping from zapata moustaches
shaped perfectly as boleros,
their memories singing images underneath shakespearean
cervantes balconies, new world don juans
smelling of cubano cigars, two broken tongues listening
lacing spanglish up into don q syllables, cuba libre
thick over sidewalks, voices
lifted & carried up into dance
up into mumbo-cha cha slick steps, these bodies
imagine themselves to be ballroom floors
rumbling car horns, *palmieri* fused
machito fired, *pachacho* tuned, barretto drums
bolero guitars wiring morse code puns, root
themselves back in villages
of don juan, romeo,
zapata, marti, in cuba writing poetic
briefs under cigar trees, the lingua-franca
of nicolas guillen, morejón, cruz & pietri
laying down expressions of what's happening now
& weaved through this pandemonium of gumbo
colors up under
the park avenue, filigreed, viaduct
criss-crossing 116th street fish smells, pinpointing
la marqueta
where elevated trains track over language
run over syllables on elevated tracks, fuse words
together, (w)rap lyrical *que pasas* on the move
ándale, spanglish harlem
nuyorican sidewalks, exploding fried bananas

■

BARRETT WATTEN

Statistics

There is no language but "reconstructed" imaged parentheses back into person "emphasizing constant" explanation "the current to run both ways." The ocean he sees when as "sour frowns of the ancients' 'signifier' " that person jumps in. We are at liberty "to take 'the' out of 'us,' " to have selves "not here" in the machinery of dramatic monologue to "smash, interrupt." To focus primarily "using examples of work" produces "difficulty": "you" in indeterminate distance "building a tower" as the circumstance of writing "to look over 'with concern' the bones of 'speech.' " Machines are "metal" words where "crystalization slipping" is "that tongue spoke" dissolved into "not it" located in constraints. "Causing 'them' to freeze and perish" has no bearing on "stumbling block" of facts "embodied" in old meanings "understood" to be "suffering 'circumstantial' distortions." "It" makes itself "by definition" into "word," missing the point "writing," wanting as "further" point "a persona" clearly named. Biochemistry adds to "average" warmth "lightly voiced" if painfully limited "rhyming with" individual "he." Those "automatons" exist who have by "progress into ground" lost use of "the raised surface" of writing. He becomes you, as "retrograde hero 'having nothing to say' " can't tell what "it" is. But a person smiles "the allowed" look at "examples of" words in front "when present." He speaks "to study inner silence" as absolute: "normally we think 'we think "we have seen 'in writing' what we have seen." ' " The figure "lightbulb turns on" of mind is not the "separate from hearing" talk in the speaker's "much more complicated" brain. One thinks hard "how to read" what "won't read autobiography" thinks "destroys no one" but invokes instants of fear "to say what 'it' wants." Remove "privilege of manifestation" to make words "active and passive" for thousands never met who might yet "passionately react." Circumstances of this writing assume "a recording" will disappear, that "self" cannot be identified as "preoccupation with voice" or "replaced with words." But "pyramids, tombs, chariots 'of personal experience' " want confusion of "schoolboy torn in half" in an odd, "theoretical" way. Transcription stood, the "8-year-old sentient gone": "speaking" twelve feet from the water, its "audience" on the rock. He wanted "baleful 'all-knowing' distance" out of this borrowed substance "often more personal than he." Disregarding if "citizens worth not one cent" listening can't speak for us "circuits not all there" themselves, he "whatever may be 'wanted' " loves to talk. "Let me in" pushed between "to have intelligibility" hopeless repetition "which takes you away."

■

TOM   WEIGEL

Invocation

Evening brings subway madonnas
after so many steps
& powerless to affect
all instant love,
you now join the ranks
   of the truly dumb
boarding the Jackson Pollock car
   of the downtown #6,
reserved for you
   & anonymous lovelies,
fingers still cold, unflinchingly numb
Like some board of trustees
Faced with a new season in poetry,
O great sky singer of modest dreams
Give me yet one more winter of harvested content;
love's familiar mantle without pain—
   such tokens when they are due;
A hand reaching for the brush
   when all else fails.

■

MARJORIE WELISH

Handwritten

An afternoon,
the unsure white space of your livelihood.
The mast of the city, like the human hand,
so near and yet so far.

Accompaniment filling the air, your hand and coffee
as you bend down to make something happen.
A pot of flowers, softspoken
and encouraging, guides your eyes to the wall,
forgotten, broken, blurred,
although there are many other dispersed
largely exploratory, places to go
when days are canceled
by unsteadiness or any of its obvious tributaries.

■

TERENCE WINCH

Ghosts

_____

In the rain falling on her.
In wide open space I think of.
I wake up without you, smoking
a cigarette, without a moment.
I have no names.
The street without looking.

I am awake. I get done in a day.
I try to remember your faults.
The ghosts are covered with footsteps,
without memory, that open like
editions of *Vogue* in the small room
without you where you see everything
without her, without emptiness
without turning to someone in bed.

■

JEFF WRIGHT

Hit or Miss

In the kitchen you are trying to make sense
out of dinner, green beans, macaroni.
The tv wants to do it for you.
Superman is on the phone. The city,
gray & busy, is out there, on the make.

You make a salad & take a breath.
Obeisance is up to you. You bet.
Where is a tear to answer to vapor?
Who will make the music of forever's fervor?
Come, fierce idol, keep the options open.

"Love once, love always." Another open book.
No telling who it is, in the dark.
And dark is falling like a bruised parachute
that knocks the fire out of us—
over the susceptible Atlantic. Soon
an overgrown child will beat his Mom or dog.

■

JOHN YAU

The Dream Life of a Coffin Factory
in Lynn, Massachusetts

Earlier in the century it was not unusual to spend
an evening on the veranda. It was a time when
movie theaters sprawled around newly constructed
lagoons, their blue concrete walls rising out of
Wisconsin snowdrifts, their tile roofs fiercely
gathering Delaware's windswept soot in March.

Every street personalized its drugstore with
mahogany stools on which one could perch
and wait for evening to unfold its newspaper,
shake out its umbrella. And at night, long
after everyone was asleep, the rows of
chrome spigots still glistened with pride.

Now it was dusk; and floating above these
warm suburbs was a tremendous dome, whose
perimeter was molded with high-relief figures
of motorcycles and pouting dancers, wagon wheels
and other things classical.

In Wisconsin's lagoons it was still considered
graceful for a man to sit in a drugstore
and wait for a hand to squeeze an orange pill.

In Delaware's soot a woman could sit on a wall
and lose hours counting clouds unfolding in
the darkness.

It was, if anything, a newly constructed century—
a time when only motorcycles sprawled fiercely
in the rain.

Behind the movie theater a warm glow spread out
from the window of the hacienda, bravely gathering
the remnants of evening to its yellow handkerchief.

Even the narrower streets had their own lagoons,
each one lined with stucco clouds on which
one could sleep, waiting for evening to deliver
its pastel uniforms. It would remain an evening
of waiting, for men and women floated above
the suburbs, pouting fiercely
in the last stages of a withered century.

In March, in Wisconsin, young men shed their moustaches.
After carefully weighing them, they were placed in
linen handkerchiefs and buried in the snow. In the
evening they ran back to the classical suburbs, where
rows of young women leaned in glistening drugstores,
waiting for the clouds to get older.

The perimeter of these suburbs was carefully outlined
by chrome spigots. Lawns rose fiercely out of the snow,
while paper bags seldom crossed the avenue. If a newspaper
floated past a window, a pale hand clutched a withered foot.
It was a time when the century had gone to sleep,
and everyone glistened with pride.

■

DON YORTY

For John Keats

I think that I'm a candle
whose flame stays round the wick
whether set in one place or carried
never wavering an inch
from where I've always been.
I hold out my hand like you did.
When I'm happy and look at it
it's not the same I see sadly,
desiring or when I'm tired;
it changes with my feelings
which usually I don't notice
like light and shadow pass over the day
revealing as the morning sun,
obscured by clouds or tears.
When you vanished, did all vanish?
With a change of heart I change the world.

■

BARRY YOURGRAU

Zoology

Out in the garden there are naked women crawling around on all
fours. Little men ride them—middle-aged, oily creeps from the
Levant, in cheap dark blue suits, shiny from use, and straw hats.
Their revelry, their contemptuous nonchalance, disgusts me. I want
to drive them off, but my companion pulls me back, back into the
house.

It's a whorehouse. "Why do you submit yourself to all this?" I
question her angrily, splashing Scotch into a tumbler. "I've turned to
it since you dropped me," she replies bitterly. I look at her. "I'm
not a *giraffe!*" I insist.

I understand what I mean to signify by this bizarre denial. So
does she—but she disagrees with me! Furiously I grab an encyclo-
pedia off a shelf and find the Giraffe entry: several giraffes are
shown in nature, in a savanna. Naturally they don't look anything
like me.

After this we keep apart in moody silence. I am sullen, insulted.
I swallow my Scotch, clenching my jaw. Out in the garden the bastards have taken off their belts and started using them as whips.

■

The Cousin

I'm down in the driveway, helping my old man clear some brush.
My mother calls from the front steps: "Stephanie's here!" The old
man and I look at each other. "Oh Jesus," I say. We go on up.
She's sitting in the kitchen drinking tea—Stephanie, my cousin, who
killed herself two years ago. Her hair is just as long and dark and
untidy as ever, but it's the disturbing whiteness of her face I notice.
The old man of course grabs her, gives her a huge hug, launches
pell-mell into a discussion of things. I peck her on the cheek quickly and take a chair and sit watching the conversation, feeling her
clamminess clinging to my lips.

A little later we walk out into the woods. She insists on showing me her wrists, not once but twice, even though I tell her it frightens me. "So what is it like—where you are?" I ask her finally in a hesitant voice. We're sitting on a log. "What's it like?" she says, and she gives me a furtive look and her upper lip quivers. "I don't know . . ." she says, and she shrugs and bites her lip, trying to suppress the giggles, thinking about what it's like. Her eyes have a wild, loony darkness in them; she just sits there, shaking with giggles, trembling with spooky, secret knowledge. She keeps it up for so long it gets really awkward, as I sit beside her, trying to grin along. I realize how absolutely little I know about her, how strange she always was. Once when she was staying with us I said something very rude and spiteful to her (about how much tea she drank), which pained me with guilt afterwards, especially after we got the news. I was going to bring it up when we came out here. But it doesn't seem appropriate now, considering the way she is. The pallor of her skin is horrifying.

We return to the house. The old man and I go back down to the driveway, to finish what we can before dinner. "How long is she going to stay?" I ask him, dropping some branches onto the pile of what he's cut. "As long as she wants," he says. His voice and face are grim, occupied. "Well, after dinner I'm going," I tell him. "I'll stay somewhere else, I can't stay in the same house with her. She gives me the creeps." "She's your cousin," he says, "and she's had a very unhappy life. You'll stay." "I'm going!" I tell him. "She scares the living piss out of me. How can you stand it?" He looks up at me, lifting an eyebrow, one of his withering, hanging-judge looks, so that I flinch. Then he reaches down for a sapling. "Your problem is you're not tough," he says, quietly, scornfully, not looking up.

■

From a Book of Hours

Beside a stream a man is reading. He sits against a tree, one knee drawn up as support for his book. Next to him a long slender pole is propped; a line dangles into the water.

The open pages of the book show an illustrated, gilded scene: a tiny figure by a stream, fields giving on to a town beyond. In the fields, men and women bend over curved bundles of wheat. Their scythes make dark punctuations of the harvest.

The man smiles, as if pleased with what he sees. Then he yawns and looks over at the pole. He shifts his gaze a bit and considers the prospect of the town in the distance: the familiar spires and gables. He surveys the fields, before returning to the book.

A shadowiness comes over the surrounding landscape, as if a cloud were passing in front of the sun. It is the man's hand, about to turn the page.

■

T R A N S L A T I O N S   I I I

Let me tell it to you all . . .

But no, the lines

the rhythm forced . . .

the heart is larger!

The collected works of

Shakespeare and Racine

are not enough for

this occurrence.

—*Marina Tsvetayeva*

from the Cycle "Wires: 2"

Trans.: Michael Chusid

and Chris Kraus

Papyrus 89

of now all

smoked around
ships, sharp
of hostile, and it dried
to the sun, recklessness
who greatly long for
you can of Naxians
and the stump of trees
men restrain
this the people'd
as not angry beside
and of brothers
some cut fig leaves
he stumbled to blows
these my heart
from the bottom

but still died

know now, if your
expressions intend
which in Thasos
and Toronaia

and who in swift ships
and . . . from Paros
and sister
heart
fire that really now around
in a suburb
they abuse the land
Erxia, ravage
equip, onto the road
and not boding good

Archilochus
Translated from the
Ancient Greek
by Vincent Katz

593

Watching the Hunt

Bone bow caws in strong wind—
The General hunting outside Wei.
Falcon eyes pierce withered grass,
Hooves slip through melting snow.

Quickly passing through "New Abundance Market,"
He returns direct to "Slender Willow Camp."
Looking back where the arrow soared—
A thousand miles of dusk level clouds.

> *Wang Wei*
> Translated from the Chinese
> by Simon Schuchat

■

From the Chinese of Sen Jou

When the moonlight is brightest
I tiptoe to open the half-open door
The night wind is sounding the wind-chimes
Is that the cricket making a suitable harmony?

Or are the singing pine-trees?
The garden reacts favourably to autumn's proposals
I walk through the garden to the shore
The horizon is at eye-level now

Fishing boats on the horizon
Why are those lights in the waves so pretty?
Why is the night wind the same temperature as me?
Gossip, I suppose.

> Translated by Steven Hall

■

Sonnet 20

Predict my future, good day, devoid of firmament
Injure Amy, slyly daunted, laughing figure
My future decries and the sands of another painting
Reconnect themselves, caught view, premier mount

Piss, the voyage of Amy is fatal
Pity, the prize of this sad adventure
And when mounted, I foresee my nature
Quiet shame that to disappearance goes the May of my ardor

Keen, used, passé, keen favor devoid of belief
That key, lay heaven is destined for the fires of nature
May, conned, I voyage to the nubilest of apertures

Vents, so cruel and such horrible. O rage
I cry questing for the infernal stops
Who from her loins orders my words, dice swaddled in an empty cloud

Louise Labé
Translated from the French by George-Thérèse Dickenson

■

Encouraging

In China swings the mandarin.
Today cocaine has killed again.
The straw is rustling: go to sleep.
Today cocaine has killed again.

Through windows of department stores
the poor see where the dollar goes.
The straw is rustling: go to sleep.
The poor see where the dollar goes.

Buy yourself sausage, buy yourself bread,
guard your life well, hold up your head.
The straw is rustling: go to sleep.
Guard your life well, hold up your head.

And one day you'll find even this:
a woman who will cook and kiss.
The straw is rustling: go to sleep.
A woman who will cook and kiss.

1927
Attila József
Translated from the Hungarian
by John Bátki

■

3 Poems

Say "Yes"!
And say "No"!
And now say "Why not?"
Thanks
I'm doing better

. . . . .

You must read Shakespeare
There was a true idiot
But read Francis Picabia
Read Ribemont-Dessaignes
Read Tristan Tzara
And you shall read no more

. . . . .

A dog is not a hammock.
Philosophy is a mélange of words.
Chaos made of mud and enigma.
I am certain of but one thing: that
I am my own pastime and a
polite enough man.

Walter Serner
Translated from the French
by Peter Frank

■

Song to a Miser

It was once discovered that a fellow had the habit of fetching meat
from his store during the night while other people in the house were
asleep. He ate his fill without letting his companions share the
enjoyment. As soon as he had finished, he wrapped the remnants in
a skin and hid them under the bed.

One of his mates later took revenge by composing the following
poem, which he recited one evening to the malicious delight of the
audience. It is said that the miser was so ashamed that he never
indulged in secret eating again:

> I put some words together,
> I made a little song,
> I took it home one evening,
> mysteriously wrapped, disguised.
> Underneath my bed it went:
> nobody was going to share it,
> nobody was going to taste it!
> I wanted it
> for me! me! me!
> Secret, undivided!

Angmagssalik, East Greenland
Translated from the Eskimo by Tom Lowenstein

■

From the Cycle *Wires: 2*

To Boris Pasternak
18 March 1923

Let me tell it to you all . . . But no, the lines
the rhythm forced . . . the heart is larger!
The collected works of Shakespeare and Racine
are not enough for this occurrence

"Everyone was crying, and if blood hurts . . .
Everyone was crying, and if there are snakes in roses . . ."
But Phaedra had one—Hippolite!
Ariadne cried for Theseus alone!

Misery! There are no shores, no roadmarks!
Yes, I agree, losing score,
okay, by losing you I lose whatever
whoever or anywhere never was!

What hope can there be—when through & through
I am drenched with you—the air knows—
When Naksos*—is built of my bone—
When under the skin my blood—runs—the River Styx!

It's useless—she's in me, everywhere—shut
eyes, she's bottomless, no day—and the date
on the calendar lies—just as you are—Severance:
I am not Ariadne and I am not Loss

Through what seas and cities
Should I look for you? (Invisible man to a visionless spectator)
Leaning up against the telegraph pole
I hand down the ritual of the road to the wires.

Marina Tsvetayeva
Translated from the Russian by
Michael Chusid and Chris Kraus

*The island where Ariadne was abandoned by Theseus.

■

The North American Military Base of Puerto Castilla

Puerto Castilla, head lowered, stands disgraced before Honduras,
that other Honduras,
the U.S.A.'s celestine,
fake Indian and keeper of the hit list
who speaks with less than decorum
as if he's propositioning a trick.

(At night depending on the whims of the sea, lighthouse beacons
enter windows or lights from windows beckon the port.)

In uniform and out on the town, apparently, Death is having a ball,
the old skull all made up, medals and stars
shining aglow
so hot so red they conduct a vertigo.

Children. Children listen to me: destroy
or burn
this jaundiced and sorry-looking portrait.

Tegucigalpa, 1984

Roberto Sosa
Translated from the Spanish by Zoë Anglesey

J./after Robert Desnos

I loved a horse—when was that?
I have dreamed so much of you
I have dreamed so strongly of you I have lost you
I loved in clear time
I have dreamt of loving
I forge ahead between the stars with two blind dogs
I think not only of the death of my guts
I said: my mother. And I thought of you, O house.
I heard a voice in those bad days
I have killed it, I killed it!
I am not only a fleeing fox, a prey on the prairies
I am as I am
I write to you from another, higher country

Translated from the French by Keith Abbott

■

Anywhere Out of the World

In the hospital of life
the patients are all mad with desire
for a change of bed

this man wants to suffer next to radiator
this imagines getting better
under the window

wherever I don't happen to be
feels good to me
my soul and I have a running discussion on that

what do you think my pale shivering
of living in sunny Lisbon
warm and alive as a lizard

they say it's built with marble
people there hate plants so much
they uproot all the trees

and it's on the seacoast
made completely of light and mineral
and water to reflect them

but my soul is not responding

well since you're so glued to peace and quiet
as long as something is moving to watch
why don't we go live in Holland

a place you think of often in art galleries
stoned by the mast-forests of Rotterdam
great ships anchored beside the houses

total silence is all that comes from this soul
say how about Batavia
where the European spirit mates with a tropical beauty

nothing—could my soul be dead already?
so down you enjoy suffering?
then let's go to some really dead places!

we'll pack our trunks for Torneo
or even farther—extreme end of the Baltic
farther—we could set up house at lifeless North Pole!

where the sun barely skims through the world
and the bare-minimum strobe of light and dark
nicely frames the monotony

which is half of the picture itself.
And we can take long baths of darkness.
For entertainment the Aurora Borealis

sometimes will color our pages
like reflections of a fireworks display
in Hell—suddenly my soul is shrieking

in its wisdom: Anywhere!
I don't care—as long as it's out
of this world!

Charles Baudelaire
Translated from the French
by David Rosenberg

■

EDITOR'S ACKNOWLEDGMENTS

The editor wishes to thank the following persons for their help with manuscript preparation: Lee Ann Brown, Reed Bye, Julia Connor, Larry Fagin, Andy Hoffmann, Anselm Hollo, Chuck Pirtle, Randy Roark, Andrew Schelling, Leland Williams, and especially Bernadette Mayer for her help with the Index. To the many editors, guest editors, and contributing editors of *The World* over the years: Sam Abrams, Charlotte Carter, Tom Clark, Cliff Fyman, Steven Hall, Daniel Krakauer, Ron Padgett, Ann Rower, Harris Schiff, Joel Sloman, Susie Timmons, Tony Towle, John Yau, and Lewis Warsh, my heartfelt appreciation. Ted Berrigan, Tim Dlugos, and Joel Oppenheimer, who have passed away during the preparation of this manuscript, were also invaluable contributors to this project.

Thanks also to Ted Greenwald, Jessica Hagedorn, Vicki Hudspith, Bill MacKay, Ron Padgett, James Ruggia, Jerome Scala, Lorna Smedman, Tony Towle, and Frances LeFevre Waldman, the editors of *The Poetry Project Newsletter*, from which some pieces were selected; John Perreault for a selection from "Out of This World," a Poetry Project publication; Ed Friedman for use of several selections from The Poetry Project Papers; and Rudy Burckhardt, Yvonne Jacquette, and Lita Hornick for their continuing presence and moral support of The Poetry Project.

Special gratitude goes to my original editor, Esther Mitgang, and to her successor, David Groff, for their perseverance. Special thanks also to Pamela Stinson and Carol Taylor at Crown.

COPYRIGHT
ACKNOWLEDGMENTS

The Contributors' Index is a selected biography, a bibliography of the particular authors in this anthology and a compendium of personal statements, reminiscences, and anecdotes associated with the activities and life of The Poetry Project over a period of twenty-five years. Contributors were invited to submit responses as to what the Project had meant to them personally and as writers, and to recollect any vivid experiences they could for this occasion. Thus the responses cover a wide range, from the early days to the more recent years. Many of the writers here actually worked at the Project and were "on the premises" for a number of years, others were frequent and loyal participants, still others were occasional guests and more distantly affiliated. And some of the authors were primarily present through publishing their work in *The World*, *The Poetry Project Newsletter*, and other Poetry Project publications. This index is not only an impressive testimony to the myriad accomplishments of the writers in this book, but also to the extensive and varied activity of a unique institution.

ABBOTT, KEITH. Born in Tacoma, Washington, in 1944. Author of *Erase Words*, Blue Wind, 1977; *Rhino Ritz*, Blue Wind, 1979; *Good News Bad News*, Doris Green Editions, 1984; *The First Thing Coming*, Coffee House, 1987; *Downstream From Trout Fishing in America, a Memoir of Richard Brautigan*, Capra Press, 1989.

ABRAMS, SAM. Born in New York in 1935. Author of *Barbara*, Ferry Press, 1966; *The Book of Days*, I. White, 1968; *The Post Maerican Cultural Congress*, Bobbs-Merrill, 1974; *The Laws*, Jargon Society, forthcoming.

THE ANARCHIST CORPORAL REPORTS

The story goes, I was outta New York City at the time but have reason to believe it was the Johnson days, with all that Office of Economic Opportunity money. This sociologist no one had ever heard of, from the New School, first he calls up Al Carmines at Judson Memorial: hello, you don't know me but I got x hundred thousand dollars I gotta give away by next Tuesday and Al hangs up—fuck off, joker. Next he calls Mike Allen (the Reverend) at St. Mark's in the Bouwerie (*sic* dammit!) and Mike says, well tell me more.

I think it was Paul Blackburn who had got the readings—they'd been floating from bar to café, into the church, and that was the seed syllable. Then came the OEO money, from which rose Theatre Genesis, Millenium Film Workshop, and the Poetry Project.

Jobs for poets as poets! A first in our gang, though the other guys had always had some lines, the consultantship, the fellowship at Rome. Joel Oppenheimer, who had been one of the original brainstormers who conceived it all, was the first one hired on, Joel Sloman the second, I was third (part-time), Anne the fourth. I don't know why Paul didn't want/get a gig, or maybe he was being paid for all that taping, every Wednesday reading and lots of the Monday opens. (And some schlep! I filled in for him a few times, the heaviest reel-to-reel deck in town.)

And, then was the mimeo revolution. Always mimeo had been the only way to home-make books/mags, cheap enough, but too messy, too crude. Suddenly new better machines, techniques, all over the country. Among the breakthrough leaders: John Sinclair's Detroit Artists Workshop, Ed Sanders's Fuck You Press, and the *glorious*, *never-to-be-forgotten* Gestefax Electronic Stencil Cutter. The production process was liberated. We could do it ourselves, without money-raising hassles, without printers' censorship hassles. Everyone was putting out decent-looking mags/books, readable, even beautiful often, for nothing, no money, home-made, and *so fast*. The Project came in just as mimeo was cresting. We put out twelve issues, averaging maybe forty big pages, of *The World* between January '67 and June '68. And the Project's mimeo equipment was pouring out lots of other mags/books. For instance, and only for instance (we were among many), Joe Early and I got out thirteen issues for our *Noose* between March '68 and March '69, using the Project mimeo. Every month, fifty or a hundred pages of *brand new* poems, from/to/for the community.

Sometimes things happen just in time. Joel and Ted would have been Joel and Ted with or without the Project, but we have, I am convinced, more of both of them on our shelves, in our heads/nerves, because of the Project.

— SA

ACCONCI, VITO. Born in the Bronx, New York, in 1940. Conceptual and performance artist, co-editor of *0 to 9*, author of *Double Bubble*, 1966, *Four Book*, *0 to 9*, 1968; *Transference: Roget's Thesaurus*, 1969; *pulse (for my mother)*, Multiplicata, Paris, 1973; *Vito Acconci* (ed. Mario Diacono), Out of London Press, 1975.

ACKER, KATHY. Born April 18, 1947, and raised in the U.S., she lives periodically in London. Author of *N.Y.C. in 1979,* Top Stories, 1981; *Hello I'm Erica Jong,* Contact Two, 1982; *Great Expectations,* Grove Press, 1982; *Blood and Guts in High School,* Grove Press, 1984; *Don Quixote,* Grove Press, 1986; *Empire of the Senseless,* Grove Press, 1988.

This is what I remember:

I was never terribly involved with The Poetry Project. I moved back to New York City around 1970; I was about twenty. I was living directly above Jerome Rothenberg. I had been sent to him by David Antin, and was very close to his group of friends, especially with Jackson Mac Low. I hung aroung The Poetry Project in 1970–71 or 1971–72. I believe that Ted Berrigan, with whom I later became friends, either called me a sex freak or called my writings those of a sex freak's. My closest friends in The Poetry Project were Bernadette Mayer and Harris Schiff, but I think they thought I was "weird."

I did read regularly, during that period, at the open readings. I was so scared to read my own work publicly, the first time I did so, I vomited. Which is strange considering that, at the time, I made my living by working (acting) in a sex show.

My overwhelming feeling, at this time, of not fitting in certainly sent me away from New York and probably made me more anxious to make and define my writing.

I think that The Poetry Project has been the main center for poets, especially younger poets, in New York City, for many years. I was helped by the Project through an interiorized antagonism, but my experience cannot be typical.

— KA

ADAM, HELEN. Author of *Ballads,* Arcadia Press, 1964; *Counting Out Rhyme,* Interim Press, 1972; *Turn Again to Me and Other Poems,* Kulchur Foundation, 1977; *Ghosts and Grinning Shadows,* Hanging Loose Press, 1979; *Stone Cold Gothic,* Kulchur Foundation, 1984.

ANDERSON, JACK. Born in 1935 in Milwaukee. Author of *The Invention of New Jersey,* The University of Pittsburgh Press, 1969; *Dance,* Newsweek Books, 1974; *The Dust Dancers,* Bk Mk Press, 1977; *The Clouds of That Country,* Hanging Loose Press, 1982; *Selected Poems,* Release Press, 1983.

The Poetry Project was important to me because it was there—and because it was close-by. I could walk to it. And because I could, the sharing of poetry became a part of my everyday life. I could not only say, "I am a poet," I could prove it in public. Yet the format of Poetry Project presentations in the sixties made it more than an ego-booster. The Monday-night open readings allowed me to acquaint my peers with my sort of standard of achievement. The poets who read then were ones that a young writer could respect—or argue against. And when one was invited to read on Wednesday, one felt one had accomplished something.

— JA

ANDREWS, BRUCE. Born 1948 in Chicago. Author of *Excommunicate*, Potes and Poets Press, 1982; *Factura*, Xeroxial Editions, 1986; *Give Em Enough Rope*, Sun & Moon Press, 1986; *Moebius*, Post-Neo, 1986; *Shut Up*, Sun & Moon Press, forthcoming. Editor of L-A-N-G-U-A-G-E (1978–1982) and co-editor of The L-A-N-G-U-A-G-E Book, University of Southern Illinois, 1984.

Off center. Things happen faster—didn't your government teach you any manners? Exaggerated injustice is poetry. Romps to stage dive to sparks max—without the yuppie reprise, ah, long-term anti-social behavior!

Minority tongue in crossoverland. Let's NOT assimilate; difference is built by power culture synonymous community. Authority means lack of language.

Yet The Poetry Project also acknowledges, calls for, openness, diversity, PLURALISM:

Nobody on nobody's side—more noise, less ratio in its many entirety; he just SOUNDS LIKE A SECTARIAN PARTY . . . dissolve audience into serial briefcases—brains without frontiers; territorial chick—no guest list!

— BA

ANGLESEY, ZOË. Born in Oregon and lives on the Lower East Side. Editor, *Ixok Amar Go:* Central American Women's Poetry for Peace. Translator of six volumes of Central American poetry. Forthcoming books: *Central to America* (poetry) and *Zazz* (short stories). Editor, anthology of contemporarary North American women's poetry to be published in Tegucigalpa, Honduras in a bilingual edition in 1989.

The crossroads for caravans of poets, a sanctuary against cant and apathy, a Manhattan poetry meeting place in the dapple Apple Village of the East of the Lower East Side Loisaida: St. Mark's Poetry Project in St. Mark's Church. If a dear poet soul is on the road for poetry's sake, over the years the microphone has been open, the community open to hearing yet another message in these most unpoetic and atomized times. If any cause is worthy of poetry, that cause and that poetry has called us together. Rites and celebrations, festivals and marathons, have assembled us to hear the word—improvising, satirizing, resonating, reeling, accusing, rapping, awakening, penetrating, commemorating, provoking, with great feelings of love. As a community and as individual poets with great feelings of love, we appreciate this liberated zone that embraces poetry.

— ZA

ANTIN, DAVID. Born in New York in 1932. Author of *Definitions*, Caterpillar Press, 1967; *Code of Flag Behaviour*, Black Sparrow Press, 1968; *Talking at the Boundaries*, New Directions, 1976; *Who's Listening Out There*, Sun & Moon Press, 1980; *Tuning*, New Directions, 1984.

The Project from its very beginning provided a central place for a community of poetry—a community you didn't have to live in to feel comforted to know that it was there.

— DA

ANTLER. Born in 1946 in Milwaukee. Author of *Factory*, City Lights Books, 1980; *Last Words*, Ballantine Books, 1986.

It was important to me being a poet from inland Ocean Realms, that my work appeared in *The World*, helping to link the east coast to the Heartland. Reading at St. Mark's in March of 1983 was a good experience of sharing my being with Mannahatta literati.

— A

ASHBERY, JOHN. Born in Rochester, New York, in 1927. Author of *Rivers and Mountains*, Holt, Rinehart and Winston, 1966; *Shadow Train*, Viking, 1981; *A Wave*, Viking, 1984; *Selected Poems*, Viking, 1985; *April Galleons*, Viking, 1987; *Flow Chart*, Knopf, 1991.

BALL, DAVID. Born February 27, 1937, in Brooklyn, New York. Author of *Two Poems*, Matrix Press, London, 1964; *New Topoi*, Buffalo Press, 1972; *The Mutant Daughter*, Buffalo Press, 1975; *Praise of Crazy*, Diana's Bimonthly, 1976, and *The Garbage Poems*, Burning Deck, 1976. His translations from the French include *Leda* by Pierre Louys, Chelonidae Press, 1985, and have appeared in *The Dice Cup: Selected Prose Poems of Max Jacob*, Sun Books, 1979; *A Big Jewish Book*, Doubleday, 1978; *French Poets of Today*, Guernica Books, 1987. His translation of Pablo Picasso's *Desire/Caught by the Tail* was performed by Eye & Ear Theatre, directed by Taylor Mead, May 1984 in New York.

BARG, BARBARA. Born in 1947 in Memphis. Author of *Obeying the Chemicals*, Hard Press, 1984.

The St. Mark's Poetry Project first came to my attention in Ted Berrigan's workshop at Northeastern Illinois University in Chicago. Berrigan brought in readers from New York for the several reading series in Chicago. By the time I actually moved to New York in 1977, I had visited the Project and given a reading there (cultural diffusion between Chicago and New York).

When I arrived, there was a spunky little scene going on. "Younger" poets inspired by the first generation of Poetry Projectarians met regularly at the readings and workshops, hobnobbed in bars and apartments, and lent their youthful highspirits. Being a student of T.B.'s, it seemed only natural that the Project become a focal point for my "talents," energies, and gossip-mongering.

At that time there were a lot of magazines, projects, etc., that came out of the minglings of those young poets. Readings in small bars, laundromats, wherever—poets' theater collaborations, bed-hopping.

As in any scene, there were gripes. Gripes were dealt with through *Caveman*, a "supplement" to the regular Poetry Project *Newsletter* edited by whoever felt the need for Caveman assertiveness at the moment. It was a beautifully merciless publication.

As the "younger" poets became more rooted, the structure began to change. An advisory board was added to either aid the director and coordinator or appease the growing community of writers. Also, community meetings were scheduled several times a year, another place to vent frustrations and air new ideas. I was serving on that board when it became expedient for the Project to incorporate, and the advisory board became the board of directors. I promise never to write a novel about those growing pains (I was going through some of my own simultaneously).

Now the cuts in funding are taking the Project through different struggles. I hope the War on Literature doesn't take too bad a toll. I'd like to see it continue for another twenty years. It represents a community, and I'd like to see that prosper. I believe we need about a thousand poets to every politician on this planet in order to achieve some global sanity. St. Mark's has its work cut out for it.

— **BB**

BARTLETT, JENNIFER. Born in Long Beach, California, in 1941. Author of *Cleopatra*, Adventures in Poetry, 1971; *History of the Universe*, Nimbus Books, 1985; *Jennifer Bartlett: Rhapsody*, Abrams, 1985. Both a writer and painter, Bartlett shows with the Paula Cooper Gallery in New York City.

BÁTKI, JOHN. Born December 15, 1942, in Miskolc, Hungary, he has lived in the U.S. since 1957—in Syracuse, where trees line the streets. He has studied at Columbia University, been a recipient of the O. Henry Award (1972), was a fellow at Stanford, and taught literature at Harvard. Author of *The Mad*

Shoemaker, Toothpaste, 1973; *Falling Upwards*, Dolphin Editions, 1976. He is the translator of *Attila József: Poems and Texts*, Carcanet, 1973/University of Iowa, 1976. Short stories appeared in *The New Yorker* and *Fiction*. Engaged since 1970 in *Kilimology*, a study of traditional weaving from the Near East. Has also been translating fiction from contemporary Hungarian writers.

Long live St. Mark's, the poetry Saint and poetry shrine of New York.

— JB

BAXTER, GLEN. Born in Leeds, England, in 1944. Author of *The Khaki*, Adventures in Poetry, 1973; *The Impending Gleam*, Alfred A. Knopf, 1982; *Atlas*, Cape, 1983; *Glen Baxter: His Life, the Years of Struggle*, Alfred A. Knopf, 1984; *Jodhpurs in the Quantocks*, Jonathan Cape, 1987. He has exhibited his work at the Gotham Bookmart Gallery, the Holly Solomon Gallery, Nigel Greenwood in London, and in Amsterdam, Paris, and New South Wales.

I became involved with the St. Mark's Project directly through Larry Fagin and Ron Padgett. The first time I ever read from my work in the world was at St. Mark's Church in 1974 on the program with Richard Snow. The enthusiasm I encountered and the encouragement I received at St. Mark's helped me to continue working in England, that great bastion of indifference, throughout the 1970s.

— GB

BEATTY, PAUL. Author of *Big Bank Take Little Bank*, New Cafe Poets #1, published by the Nuyorican Poets Cafe, 1991.

BERKSON, BILL. Born in New York City in 1939. *Shining Leaves*, Angel Hair Books, 1969; *Ants*, Arif, 1975; *Red Devil*, Smithereens, 1983; *Lush Life*, Z Press, 1984.

In the sixties, Anne Waldman skyrocketed The Poetry Project, and by the time I caught on (late, around 1967), the local energy display was already tremendous. How did it affect and contribute? A succession of readings that opened one door after another, beginning with the first (for me) by Ted Berrigan in the Parish Hall, and continuing through the variety jumble: John Wieners, Joe Brainard, Fielding Dawson, Kenward Elmslie, John Ashbery, and Ray Bremser, among the top performers. The doors were called Style, Intimation, and Tone. Pluses: a live audience of peers who came early and stayed late; a much-missed magazine which had both standards of energy and community spirit; a neighborhood, which continues (although the art parvenues forget, think they invented it), the stations of that crosstown line struck by St. Bridget's (Tompkins Square), St. Mark's

(Second Avenue), and Grace Church (Broadway, across from which Frank O'Hara lived and Poe wrote his "Bells"). The readings one heard about and missed and heard later on tape: Clark Coolidge, Charles Reznikoff, F. T. Prince. The specific sense that one's own upcoming reading at the church was "it," the stage, professionally, for contemporary writing, much as the Met is "it" for singers, where you go to be heard.

— BB

BERNSTEIN, CHARLES. Born in New York in 1950. Author of *Disfrutes*, Potes and Poets Press, 1981; *Islets/Irritations*, Jordan Davies, 1983; *The Occurrence of Tune*, Segue, 1981; *Resistance*, Awede Press, 1983; *The Sophist*, Sun & Moon Press, 1986; *Content's Dream: Essays, 1975–1984*, Sun & Moon Press, 1986. Editor of *The Politics of Poetic Form*, Roof Press, 1990. Co-editor of *The L-A-N-G-U-A-G-E Book*, Southern Illinois University Press, 1984.

For me, St. Mark's provided an important alternative to the low-energy, formally inert poetry of official verse culture, such as that presented at the 92nd Street Y's poetry program. At its best, St. Mark's has stood for the possibilities of difference in American poetry. This is a much broader—national—commitment that any of the various stylistic tendencies have sometimes been identified with the Project. It is also a commitment that the Project has not always wanted to foreground, lest it seem too inclusive or, paradoxically, not pluralistic enough. The famous Ginsberg-Lowell reading of the late 1970s seemed symptomatic of a certain refusal to stand by one's stands, as if fame superceded ideological or aesthetic oppositions, or as if opposition had no place in poetry; in contrast, a certain preference for the local (the neighborhood) and the stylistically familiar (tried) has sometimes clouded a larger view of what is happening in the art. I dwell on these things because I take the place seriously and the many conversations I have had with people about the "church" have been related to them. It is a measure of the power of St. Mark's as a symbol of the many and contradictory wakes of the New American Poetries, chronicled by Don Allen in his 1960 anthology, that getting a reading there has been a goal of many poets and not getting one a sour irritation. This is an intimate part of the aura (or should I say seductiveness) of the place; it's always awkward, of course, to plunge into such matters.

— CB

BERRIGAN, SANDRA. Born in Detroit in 1942. Author of *Daily Rites*, Telephone Books, 1972; *Summer Sleeper*, Telephone Books, 1981.

The Poetry Project was an idea and a family. We all went to the readings, including children. There was a tribal sociability about the Project. At the time I had no writing or writing career. Now I love to write when I can but still no career. I was then the wife of Ted Berrigan ("The Elder"). He was part of the beginnings of The Poetry Project. Later, when I left New York, I used to get copies of *The World*, but there were so many poems and new poets, I couldn't keep track. Whenever I made a visit to New York I was happy to be able to go to readings in a place that was decent and which paid poets a few dollars. The last time I was there I heard Barbara Guest read. I have always liked her work and so it was a traveling gift. She read about blue and the sea and reminded me of H.D.

— SB

BERRIGAN, TED. 1934–1983. Born in Providence, Rhode Island. Author of *A Lily for My Love, Seventeen* (with Ron Padgett), *Bean Spasms* (with Ron Padgett and Joe Brainard), *Many Happy Returns, Double Talk* (with Anselm Hollo), *In the Early Morning Rain, Guillaume Apollinaire Ist Tot* (Marz Verlag, Germany), *Back in Boston Again* (with Ron Padgett and Tom Clark), *Memorial Day* (with Anne Waldman), *A Feeling for Leaving, Red Wagon, Clear the Range, Nothing for You, Train Ride, Carrying a Torch, Yo-Yo's With Money* (with Harris Schiff), *So Going Around Cities, In a Blue River,* and *The Sonnets,* among other works.

BERSSENBRUGGE, MEI MEI. Born in 1947 in Beijing, China. Author of *Fish Souls,* Greenwood Press, 1971; *Random Possession,* I. Reed Books, 1979; *The Heat Bird,* Burning Deck Press, 1984; *Empathy,* The Figures, 1987.

I spent a day with a painter at her house, here in New Mexico, an autumn day, and she told me about giving a talk to "the poets," meaning at St. Mark's. She told me the poets hadn't liked her talk, because she said there was no "I" in poetry. At St. Mark's! And then we talked about Walt Whitman. And I have decided The Poetry Project has as much and as little "I." Brilliant, potent, individual visions like shards. A devotion to world poetics without boundaries, a public work. Speaking, and hearing these voices, has been so precious to me.

— MB

BIJOU, RACHELLE. Born April 4, 1947, in New York City. Author of *Entrance to the City,* Buffalo Press, 1978. Published in *Transfer, The World, Telephone,* and the *Poetry Project Newsletter.*

BLACKBURN, PAUL. 1926–1971. Born in Vermont. Author of *The Cities,* Grove Press, 1967; *The Journals,* Black Sparrow Press, 1968; *Against the*

Silences, Permanent Press, 1980; *The Collected Poems of Paul Blackburn*, Persea Books, 1985; *The Accumulated Criticism of Paul Blackburn*, Bibliophasia Reprint Service, 1988.

BOUDIN, JEAN. Born in 1912 in Philadelphia. Author of *Miranda's Music*, Crowell, 1967; *Some of the Parts*, The Pomegranate Press, 1982.

I became a workshopper at The Poetry Project even before it took its name. Anne Waldman was sweeping up the junk at the old dilapidated ex-courthouse and was in charge. Joel Oppenheimer ran the poetry sessions . . . and gradually St. Mark's evolved. Filled with visions of song, dance, craft, and arts, it became a routine part of my dear friend Frances Waldman and my lives. A minimum of twice a week we walked crosstown from the West Village to Tenth and Second. We vied in workshops with Peter Schjeldahl, with Ron Padgett. There were occasional classes with Anne Waldman, with Lewis Warsh; clutching a poem in our hot hands, an opportunity always to read aloud and to hear what the others had to say. Some nights three in a class, some nights the room so jam-packed you could barely get in the door.

How happy I was when I gave my first reading; how special the New Year's Day nights which so many of us participated in and enjoyed through the small hours. For me, St. Mark's was a time of growing and feeling my poems do the same.

— JB

BOWLES, PAUL. Born in 1911. Author of *The Collected Stories, 1939–1976*, Black Sparrow Press, 1979; *Let It Come Down*, Black Sparrow Press, 1980; *Midnight Mass*, Black Sparrow Press, 1981; *Next to Nothing, Collected Poems, 1926–1977*.

BRAINARD, JOE. Born in 1942, in Salem, Arkansas, Brainard is both a writer and artist. Author of *Nothing to Write Home About*, Kulchur Press, 1970; *I Remember*, Full Court Press, 1975.

My involvement with The Poetry Project has been as a reader and a listener for God only knows how many (so many!) years that I can only think of it as an old friend: consistently there.

— JB

BRAUTIGAN, RICHARD. 1933–1984. Author of *Trout Fishing in America*, Four Seasons Foundation, 1967; *The Abortion, A Historical Romance*, Simon & Schuster, 1971; *The Hawkline Monster*, Simon & Schuster, 1974; *Dreaming of Babylon*, Delacorte Press, 1977.

BREMSER, RAY. Born in Jersey City in 1934. Author of *Angel*, Tompkins Square Press, 1967, and *Blowing Mouth/The Jazz Poems*, Cherry Valley Editions, 1978.

BRODEY, JIM. Born in Brooklyn, New York, in 1942. Author of *Fleeing Madly South*, Clothesline Editions, 1966; *Identikit*, Angel Hair Books, 1967; *Blues for the Egyptian Kings*, Big Sky Books, 1975; *Unless*, Jawbone, 1977; *Judyism*, United Artists, 1980.

Before the literary magazine of The Poetry Project, *The World*, got going, there was a little well-done book called *A Genre of Silence*, which I was lucky to be included in. I got into it because Ted Berrigan was so hot for it. We'd been hanging around the church since before the Project got going, and now it finally looked like something very big and very us was about to blossom. *A Genre of Silence* was just the first geyser of poetic flame, but it started a whole other gushflood of mimeo magazines. I can recall the excitement around the early Project office. I'd drop in and Ted and Anne and I would live poetry and write and talktalktalk.

Anne edited *The World* like a telephone book, fat and bulky big, with huge staples like spikes in the railroad ties of a new exploding-with-glee generation of mimeo maniacs. All of us got the poetry fever in big doses . . . endless scroll speeding down the Verbal highway out towards infinity, crisscrossed schools and styles rip by puncturing little pinpoint holes in the very velvet of gigantic pills. *The World* took it all and stuck it together and gave it a name and a face and a body that knew how to write itself back into History. The Poetry Project is not only a physical place, it's a force and a faith. Without it I'd never have had a career. I can think of about thirty other poets I can easily say that about as well.

— JB

BROTHERSTON, GORDON. Author of *Latin American Poetry, Origins and Presence*, Cambridge University Press, 1975; *The Emergence of the Latin American Novel*, Cambridge University Press, 1977.

BROWN, LEE ANN. Born in 1963 in Tokyo, Japan. A poet with recent work in *Cuz*, *Archeus*, and *Tyuonyi* magazines. She also makes experimental films. She was the Monday Night Series coordinator at The Poetry Project and is the editor and publisher of Tender Buttons books.

BROWN, REBECCA. Born in 1948 in Louisville, Kentucky. Author of *Three Way Split*, Telephone Books, 1979.

St. Mark's was a refuge for us in the late sixties and early seventies—free workshops for those of us who lived off air then, those days, when my Mott Street apartment cost eighty-nine dollars a month. St. Mark's provided us with opportunities to publish, and we also found out where the good parties were.

— **RB**

BROWNSTEIN, MICHAEL. Born in Philadelphia in 1943. Author of *Brainstorms*, Bobbs-Merrill, 1971; *Country Cousins*, George Braziller Inc., 1974; *Strange Days Ahead*, Z Press, 1975; *When Nobody's Looking*, Rocky Ledge Editions, 1981; *Oracle Night: A Love Poem*, Sun & Moon Press, 1982.

My involvement with The Poetry Project came about as a result of meeting dozens of writers and artists on the Lower East Side after I moved to New York in 1965. Only some of these people were connected to The Poetry Project in any direct sense, but many, including myself, gave numerous readings and performances at the church and, more importantly even, spent vast amounts of time with one another, at all hours of the day and night. The Poetry Project provided a context, a forum, a focus for what we wanted to say, which varied, from person to person, to a greater degree than we were perhaps aware of at the time. Collaboration, for instance—two or more poets writing all sorts of works together at the drop of a hat—was less important for me than for other poets, and yet the idea that we would take such a form seriously reveals the unique air of cross-pollination and openness prevailing in America in the sixties.

For me, the influence of The Poetry Project in the late sixties and early seventies was indirect, even if it was also intense. The greatest influence came not from any specific aesthetic, but rather from the personal example of certain poets whose lives were bound up with the Project then. Above all, I'm thinking of Paul Blackburn; and of Ted Berrigan, who at a crucial time in my life insisted on the importance of following the vision I had as a writer, rather than dutifully turning tail in order to obtain advanced degrees and a secure position on the academic ladder. He *insisted*—and anyone who knew Ted will vouch for the aptness of that word—that the most important thing I could do would be to remain true to that vision. What a crazy thing to tell somebody. But I believed him—and he was right!

— **MB**

BRUTUS, DENNIS. Born in 1924 in Horare, Zimbabwe. Author of *Knuckles Boots*, Northwestern University Press, 1963; *Letters to Martha*, Heinemann,

1968; *Poems from Algiers*, University of Texas, 1970; *A Simple Lust*, Hill and Wang, 1973.

A very useful and stimulating experience—most useful in the exchanges between poet and audience after readings (and between) on both subject matter and craft. It helps writers to discover *other* possible ways of writing and generates creative energy and confidence in both writers and potential writers.

— DB

BURROUGHS, WILLIAM S. Born in 1914 in Kansas City, Missouri. Author of *Nova Express*, Grove Press, 1964; *Naked Lunch*, Grove Press, 1966; *Exterminator!*, Viking, 1973; *The Last Words of Dutch Schultz*, Viking, 1975; *Cities of the Red Night*, Holt, Rinehart & Winston, 1981; *Queer*, Viking, 1985.

In 1974 I returned to the U.S. after many years living abroad. Before that time I had given a handful of readings in New York, London, and Chicago, but did not seriously consider the possibilities inherent in the live performance of my writing. That spring I was living in New York, and The Poetry Project invited me to read at St. Mark's Church. This event was a resounding success, both in terms of attendance and the audience's enthusiastic reception, and it marked the beginning of a period (1974–1984) when I gave readings all over the U.S.A. and Europe, sometimes as many as fifteen a year. I have always felt that the especially warm reaction of the St. Mark's audience that first night was the gateway to a new dimension in my life as a writer: to see at first hand, to meet and talk with, the people who actually read my works. It led to many contacts with interesting persons and projects; to various recording projects; and to a new sense of the sound of the words themselves as I continued writing *Cities of the Red Night, The Place of Dead Roads*, and *The Western Lands*.

— WB

BYE, REED. Born in 1948 in Plainfield, New Jersey. Author of *Some Magic at the Dump*, Angel Hair Books, 1978; *Erstwhile Charms*, Rocky Ledge, 1980; *Border Theme*, Z Press, 1981; *Heart's Bestiary*, Rocky Ledge, 1986.

FROM A JOURNAL, JULY 27, 1978

Morning see Edwin off at 21st Street; Jacob Burckhardt driving him to LaGuardia. I decide to go over to St. Mark's tomorrow for further roofing consultation re: the new church roof. Steve Facey expected back today. Back to Macdougal. Frances gets a call around 1:30 P.M. from Leandro Katz. Says he's just heard on the radio St. Mark's

Church is burning! Frances & I go over together in a cab. Smoke billowing from the steeple—all windows smashed, including the new stained glass. Now, pulling up to 2nd Avenue & getting out, we see most of the roof is gone. Beams all surely burned too. Flames shooting out through roof. Five years of Preservation Youth Project work going up in flames! Two days ago I was there on the roof as David Perez was beginning to use the oxyacetylene torch to weld holes in the copper gutter—I never considered the fire hazard. Now on TV news they say this is how fire probably started (maybe in welding new copper downspout sleeves from gutter). Roof, second floor of church & roof beams gone! The bell fell from the base of the steeple down to the entry & cracked.

Church 179 years old, oldest continually active one in the city. Built in 1799 on site of previous church, built, I think, in 1660 by Peter Stuyvesant as his family chapel. Second oldest public building in New York. Stuyvesant's "bouwerie" (Dutch for "farm") stretched from Broadway to the East River & from 5th to 17th Streets. It was a journey, they say, from this country estate to New Amsterdam Village near present Wall Street, bad roads and wolves, Indian attacks.

[Steve Facey and the Preservation Youth Project crew will begin to work again, first clearing out the burned & broken beams & rubble . . . Another 3 years until the (once more) newly restored St. Mark's would open its main sanctuary doors.]

— RB

CAPONEGRO, MARY.   Author of *Tales from the Next Village*, Lost Roads Press; *The Star Cafe*, Charles Scribner's Sons, 1990.

CAREY, STEVE.   Born in Washington, D.C., in 1945. Died in 1989. Author of *Fleur-de-Lis*, Blue Suede Shoes, 1972; *Gentle Subsidy*, Big Sky, 1975; *The Lily of St, Mark's*, "C" Books, 1978; *The California Papers*, United Artists, 1981; *A.P.*, Archipelago Books, 1984.

St. Mark's gives me a chance to hear what other poets are doing, gives me a sense of community that is invaluable. It also gave me a chance to teach what I was up to in a workshop. (1988)

— SC

CARROLL, JIM.   Born in 1950 in New York City. Author of *Organic Trains*, Penny Press, 1966; *Living at the Movies*, Viking, 1972, reissued by Penguin, 1982; *The Basketball Diaries*, Bantam, 1979; *The Book of Nods*, Viking/Penquin Books, 1986. Recordings include *Catholic Boy*, 1980; *I Write Your Name*, 1983.

CARTER, CHARLOTTE. Born in 1947 in Chicago. Author of *Sheltered Life*, Angel Hair Books, 1975; *Personal Effects*, United Artists Books, 1991.

It was my good fortune to find my way to The Poetry Project in 1973. It quite literally altered the course of my life, as I would never have had the courage to write had it not been for the generosity and kindness of people like Bernadette Mayer and Anne Waldman. As is the case with most people who connect with the Project, there will always be a little New York School in everything I do.

— CC

CATALDO, SUSAN. Born in the Bronx, New York, in 1952. Author of *Brooklyn-Queens Day*, Telephone Books, 1982.

In 1978 Susie Timmons took me to Ted Berrigan's last summer workshop. Jim Brodey belched through the entire workshop and Eileen Myles read a poem. I was in college studying journalism and Susie babysat my son Kris while I was in class. We talked a lot about poetry. Susie gave me *Dodgems* to read. Less than a year later I was publishing my magazine *Little Light* out of the Poetry Project office with much support from Maureen Owen, Ron Padgett, and Gary Lenhart, who ordered the paper and made sure the mimeo machine was in working order.

My first Wednesday-night reading was in 1980. I read with Diane Ward on the eve of Christmas Eve and there was a terrific party afterwards in my apartment. I remember Ted told me the line he liked best of all from the poems I read and I remember which one it was and I remember we were standing in my bedroom doorway and Ted was picking all the pill bottles off Steve's shelf and reading the labels. Harris Schiff does that too. I could go on. Bernadette Mayer asked me to teach the children's poetry workshop and I did it and those kids are teenagers now and we still teach each other poetry.

— SC

CEELY, JOHN. Born August 29, 1936, in Springfield, Massachusetts. Author of *The Country Is Not Frightening*, Neon Sun, 1976. Now translating fifteenth- and sixteenth-century Aztec Songs.

CERAVOLO, JOSEPH. 1934–1988. Born in New York City. Author of *Fits of Dawn*, "C" Press, 1965; *Wild Flowers Out of Gas*, Tibor de Nagy Editions, 1967; *Spring in This World of Poor Mutts*, Columbia University Press, 1968; *INRI*, Swollen Magpie Press, 1979; *Transmigration Solo*, Toothpaste Press, 1979; *Millenium Dust*, Kulchur Foundation, 1982. Forthcoming collected poems.

I've always felt free to read my earliest, my latest, or my most experimental poems at St. Mark's. The atmosphere was open and receptive, sometimes even exuberant. This provided the best encouragement and reinforcement of the work that a poet could ever ask for and actually get in return.

The weekly readings in that marvelous setting of St. Mark's Church gave me many invaluable experiences and opportunities to meet with other poets and hear the works of my contemporaries. Lasting friendships were formed and cultivated, making the isolation the poet can easily feel at certain times more bearable, and more importantly, to break through and go on with the work, no matter what.

Many times, I've read in the small back room and the same feeling pervades, as the people came crowding in. I've even had the opportunity to put on an art performance with the artist Mona da Vinci.

But the major thrill is someone coming up to you years later, telling you they vividly remember and will never forget a certain poem in a reading or performance that you had thought was lost forever. (1988)

— JC

CHUSID, MICHAEL. A writer living in New York.

CLARE, JOSEPHINE. Author of *Deutschland & Other Places*, North Atlantic, 1974; *Mammatocumulus*, Ocotillo, 1977.

CLARK, TOM. Born in Chicago in 1941. Author of *When Things Get Tough on Easy Street: Selected Poems, 1963–1978*, Black Sparrow Press, 1984; *Jack Kerouac*, Harcourt Brace Jovanovich, 1984; *Paradise Revisited: Selected Poems, 1978–1984*, Black Sparrow Press, 1985; *The Exile of Céline*, Random House, 1987; *The Allegory of a Poet's Life*, an autobiography of Charles Olson, W. W. Norton & Co., 1991.

My "involvement in the St. Mark's Poetry Project" is no less difficult to "assess" than any other sector of personal history. I mean, "assessment" is so *cold*—I want to say, hey, wait a minute, don't put that in the freezer yet! How would one's life be different if one hadn't lived it? Easier to stick to the facts, I guess, which for me are as follows: First encounter, spring 1967, when Ted Berrigan dragged me along to a reading in the parish hall. David Antin was reading. My chief memory is of Ted "digging the reading" while simultaneously insinuating a trained hand inside Martha Diamond's sweater. Great moments . . . also some not so great ones. Many times did I help to put up and take down the folding chairs for five dollars. One night, while waiting in the kitchen of the parish hall for Jackson Mac Low to get through a multi-tape-recorder "reading" that seemed to go on forever, Sam Abrams and I (we were supposed to put away the chairs) got into some bird-call imitations that made Jackson stop the "reading" and come back to bawl us out. Our casual assumption that we'd be accepted as part of the "context" made Sam and me twenty years ahead of our time, I guess (pardon the assessment). Later I got married in St. Mark's Church, with poets playing all the roles except that of the bride (who was a normal human being, and should have known better!). Who could assess a thing like that and live to tell about it? Present "involvement," uh . . . dormant, un-accessed, non-accessable.

— TC

CODRESCU, ANDREI. Born in 1946 in Sibiu, Romania. Author of *The Life & Times of an Involuntary Genius*, George Braziller Inc., 1976; *For the Love of a Coat*, Four Zoas, 1978; *Necrocorida*, Panjandrum, 1980; *Selected Poems: 1970–1980*, Coffee House Press, 1983; *Comrade Past & Mister Present*, Coffee House Press, 1986; *A Craving for Swan*, Ohio State University, 1986; *The Hole in the Flag*, William Morrow, 1991. Editor of *Up Late: American Poetry Since 1970*, 4 Walls & Windows Press, 1989.

I'm lucky. When I came to America in 1966, I landed in the Lower East Side of New York and found myself in a vibrant poetry scene. Ted Berrigan, who enjoyed my rudimentary English, taught me the poetry of the New World. It was a whole new kind of poetry: alive, anti-academic, bohemian, streetwise, political, open. In 1967 Anne Waldman published me in *The World*, and I read at St. Mark's. I have since lived in many places, but the New York School connection has been unbroken. There is a strong surrealist element in the New York School since Frank O'Hara, and I've done my best to keep up that end of it. The scene has always been a "conspiracy of inclusion," a notion of particular interest in the severely constricted decade of the eighties: it made room for sheer aliens like myself, and it joined easily with the poetries of black, Chicano, and performance poets. St. Mark's is a church in the most exalted sense: it's been possible to worship and celebrate one's possibilities there.

— AC

COLLOM, JACK. Born in 1931 in Chicago. Author of *Blue Heron & IBC*, Grosseteste Press, 1972; *Ice*, Lodestar Press, 1974; *Squirrel Tails*, Lodestar Press, 1976; *The Fox*, United Artists, 1981; *Moving Windows: Evaluating the Poetry Children Write*, Teachers & Writers Collaborative, 1985; *Arguing With Something Plato Said*, Rocky Ledge Editions, 1990.

I'd heard about St. Mark's for years, a rare center where most of the current poetry I admired was kept alive and kicking. I was invited to read and give a workshop in the early seventies, an (over) exciting trip. When I moved to New York City in 1980, St. Mark's became the single extra-domestic focus of my life, or almost domestic. I read there a few times, always the reading highlight for me. Later I conducted a weekly workshop for two years, leaving many fond and vivid memories. Almost weekly I attended readings, many so good as to be confusing, therefore educational. Various as hell, or ideas of it.

The night before my January 1981 reading I got drunk as a loon . . . lay there all day—no music, no food, nothing to drink more consoling than water. At 6 P.M. sharp I poured a waterglass of wine and put Jimmie Rodgers and Ewan MacColl (not concurrently) on the record player. Ate some toast, yodeled a little, drank another glass of wine. Walked over, listened to young Elio Schneeman give a reading of beautiful promise and no promises. Then I read. There's no point to this story, except that present in the audience were so many of the pairs of ears one wants to penetrate that the gratification was full, thus emptied out and led onward.

— JC

COOLIDGE, CLARK. Born in Providence, Rhode Island, in 1939. Author of *Space*, Harper & Row, 1970; *The Maintains*, This Press, 1974; *Polaroid*, Adventures in Poetry/Big Sky, 1975; *Smithsonian Depositions & Subject to a Film*, Vehicle Editions, 1980; *American Ones*, Tombouctou, 1981; *Mine: the one that enters the stories*, The Figures, 1982; *The Crystal Text*, The Figures, 1986; *Solution Passage: Poems, 1978–1981*, Sun & Moon Press, 1986; *At Egypt*, The Figures, 1988. Also: *Flag Flutter & U.S. Electric, Ing, Own Face, The So, Suite V, Quartz Hearts, Melencolia*, and *Mesh*. Most recently, *Sound As Thought: Poems 1982–1984*, Sun & Moon, 1990.

For me St. Mark's was, among other values, the beginning of when everything began to exist again on tape and everybody got a second chance at the sound. The feeling that every syllable, grunt, scream ever read or said or whispered in the interstices of the church continues to exist and, given several lifetimes, you could play it *all* back. This notion probably arises from the very fact that Larry Fagin and I spent years once editing years of St. Mark's readings from cassettes to reel-to-reel tapes. I may not have been to many of the readings, but I certainly heard most of them. Thanks to all the various machines nobody in the place ever seemed to be exactly expert at: that podium amp that usually provided backfires of heavy-metal accompaniment, and the later one that seemed to have a rock station aimed at it, and the ones that somebody forgot to turn on or reverse the cassette of or bring in at all. The labyrinthine wiring of poetry. The color of its oxide tracings. Ted Berrigan stood in front of the Parish Hall mantelpiece the first time I walked in, spring of 1966. That's where we started our part in the discontinuous but endless conversation. Someday I must find that tape.

— CC

COOPER, DENNIS. Born January 10, 1953, in Pasadena, California. Author of *Tiger Beat*, Little Caesar Press, 1978; *Idols*, The Sea Horse Press, 1979/ Amethyst Press, 1989; *Tenderness of the Wolves*, Crossing Press, 1982; *The Missing Men*, Am Here Books/Immediate Editions, 1982; *Safe;* The Sea Horse Press, 1984; *He Cried: Poems & Stories*, Black Star Series, 1984; *Closer*, Grove Press, 1989. Writer for *Artforum* and *Artscribe*.

When I was first getting serious as a teenaged writer in Los Angeles, most of my favorite poets were involved with St. Mark's in one way or another: Ashbery, Schuyler, Elmslie, O'Hara . . . just to start. To me the "New York School" was holy, and St. Mark's was literally its heart, its church. I longed for a local equivalent. When I got the chance to program readings and performances at the Beyond Baroque Literary/Arts Center in Venice, California, in the early eighties, St. Mark's was my role model.

— DC

CORBETT, WILLIAM. Born in 1943 in Norfolk, Virginia. Author of *Three New Poets*, Pym-Randall, 1966; *Columbus Square Journal*, Angel Hair, 1975; *St. Patrick's Day*, Arion's Dolphin, 1976; *Spoken in Sleep*, United Airlines, 1979; *Schedule Rhapsody*, Pig Press, 1980; *Runaway Pond*, Applewood Press, 1981; *Collected Poems: City Nature*, National Poetry Foundation, 1984; *Remembrances*, The Figures, 1987; *On Blue Note*, SUN Press, 1989.

The Poetry Project has treated this visiting fireman very well. I have read with Sidney Goldfarb, Fanny Howe (perhaps the first all-Boston reading at the church), Michael Palmer, and Charles Bernstein. All these gave me pleasure, but the reading I treasure most is the memorial evening for Philip Guston. Meyer Schapiro, a hero of mine, came up to me afterward, shook my hand, and said a word of thanks. This could only have happened at the Project, and I'm grateful for it. I do regret never making a New Year's Day marathon, and I wish I'd been in New York on Wednesday night, any Wednesday, just to be able to drop in and try potluck.

— WC

CORSO, GREGORY. Born in 1930. Author of *Bomb*, City Lights, 1958; *The Happy Birthday of Death*, New Directions, 1960; *Gasoline*, City Lights, 1968; *Elegiac Feelings American*, New Directions, 1970; *Herald of the Autochthonic Spirit*, New Directions, 1981; *Some of My Beginnings and What I Feel Now*, Aquila, 1982.

COTT, JONATHAN. Author of *City of Earthly Love*, Stonehill Publishing, 1975; *The Roses Race Around Her Name*, Stonehill Publishing, 1975; *Forever Young*, Random House, 1977; *The Ballad of John and Yoko*, Doubleday, 1982; *Charms*, Toothpaste Press, 1988.

CREELEY, ROBERT. Born in 1926. Author of *For Love*, Scribner's, 1965; *The Gold Diggers*, Scribner's, 1965; *As It Would Be Snow*, Black Sparrow Press, 1970; *Later*, New Directions, 1979; *The Collected Poems, 1945–1975*, The University of California Press, 1983; *Mirrors*, New Directions, 1983; *The Collected Prose*, University of California Press, 1988; *The Collected Essays*, University of California Press, 1989.

I've read at St. Mark's since its initiation and I can think of no audience more responsive or defining of what I'm trying to do as a poet. They hear with such specific, hip clarity, and that's immensely useful to anyone trying to work in this art. Otherwise, they've been immensely patient with me—like the time I seemed to have partially eaten the microphone at a rally for McGovern or inadvertently fallen briefly in with macho young companions in the foyer of the charming church from which unrecognized threat to existence the amply provident Ted Berrigan rescued me, so that I might then read in the proverbial "one piece." The point is that I always had a home there. There was always a light in the window.

— RC

CRUZ, VICTOR HERNANDEZ. Born in Aguas Buenas, Puerto Rico, in 1949. Author of *Snaps*, Random House, 1969; *Mainland*, Random House, 1973; *Tropicalization*, Reed Cannon & Johnson, 1976; *By Lingual Wholes*, Momos Press, 1982.

CURTIS, JACKIE (JOHN HOLDER) Born February 19, 1947, in New York City, died in 1985. Curtis performed in the plays *Scrooge, This Was Burlesque, The Life of Lady Godiva, Trojan Women, Les Precieuses Ridicules, A Modern Hamlet, Americka Cleopatra, I Died Yesterday, Miss Nefertiti Regrets, Tyrone X, Flop—A New Hit,* and *Champagne.* Author of the plays *Glamour, Glory, and Gold: The Life and Legend of Nola Noonan, Goddess and Star, Lucky Wonderful: Thirteen Musicals About Tommy Manville, Heaven Grand in Amber Orbit, Femme Fatale: The Three Faces of Gloria,* and *Vain Victory: The Vicissitudes of the Damned.*

Screenplays: *Flesh, Big Badge: The Brigid Polk Detective Story, WR—Mysteries of the Organism, Tits,* and *Women in Revolt.* Film appearances: *WR—Mysteries of the Organism, Flesh, Women in Revolt, Big Badge, Keyholes, The Audrey Hepburn Story, Underground U.S.A., The Sissy Upton Story,* and *Burroughs.* TV appearances: "The Joe Franklin Story," "The David Susskind Show," "Midday Live," "Straight Talk," "Free Time," "NBC Live," "Rhoda," "Saturday Night Live," and "Loud: An American Family." Author of many songs; *Wild Orchids,* poems forthcoming from Accent Editions; and his memoirs, with David Dalton, also forthcoming.

DAVIES, ALAN. A critic and a poet. He has published in numerous literary magazines. He is the author of *Active 24 Hours,* Roof, 1982; *Name,* This, 1986; *Signage,* Roof, 1987; and *Candor,* O Books, 1990.

DAWSON, FIELDING. Born in 1930 in New York City. Author of *An Emotional Memoir of Franz Kline,* Pantheon, 1967; *The Sun Rises Into the Sky,* Black Sparrow Press, 1974; *The Dream/Thunder Road,* Black Sparrow Press, 1978; *Krazy Kat & 76 More: The Collected Stories,* Black Sparrow Press, 1982; *Tiger Lillies: An American Childhood,* Duke University Press, 1984; *Virginia Dare,* Black Sparrow Press, 1985; *The Trick: New Stories,* Black Sparrow, 1991.

Like Black Mountain was, Naropa is, and St. Mark's was, is and will be what it will be because of the people there. Today it seems a pleasant, in-group club, members writing rave reviews of each other's work in the *Newsletter.* I wrote a letter to the editor critical of Maureen Owen's long poem "AE," saying she, like Jessica Lange, had a problem with her voice (meaning "AE" was the end of the prototypical Maureen Owen poem, and her new book, *Zombie Notes,* is a departure). Well, in the next issue of that publication a letter of rebuttal, nice and nasty, from some Si Shoo-Fly-Pie cat using my nickname like a caraway seed stuck in his teeth, and at the end, after his name, dig, Harvard University—!!! All this pissed me off, unh-huh, poets, writers, writers, but poets worse, such babies, so talking with George Butterick in Baltimore, not long after Si Cat's letter appeared, George said, "If he has to use Harvard, he's *nobody!*"

In the fall of 1969 I led a writing workshop at St. Mark's, and failed in the effort. Krim had gotten me the job, to replace him, but the group was very keen on him, and I went in with two strikes, drinking heavily in those days it seemed, those Monday nights, I would never get over being self-conscious, and be able to face a group, like this group, hostile but courteous. Clark Whelton and Bill Amidon were there, very direct voices, formed and encouraged by Krim, his vision and journalistic discipline whereas mine was and is poetic. I was pretty bad. That failure underlies much of what I recall and think about St. Mark's, because a sustained failure before a group is as memorable an experience as any I know.

One night while reading at St. Mark's, at the climax of a dramatic short story, a chunk of the ceiling fell to the floor injuring no one: cheers, laughter, applause. At Dr. Generosity's too (don't we miss that great place!!!), reading the high-school Peeping Tom passage from "The Mandalay Dream" that night, at the crucial, tingling suspense peak, the lights went out. Wonderful reactions. And again at St. Mark's on yet another night, reading a high-intensity story, "The Face in the Casket," a bolt of lightning turned the church flashbulb white, in a blast of thunder, everybody impressed, quite so: scared the wits out of me.

— FD

DENBY, EDWIN. Born in Tientsin, China, in 1903, and raised in China, Austria, and the United States. He attended Harvard and later studied dance in Vienna, after which he and a friend formed a dance company that performed in Germany from 1928 to 1933. After 1935, he lived mainly in New York. He died in Searsmont, Maine, in 1983. Poetry: *In Public, in Private*, The Press of James Decker, 1948; *Mediterranean Cities*, Wittenborn, 1956; *Snoring in New York*, Angel Hair/Adventures in Poetry, 1974; *Collected Poems*, Full Court Press, 1975: *The Complete Poems*, Random House, 1986. Fiction: *Mrs. W's Last Sandwich*, Horizon, 1972; *Scream in a Cave*, Curtis Books, 1973. Librettos: *The Second Hurricane*, Boosey & Hawkes, 1957. Criticism: *Dancers, Buildings, and People in the Streets*, Horizon Press, 1972; *Dance Writings*, Alfred A. Knopf, 1986.

DICKENSON, GEORGE-THÉRÈSE. Born October 23, 1951, in Napa Valley, California. Author of *Transducing*, Segue, 1985; *Striations*, Good Gay Poets, 1976. Editor of *Assassin; Black Rose: A Journal of Contemporary Anarchist Thinking;* and *Incisions: Prison Ward Poetry*.

DINE, JIM. Born in 1935. Author of *The Adventures of Mr. & Mrs. Jim & Ron* (with Ron Padgett), Grossman Viking, 1970; *Jim Dine Figure Drawings*, Harper & Row, 1979; *Jim Dine, November 6–December 5, 1981*, Pace Gallery, 1981; *Jim Dine, Five Themes*, Abbeville Press, 1984; *Jim Dine Drawings*, Abrams, 1985.

DI PRIMA, DIANE. Author of *Various Fables from Various Places*, G. P. Putnam's Sons, 1960; *War Poems*, Poets Press, 1968; *Revolutionary Letters*, City Lights Books, 1971; *Rising Tides*, Washington Square Press, 1973; *Selected Poems, 1956–1976*, North Atlantic, 1977; *Loba*, Wingbow Press, 1978; *Pieces of a Song: Selected Poems*, City Lights, 1990.

DLUGOS, TIM. Born August 5, 1950, in Springfield, Massachusetts, died in 1990. Author of *High There*, Some of Us Press, 1973; *For Years*, Jawbone, 1977; *Je Suis Ein Americano*, Little Caesar Press, 1979; *Entre Nous*, Little Caesar Press, 1982; *A Fast Life*, Sherwood Press, 1982.

DORN, EDWARD. Born in 1929. Author of *Collected Gunslinger (with Book IV)*, Wingbow, 1974; *Collected Poems, 1956–1975*, Four Seasons Foundation, 1975; *Hello La Jolla*, Wingbow, 1978; *Selected Poems*, Grey Fox Press, 1978; *Yellow Lola*, Cadmus Editions, 1981; *Abhorrences*, Black Sparrow Press, 1990.

DUBRIS, MAGGIE. Born in Georgia, grew up in the Southeast and Michigan. She has worked as a paramedic in New York City for the past eight years. The material used in this anthology has been taken from a book-length work in progress called *WillieWorld*. She is currently writing songs and playing guitar in two bands: Fleurs du Mal and The Dish That Flew Away.

EIGNER, LARRY. Born in 1927 in Lynn, Massachusetts. Author of *On My Eyes*, Jargon Society, 1960; *Air the Tress*, Black Sparrow Press, 1967; *Selected Poems*, Oyez, 1971; *The World & Its Streets, Places*, Black Sparrow Press, 1977; *Earth Birds*, Circle Press, 1981; *Areas Lights Heights: Writings 1954–1989*, Roof, 1989.

 Nice if the greater city, state, world could be as fine and hearthy a place. Nobody can put it more than miles or yards behind us, of course. And *The Wor(l)d* reaches out, and The Poetry Project. (There's also, for example, Lincoln Center, which I see by TV.)

                — LE

ELMSLIE, KENWARD. Born in New York in 1929. Author of *The Champ* (with Joe Brainard), Black Sparrow Press, 1968; *Motor Disturbance*, Columbia University Press, 1971; *City Junket* (a play), Adventures in Poetry/Boke Press, 1972; *The Alphabet Work*, Titanic Books, 1977; *26 Bars* (with Donna Dennis), Z Press, 1986.

 "At the Controls" evolved into "Eggs," a poem-song, which I set to music improvising at the piano, cutting the text slightly, and, eventually, adding new lines (smelly eggs/deli eggs)—in part because I tested the waters, at The Poetry Project, several times, evolving from talking poet to talking and singing poet, and finally to ninety percent singing poet by 1984. When record impressario Ben Bagley asked me to put together an LP for his "Visited" series, which honored theater song maestros such as Lorenz Hart, John Latouche, Cole Porter, and Ira Gershwin, I devoted Side B to poem-songs and two scenes from an opera, *Washington Square*. At The Poetry Project, again and again, I found an audience that welcomed these poem-songs, and, gradually,

I gained confidence—and know-how—as a singer, so that I could project the songs steadily enough to give the material a fair shake. One time, singing "Bang-Bang Tango," the audience response was so wild, I became terrified and fled from the podium. Another time, at a New Year's benefit, video cameras lunged as I sang "Who'll Prop Me Up in the Rain?" The performance, including my low-tech hesitance pressing the right button on my accompaniment (ghetto blaster), ended up in a performance poet movie, *Poetry in Motion*. I'll always be grateful to The Poetry Project for giving me a chance to sing, and to hone my vocal craft a bit, and for providing a gathering place for an audience that is a joy, for me, to perform for.

—KE

ELOVICH, RICHARD. Born in New York City in 1954. Director, writer, and performer.

EQUI, ELAINE. Born on July 24, 1953. She is the author of *Shrewcrazy*, Little Caesar Press; *Views Without Rooms*, Hanuman Books, 1989; *Surface Tension*, Coffee House Press, 1989.

FAGIN, LARRY. Born in New York in 1937. Author of *Parade of the Caterpillars*, Angel Hair Books, 1968; *Brain Damage*, Sand Project Press, 1971; *Rhymes of a Jerk*, Kulchur Foundation, *I'll Be Seeing You: Selected Poems, 1962–1975*, Full Court Press, 1978; *The List Poem*, Teachers & Writers Collaborative, 1991.

I worked at The Poetry Project through the early 1970s. The scene around St. Mark's was one of the reasons I moved to the neighborhood in '69. Socially, the spots to be were the Warsh/Waldman, Berkson, and Schneeman apartments, all within shouting distance of each other and the church. From 1967 through maybe '74, it was go-go-go with readings, dance events, concerts, art openings, workshops, little mags, collaborations, parties, bar scenes, weddings, friend-ships, gossip, suicides, breakups, and punch-outs. I enjoyed helping Anne Waldman schedule events and plan issues of *The World*. Then we'd struggle through the realities: a reader's (pitiful) check wasn't "ready"; a surly drunk or hideous crazy of indeterminate sex would rise out of the audience and begin to shriek; power blowouts; mimeo breakdowns; Kenneth Koch "shot" through the heart; tech screwups; endless egopsychobabble. Mostly we had fun. It was a night scene. After a "totally great" reading and a hasty clean-up, there'd be a party for the poets at Anne's or Bill's and after that maybe we'd move on to Ratner's to check out the soup and Barbara Rubin or S. J. Perelman at 4 A.M. Though there were a fair number of lame readings (failed experiments, bad timing, or just lame), *most* performances, astonishingly, ranged from fresh to sublime or "totally great." To mention a paltry few: the evening of goofy improvisation by Ginsberg and Koch; the resuscitation of Charles Reznikoff; John Wieners's dreamy "movie star" reading; René Ricard's electrifying "attack" poem on a stoic Steven Hall; and memorable star turns by Padgett, Corso, Berrigan, Creeley, Bremser, Elmslie, Coolidge, Bukowski, Mayer, Ashbery, and Lowell. Come July, we were ready for our summer vacations.

I became an editor (*Adventures in Poetry, Un Poco Loco*) at the Project. A reading was an optimum situation to screen material and get the writer to submit a piece on the spot. A magazine or pamphlet might be "run off" in the afternoon, collated during dinner (deli sandwiches to go), and distributed at that night's event.

Around 1975 I began to devote most of my time to Danspace, the dance program at St. Mark's founded the year before by Barbara Dilley and myself. We managed to survive the great fire in the summer of '78, and, while rebuilding was going on, Project and dance activities moved across the street to the music school. By then, the adolescence of the scene was over, and the era of grants and advisory boards had dawned.

— LF

FEIN, CHERI.   Born in 1950 in Philadelphia. Since 1978 she's been making her living as a freelance journalist. She has published three books: *Getting Into Money*, Ballantine Books; *How to Get Your Child Into Modeling and Commercials*, Fireside/Simon & Schuster; and *New York: Open to the Public*, Stewart, Tabori & Chang). Articles have appeared in *Connoisseur, Cosmopolitan, Glamour, Mademoiselle, Details, L'Officiel/USA, American Arts,* and *Camera Arts*. Book reviews (of poetry and literary fiction) have appeared in *The New York Times Book Review, Washington Post Book World, The Village Voice,* and *Vanity Fair*.

I came to New York City in 1971 to work as an apprentice to Kenneth Koch. That year turned out to be pivotal; in fact, I really don't think I'd have continued writing if it weren't for the time I spent with Kenneth and at The Poetry Project. At that time Kenneth was already a senior statesman of the New York School. He was my teacher and my mentor, but it was at The Poetry Project that I found poets of my own generation. It's where I gave my first reading and where I first published—through an all-day round-robin collaboration led by Bernadette Mayer. We wrote something, put it on a table, picked up someone else's piece, and continued it. By the end of the day, no one knew which parts they had written. The entire work was published through The Poetry Project; it was called *Unnatural Acts*. What energy! What creativity! Who wouldn't have been inspired.

— **CF**

FERRARI, MARY. Born in New Orleans in 1928. Author of *The Flying Glove*, Adventures in Poetry, 1973; *The Mockingbird and Other Poems*, Swollen Magpie Press, 1980; *The Isle of the Little God: Poems, 1964–1980*, Kulchur Press, 1981.

Kenneth Koch's poetry workshop at the New School began my career as a poet, and St. Mark's Poetry Project continued it. I was invited to give poetry readings at St. Mark's beginning in 1968, and numerous poems were published in St. Mark's publications. I taught a poetry workshop there in 1978, thanks to Maureen Owen's invitation. I've also attended many wonderful poetry readings, as well as Bill Zavatsky's memorable workshop. Poets met there, especially Anne Waldman, Larry Fagin, Maureen Owen, and Charles North, were responsible for bringing my poetry to the attention of other poets, through inviting me to give readings and/or by publishing my work. St. Mark's is a world in which I feel at home. When I heard about the fire in July of '78, I felt as if my house had been devastated.

— **MA**

FLANAGAN, BOB. Born December 26, 1952 in New York City. Coauthor with David Trinidad of *A Taste of Honey*, Cold Calm Press 1990; author of the infamous *Fuck Journal*, Hanuman Books, 1989.

FOX, ELIZABETH. Born in 1956 in Connecticut. Author of *Limousine Kids on the Ground*, Rocky Ledge Cottage Editions, 1983.

FRANK, PETER. Born in New York in 1950. Author of *The Travelogues*, Sun & Moon Press, 1982; *Something Else Press: An Annotated Bibliography*, McPherson & Co-Documentext, 1983; *New, Used and Improved* (with Michael McKenzie), Abbeville Press, 1987.

I was born a few blocks away from St. Mark's Church, a few years too early to be weaned on Poetry Project events. I made up for lost time during my college years, frequently attending readings and acquiring (with embarrassing voraciousness) Project publications. The Project activities and the circle of writers involved in them, however cliquish and hierarchical, always seemed congenial. I never allowed myself to feel part of the gang, junior league or otherwise, but

I was never discouraged from hanging around. Indeed, the Project folks rather indulged me.

As a critic of performance for the *Soho Weekly News* in the mid-seventies, I often found myself back at the church, witnessing acts of art sponsored by the Project in the same spirit of relaxed, convivial adventure with which it continued to present "straight" poetry readings. Professional concerns now lead me far from the church, but every once in a blue moon I return. The atmosphere is more tattered and more ecumenical than ever. When, after an event, the assembled multitude spill out for a beer at a nearby joint, I now run into East Village artists and gallerists, not just other poets. It is nice to think of the church and its Project as links between two surges of Lower East Side artistic vitality. Here's praying that St. Mark's links us up to the next surge as well.

— PF

FRASER, KATHLEEN. Born in Tulsa in 1937. Author of *Change of Address*, Kayak Books, 1966; *Each Next, Narratives*, The Figures, 1980; *Something (even human voices) in the Foreground, A Lake*, Kelsey St., 1984; *In Defiance of the Rains*, Kayak Books, 1989.

FRIEDMAN, ED. Born in Los Angeles in 1950. Author of *The Black Star Pilgrimage*, Frontward Books, 1977; *Lingomats*, Helpful Book, 1980; *The Telephone Book*, Telephone Books/Power Mad Press, 1980; *La Frontera*, Helpful Book, 1983; *Humans Work, Poems 1982–1986*, Helpful Book, 1988.

This was in May of 1972. . . .

After a reading there was a party at Lita Hornick's. I was very nervous about not having an invitation, but Bernadette and Jerry Rothenberg assured me I'd get in okay, so I went. I hate going places without invitations. Anyhow, it was a pretty good party, I guess, but the main thing was that that was the first night Bernadette and I kissed. I'd been in love with her since I started going to her workshop at The Poetry Project the previous October. So we kissed and made out all the way from Lita's house back to the 92nd Street Y, where I was living that year. I lived there?! Unbelievable!! Oh, but that was the night before. I want to get to the next day, the day of the marathon Gertrude Stein reading that Bernadette and Jerry were hosting at the church. I was supposed to get down there early to get some Stein books that only Lenny had copies of. Actually, they were Lenny's *and* Kathy's, but that's another saga. So I met Lenny. It was a beautiful warm spring morning. He was sitting on a bench out in front of the church waiting for me. He gave me the books and went off to work.

Then Anne came along to open up the church. We were going to start the marathon together. I was still all shaky inside from kissing Bernadette, and extra shaky being around Anne, who I also had a crush on. Anne said, "Go ahead and start, I have to go upstairs for a minute." So I sat down at a table in the middle of the church and began reading "Lifting Belly" from my copy of *Bee Time Vine*. "I have been heavy and had much selecting. I saw a star which was low. It was so low it twinkled. Breath was it." Then I felt a hand on my shoulder, Anne's. And it was so beautiful in the church, dark except for the sunlight streaming through the stained-glass windows—fire. And we were reading. Trading lines back and forth.

Anne: "I am with her."

E: "Lifting belly to me."

Anne: "Very nicely done."

E: "Poetry is very nicely done."

— EF

FYMAN, CLIFF. Born in New York in 1954. Author of *Stormy Heaven*, Misty Terrace Press, 1981.

In 1978 I attended a workshop at The Poetry Project at the suggestion of a friend, and it was wonderful. All week I looked forward to those Sunday nights in the parish hall. There was a religious fresco high on the wall, an old abandoned fireplace, tall windows looking out on the night, and the privacy of the silent church. The students got along well together, and we rolled on week after week through the fall, winter, and spring.

— CF

GALLUP, CAROL. Born in 1942.

GALLUP, DICK. Born in 1941 in Greenfield, Massachusetts. Author of *Hinges*, C Press, 1965; *The Bingo*, Mother Press, 1966; *Where I Hang My Hat*, Harper & Row, 1967; *Plumbing the Depths of Folly*, Smithereens Press, 1983.

Early memories about something that continued to change and have relevance for a long period of time are always liable to be colored by later experience.

The old family/neighborhood courthouse at Second Street and Second Avenue was a very creepy place. Wandering around the place . . . the holding cells and narrow staircases, dark and musty, were only slightly more sinister than the trashed-out courtrooms. Ted Berrigan held a totally outrageous workshop in a jury room. Anne Waldman's arrival, fresh from Bennington, was a bright occasion— one which still sparkles, like the sunlight, which arrived in shafts throughout the iron trellises covering the broken windows, sparkled with years of dust from the real Lower East Side. Just seeing Anne sitting in the "office" made it obvious we'd soon get a better place from which to create the Great Society.

— DG

GERSTLER, AMY. Born in San Diego in 1956. Author of *Christy's Alpine Inn*, Sherwood Press, 1982; *Early Heaven*, Madness Press, 1984; *White Marriage/Recovery*, Illuminati Press, 1984; *Martine's Mouth*, Illuminati Press, 1985; *The True Bride*, Lapis Press, 1986.

From here in Los Angeles, at least to me, St. Mark's was something to aspire to. A place with weight and history . . . the breeding ground, a mysterious spot with a holy-sounding name that had apparently provided a forum for some of my literary heroes. To certain of us "out here," both the work generated by these writers on the opposite coast, and even the sound of the phrase "the New York School," had a tantalizing ring. Having the opportunity to travel east to read (preferably during some exotic season Southern California doesn't provide, like "autumn") at "St. Mark's Church in the Bowery" (what was a bowery . . . skid row? a neighborhood from an old and now nearly incomprehensible TV slapstick comedy, where Bowery Boys romped? a flower bed?) seemed marvelous. Also frightening: to meet and shake hands with writers I'd admired, and to have to attach those pages I'd pored over in books to real faces and voices and clothes. To contend with subways and New York foreign currency: subway tokens. To read on the East Coast seemed a dream, to an audience of writers or their fans, followers, or descendants who sounded like they lived on Pepsi, coffee, speed, and potato chips, never slept, were impervious to cold but not love and grief, fucked around, fought, made scenes, loved painting, devoured books, and wrote themselves senseless. Dennis Cooper, a writer who showed me millions of things, also introduced me to "New York School" writers, and St. Mark's *Newsletter*, and numerous East Coast small-press magazines and anthologies. Those introductions provided me with what felt at the time like a direction. It also gave those of us who felt a lack of connection with the literary history on the West Coast another choice, another tradition to use, feel affinity with, plunder, embrace, or reject.

— AG

GILLFILAN, MERRILL. Born in Mt. Gilead, Ohio, in 1945. Author of *To Creature*, Blue Wind Press, 1975; *Light Years: Selected Early Work*, Blue Wind Press, 1977; *River Through Rivertown*, The Figures, 1982.

GINSBERG, ALLEN. Born in New York in 1926. Author of *Howl & Other Poems*, City Lights Books, 1956; *Collected Poems, 1947–1980*, Harper & Row, 1984; *Scenes Along the Road*, City Lights, 1985; *White Shroud: Poems, 1980–1985*, Harper & Row, 1986; *Annotated Notes to "Howl,"* Harper & Row, 1986; *White Shroud: Poems 1980–1985*, Harper & Row, 1986. (See Preface)

GIORNO, JOHN. Born in Tupelo, Mississippi, in 1935. Author of *Birds*, Angel Hair Books, 1965; *Manifestoes*, Ultramarine, 1967; *Balling Buddha*, Kulchur Foundation, 1970; *Cum*, Adventures in Poetry, 1971. Head of Giorno Poetry Systems.

GODFREY, JOHN. Born in 1944. Author of *26 Poems*, Adventures in Poetry, 1971; *The Music of the Curbs*, Adventures in Poetry, 1976; *Twelve Hundred & Four—The Unholy Crusade*, Oxford University Press, 1980; *Dabble: Selected Poems*, Full Court Press, 1982; *Where the Weather Suits My Clothes*, Z Press, 1984; *Midnight on Your Left*, The Figures, 1988.

GOOCH, BRAD. Born in 1952 in Kingston, Pennsylvania. Author of *The Daily News*, Z Press, 1977; *Jailbait and Other Stories*, Sea Horse Press, 1984.

GREENWALD, TED. Born in Brooklyn, New York, on December 19, 1942. Author of *Making a Living*, Adventures in Poetry, 1973; *Makes Sense*, Angel Hair Books, 1975; *You Bet!*, This Books, 1977; *Smile*, Tuumba Books, 1977; *Common Sense*, L Publications, 1979; *The Licorice Chronicles*, Kulchur Foundation, 1980; *Exit the Face*, The Museum of Modern Art, 1982; *Young and Restless*, Segue Foundation, 1984; *Word of Mouth*, Sun & Moon Press, 1985.

GRENIER, ROBERT. Born in Minneapolis in 1941. Author of *Sentences*, Whale Cloth Press, 1978; *Series (Poems 1967–1971)*, This Press, 1978; *A Day at the Beach*, Roof Books, 1985; *Phantom Anthems*, O Books, 1986; *Attention*, Institute of Further Studies, 1988.

    I've read at St. Mark's twice, through the grace of Bernadette Mayer and Bob Holman, on the second occasion lecturing also. I always felt it was something to do—i.e., that the circumstance required preparation and focus, being given the chance to show what I'd made in the interim and "say what I knew"—thus, much to look forward to, for me, as regards such expectation and the use and stimulus that means. Also, fun to actually be there, to eat and speak in such a forum of exchange amongst makers and friends. With the passage of time (something further to bring, to mean), "I'd do it again!"—gladly. Don't know any place like it, with that pitch of senses indicated.

— RG

GUEST, BARBARA. Born in North Carolina; lives in New York. Author of *The Blue Stairs*, Corinth Books, 1968; *Moscow Mansions*, Viking, 1973; *The Countess from Minneapolis*, Burning Deck, 1976; *Seeking Air*, Black Sparrow Press, 1978; *Biography*, Burning Deck, 1980; *Herself Defined: The Poet H.D. & Her World*, William Morrow, 1985; *Fair Realism*, Sun & Moon, 1988.

The Project and its unique environment are now a landmark in American Poetry. Ruled over by Empress Anne, who alleviated and adjucated the Poets' Wars, St. Mark's with its enveloping Project became a medieval haven in the din of furor that is New York City. Since its early founding, subsequent directors have carried the crown with panache and distinction. The Project offers hope to the young poets, and to the older poets a necessary provocation to accept the fertilization of outrageous talent.

— BG

HACKER, MARILYN. Born in the Bronx, New York, in 1942. Author of *Presentation Piece*, Viking, 1974; *Separations*, Alfred A. Knopf, 1976; *Taking Notice*, Alfred A. Knopf, 1980; *Assumptions*, Alfred A. Knopf, 1985; *Love, Death, and the Changing of the Seasons*, Arbor House, 1986.

HAGEDORN, JESSICA. Born in 1949 in the Philippines. Author of *Dangerous Music*, Momo's Press, 1983; *Breaking Silence: Asian American Poetry Anthology*, Greenfield Review Press, 1984; *Art Against Apartheid*, Ikon, 1986.

HAHN, KIMIKO. Born in 1955 in Mt. Kisco, New York. Author of *We Stand Our Ground* (with Gail Jackson and Susan Sherman), Ikon, 1986; *Air Pocket*, Hanging Loose Press, 1989.

1/1. 11 P.M. At the mike I know I am a poet and in NY. See the poets.

— KH

HALL, DONALD. Born in 1928. Author of *The Yellow Room, Love Poems*, Harper & Row, 1971; *The Toy Bone*, Boa Editions, 1979; *The Happy Man, Poems*, Random House, 1986; *The Ideal Bakery*, North Point Press, 1987.

HALL, STEVEN. Born in Scotland in 1957. Author of *Style*, Shell Press, 1980; *My Newport*, Shell Press, 1981; *White Rice*, Chelsea Copy, 1982; *Black Watch*, Shiny Books.

I got involved when I was a junior in high school visiting Larry Fagin on a regular basis from Wilmington, Delaware. I was happily corralled into collating issues of *The World* and *Adventures in Poetry*, during which I met various other poets. I felt from the beginning that a community already existed for me and dreamed of moving to the

Lower East Side and living in the Poetry Building (437 East Twelfth Street) and doing collaborations all day long with the artists, writers, and dancers who seemed to be everywhere—and it was almost like that when I did move to New York! Except the scene had become more polarized, contingent with the shift away from New York as the only center of cultural fashion.

My first reading was at the church, age eighteen, and I continued to attend readings and performances up to the present, sometimes helping out. I learned not only how to write from people I met there who were centered around St. Mark's, but how to bring it to life in a responsive circle, including talking back—my favorite readings were when Gregory Corso or Ted Berrigan were present and making hilarious remarks. The last time I saw Ted was outside St. Mark's after a reading—I was making some bitchy remarks about the poet performing that evening and Ted laughed and gave me a very powerful bear hug.

— SH

HARRYMAN, CARLA. Born in Orange, California, in 1952. Author of *Percentage*, Tuumba, 1979; *Under the Bridge*, This Press, 1980; *The Middle*, Gaz Press, 1983; *Animal Instincts*, This Press, 1986; *Vice*, Potes and Poets Press, 1986.

HARTMAN, YUKI. Born March 25, 1939, in Tokyo. Author of *A One of Me*, Genesis: Grasp Press, 1970; *Hot Footsteps*, Telephone Books, 1976; *Red Rice*, Swollen Magpie Press, 1980; *Ping*, Kulchur Foundation, 1984.

It has been a rewarding experience personally to have contact with many wonderful poets at The Poetry Project. May you thrive, my friends.

— YH

HARWOOD, LEE. Born in England. Author of *Title Illegible*, Writers Forum, 1965; *The Man with Blue Eyes*, Angel Hair Books, 1966; *The White Room*, Fulcrum Press, 1968; *Landscapes*, Fulcrum Press, 1969; *Freighters* from *Notes of a Post Office Clerk*, Pig Press, 1975; *All the Wrong Notes* (with Judith Walker), Pig Press, 1981.

HAWKINS, BOBBIE LOUISE. Born in Abilene, Texas. Author of *Own Your Body*, Black Sparrow Press, 1973; *Fifteen Poems*, Arif Press, 1974; *Frenchy and Cuban Pete*, Tombouctou, 1977; *Back to Texas*, Bear Hug Books, 1977; *Enroute*, Little Dinosaur, 1982; *Almost Everything*, Coach House Press/Longriver Books, 1982; *One Small Saga*, Coffee House Press, 1984; *My Own Alphabet*, Coffee House Press, 1989.

When I was just beginning to admit that I was a secret writer, when I was going slightly nutty from having concealed it so long, when I had published very little and needed to be taken seriously by someone other than my mother, I was given a reading at the St. Mark's Poetry Project. It mattered enormously to me.

Since then I've read at St. Mark's whenever I've had the chance and it continues to matter to me.

For those of us who live elsewhere and get to New York City only occasionally, a reading at St. Mark's guarantees a knowledgeable audience of writers and readers and friends.

There's no place like it.

— BLH

HEJINIAN, LYN. Born in California in 1941. Author of *A Thought Is the Bride of What Thinking*, Tuumba, 1976; *A Mask of Motion*, Burning Deck, 1977; *Gesualdo*, Tuumba, 1978; *The Guard*, Tuumba, 1984; *My Life*, Sun & Moon Press, 1987.

HELL, RICHARD. Born in Lexington, Kentucky, in 1951. Author of *Wanna Go Out?* (with Tom Verlaine), Dot Books, 1973. Recordings: *Blank Generation*, *Destiny Street*, and *R.I.P.* Founder, "Voidoids." Starred in the movie *Smithereens*. Editor of *Cuz* magazine; former booker of The Poetry Project's Monday-night reading series.

I bought a little tabletop offset press and began editing and publishing books and broadsheets and a magazine myself. That was about the most satisfying work I ever did. I remember reading in an interview with Anne Waldman (in the early seventies) her answer to a question about how one goes about getting published, which was something like, "Start a magazine!" (I can't help associating exclamation points and quotation marks with New York poetry—there must have been enough of them in those *World*s to build a house.) That was about the best, most honest advice for a lonely, determined young writer I'd ever heard. There's a great New York tradition of "doing it yourself" in the arts. Just bypass the big office buildings and go straight to the streets. Then the buildings come to you and you can do with them as you will.

I got a reputation as a writer through my rock 'n' roll lyrics. Then St. Mark's came to me (which is what I'd always secretly wanted). *The World* published some of my stuff (thanks to Ann Rower!), and I made them some money playing a benefit at CBGB's when the church burned down. (It was a great night, with Elvis Costello joining me onstage, Ted Berrigan calling out requests, and Allen Ginsberg dancing among the punks.) I ended up M.C.ing the Project's first two rock 'n' roll fund-raisers. I even gave my own Wednesday-night reading a couple of years ago. Poets have a hard life in this time and place, and The Poetry Project is one inspiring and indispensable means for helping to make the best of it.

— **RH**

HENDERSON, DAVID. Born in Harlem, New York; lives on the Lower East Side and in Berkeley, California. Author of *Felix of the Silent Forest*, The Poets Press, 1967; *Jimi Hendrix: Voo Doo Child*, Doubleday, 1978; *The Low East*, North Atlantic Books, 1981.

HOLLO, ANSELM. Born in Helsinki, Finland, in 1934. Author of *And It Is a Song*, Migrant Press, 1965; *Maya: Works, 1959–1969*, Cape Goliard/Grossman, 1970; *Finite Continued*, Blue Wind Press, 1979; *No Complaints*, Toothpaste Press, 1983; *Pick Up the House: New & Selected Poems*, Coffee House Press, 1986; *Outlying Districts*, Coffee House Press, 1990; *Near Miss Haiku*, Yellow Press, 1990.

First visit to St. Mark's, and reading, chaired by Paul Blackburn, in 1965. Wonderful time listening to Blackburn's amazing tape collection. Many subsequent visits and readings, for over twenty years now. The St. Mark's Poetry Project and its many offshoots (publications, records) have always seemed to me representative of what has been most exciting and important on the North American poetry scene during those decades, especially in the seventies, when it was a center, and program, for poetry readings unrivaled anywhere on the continent. While never a resident of New York City, I knew where to go when I was looking for poetry there: St. Mark's, *c'est tout*.

— **AH**

HOLMAN, BOB. Born in 1948 in LaFollette, Tennessee. Author of *Bicentennial Suicide*, Frontward Books, 1976; *The Rainbow Raises Its Shoulder/When a Flower Grows*, Chinatown Planning, 1979; *Tear to Open*, Power Mad Press, 1979; *Eight Chinese Poems*, Peeka Boo Press, 1980; *Sweat & Sex & Politics!* Peeka Boo Press, 1984; *Panic DJ*, VRI Theatre Library, 1987. Director of plays including: *The Cause of Gravity, The Wizard of Oz, The Gas Heart, Jet of Blood, Mayakovsky, a Tragedy, Clear the Range, Four Plays by Edwin Denby, The White Snake, Paid on Both Sides, Eat Rocks!* and *She Is in Tangier: Life and Work of Jane Bowles*.

The solitary poet sits in her garret and chews a nib . . . it's all a myth take! which the Poetry Project shatters: light through stained glass falls on an open book. "Community," buzzword of a decade ago, now verboten as (1985) NEA awards $20,000 each to 100-plus individual poets, and $15,000 to the Project that nurtures established poets, up-and-coming poets, poets-to-be, audience, and "community" (buzz) via all means possible (and im-).

Still, Project at 20 survives, site of the living tradition of poetry. Here, you don't have to dust before reading. A poetry that confronts, performs, demystifies, takes its clothes off, launches rockets to the unconscious, outlaws, in-laws, stop me quick lest I go on, Poetry Project, I love you, *aqui se habla poesia.*

1972: Attend New Year's reading, discover *World* is all poets. 1974–76: Attend Alice Notley workshop, receive education in inspiration; Ed Friedman's Monday nights invent performance poetry; with Bob Rosenthal write and produce all-poet productions of plays *The Cause of Gravity, The Whore of the Alpines, Bicentennial Suicide.* 1977–78: Lead two Poets' Theater Workshops; as CETA poet, write and perform *An Oral History of the Poetry Project,* discover there is no such thing as history. 1978–80: Coordinator, Monday-night poetry/performance series. 1980: Poetry Project Coordinator.

— **BH**

HOWE, FANNY. Born in Buffalo, New York, in 1949. Author of *Eggs*, Houghton Mifflin, 1970; *The Amerindian Coastline Poem*, Telephone Books, 1975; *Bronte Wild*, Avon Books, 1976; *First Marriage*, Avon, 1976; *Alsace-Lorraine*, Telephone Books, 1982; *For Erato: The Meaning of Life*, Tuumba, 1984; *Robeson Street*, Alice James Books, 1985; *Introduction to the World*, The Figures, 1986; *The Lives of a Spirit*, Sun & Moon Press, 1987; *The Vineyard*, Lost Roads, 1988.

Many years ago—in the sixties—I lived on St. Mark's Place and attended readings and, being a writing person, aspired to that platform. It seemed to attract and contain the best among us, and not always those most lighted or secure. As I feel that great work tends to emerge from obscurity and is made in hidden places, I continue to see the church project as sustaining those who dare to stay down. The fact that the Project is located in a setting which is dedicated to the message "Ubi caritas, ubi deus est," only increases the potent quality of the place. I have read there a few times—always in atrocious weather (hailstorms, blizzards, and gales)—and have had a wonderful audience nonetheless. Once, however, when I was giving a talk, no one came. Ron Padgett recorded me as I read to him alone, and then a mad woman roamed in from the wet streets and tore my talk to shreds. Another time I wore cheap high heels with plastic soles through the rain to get there, teetered through my reading, and fell flat on my back when I left the podium in my slick shoes. Maureen

Owen said it looked as if an angel had tackled me from behind. Perhaps one had—for getting too proud at being invited to read there.

— FH

HUDSPITH, VICKI. Born in Winterset, Iowa, in 1952. Author of *White and Nervous*, Bench Press, 1982; *Limousine Dreams*, Bench Press, 1986.

When I moved to New York via Tehran, Iran, it took a year or so to find The Poetry Project. I took Ted Berrigan's workshop and he later said to me over a bowl of rice pudding at the L&M Coffee Shop, "Hang around ten years and see what happens." So I did. The Poetry Project has been both an artistic and emotional refuge—challenging and supportive. "A room of one's own" filled with the kindest, toughest audience I've ever read my poems to. The Poetry Project is to poets what the Cedar Tavern was to painters in the fifties: a place to try ideas, change, and grow—artistically and personally.

— VH

HUGHES, HELENA. Born in Bristol, England, in 1951, came to the U.S.A. in 1978. Author of *Kiss My Lips*, Andrea Doria Books, 1979.

JONES, PATRICIA. Born in Forest City, Arkansas, 1951. Author of *New York: Poems*, Avon Books, 1980; *Knock Knock*, Bench Press, 1981; *Home Girls*, Kitchen Table Books, 1983; *Bessie Smith for Beginners*, Writers & Readers, 1987.

My two years of being program coordinator at The Poetry Project were exhilarating and frustrating! There are so many poets, so many divided loyalties, and so little time and money. I sometimes marvel that I was able to write well during my tenure, but I did. I enjoyed putting together (with Eileen Myles) oddball combinations of poets— seeing when their works and audiences meshed and when they didn't. My only regret was having only twenty people attend the wonderful program of noted Argentinian novelist Luisa Valenzuela and Afro-American poet Melvin Dixon. The thing aesthetically that got to me at the Project was (is) the Euro-centric vision whereby people can quote obscure Dadaist poets, but have no knowledge or concern with, say, the work of Chicano poets or obscure American regionalists or South American poetry. I'm not saying that the Project needs to look further than its own backyard, but we (American poets) need to realize more the tremendous intellectual basis that is New World–born and –raised. The Poetry Project, at its best, remains open and willing to take chances on contemporary poets. Sometimes it errs toward one set or other, but more than anywhere else, it remains passionately committed to the value of poets and their *living work*. There just is no way to describe how, after a day of hustling funders, calling the press, answering stupid questions, reading yet another request for a reading from yet another obnoxious person, one feels as if the whole church will crumble.

Poets are the true and honest historians of any and all cultures. To know what we are and, as well, who we are is the stuff of great poetics; the stuff of The Poetry Project.

— PJ

JORDAN, JUNE. Born in Harlem, New York, in 1936. Author of *Dry Victories*, Holt, Rinehart & Winston, 1970; *Things That I Do in the Dark: Selected Poems, 1954–1977*, Beacon Press, 1980; *Civil Wars, Selected Essays, 1963–1980*, Beacon Press, 1981; *Kimako's Story*, Houghton Mifflin, 1981; *Living Room, New Poems, 1980–1984*, Thunder's Mouth Press, 1985.

Reading at St. Mark's Poetry Project has always represented the chance to test my work among my true peers—competitive, serious poets intent upon making a difference through their art.

— JJ

KASHNER, SAM. Born in Brooklyn, New York, in 1954. Author of *Driving at Night*, Hanging Loose Press, 1976; *No More Mr. Nice Guy*, Telephone Books, 1979.

KATZ, VINCENT. Born June 4, 1960, in New York City. Author of *Rooms*, Open Window Books, 1978; *A Tremor in the Morning* (linocuts by Alex Katz), Peter Blum Editions, 1986; *Cabal of Zealots*, Hanuman Books, 1988; *New York Hello!* (with photographs by Rudy Burckhardt), Ommation Press, 1991.

Encouragement is, like, I'm reading at one of those huge St. Mark's New Year's benefit readings with hundreds of people in the audience. The five readers before me seem interminable, I'm so damn nervous. Finally, Bob Rosenthal is blurting something out about The Throbbers, and I step up, Allen Ginsberg smiling and saying, "Have a ball" as I trip lightly up. So I read this poem about Edwin Denby with tons of sentiment and emotion in it. I was sure it was the right thing to do, but it was a little weird in the days of "blue window flux towards minute" poetry. Then, in a natural speaking voice, but somehow resonating across that whole auditorium, I hear Ted say, "Right on, Vinny." He said it so calmly, but I heard it, and he knew I heard it. I stood there a moment shivering, then I walked off the stage.

— VK

KELLY, ROBERT. Born in 1935. Author of *The Loom*, Black Sparrow Press, 1975; *The Flowers of Unceasing Coincidence*, Station Hill Press, 1979; *Kill the Messenger Who Brings Bad News*, Black Sparrow Press, 1979; *The Alchemist to Mercury*, North Atlantic Books, 1981; *The Scorpions*, Station Hill Press, 1985; *A Transparent Tree: Fictions*, McPherson & Company, 1985; *Doctor of Silence*, McPherson & Company, 1988.

KIM, ANN. Born in Boston. Author of *18 Poems*, Shell, 1980; *A Color Refractory*, forthcoming.

KNOWLES, CHRISTOPHER. Author of *Typings*, Vehicle Editions, 1979.

KOCH, KENNETH. Born in 1925 in Cincinnati. Author of *The Art of Love*, Random House, 1975; *The Burning Mystery of Anna in 1951*, Random House, 1979; *Days and Nights*, Random House, 1982; *Selected Poems, 1950–1982*, Random House, 1985; *On the Edge*, Penguin, 1986. His educational works include: *Wishes, Lies, and Dreams: Teaching Children to Write Poetry; Rose, Where Did You Get That Red?: Teaching Great Poetry to Children; I Never Told Anybody: Teaching Poetry Writing in a Nursing Home; Sleeping on the Wing: An Anthology of Modern Poetry* (with Kate Farrell).

What I've always liked best about reading my poems at St. Mark's—and also somewhat dreaded, but I figured it was good for me in the end—is knowing I had an audience, or at least part of an audience, who were crazy about poetry, kept up with what was going on in it, and, in many cases, wrote it themselves. Paul Valéry said it's not true, as some say, that not many people like poetry; quite a lot like it. What is true, he said, is that there are very few people for whom poetry is necessary. St. Mark's has always had more of that precious few there listening than any other place I've known. In that way alone it's been a means of raising standards, of making some poems better than they'd otherwise have been, even of causing certain poems to exist. I imagine I'm not the only poet who's worked hard on a poem or written a new one because of having a reading there, or who's gotten some new ideas from having done so. The good effects it has, of course, are greatly magnified by the remarkable consistency with which St. Mark's has kept audiences, and poets, coming year after year after year.

— KK

KOCHAN, MUSHKA. Born February 6, 1950, in Los Angeles. Winner of First Place, Mid-Atlantic, National Association of Teachers of Singing—mezzo soprano—in 1988. Currently working as a teacher of music and composing "Song Cycles" of American poets. Author of *Time on Two Feet*, Bench Press, 1980.

KRAKAUER, DANIEL. Born in 1923 in Beuthen, Germany. Author of *Poems*, Frontward Books, 1979.

Because of all the splendid things it offered . . .

As I got more turned on, I became more actively involved. I began to give readings myself—at the Project and other locations. I participated in a few performances, became an actor of sorts. And four of my own plays were produced—three at the Project, the last one, *Jack Who Yawned*, in May 1986, directed by Johnny Stanton.

Moreover, it was the Project that gave me the opportunity to conduct a poetry translation workshop (I had a lot of fun doing this while participation fluctuated between two and nine poets), as well as to edit a translation issue of *The World* (#35). At the time I thought it was the best thing I had ever accomplished in the field of poetry.

— DK

KRAUS, CHRIS. A writer and filmmaker who has had a one-woman show at The Anthology Film Archives in New York City.

KRAUSS, RUTH. Born in Maryland in 1911. Author of *Under Thirteen*, a Sharp Book, distributed by Bookstore Press; *This Breast Gothic*, Bookstore Press; *There's a Little Ambiguity Over There Among the Bluebells*, Something Else Press; *If I Were Freedom*, Toothpaste Press.

It seems, looking back, that I was mostly trudging through blizzards on lower Second Avenue to get to the workshops of Joel S. and Joel O. held in that dark building among smells of garbage and bourbon.

— RK

KRAUT, ROCHELLE. Born January 30, 1952, in Germany. Author of *Circus Babys*, Frontward Books, 1975. Work has appeared in *Up Late*, *Cuz*, *Long Shot*, *Little Light*, *The World*, *Tangerine*, *Mag City*, *432 Review*, and *Bombay Gin*.

In 1973, I moved to New York City and began to attend readings at the Project. One of the most important "messages" I tuned in on was that it was possible to really live the life of a poet, writer, artist. Every poet who read reinforced that idea: that it was possible and it was sane and it was a reasonable, practical goal!

Younger writers were growing up there. A new community. Wednesday-night readings of "established" writers gave courage that it was possible to live as a writer . . . support in numbers that continues now against economic realities. While I comb the "normal job" market to make ends meet, I know where I belong, whatever I may have to do at times. Most important in all this was the listening, the oral development of my "ear." Now I can hear things! Providing amusement, pleasure, and music every day.

— RK

KUPFERBERG, TULI. Born September 8, 1923. Poet, songwriter, cartoonist. Founding member of the Fugs. Thirty-five booklets of poetry and cartoons, including *Kill for Peace (Again)*. He has a recent record album entitled *Tuli and Friends*.

KUSHNER, BILL. Born in New York City in 1931. Author of *Night Fishing*, Midnight Sun, 1976; *Head*, United Artists Books, 1986.

I took a workshop there with Lewis Warsh & think
It was 1974 it was either that or commit suicide I
Was so depressed & it was free I was broke it was
A cool casual place to go & he kept asking of us
"What did you do today?" week after week I
Think it was Friday nights we met & I'd think
What has doing this today thing got to do with any
Thing to do with POETRY? well having been taught in
The great public school system of the late 30's, early
40's which said poetry came from The Beauty School
Of Beautiful Thoughts & sorry but my thoughts were
Well not all that beautiful mostly about hot sex
& movies I loved & still do & men's rooms & being
& walking along & looking at all this cracked beauty
But never really connecting myself as being a part
Of all that no I was in my mind outside & apart &
Eventually tho I saw a lot of great poetry readings
There & began feeling less of a stranger among stranger
Strangers & Lewis usually wearing these great looking
Shirts spoke about Edwin Denby "this guy he writes
These great sonnets" & so I read them & read them & I
Thought "Amazing!" & I still do that was true true love
& it still is but I perhaps realized more & more
That for a neurotic gay balding guy like huh who me?
That being in poetry was not such a bad place to be that
There was a place for me like a line of dancing Rockettes
There we all are kicking all our heels high up
From Walt Whitman to little me & all you guys/ladies in
Between you know who you are & so there I became a poet
Yes even more important is to be one's self, true
The finding of that self. That's what the poem is

About always about. "Something happened to you, Bill"
Lewis said at the end of one class & he meant I guess he
Finally liked a poem I'd wrote, ahh that sweet night
It was like that moment in *The Miracle Worker*, remember?
When little blind dead mad Helen suddenly realized what
The hell all that writing on her hands was is all about
Wow! I know what this word means & that! Wow!
Today I try to write like a good boy/girl scout every day
In every way because that way you're not so that involved
With this business of having to "say something" ugh if
Something's there it says itself, you do it by doing it
This weird person in space in motion in body motion in
Mind emotion & so you simply say this is what I did today
I am doing right now or dreaming of doing these forbidden
Things to you there right now at this very precious moment
You put your life in your hands & you write it down
& if someone says that's Edwin in your poem or that's Frank
That's Walt or Wieners or Waldman that's quite all right
In fact that's great because I truly feel that's a part
Of it what I'm saying & of whatever else the poem is doing
These lives they still live reside with me I speak proudly
In these tongues these voices they are me, I do proudly put
You & you in this poem of mine for all the cruel world to see

— **BK**

KYGER, JOANNE. Born in 1934 in Vallejo, California. Author of *Joanne*, Angel Hair Books, 1970; *Place to Go*, Black Sparrow Press, 1970; *All This Everyday*, Big Sky, 1975; *The Wonderful Focus of You*, Z Press, 1980; *Mexico Blond*, Evergreen Press, 1981; *Going On: Selected Poems, 1958–1980*, National Poetry Series, 1983; *Phenomenology*, Institute of Further Studies, 1990.

LALLY, MICHAEL. Born in New Jersey in 1945, lives in California. Author of *Attitude*, Hanging Loose Press, 1982; *Hollywood Magic*, Little Caesar Press, 1982.

LA LOCA. Author of *The Mayan*, Bone Scan Press, 1988, and *Adventures on the Isle of Adolescence*, City Lights, 1989.

LAUTERBACH, ANN. Born September 28, 1942, in New York City. Author of *Vertical, Horizontal*, Seafront Press, 1971; *Book One*, Spring Street Press, 1975; *Many Times, But Then*, Texas University Press, 1979; *Later That Evening*, Jordan Davies, 1981; *Closing Hours*, Red Ozier Press, 1983; *Sacred Weather*, The Greenfell Press, 1984; *Greeks* (with Jan Groover and Bruce Boice), The Hollow Press, 1984; *Before Recollection*, Princeton University Press, 1987.

LENHART, GARY. Born in Newark, Ohio, in 1947. Author of *Bulb in Socket,* Crony Books, 1980; *One at a Time,* United Artists Books, 1983.

In the mid-seventies I attended workshops led by Ted Berrigan, Alice Notley, and Jim Brodey. I learned a lot about poetry and was introduced to many poets, old and young, living and dead, who for various reasons hadn't made it into the academic canon. I learned how poets worked, how they talked about their work, how they fit their dedication to an unremunerative calling into their lives. And I learned a lot about competition. Most important, I learned that poems were social acts, to be received as they were offered, that no matter how talented, you must remain vulnerable to inspiration.

I accepted eagerly when Ron Padgett and Maureen invited me to work in the office as a jack-of-all-tasks, and was pleased to continue when Bernadette Mayer and Bob Holman took over. Subsequently, I coordinated the lecture series for two years. So for seven years I was at the church three or four times a week, and many days. When I wrote reviews, they were for the *Newsletter.* My first two books of poems were mimeographed on the Project machine. All this has obviously affected my writing. Principally, I discovered a community of poets whose shared views help dispel the paranoia that often is attached in the U.S. to being a poet without money or academic affiliation.

— GL

LESNIAK, ROSE. Born in Chicago in 1955. Author of *Young Anger,* Toothpaste Press, 1979; *Throwing Spitballs at the Nuns,* Toothpaste Press, 1980.

After college and at the advice of Ted Berrigan, I moved to New York City to pursue my artistic dream of becoming a poet. This was in 1975.

When I arrived at St. Mark's, the community of poets was like a family. Not only did we write together, but we played together. We would meet at someone's house and work on collaborative poems. We would gather at St. Mark's readings to hear each other or new poets.

I doubt very much I would have continued writing if I wasn't involved in The Poetry Project.

— RL

LEVINE, STEVE. Born in Brooklyn, New York, in 1953. Author of *Three Numbers* (with Jim Hanson), Toothpaste Press, 1976; *A Blue Tongue,* Toothpaste Press, 1976; *Pure Notations,* Toothpaste Press, 1981; *The Cycles of Heaven,* Coffee House Press, 1987.

As an individual in America, my education has been for the most part formal, though any degree I've received in this regard is not worth mentioning. As an American poet, or just a poet, my education is, as they say, "ongoing," and involves the reading of books and signs, the conversations of strangers, enemies, friends, breathing and seeing. The awards I've received are the poems I've written. All citations have been for exceeding the limit.

— SL

LEWIS, JOEL. Born May 26, 1955, in Brooklyn, New York. He is a life-long New Jerseyan currently in residence in Hoboken. Author of *Three Works*, Gaede's Pond Press, 1983; *Entropia*, Gaede's Pond Press, 1986. New Jersey State Council of the Arts Fellow, 1983–84. New Jersey's unofficial poetry goodwill ambassador to the world.

LIPPARD, LUCY R. Born in New York City in 1937. Author of *Overlay: Contemporary Art and the Art of Pre-History*, Pantheon, 1983; *Get the Message*, E. P. Dutton, 1985.

The Poetry Project was/is unique in bringing together "poetry" and "the real world." (Is there really a difference?)

— LRL

LOWENSTEIN, TOM. Born in 1941 in Buckinghamshire, England. Author of *The Death of Mrs. Owl*, Anvil Press, 1977; *Booster, A Game of Devination*, The Many Press, 1977; *The Shaman Aningatchag*, The Many Press, 1981; *Ancient Land: Sacred Whale: Four Essays on the Tikigag Coast as Experienced Through Tradition*, North Slope Borough, 1987; *Filibustering in Samsara*, The Many Press, 1987.

LYONS, KIMBERLY. She is the author of three chapbooks: *Six Poems*, Lines, and *Strategies*, Prospect Books, and *In Padua*, St. La Zare Press. She was program coordinator for The Poetry Project, St. Mark's Church, from 1987 to 1991.

MACADAMS, LEWIS. Born in San Angelo, Texas, in 1944. Former editor, *Mother Magazine*. Author of *Live at the Church*, Kulchur Foundation, 1977; *Africa and the Marriage of Walt Whitman and Marilyn Monroe*, Little Caesar, 1982. Co-director *What Happened to Kerouac?* 1987; producer and director of the *Battle of the Bards* video, Lannan Foundation, 1990, and other Lannan archival videos.

Perhaps because of Anne's longtime involvement with it (or Allen G's?), I've always considered St. Mark's the Mother Church of American Poetry. I named my comeback (from hepatitis) book *Live at the Church* because I thought of the church as glamour, high energy, intrigue, social life, and drama; and I always liked to be associated with it.

One of my best memories of the church would have to be the fine spring day the Episcopalian Diocese of New York rededicated the church. Larry Fagin, Anne Waldman, and I planted three fruit trees by the churchyard north fence in honor of three poets who had been St. Mark's parishioners (in the sense that they lived in the neighborhood and inspired us all poetically): W. H. Auden, Frank O'Hara, and Paul Blackburn. Then we each read a poem by one of them. I can't remember what poems Larry and Anne read of Blackburn's and Auden's, but I happily read O'Hara's "Aus Einem April" ("We dust the walls/And of course we are weeping larks . . ."). I remember the wind rattling through the leafy trees, everybody dressed up like at a reunion, and the archbishop of New York in full regalia spritzing holy water on the side of the church with his wand.

— **LM**

MCCLURE, MICHAEL. Author of *Hymns to St. Geryon & Dark Brown*, Grey Fox Press, 1980; *Josephine the Mouse Singer*, New Directions, 1980; *Fragments of Perseus*, New Directions, 1983; *Specks*, Talonbooks, 1985; *The Beard & Victims: Two Plays*, Grove Press, 1985; Selected Poems, New Directions, 1985; *Rebel Lions*, New Directions, 1991.

MACINNIS, JAMIE. Born in 1943 in San Francisco. Author of *Hand Shadows*, Adventures in Poetry, 1974; *Practicing*, Tombouctou, 1980.

MAC LOW, JACKSON. Born in Chicago in 1922. Author of *Bloomsday*, Station Hill Press, 1984; *The Virginia Woolf Poems*, Burning Deck, 1985; *Representative Works, 1938–1985*, Roof Books, 1986; *Pieces O' Six*, Sun & Moon Press, 1987.

As a continuation of the reading and discussion series at the Tenth Street Coffeehouse, Les Deux Megots, and Le Metro, which began in 1960, the St. Mark's Poetry Project has given me many opportunities to share my work both with other writers, musicians, and artists, and with a wider audience. It has also allowed me to hear the work of a great variety of other writers, as well as to witness various types of performances, and in the Talks series organized by Charles Bernstein, to take part in far-ranging discussions both of writing and other arts, and of their relations to wider social concerns. Its greatest virtues have been its unashamed eclecticism and the tremendous *variety* of the voices, "schools," and approaches to the arts that have been represented in its programs. It thus can afford the pleasures of surprise as well as being a forum where those representing many different tendencies can mingle and interact.

— **JM**

MALANGA, GERARD. Born in the Bronx, New York, in 1943. Author of *Chic Death*, Pym Randall Press, 1971; *Ten Years After/The Selected Benedetta Poems*, Black Sparrow Press, 1977; *Angus Maclise Checklist, 1959–1979*, DIA Art Foundation, 1981; *Autobiography of a Sex Thief*, Lustrum Press, 1984; *Radar: Gerard Malanga in His Time*, 1984.

In 1971 Ted Berrigan, during an all-day in the streets of New York photo session, confided in me that he noticed that the majority of those poets associated with the St. Mark's poetry scene were envious of "my life existing without me" in the social and media strata of New York night life that had somehow eluded them, and that they had formed a competitive flank to keep me out of certain situations that would have been beneficial in subsidizing my existence as a poet on a full-time basis. What these poets failed to see was my ability to actually transcend all the glitz and remain humanly centered through it all.

Whereas I could always count on Ted and, to a greater extent, Anne Waldman to champion my work in whatever projects they were involved with from time to time, I could not expect the same respect from other poets (some of whom were in positions of power). Elsewise, luckily for me I'm blessed with talents in the visual arts in that I don't have to rely solely on the poetry world for my bread and butter. If I had, I would've been extinguished a long time ago.

— GM

MALMUDE, STEVE. Born on January 4, 1940, in New York City. Author of *Catting*, Adventures in Poetry, 1972; *From Roses to Coal*, Shell Press, 1980. His work has appeared in *The World, Adventures in Poetry, Sun, Telephone, The Harris Review*, and *Un Poco Loco*.

I went to The Poetry Project when I had poems. I'd give a reading and spot on a few faces. This was what I wrote for. I rhymed a lot; it meant good luck, the election of lines and stanzas. And rhyming prolonged composition, nights with the feeling of the audience all to myself. It was a matter of pacing delicious cycles without hangovers, climbing and coasting down highs safely. I wanted to be a durable example of that fragile culture.

Oh, I've stomped out on poems, mine and others' when they disappointed the focus, wasted the time. But when the poem is great, so is the party afterwards. There are many, many works about this, and I hope you get to read them.

Love to Anne for her protection, to Larry for his company, and to all the poets for their works and ears.

— SM

MASTERS, GREG. Born in Passaic, New Jersey, in 1952. Author of *In the Air, Remember I Did This For You*/Power Mad Press, 1978; *My Women and Men, Part Two*, Crony Books, 1980.

I first came around The Poetry Project in 1975 and was immediately drawn in 'cause here was a place where people were writing poems with The Kinks in them, workshops were informal, so comfortable (you didn't have to attend every week) and charged and enthusiastic, and then, with Gary Lenhart, I was offered the job of setting up chairs, microphones, and tape recorder for the readings. Did that for practically every reading for three years, became administrative assistant, and then Ron Padgett, director at the time, asked if I'd like to be *Newsletter* editor. I said, "Let me think about it over tonight," and a minute later said yes. I had fun with that for three years.

— GM

MATHEWS, HARRY. Born in New York in 1930. Author of *The Sinking of the Oradek Stadium*, Harper & Row, 1975; *Trial Impression*, Burning Deck, 1977; *Country Cooking and Other Stories*, Burning Deck, 1980; *Cigarettes*, Weidenfeld and Nicolson, 1987; *Armenian Papers: Poems, 1954–1984*, Princeton University Press, 1987.

Heraclitus wrote that one bathes in the same river but never in the same waters. I can imagine as corollaries to his statement that it is because the waters are never the same that one is always refreshed by them; and that should the river dry up, one would weep with exasperated regret. For a poet in New York (for this poet certainly), St. Mark's for twenty-five years has been a fountain of rejuvenation and recommitment.

— HM

MAYER, BERNADETTE. Born in Brooklyn in 1945. Author of *Story*, 0 to 9, 1968; *Moving*, Angel Hair Books, 1971; *Memory*, North Atlantic Books, 1976; *Studying Hunger*, Big Sky/Adventures in Poetry, 1976; *Poetry*, Kulchur Foundation, 1976; *Eruditio ex Memoria*, Angel Hair Books, 1977; *The Golden Book of Words*, Angel Hair Books, 1978; *Midwinter Day*, Turtle Island Foundation, 1982; *Utopia*, United Artists, 1983; *Sonnets*, Tender Buttons Books, 1990.

I gave my first reading at The Poetry Project nearly twenty-five years ago. Both Anne Waldman and Joel Oppenheimer encouraged me to do it, for which I may never forgive them. I had felt that writing the poetry was difficult enough without having to stand up in front of a sophisticated audience at a wooden podium in an actual church and read it. It made me very nervous to read the poems that my teacher at the New School for Social Research, Bill Berkson, had just told me sounded like Gertrude Stein before I had even heard of her. Later I worked as an assistant in the office, running off the mimeographed *Newsletter* when Billy McKay was editor. He and I were both efficient and graceful in our tasks, though we received much criticism, as has been the consistent fate of workers at The Poetry Project, perhaps because of the combination of its sublime importance with its some-what communal modesty. Also, many of the poets involved were too inspired and were being enabled to write, speak, and even publish and teach, and too, they were having too much fun. Very lively uses of the office mimeo machine were being made, including, of course, the frequent and highly democratic publication of *The World,* a magazine which at the time I felt was a bit old-fashioned.

Artists and lovers of poetry of all kinds became involved with The Poetry Project, and sometimes we poor poets would find ourselves entering some of New York's most glamorous spheres. Once I was invited to a dinner party where all the knives and forks and spoons were made of gold! It was around this time that Harris Schiff and I decided to foment an anarchist revolution at the Project, but he got fired and/or disappeared. Group readings for political causes and moments and organized and disorganized political activity were happening all the time, both at the Project and in the larger church. In 1971 I began to teach a workshop at St. Mark's which I called Experimental Writing. During the second session Steve Malmude took issue with me about introducing Wittgenstein. Some years later our workshop became a group with a revolving leadership and it was around that time we introduced an interdisciplinary lecture series. As I had already found that my work at the Project enabled me to correspond with practically any living poet, so we found that other kinds of experts were inspired to come to talk to a finitely assembled group of poetry students.

When our workshop was concluded, I moved to the country and after five years there I received a phone call from Ron Padgett, asking if I would consider the job of Poetry Project director, which I did become for four years, working with Bob Holman, who would agree that no such task can be conceived of by any current CEOs. Although here was one of the most worthwhile tasks in the universe, there was the embarrassment among other poets of running a poetry "institu-tion"! Once Allen Ginsberg came into the office and asked what I was so busy at and I had to admit to him I was working on the membership drive. Suddenly it seemed there was nothing sublime about it all, yet the incessant readings in the old church building, where even the newly plastered walls are so absorbent of so much poetry, proved that not to be so, and The Poetry Project's historically non-academic variousness makes it like an ideal public school—no privilege and lots of measure. (In fact, despite its otherwise pretty formal importance now, it's the Project's inadvertent and also downtrodden sort of role to hold the cup of measure to be filled with non-measure, if you will. Nobody else is going to do it right!) It was while I was working as the director of the Project that I decided to write a utopia because at last poetry (and my having at the same time thrust my children into P.S. 19) had situated me in the world not just cosmologically, which I already knew about from the muse, but also momentarily in a way that previous political work or thought and understanding of human nature had never mentioned to me.

— BM

MAYER, ROSEMARY. Born in Brooklyn, New York, in 1943. Author/illustrator of *Surroundings*, Art-Rite Inc., 1977; author/translator, *Pontormo's Diary*, Oolop Press, 1983. Contributor to *Individuals*, E. P. Dutton, 1977; *Beauty & Critique*, Time/Space Limited, Mussman Bruce, 1983; *Heresies, White Walls, New Observations, United Artists*, and *Tracks*.

MESSERLI, DOUGLAS. Born in 1947. *Djuna Barnes, A Bibliography*, D. Lewis, 1975; *Some Distance*, Segue, 1983; *Contemporary American Fiction*, Sun & Moon Press, 1983; *"Language" Poetries, An Anthology*, New Directions, 1987.

MOORE, HONOR. Born in New York City in 1945. Author of *Leaving and Coming Back*, Ellie's Press, 1981; *Firewalker*, Chicory Blue Press, 1987.

I love that I saw Gregory Corso streak Allen Ginsberg's reading at a New Year's or Valentine's marathon years ago. I love that there is a place that welcomes James Merrill, naked Gregory Corso, radical lesbians, performance art, and me with my sestinas and syllables. I was there the first Easter of the new sanctuary and saw poets and painters I knew, which reminded me of the sacred origins of poetry and that anything can rise again from its ashes if faith is there.

— MH

MORLEY (WOLPE), HILDA. Was born September 19, 1921, in New York City and educated in New York City, Israel, London, and Black Mountain College in North Carolina. Author of *A Blessing Outside Us*, 1976; *What Are Winds and What Are Waters*, Matrix Press, 1983; *To Hold in My Hands: Selected Poems, 1955–1983; Cloudless at First*, Moyer Bell Ltd., 1988. Recent work appears in *Sulfur, Partisan Review, Tri Quarterly*, and *Ironwood*.

MUELLER, COOKIE. (1949–1989) Born in Baltimore. Author of *How to Get Rid of Pimples*, Top Stories, 1984; *Wild History*, Tanam Press, 1985.

It must have been New Year's 1981. It was the first year I read at the New Year's Day St. Mark's annual. I had not been formally invited.

I had gone to the reading with an old friend, an invited writer, Gregory Corso. He told me to bring one of my shortest short stories. He would ask them if I could read. I liked the idea well enough at home, but when I got there I chickened out. That didn't hold a lot of weight with Gregory, so he introduced me anyway right after he read. I didn't have much choice then.

I read a piece of about four paragraphs. Formally, this story had been a sort of mini-novel that I edited and condensed down to three quarters of a page. I figure that these days not many people have the attention spans to listen to or even read novels.

That night the audience was incredibly responsive, so I began to believe in my work. The St. Mark's Poetry Project really gave me my first audience; I don't think I'd have a public writing career without them. (1987)

— CM

MURRAY, CATHERINE. Born April 12, 1918, on Staten Island, New York City; died 1990. Author of *The Transatlantic Flight of the Angel Death*, New Rivers Press, 1980. Contributor to *Art and Literature*, *Angel Hair*, *The Virginia Quarterly Review*, *Prairie Schooner*, *Extensions*, *Mother*, *Bones*, *Commonweal*, *The World*, *Earthship*, *Glassworks*, and *Gallimaufry*.

MYLES, EILEEN. Born in Cambridge, Massachusetts, in 1949. Author of *The Irony of the Leash*, Jim Brodey Books, 1978; *Polar Ode* (with Anne Waldman), Dead Duke Books, 1979; *A Fresh Young Voice from the Plains*, Power Mad Press, 1981; *Sappho's Boat*, Little Caesar, 1982; *Bread and Water*, Hanuman Press, 1986; *Not Me*, Semiotexte, 1991.

I was educated here. In poetry, anyhow. I was a graduate-school dropout in New York City and was looking for a structured take on what was going on in poetry, and everyone I met in New York told me something different. You know, someone would tell you to read A. R. Ammons and someone else Paul Blackburn, and my graduate-school instructor told me about James Schuyler and Frank O'Hara being members of the New York School of Poetry, denizens—not either of these guys, but somehow the "school"—of St. Mark's Church. So I first came around because it seemed like a place to go, and therefore more trustworthy than people. Like the building would exude opinions. It was a little distressing that it seemed only men read poetry there, but there were plenty of women in the workshops, where I started out, and it seemed like things were bound to change. I went to Alice Notley's workshop in '76 and there all the younger poets assembled: Susie Timmons, Michael Scholnick, Jeff Wright, Steve Levine, Shelly Kraut, Bob Rosenthal, Bob Holman, Simon Schuchat. It was Friday night, which was great since we'd all bring beers into the workshop and it would continue into El Centro, a bar on St. Mark's Place. Alice would invite older poets like Anselm Hollo along to the bar, but mostly it was all about us, being a particularly anarchic period in the church's history when it just seemed like the readings were where you went to meet friends, we went to all the readings, and if you didn't like the poet, you could laugh at him or her and would have plenty of support.

Being a poet seemed to have a lot to do with advocacy. We were all starting magazines—*Mag City, Roof, Dodgems*—also we had something to define ourselves as a group with, and we could invite the more established poets to make it seem "heavier." I think the Project invited us all in to do it ourselves. It wasn't only stapling or making your own magazine—you were literally given a space to take over and occupy as your poetic stomping grounds. Kind of a little clubhouse, fanning out through the East Village, which was not yet trendy. Pre-trendy, I guess. The fire changed things because the building was not to be "tampered" with then; it was supposed to be immaculate and always considered before putting a cigarette out on the floor. There's a new group of younger poets around now, though I'm told they have to defend the cleanliness of the place to more Avenue C people who see it as not decayed enough looking. I think people occupy St. Mark's when their poetry flame is most high, and begin to drop out and away when jobs, relationships, lack of passion dissuade them from being involved. I don't think the economy or any of those externals have really affected who comes or not. The place is more public because it's over twenty years old and the reputation has developed and poets from all walks want to read. It's a broader school now, which has to be, I suppose, because the third- or fourth-generation New York School is too decadent to be believed, and the original impulse is too watered down to inspire anyone. I feel like I watched a piece of history happen by coming here for the past ten years. I haven't learned any more about The Poetry Project by having run it. It's really all about itself, poetry, and people who care about that.

— **EM**

663

NASDOR, MARC. Born in Baltimore in 1958. Coordinator for the Committee for International Poetry. Translator from Spanish and Hungarian. A recent work, "Trene in Partenza," appears in *Temblor #7.*

In 1981, I met Bob Rosenthal and Rochelle Kraut, who took me on as their assistant on the Monday-night poetry series. I stayed with the series all the way to 1985, as coordinator with Chris Kraus. Chris and I booked lots of different kinds of poetry and performance, but after we left, the series went almost all the way over in the direction of performance, so then later there was a backlash when Richard Hell took over, who moved things back over to mostly poetry, which I think was a good idea.

However, I think to mention a juicy "incident." For our last gig on the Monday nights, I booked a performance artist who did some kind of a sexy Classical Greek piece; opposite her, I booked a friend of mine from Baltimore named Tentatively, A Convenience, a filmmaker and conceptual performance artist. "Tent" went first with some Church of the Sub-Genius films, including one where his girlfriend peed about a gallon of pee into his mouth. Another film had him in London on all fours with a Seeing Eye dog harness and mask on, leading around a mutual artist friend of ours who was losing her eyesight; they went on the double-decker buses, and Gail (our friend) bought him some doggy sweets as a reward. During another film, Tent, who throughout the performance wasn't wearing any pants and wore three pairs of rubber breasts (like a she-wolf), began carving circles, squares, and triangles into his legs with an X-acto knife. More than half of the audience was there to see the sexy Classical Greek performer. During Tent's performance, this portion of the audience yelled at me to turn off the projector, and some of them pointed their fingers at me like they were giving me the evil eye or something. I kept assuring them, "It will be over in five minutes or so," every ten minutes or so. One audience member tried forcibly to turn off the projector.

My favorite experience during an annual New Year's marathon reading was on January 1, 1982, when the benefit was held in the hall of the Ukrainian National Home. On that occasion, I had the pleasure of reading a long poem—in East Baltimore dialect—about what happened in that city on the day Elvis died.

— MN

NAUEN, ELINOR. Born in South Dakota. Author of *Cars & Other Poems,* Misty Terrace Press, 1980. Has published in *Exquisite Corpse* and *Fiction* magazines.

When I came to New York, I immediately went to my first poetry reading ever, the Frank O'Hara memorial, in November of '76. "Everybody" read and I was stunned. Glamour, beauty, wit. I never left. So I've been a/with/part of the Project for half its existence, and I wouldn't be the poet I am without it. That community of poets listening intelligently (often enough). The great big party that made poetry seem the most exciting thing you could possibly do.

— EN

NOEL, SUSAN. Born in Lexington, Kentucky, in 1953. Author of *Bronze Age*, Rocky Ledge Cottage Editions, 1980; *Speak Gently in Her Bardo* (with Anne Waldman), Rocky Ledge, 1991.

NOLAN, PAT. Born September 3, 1943, in Montreal, Quebec, Canada. Author of *Rock Me Roll Me Vast Fatality*, Snazzy Wah Press, 1970; *Bob Hope In a Buick*, Blue Suede Shoes, 1971; *Our Fashion Plate*, The End (& Variations), 1972; *The Chinese Quartet*, Cranium Press, 1973; *Counterintelligence*, Doris Green Editions, 1975; *Obvious Forgeries*, Famous Last Words, 1976; *Fast Asleep*, Z Press, 1977; *Drastic Measures*, Telephone Books, 1981; *Fundamental*, Doris Green Editions, 1982; *The Great Pretenderer*, Doris Green Editions, 1984.

NORTH, CHARLES. Born in New York City in 1941. Author of *Lineups*, 1972; *Elizabethan & Nova Scotian Music*, Adventures in Poetry, 1974; *Six Buildings*, Swollen Magpie Press, 1977; *Leap Year: Poems, 1968–1978*, Kulchur Foundation, 1978; *Gemini* (with Tony Towle), Swollen Magpie Press, 1981.

The Poetry Project has meant a great deal to me. The first poems I published, hesitantly, were in *The World* (1968), the first reading I gave was there in 1970, and the first publisher I had was Larry Fagin's Adventures in Poetry. I was also encouraged tremendously by sitting in for a couple of months on a workshop given by Tony Towle in 1970, without which, who knows. This isn't to minimize the differences I've had with prevailing styles and attitudes there (as Frank O'Hara said, "a useful thorn to have in one's side"), nor my own private share in the disgruntlements, disenchantments, and entropies that have been part of the St. Mark's aura for over twenty years. Nor have I, despite all the readings, collatings, and magazines, teaching a workshop and serving on the advisory board, lost the feeling of being a visitor (partly because it takes me forty minutes to get there by subway). But really, there is no other *center* as far as I'm concerned. Where else do you go to hear those who inspire you? What other reading every two years (it used to be) is the equivalent of a vernissage? Where else have I taught a workshop with Yuki Hartman as a student? The place has also been a lot more inclusive than its professional detractors have been willing to let on, and its array of publications (remember that early comment about a "runaway A.B. Dick machine"?) the equal, mimeo notwithstanding, of anyplace in the country.

— CN

NOTLEY, ALICE. Born in Bixbee, Arizona, in 1945. Author of *Songs for the Unborn Second Baby*, United Artists, 1979; *Dr. Williams' Heiresses*, Tuumba, 1980; *How Spring Comes*, Toothpaste Press, 1981; *Sorrento*, Sherwood Press, 1984; *Margaret & Dusty*, Coffee House Press, 1985; *At Night the States*, Yellow Press, 1987; *Homer's Art*, The Institute of Further Studies, 1990.

OBENZINGER, HILTON. Born in Brooklyn, New York, May 22, 1947. Books published include *This Passover or the Next I Will Never Be in Jerusalem*, which won the Before Columbus Foundation's American Book Award, Momo's Press, and *The Day of the Exquisite Poet Is Kaput*, FITS. *New York on Fire*, a series of narratives on the history of New York City from the point of view of its fires, is published by The Real Comet Press. Co-editor of *Palestine Focus*, a national newspaper on the Palestinian-Israeli conflict.

O'HARA, FRANK. 1926–1966. Born in Baltimore. Author of *Meditations in an Emergency*, Grove Press, 1957; *Lunch Poems*, City Lights Books, 1964; *The Collected Poems of Frank O'Hara*, Alfred A. Knopf, 1971; *Selected Poems*, Random House, 1974; *Art Chronicles: 1954–1966*, George Braziller Inc., 1975; *Poems Retrieved*, Grey Fox Press, 1977; *Selected Plays*, Full Court Press, 1978; *Standing Still and Walking in New York*, Grey Fox Press, 1983.

OPPENHEIMER, JOEL. 1930–1988. Born in Yonkers, New York. Author of *The Dutiful Son*, Jargon, 1956; *The Wrong Season*, Bobbs-Merrill, 1975; *At Fifty*, St. Andrew's Press, 1978; *Houses*, White Pine Press, 1980; *Just Friends/Friends & Lovers*, Jargon, 1981; *Del Quien lo Tomo*, Perishable Press, 1983; *The Ghost Lover*, Mann Kaye, 1983; *New Spaces*, Black Sparrow Press, 1985; *Names and Local Habitations: Selected Earlier Poems 1951–1972*, Jargon Society, 1988.

In the spring of '66 I was working in a print shop and getting ready to get married for the second time. I was thirty-six, and as everyone knows by now, that's an age where you are at the top of your game, in control, ready to move out, etc.

Marty Moskof, an old friend from Black Mountain days, called and invited me out for a drink with him and Bob Amussen so Bob and I could size each other up. After the introductions, Marty left, and Bob told me about the federal grant that would allow St. Mark's to get actively engaged in the arts. He said that I'd been mentioned as a possible director of the poetry end of things—it wasn't till a month or so later that I learned I'd been acceptable to the clique of "Metro poets" who'd been using St. Mark's, because the first person suggested "was a terrible womanizer, the second was a terrible lush, and Oppenheimer, while both, was not as bad as either."

So it was another case of overall performance counting for more than specialization, I guess. In any event, when Bob and Mike Allen offered me the job, I quit the print shop and started a new career.

I remember the first time I was shown the church by Mike. We were standing in the vestry and it suddenly occurred to me that this nice Jewish boy was going to work for the goyim, and I had no idea what kind of goyim Episcopalians were. So I asked Mike if there were any problems with drinking or smoking as far as his religion was concerned. He laughed and told me his first act as rector had been to get rid of the cheap sherry they'd been using for communion wine, and substituting some good stuff.

Well, we did get off the ground, despite the hassles getting a place to start from, and the flak from the old guard, and the red tape from the government, and the internecine sniping between film and the rest of the gang, and the raids on the courthouse by the neighborhood gangs, etc. etc. etc.

As far as my own work went, St. Mark's (and particularly Joel Sloman) convinced me that poetry could carry a political content—and sometimes, indeed, had to!

I'm proud that the New Year's Day reading goes on; that the Project goes on; that the publishing begun by "The Genre of Silence" and *The World* goes on. Anne and I met at the HD conference up in Orono this summer and we both were startled to realize that we'd met twenty years ago! (1987)

— JO

ORLOVSKY, PETER. Born in 1933. Author of *Clean Asshole Poems & Smiling Vegetable Songs*, City Lights Books, 1978; *Straight Heart's Delight, Love Poems and Selected Letters, 1947–1980* (with Allen Ginsberg), Gay Sunshine Press, 1980.

OWEN, MAUREEN. Born in Graceville, Minnesota, in 1943. Author of *Country Rush*, Adventures in Poetry, 1973; *No Travels Journal*, Cherry Valley Editions, 1975; *Hearts in Space*, Kulchur Foundation, 1980; *AE*, Vortex Editions, 1984; *Zombie Notes*, SUN Press, 1985.

The Poetry Project was my formal education. In the span of years I worked at St. Mark's I heard more poets read, talked to more writers, worked with more poets, writers, editors, saw more performance poetry, more poetry film, helped collate more magazines and small-press books, attended more workshops and talks by visiting writers, had lunch with more poets, was exposed to more poetry than anyone ever could possibly be in any writing program in any university anywhere. When I came to New York City in the late sixties from Japan and San Francisco, I was blown away by the incredible LIFE that was going on at The Poetry Project. Living on the Lower East Side and meeting many poets whose work really excited me (especially women writers who didn't seem to be getting published at the time), I wanted to do a little poetry magazine. I had never run a mimeograph machine, but I asked Anne if I could run off my first issue at the Project and she magnanimously said, "Of course!" Amazed by the openness and helpfulness of the place, I talked to Larry Fagin, who arranged a time for me to mimeo, and the final amazement—Tom Veitch, who I barely knew, offered to run the entire issue off for me! I'd never encountered such a generous attitude in any other poetry community that I'd been part of. It's a rare distinctive quality of the Project. A one-of-a-kind place. There is no place in New York City or elsewhere that even comes close to it. Some rag on it, some applaud it, but all agree it is a magnet, a center almost inexplicable in its importance.

— MO

PADGETT, RON. Born in Tulsa, Oklahoma, in 1942. Author of *Bean Spasms* (with Ted Berrigan), Kulchur Foundation, 1967; *Great Balls of Fire*, Holt, Rinehart, 1969; *Antlers in the Treetops* (with Tom Veitch), Coach House Press, 1970; *The Adventures of Mr. & Mrs. Jim & Ron* (with Jim Dine), Grossman, Viking, 1970; *Toujours L'Amour*, SUN Press, 1976; *Arrive by Pullman*, Generations, 1978; *Tulsa Kid*, Z Press, 1979; *Triangles in the Afternoon*, SUN Press, 1979; *How to Be a Woodpecker*, Toothpaste, 1983; *How to Be Modern Art*, Coffee House Press, 1984; *Among the Blacks*, Avenue B, 1988. Translations: *Dialogues with Marcel Duchamp* by Pierre Caban, Viking, 1971; *The Poems of A. O. Barnabooth* by Valery Larbaud, Mushinsha, 1977; *The Poet Assassinated and Other Stories* by Guillaume Apollinaire, North Point Press, 1984; *The Big Something*, The Figures, 1990.

At various times at The Poetry Project I have been a reader, a member of the audience, a volunteer magazine collator, an informal janitor, a proofreader, a guest-editor, a newsletter founder/editor, a workshop teacher, an advisory board member, and director. Since

1966 The Poetry Project has radiated a tremendous amount of energy, and I, among others, have been vitalized by it.

— RP

PALMER, MICHAEL. Born in New York City in 1943. Author of *Without Music*, Black Sparrow Press, 1977; *Alogon*, Tuumba, 1980; *Transparency of the Mirror*, Little Dinosaur Press, 1980; *Notes for Echo Lake*, North Point Press, 1981; *First Figure*, North Point Press, 1984; *Sun*, North Point Press, 1988. Editor, *Code of Signals, Recent Writings in Poetics*, North Atlantic Books, 1984.

St. Mark's: my first New York reading, a benefit. Noticing me trembling, Joel Oppenheimer kindly offered his flask. I read so as not to be heard. Just as well. Later readings with David Meltzer, Joe Brainard, et al., Berrigan's barking laugh, half challenge, half support, in the background. Now jostling Auden's ghost in the aisles? Most recently a reading with Charles North and a Sunday "conversation" with Clark Coolidge and audience about desire, silence, narrative, subversion, loss, subject, Sade, Bataille, Blanchot, Olson, hymns, and fragments. Anne extended the first invitation. Padgett, Fagin, Mayer, Bernstein gave others. Over time, St. Mark's has been the one enduring place to come to read and to listen, for those of us on the fringe of that tired concordance elsewhere designated as "literature."

— MP

PERREAULT, JOHN. Born in New York City in 1937. Author of *Camouflage*, Lines Press, 1966; *Luck*, Kulchur Foundation, 1969; *Harry*, Coach House Press, 1974; *Hotel Death and Other Tales*, Sun & Moon Press, 1987.

I remember I did my first poetry event at St. Mark's in 1967. Using a tape recorder, I interviewed myself. And I also remember during a pre-recorded rendition of my long poem called "Hunger" I had color slides projected on my naked back. I remember seeing the drops of sweat from my armpits on my shadow on the wall in front of me. A little later I made someone in the audience get up and give me his chair and then licked the chair all over. In 1969 we did an all-media version of the Fashion Show Poetry Event. This was a collaboration— Hannah Weiner, Eduardo Cost, and myself—that featured clothing made by artists, with a fashion commentary written by the three of us. Other artists involved were Andy Warhol, Claes Oldenburg, Alex Katz, Marisol, James Rosenquist, James Lee Byars, and Alan D'Arcangelo. And we, as poets, did clothing too. Eduardo showed his gold ears; Hannah invented a travel cape that had so many pockets the wearer didn't need to use luggage; I showed my "Hair Line"—very minimal clothing made out of a frontless and backless blouse, tied around the waist to make a mini-skirt, or—in the grand climax—worn tied around the forehead as a wedding veil. I'm not sure anybody liked what I was up to, or got it. But here's the real point: Where else could I have done such things if the St. Mark's Poetry Project hadn't existed?

— JP

PICKARD, TOM. Born in Newcastle Upon Tyne, England, in 1946. Author of *Guttersnipe*, City Lights Books, 1971; *The Order of Chance*, Fulcrum Press, 1971; *Hero Dust, New and Selected Poems*, Schocken Books, 1979; *OK Tree*, Pig Press, 1980; *Custom and Exile*, Schocken Books, 1985.

Always found it an open and welcoming place since 1968 when I first read there. Always a good place to stop off and see friends, to hear innovative verse and get a good audience.

— TP

PLYMELL, CHARLES. Author of *Apocalypse Rose*, Dave Haselwood Books, 1967; *Neon Poems*, Atom Mind Productions, 1970; *The Last of the Moccasins*, City Lights Books, 1971; *Moccasins Ein Beat*, Kaleidoskop, 1980; *Over the Stage of Kansas*, Telephone Books, 1973; *The Trashing of America*, Kulchur Foundation, 1975; *Blue Orchid Numero Uno*, Telephone Books, 1977; *Panik in Dodge City*, Expanded Media Editions, 1981; *Forever Wider*, Scarecrow Press, 1985.

PORTER, FAIRFIELD. 1907–1975. Born in Winnetka, Illinois. Realist painter whose first show was in 1952 at the Tibor de Nagy Gallery. He taught at Yale University, the Skowhegan School of Painting and Sculpture, Amherst College, and the Art Institute of Chicago. A twenty-year retrospective of his work took place at the Heckscher Museum on Long Island, the Queens Museum, the Montclair Art Museum in New Jersey, the Boston Museum of Fine Arts, and in the later years of his life, his works were shown at the Hirsch & Adler Gallery.

RATCLIFF, CARTER. Born in Seattle in 1941. Author of *Fever Coast*, Kulchur Foundation, 1973; *John Singer Sargent*, Abbeville Press, 1982; *Give Me Tomorrow*, Vehicle Press, 1983, *Andy Warhol*, Abbeville Press, 1983; *Robert Longo*, Rizzoli Books, 1985; *Pat Steir*, Abrams 1986; *Komar and Melamid*, Abbeville Press, 1989.

About the Poetry Project—I remember it in what might seem an odd way, as a Utopia, not in theory or in structure or in its day-to-day functioning, but in spirit, as a place where, as nowhere else, poetry was the most important thing.

— CR

RATTRAY, DAVID. Born in Southampton, New York, in 1936. Author of *A Red-framed Print of the Summer Palace*, Vincent FitzGerald Company, 1983; *To the Consciousness of a Shooting Star*, Vincent FitzGerald Company, 1986.

I've been attending readings at The Poetry Project ever since it began. Around 1982, I made friends with poets who were involved with the Project, and they gave me encouragement and support at a point when I had come to believe that my life was at a dead end. What I got from them wasn't the secret of a privileged elite, it was more like music on the air waves, an unspoken awareness that is a common knowledge of poets and their audiences anywhere; but the place it first came to me, bringing me out of a lifelong isolation, was The Poetry Project. The Project's contribution to my career was decisive. I could go on and list unforgettable evenings at the Project that inspired me personally, but this might tend to reduce the Project to the level of a mere temple of consumption in which the adulation of the star, and of course the hermetic separation of the audience from the star, is the basic operating principle. The Poetry Project, reflecting the Utopian ideas of its founders, has been largely successful in avoiding such separations, so as to provide a sheltered space in which talents could develop and flourish.

— DR

RAWORTH, TOM. Born in London, in 1938. Author of *Levre de Poche*, Bull City Press, 1982; *Writing*, The Figures, 1982; *Tottering State: Selected and New Poems, 1963–1983*, The Figures, 1984; *Heavy Light*, Actual Size, 1984; *Lazy Left Hand*, Actual Size, 1986.

I first visited the United States in 1970, thanks to Kenneth Koch, who invited me to read at the Loeb Student Center. My second reading was at St. Mark's. I remember getting there early and meeting Ted Greenwald, who was setting out chairs: the start of a long friendship. In fact, I spent my first night in the U.S. in Anne Waldman's apartment (she was away) talking with John Godfrey (another valued friend), who was briefly staying there. I'm grateful to everyone connected with the Project, then and now, for their energy, generosity, and hospitality to me and to writers from many countries.

— TR

671

REED, LOU. Born in Brooklyn, New York, in 1942. Recordings include: *Transformer*, 1972; *Berlin*, 1973; *Sally Can't Dance*, 1974; *Metal Machine Music*, 1975; *Rock and Roll Heart*, 1976; *Walk on the Wild Side: The Best of Lou Reed*, 1977; *Street Hassle*, 1978; *The Bells*, 1979; *Growing Up in Public*, 1980; *The Blue Mask*, 1982; *Legendary Hearts, 1983; New Sensations*, 1984; *Mistrial*, 1985; *New York*, 1988; *Songs for Drella* (with John Cale), 1990.

RICARD, RENÉ. Born in Boston. Author of *René Ricard*, DIA Foundation. Also an art critic and actor, he appeared in Warhol's *Chelsea Girls* and in John Vaccaro's *Conquest of the Universe* and other theater spectacles.

ROBINSON, KIT. Born in Evanston, Illinois, in 1949. Author of *Down and Back*, The Figures, 1978; *Tribute to Nervous*, Tuumba, 1980; *Riddle Road*, Tuumba, 1982; *Windows*, Whale Cloth, 1985; *A Day Off*, State One, 1986; *Ice Cubes*, Square Zero, 1986.

In 1969, Anne Waldman, Peter Schjeldahl, Michael Brownstein, Bill Berkson, Lewis Warsh, and John Giorno gave a reading at Branford College, Yale. The following year, Berkson, Schjeldahl, and Ted Berrigan came to teach weekly workshops. I made several trips to New York to hear readings, including a monster reading at St. Mark's Church.

The esprit de corps of the New York poetry scene partly inspired various group activities among actors and writers at Yale, including an all-night production of *Hamlet* during a student strike in support of seven Black Panthers jailed in New Haven on murder charges.

When I moved to San Francisco in 1971, I imagined I'd return to St. Mark's, armed with terrific new poems. In 1978, later and much differently than expected, my dream came true. Ron Padgett invited me to read with Jackson Mac Low. In the audience were John Cage (to hear Jackson), Ted Berrigan and Greenwald (to hear me), and some new friends I've continued to know and work with since.

— KR

ROSENBERG, DAVID. Born in Detroit in 1943. Author of *Leavin' America*, Coach House Press, 1972; *Blues of the Sky*, Harper & Row, 1976; *Job Speaks*, Harper & Row, 1977; *A Blazing Fountain*, Schocken Books, 1978; *Chosen Days*, Doubleday, 1980; *The J Book* (with Harold Bloom), Grove Press, 1989.

The Poetry Project embodied performance in writing the poem in living, printing, and reading it. Even this act of assessment, or criticism, begs for more of the same performance. The curriculum was that all—each minute—is a performance, and poetry, in its most refined expression worked best in the illusion of immediate speech, an illusion of reality. Many graduated, some to other religions, which I did too, as a student of Judaism. As a Poetry Project alumnus, I'm not yet ready to resist my education and venture the serious criticism it deserves. It's still too early for that, too close to the event. Yet now, as a student as well of Freud, the price of an unexamined past grows increasingly visible. The Poetry Project supported a strategy of confronting an intolerable culture, and the price was a deflation of time. Properly deadpan, though dressed with visible irony, I was also a Vietnam draft resister who could not return for almost six years: The Poetry Project functioned as my Voice of America and I an ambassador in Toronto and world travels. At the time, then, poetry as a method of survival, a weapon for a vulnerable heart and mind, precluded critical tools, the examination of our latest reality myths. Yet the Project was a typically myopic university; I felt privileged to be there, anxious to be accepted as a humble genius, and also anxious to get out on my own, away from the herd.

I miss my youth, but also recognize I lived a prolonged adolescence on the poetry front. During that time, the Project was not so much a home—and certainly much more than a cultural center—it was, alas, a church, with poetry in the moment its liturgy. We wrote thousands of individual (personism) prayers, mostly asking for forgiveness (we were living dangerous lives, blind to our pasts). Each week at the readings we kept up with the latest in petitions, which also served as an intimate social arena, for the household gods were within us.

— DR

ROSENTHAL, BOB. Born in Chicago in 1950. Author of *Morning Poems*, Yellow Press, 1972; *Sweet Substitute*, Yellow Press, 1973; *Cleaning Up New York*, Angel Hair Books, 1977; *Lies About the Flesh*, Frontward Books, 1977; *Rude Awakenings*, Yellow Press, 1982.

The Poetry Project, a mythical place in a church in New York City, Send $10. and receive *The World*./1973 move to New York City, onto St. Mark's Place, surprise to see the weather vane atop St. Mark's Church from window./Lie down in the pews during reading or actually try to read the hymn books./Giant New Year's Day marathon—I'm invited to read! Larry Fagin puts me between Abbie Hoffman and Allen Ginsberg. As I walk to the podium, feel glad Tuinal is kicking in./Gregory Corso streaking at Ginsberg, McClure reading, Corso yelling, "I am the first poetry streaker!"/Bernadette Mayer experimental writing workshops, learn to embody the critical./Help at New Year's Marathon, Larry (Quasimodo) Fagin holds back the hordes crushing in the door./The amazing Monday nights (host Ed Friedman) birthing The Kitchen with no budget./Jim Brodey doesn't show up and people get up from the audience and read poems they have with them./Brodey does show up and brings a sitar player and asks the musician if he can play like Miles on "Sketches of Spain."/ John Wieners starts his reading fifteen minutes early and finishes at five minutes to Eight./Alice Notley introduces a generation of poets to themselves in 1977./Poets say the Project died in 1970./Poets say the Project died in 1974./Hearing poets comment that the Project died in 1979./Maybe the Project will die next year./Philip Whalen read forever!/Open Reading where author of "Death's Tit" rips wooden podium apart./Robert Creeley meandering around the poem for most of an hour, then reads three poems flawed with real beauty./Open Readings fertile meeting ground poets from New Jersey meet the poets from the Bronx and visiting poets from Yugoslavia./Mimeo machine ready for your stencil./The gathering place between the civilized and the less so, the streets to the academy, poetry is the only survivor.

— BR

ROTHENBERG, JEROME. Author of *Poland, 1931*, New Directions, 1974; *Poems for the Game of Silence*, New Directions, 1975; *The Notebooks*, Membrane, 1977; *Pre-Face & Other Writings*, New Directions, 1981; *Altar Pieces*, Station Hill Press, 1982; *New Selected Poems, 1970–1985*, New Directions, 1986. Anthologies include *America A Prophecy*, Random House, 1973; *Technicians of the Sacred*, University of California Press, 1985.

It's hard to get it back into focus—the beginnings directed by Paul Blackburn and seeming even more so in the aftermath of his death, now itself fifteen years into the past. I was on the committee from the start, but Blackburn was its assembler and organizer, who sensed and promoted the "reading" as crucial to the work at hand. I had met him first at an earlier series he was running at the Café Borgia— Macdougal Street, across the corner from Figaro and the San Remo. It was the late fifties and Levertov—whom I had just gotten to know— was the reader. I was immediately aware of Blackburn: curiously professional in manner and cultivated in his voice and in the words he spoke as introduction. In memory he becomes the guide from there through other venues—coffee shops and little theaters and galleries—to the discovery (after the retreat from Café Metro on Second Avenue) of the church, which was open and available and had the promise, only a glimmer at first, of a still larger venture.

In the years since, St. Mark's and its Poetry Project have provided an ongoing home for the full range of poetry activity in our time. Without it, the work of the most adventurous poets of the last three decades would have been without its own space in the great kulchuropolis, whose established institutions have favored (too often) the conservative and mediocre. I do not mean by this that the Project has been important as an *alternative* space but as a public arena and school for the *dominant* poetry of the twentieth century as it continues to flourish among us. Walking with Paul to find it was, then, one of the blessed moments of my life.

— JR

RUGGIA, JAMES. Born in Hackensack, New Jersey, in 1954. Author of *New Blood*, Artz Press, 1984; *Big Scream*, Nada Press, 1986; *Crossing the Border: My Selected Poems*, Nada Press, 1986.

The dome of San Marcos is covered with beautiful mosaics which detail the creation; outside the stolen horses of Byzantium stare out on the Venetian lion. Likewise the rafters of St. Mark's are cluttered for me with important arguments, lines of poetry and other more visual memories of Berrigan in his bed, of Maureen Owen enraged at Gregory Corso's rage for Robert Lowell. When all is said and done, with all its posing, its conniving and egocentricities, poetry just transcends. And the poetry of St. Mark's, at its best, has the hard edge, the eloquence, the commitment and the glee to be contemporary American poetry's best chance.

— JR

SANCHEZ, SONIA. Born September 9, 1934, in Birmingham, Alabama. Author of *Homecoming*, Broadside Press, 1969; *We are a BaddDDD People*, Broadside Press, 1970; *It's a New Day: Poems for Young Brothers and Sisters*, Broadside Press, 1971; *A Blues Book for Blue Black Magical Women*, Broadside Press, 1974; *Love Poems*, Third Press, 1974; *I've Been a Woman: New & Selected Poems*, Black Scholar Press, 1978, Third World Press, 1985; *Sound Investment*, Third World Press, 1980; *Homegirls & Handgrenades*, Thunder's Mouth Press, 1984; *Under a Soprano Sky*, Africa World Press, 1987.

SANDERS, EDWARD. Born August 17, 1939, Kansas City, Missouri. B.A. in Greek from New York University. Founding Member of The Fugs, publisher of *Fuck You: A Magazine of the Arts* (1962–1965), proprietor of Peace Eye Bookstore (1965–1970). Among his many books of poetry, fiction, and investigative journalism are *Poem from Jail*, City Lights, 1963; *The Family*, Dutton, 1971; *Egyptian Hieroglyphs*, Institute of Further Studies, 1973; *Investigative Poetry*, City Lights, 1976; *Fame and Love in New York*, Turtle

Island, 1980; *Thirsting for Peace in a Raging Century*, Coffee House Press, 1987—American Book Award Winner, 1988; and *Tales of Beatnik Glory*, Vols. I and II, Citadel, 1990. He is the inventor of several electronic musical instruments designed for the accompaniment of poetry, including the Talking Tie and the Singing Quilting Frame. He lives in Woodstock, New York, where he is active in the environmental movement.

SAROYAN, ARAM. Born in New York in 1943. Author of *Aram Saroyan, Poems*, Random House, 1968; *Genesis Angels: The Saga of Lew Welch and the Beat Generation*, William Morrow, 1979; *Last Rites: The Death of William Saroyan*, William Morrow, 1982; *The Intimate Friendship of Oona Chaplin, Carol Matthau, and Gloria Vanderbilt*, Simon & Schuster, 1985.

SAVAGE, TOM. Born July 14, 1948, in New York City. Author of *Personalities*, Jim Brodey Books, 1978; *Slow Waltz on a Glass Harmonica*, Nalanda University Press, 1980; *Filling Spaces*, Nalanda University Press, 1980; *Housing, Preservation and Development*, Cheap Review Press, 1988; *Processed Words*, Coffee House Press, 1990. Editor, *Gandhabba* magazine and *Connaissez-Vous Maitre Eckhart* (based on Ron Padgett's translation workshop). Co-founder and editor of *Roof*; coordinator, "Words Music Words."

SCHIFF, HARRIS. Author of *Secret Clouds*, Angel Hair, 1970; *Easy Street*, No Books, 1972; *I Should Run for Cover But I'm Right Here*, Angel Hair Books, 1978; *In the Heart of the Empire*, United Artists, 1979.

In November 1970 I came back to New York from Morningstar Commune in Northern New Mexico to read at The Poetry Project with Johnny Stanton. I was planning to stay about six weeks. A few days after the reading I went out to Southampton to stay with Ted Berrigan and Alice Notley. Ted suggested that I might ask Anne Waldman to give me the job of running the open readings at St. Mark's every Monday and so I did and she did. I wound up staying for eighteen months.

I ran the open readings according to the principles of Morningstar Commune's "Land—Access to Which Is Denied No One." The open readings mushroomed. Sometimes as many as forty or fifty readers with huge audiences. All the East Village crazies and serious poets too. Olsen MacIntosh, Steve Raven (who performed as Ralston Farina), Anne Waldman, Lisa Galt, Margo Da Silva, Ted Berrigan, Ed White, Kathy Acker, Larry Fagin, Frank Murphy, and many others would read regularly. There was a great feeling of something happening, coming together. Strange forces surged through the room. Once when Nixon was about to give a speech to announce the bombing of

Cambodia, I put a radio up on the podium. Timing was perfect. I turned it on and a voice said, "Ladies and gentlemen, the President of the United States." Then the radio literally flew off the podium, crashing to the floor and scattering its batteries.

In 1978 I was hired to run a poetry workshop and had great success. I was voted on to the advisory board in 1980 and was editor of *The World* in 1982.

— SH

SCHJELDAHL, PETER.   Born in Fargo, North Dakota, in 1942. Author of *White Country*, Corinth, 1968; *An Adventure of the Thought Police*, Ferry Press, 1970; *Dreams*, Angel Hair Books, 1971; *Since 1964: New and Selected Poems*, SUN Press, 1978; *The Brute*, Little Caesar, 1981.

SCHNEEMAN, ELIO.   Born October 16, 1961, in Taranto, Italy. Author of *In February I Think*, C Press, 1978. Contributor to *Mag City, United Artists, Transfer*, and *Open Window*.

SCHNEEMAN, PAUL.   Born in Siena, Italy, in 1960. Author of *Out Will Return*, Open Window Books, 1978.

SCHOLNICK, MICHAEL.   (1953–1990). Born in Queens, New York. *A Hot Little Number & Nations and Peace* (with Tom Weigel), Andrea Doria Books, 1978; *Perfume, Remember I Did This for You*, Power Mad Press Books, 1978; *Beyond Venus*, Crony Books, 1980.

The stimulating thread of readings and other events, bringing together poets of different generations and locales, allow for intimacies to blossom which might otherwise never take place. But doesn't the emphasis on gatherings, you say, lead to a dangerous kind of provincialism? Not necessarily. Home in New York City with one's consciousness and tasks, a poet has ample opportunity to remain in touch with more distant vanguards. Often, labeling poets elite, and rating poems obscurely according to insignificant aesthetic opinions, is to mistake the created thing for incidental issues. One's critical intelligence concerning the product at hand matures, and must be weighed, independently of one's biographical successes, however indispensable and fulfilling relationships with peers and mentor has proven. Let the informed reader, therefore, be discrete and the soul of sublimity (1989).

— MS

677

SCHUCHAT, SIMON. Born July 21, 1954, in Washington, D.C. Author of *Svelte*, Genesis: Grasp, 1971; *Blue Skies*, S.O.U.P., 1973; *Light and Shadow*, Vehicle Editions, 1977; *At Baoshan*, Coffee House, 1987.

SCHUYLER, JAMES. (1923–1991) Born in Chicago. Author of *The Crystal Lithium*, Random House, 1972; *What's for Dinner*, Black Sparrow Press, 1979; *The Morning of the Poem*, Farrar, Straus, Giroux, 1980; *A Few Days*, Random House, 1985; *Alfred and Guinevere*, Harcourt, Brace, Jovanovich, 1986; *Selected Poems*, Farrar, Straus, Giroux, 1988.

SHAPIRO, DAVID. Born in Newark, New Jersey, in 1947. Author of *January*, Holt, 1965; *Poems from Deal*, E. P. Dutton, 1969; *A Man Holding an Acoustic Panel*, E. P. Dutton, 1971; *The Page-turner*, Liveright, 1973; *Lateness*, Overlook, 1977.

SHEPARD, SAM. Born in Fort Sheridan, Illinois, in 1943. Author of *A Lie of the Mind, Curse of the Starving Class, True West, Fool for Love, Buried Child, Red Cross, Icarus's Mother, Action, La Turista, Seduced, Tongues, Savage/Love, Back Bog Beast Bait, Angel City*, and other plays.

SHERRY, JAMES. Born in Philadelphia in 1946. Author of *In Case*, Sun & Moon Press, 1980; *Converses*, Awede Press, 1983; *Popular Fiction*, Roof Books, 1985; *Lazy Sonnets*, Abacus, 1986; *The Word I Like White Paint Considered*, Awede Press, 1986.

> Out of Naropa came *Roof* magazine, which I co-edited in New York, first with Tom Savage, then Vicki Hudspith, and finally Michael Gottlieb. The development of over ten issues marks the effect of the Project on my poetics more clearly than in my own published work as I became increasingly aware of who, to me, were the most interesting writers of my generation. I spent a good deal of time at Poetry Project events, and until the Ear Inn began regularly presenting poets, The Poetry Project was the main sieve of my poetics, apart, of course, from an increasingly wide correspondence generated by my editorial work.

> — JS

SINGH, RAVI. (nee Neil Hackman). Born in Chicago, 1943. He attended Northeastern Illinois University, where he studied with Ted Berrigan and founded and edited *Out There* magazine. In 1974 he moved to New York City. Author of *Ode to Jack Spicer and Other Poems*, Northeastern Illinois University Press, 1975; *Small Poems to God*, Frontward Books, 1979; *Long Song to the One I Love*, White Lion Press, 1986; and *Kundalini Yoga for Body, Mind, and Beyond*, White Lion Press, 1988.

SMEDMAN, LORNA. Born June 6, 1956, in Kingston, New York. Author of *Dangers of Reading*, Prospect Books, 1983.

SMITH, PATTI. Born in Chicago. Author of *Witt: a Book of Poems*, Gotham, 1973; *Babel*, G. P. Putnam & Sons, 1978. Recordings include *Horses*, 1975; *Radio Ethiopia*, 1976; *Easter*, 1978; *Wave*, 1979; *Dream of Life*, 1988.

SMOLARSKI, ARLETTE. Born in Grenoble, France, she has worked as a designer.

SNYDER, GARY. Born May 8, 1930, in San Francisco. Author of *Riprap and Cold Mountain Poems*, Four Seasons, 1959; *Myths and Texts*, New Directions, 1960; *Six Sections*, Four Seasons, 1965; *Back Country*, New Directions, 1968; *Earth House Hold*, New Directions, 1969; *Regarding Wave*, New Directions, 1970; *The Fudo Trilogy*, Shaman Drum 1973; *Turtle Island*, New Directions, 1974; *The Old Ways: Six Essays*, City Lights, 1977; *Myths & Texts*, New Directions, 1978; *He Who Hunted Birds in His Father's Village*, Grey Fox Press, 1979; *The Real Work*, New Directions, 1980; *Axe Handles*, North Point Press, 1983; *Passage Through India*, Grey Fox Press, 1984; *Left Out in the Rain*, North Point Press, 1986; *The Practice of the Wild*, North Point Press, 1990.

Walking down the rainy street, the iron fence stakes of St. Mark's flashing past in the streetlight. People gathering from different streets and alleys, converging. Into the churchyard and the big hall, bright full! Still gathering and filling, up into the balcony. The warmth, conviviality, comradeliness of hundreds, gathered out of the web of the city, and so many people I knew! My reading at St. Mark's, some time in the seventies, still shy of New York City and surprised here at the spirit. That contact, and the *Newsletter*, gave me a sense of place and base in the East Coast world of poetics and poets. It bridged the continent for me—for many of us out west—and was the beginning of new friendships. How valuable.

— GS

SPICER, JACK. (1925–1965). Author of *The Red Wheelbarrow*, Arif; *The Collected Books of Jack Spicer*, Black Sparrow Press, 1975; *One Night Stand & Other Poems*, Grey Fox Press, 1980.

STANTON, JOHNNY. Born in New York City in 1943. *Slip of the Tongue*, Angel Hair Books; *Mangled Hands*, Sun & Moon Press, 1986; *Sons of Xavier Keep Marching*, Sun & Moon Press, 1989.

Johnny Stanton leaped from the barb-wire womb and hurled his first literary grenade in 1943, New York City. That's the truth, folks. Since then he's been riding the nonstop train to oblivion. He knows it.

He knows it so well but he doesn't let it give him the fears. No, instead he's like a man possessed, standing one day atop the baggage car throwing assorted shit-bombs in the direction of the police, sitting the next day out in the dining car smoking his Havana-Havana, drawing detailed plans on the tablecloth for his impending attack on the City of Success. And in between all this frenzy, all this madness, all this struggle with the Big Lie, old Johnny—what's left of him— just takes it easy in his private Pullman, pulling his doggy, making love to his ever-lovin', eating endless heaps of French toast, and digging the Culture Spasms as they come off the wire . . .

St. Mark's Poetry Project
has ruined my life
utterly,
completely,
totally.
St. Mark's would've been
my Lower Depths.
Long live poetry,
Death to all poets.

— JS

STEPANCHEV, STEPHEN. Born January 30, 1915, in Yugoslavia. Author of *American Poetry Since 1945: A Critical Study*, Harper & Row, 1965; *What I Own*, Black Sparrow Press, 1978; *Descent*, Stonehouse Press, 1988.

THOMAS, LORENZO. Born August 31, 1944, in the Republic of Panama. He is the author of *Chances Are Few*, Blue Wind Press, 1979; *The Bathers*, Reed & Cannon, 1981. He is a member of the English Department at the University of Houston in Houston, Texas. Previous academic appointments include Texas Southern University and Florida A&M University. Since 1976, he has also served as writer-in-residence for the Arkansas Arts and Humanities Office. A winner of the Lucille Medwick Prize, Mr. Thomas is co-editor of *Roots Magazine* and an advisory editor for *Hoodoo*, *Black Box*, and *Nimrod*. His critical and historical studies of American music, folk art, and poetry have been published widely in the U.S. He has served for four years as a member of the Literature Panel of the Texas Commission on the Arts and Humanities. A collection of his writing is forthcoming from Callalloo Press.

THORPE, JOHN. Author of *Five Aces & Independence*, Tombouctou, 1981.

TILLMAN, LYNNE. Writer and filmmaker who lives in Manhattan. Her most recent book, *Haunted Houses*, was published by Poseidon Press. Her short fiction and essays appear in *Bomb, Between C & D, The Village Voice*, etc. She is the co-director and writer of *Committed*, an independent feature film about Frances Farmer.

TIMMONS, SUSIE. Born in Chicago in 1955, she grew up in New Jersey and moved to New York in 1975. Author of *Hogwild*, Frontward Books, editor of *Bingo*, contributing editor to *Caveman*, teacher at The Poetry Project, co-founder of the New York City Poetry Calendar, and contributor to the anthologies *Fresh Paint* and *Ladies Museum*. Winner of the Ted Berrigan/Yellow Press Award for her manuscript *Locked From The Outside*, now in print, from Yellow Press, Chicago, 1990.

TOWLE, TONY. Born in New York City in 1939. Author of *After Dinner We Take a Drive into the Night*, Tibor de Nagy, 1968; *Autobiography and Other Poems*, SUN/Coach House South, 1977; *Gemini*, collaborations with Charles North, Swollen Magpie Press, 1981; *Works on Paper*, Swollen Magpie Press, 1981; *New and Selected Poems, 1963–1983*, Kulchur Foundation, 1983.

The first time I read at The Poetry Project was in 1968 (twenty-three years ago!). I was scheduled to read with my old friend Frank Lima, who unfortunately was unable to show up that evening. The next year I was asked to conduct one of the evening poetry workshops for the 1969–70 season, and I discovered a didactic streak I didn't know I had. In the Frank O'Hara tradition (from his 1963 New School workshop, the only one he ever gave), I would go out after class to a nearby bar (the Orchidia, now defunct) and have a few drinks and conversation with any of the students who cared to come along.

— TT

TRINIDAD, DAVID. The author of *November*, Hanuman Books; *Pavane*, Sherwood Press, 1981; *Monday, Monday*, Cold Calm Press, 1985.

TROUPE, QUINCY. Born in New York City in 1943. Author of *Snake-Back Solos*, I. Reed Books, 1978; coauthor with Miles Davis of *Miles, The Autobiography*, Simon and Schuster, 1989; editor of *James Baldwin: The Legacy*, Simon and Schuster, 1982 and *Giant Talk: An Anthology of Third World Writings*, Vintage, 1975. He teaches at Columbia University and the City University of New York.

TYSH, GEORGE. Born in Passaic, New Jersey, in 1942. Author of *Cheapness Means Forgiveness*, Sand Project Press, 1970; *Mecanorgane*, Burning Deck Press, 1979; *Ovals*, In Camera, 1985.

For years before I actually read there, and particularly during eight years in Parisian exile, St. Mark's was a distant idea, a model of excellence, the mythic scene of joy in language that now has spread, in reality, to many parts of the country. When we put together "Lines: New Writing at The Detroit Institute of the Arts," the program of readings, talks, and workshops I've coordinated since 1980, The Poetry Project was the main reference point, a persistent background murmuring the ambient music of our times.

— GT

VEGA, JANINE POMMY. Author of *Morning Passage*, Telephone Books, 1976; *Here at the Door*, Zone Press, 1978; *Journal of a Hermit*, Cherry Valley Editions, 1979; *The Bard Owl*, Kulchur Foundation, 1980; *Apex of the Earth's Way*, White Pine Press, 1984; *Ave Salvajex Del Corazon*, Lluvias Press, 1987.

VEITCH, TOM. Author of *Antlers in the Treetops* (with Ron Padgett), Coach House Press, 1973; *Eat This!*, Angel Hair Books, 1974; *The Luis Armed Story*, Full Court Press, 1978.

VIOLI, PAUL. Born in New York City in 1944. Author of *Waterworks*, Toothpaste Press, 1972; *In Baltic Circles*, Kulchur Foundation, 1973; *Marmatan*, SUN Press, 1977; *Splurge*, SUN Press, 1981; *Likewise*, SUN Press, 1987.

WAKOSKI, DIANE. Born in Whittier, California, in 1937. Author of *Coins & Coffins*, Hawk's Well Press, 1962; *Cap of Darkness*, Black Sparrow Press, 1982; *The Magician's Feastlets*, Black Sparrow Press, 1982; *The Collected Greed: Parts I–XIII*, Black Sparrow Press, 1984; *The Rings of Saturn*, Black Sparrow Press, 1986; *Emerald Ice*, Black Sparrow Press, 1988.

For me, St. Mark's provided a continuation of the coffeehouse and bar poetry reading scene which I participated in from the time I came to New York City in 1960 until I left in 1973. Because there was funding for the readings and a teaching connection was established, the readings both open and scheduled took on a more authoritative reality, as well as providing more establishment approval. However, the original energy for the coffeehouse scene was not immediately lost in spite of the legitimacy conferred on St. Mark's. Young poets still had to earn some kind of "popular" respect, not just the accolade of teachers, critics, and hierarchical figures. It was this combination of the popular and the critical that gave the whole East Side poetry scene its vitality from about 1960 to 1980. After I moved away from New York, I lost the sense of what was going on at St. Mark's and feel in no position to evaluate its continuing effectiveness, but for me it was a vital center during the last five years that I lived in New York. I doubt if a university could provide such an atmosphere for its students today.

— DW

WALDMAN, ANNE. Born in Millville, New Jersey, in 1945. Grew up in New York City. Assistant Director, The Poetry Project, 1966–1968; Director, The Poetry Project, 1968–1978. Currently, Director, The Department of Writing & Poetics at The Naropa Institute in Boulder, Colorado. Author of *Giant Night*, Corinth Books, 1970; *Baby Breakdown*, Bobbs-Merrill, 1970; *No Hassles*, Kulchur Foundation, 1971; *Life Notes*, Bobbs-Merrill, 1973; *Fast Speaking Woman*, City Lights, 1975; *Journals & Dreams*, Stonehill, 1976; *Cabin*, Z Press, 1981; *First Baby Poems*, Rocky Ledge 1982/Hyacinth Girls, 1983; *Makeup on Empty Space*, Toothpaste Press, 1984; *Invention* (with Susan Hall), Kulchur Foundation, 1985; *Skin Meat Bones*, Coffee House Press, 1985; *The Romance Thing*, Bamberger Books, 1987; *Blue Mosque*, United Artists Books, 1988; *Helping the Dreamer: New & Selected Poems, 1966–1988*, Coffee House Press, 1988; *Not a Male Pseudonym*, Tender Buttons, 1990; *Shaman/Schamane*, Apartment Editions, 1990. Editor of *The World Anthology*, Bobbs-Merrill, 1969; *Another World*, Bobbs-Merrill, 1972; *Talking Poetics*, Vols. I and II (with Marilyn Webb), Shambhala Publications, 1978; *Nice to See You: Homage to Ted Berrigan*, Coffee House Press, 1991; Cassettes include *Crack in the World*, *Assorted Singles*. Videos: *Eyes in all Heads*, *Battle of the Bards*, *Live at Naropa*.

Edwin Denby, celebrated dance critic, fine poet, and a mentor for me and many others, was always attracted, he said, to the "atmosphere" of The Poetry Project. This was important, he would add, because the sound system in the large sanctuary where many of the big readings and events were held was perfectly *awful*. He used to say this so politely as if it didn't matter in the least that you couldn't hear the poets without straining. At the same time, he spoke of the "highly attuned" sensibility of the audience and how nowhere else on earth had such a cultivated "ear" for poetry. Well with all that strain, you'd have to think your hearing capacity and tolerance would become more refined. He was exceedingly loyal to the Project, literally attending hundreds of readings until his death in 1983. We used to call him St. Edwin. When at the memorial celebration Maria Calegari and Edward Villela—principal dancers from the New York City Ballet—performed a duet in his honor, it felt as if Edwin Denby's world of poetry and dance were mystically joined for a few breathtaking moments. It seemed only at St. Mark's that such a conjunction could occur. (See Introduction)

— AW

WALDMAN, FRANCES LEFEVRE. 1909–1982. Born in York, Pennsylvania. Author of *Amor à Mort*, translations of Cesar Moro, The Vanishing Rotating Triangle Press, 1973; *The Borderguards*, translations of Angelos Sikelianos, Rocky Ledge Cottage Editions, 1982.

WARSH, LEWIS. Born in New York City in 1944. Author of *Methods of Birth Control*, Sun & Moon Press, 1983; *Agnes & Sally*, Fiction Collective, 1984; *The Corset*, In Camera, 1986; *Information from the Surface of Venus*, United Artists Books, 1986; *A Free Man*, Sun & Moon Press, 1989.

WATTEN, BARRETT. Born in California in 1948. Author of *Opera*, Big Sky, 1975; *Decay*, This Press, 1977; *Plasma/Parallels/"X"*, Tuumba, 1979; *1—10*, This Press, 1980; *Complete Thought*, Tuumba, 1982; *Total Syntax*, Southern Illinois University Press, 1984; *Progress*, Roof, 1985; *Conduit*, Gaz, 1988.

Thinking back on The Poetry Project, I am reminded of an absurdist question posed by Gerard Malanga to Charles Olson in *The Paris Review:* "A school is a place where one can learn something. Can a school lose by giving away its knowledge?" From my first involvement with it in about 1972, The Poetry Project seemed a place where a school of poetry—the New York School—was physically embodied in a group of writers who felt free to develop in the confidence of their mutual (and contending) assumptions, and I certainly learned something from that. Its "effect on my writing career" came directly from the social confidence of that school, its urban directness and aesthetic autonomy, which I consider to be unique in American literature. Yet at the same time its literary moment seemed fragile, and in "giving away its knowledge" it did not seem able to reconstitute itself as an unambiguous cultural fact as the seventies turned into the eighties. Perhaps it could have otherwise; rather than a romance of beginnings that turned into a looking backward to sources in the Beats—as, say, Ted Berrigan's interpretation of his work veered from the terrorist implications of cut-up to the recuperative ones of autobiography—there might have been more of an opening, for instance, to issues in other arts and modes of thought, to a wider intellectual life. This may be more of a problem for poetry in general than for The Poetry Project, so I would say that the question of a school changing as it gives itself up in the course of its development (and I can think of other schools) has led me to a desire for a literature less insular in its relation to everything else! But for an anecdote, how about this: The first thing I did when I got to the East Coast, as a student at MIT in 1965, was to go straight to the church, where Lee Crabtree offered me a swig of the crème de menthe he was drinking while playing piano for the Fugs, and I'm sure that changed my life.

— BA

WEIGEL, TOM. Born October 14, 1948, in New York City. Grew up in Northport and East Northport, Long Island. Schools: St. Philip Neri's, Northport High, and Parsons School of Design. Moved to New York in 1970 later lived in Buffalo and Louisville. Back to New York in 1977, joining The Poetry Project and meeting Jackie Curtis in poets theater collaborations, including *Blob-Blob* (1972), performed at St. Mark's Poetry Project in October 1978. Published poems in *Telephone, Little Caesar, Cover Arts N.Y., The Paris Review, The World, Mag City, Little Light, Not Guilty, The Little Magazine,* and others. Began Andrea Doria Books as editor and publisher in 1978. Collaborations with Michael Scholnick, Greg Masters, Steve Levine, Bill Kushner, Will Bennett, Jeff Wright, Rose Lesniak, and others. Began publishing *Tangerine* in 1982 (the last issue was in 1986) and two *Full Deck* anthologies in this same span. Books include *Panic Hardware*, Andrea Doria Books, 1979; *Audrey Hepburn's Symphonic Salad & the Coming of Autumn*, Telephone Books, 1980; *Sonnets*, Accent Editions, 1980; *Little Heart*, Accent Editions, 1981; *A Hot Little Number* (with Michael Scholnick), Andrea Doria Books, 1979; *Nations & Peace* (with Michael Scholnick), Misty Terrace Press, 1980; *Twenty-four Haiku After the Japanese*, Telephone Books, 1982. Poem collage exhibit at 9 Carroll Place Gallery, Staten Island, New York, in 1982.

WEINER, HANNAH. Born in Providence, Rhode Island, in 1928. Author of *Clairvoyant Journal*, Angel Hair Books, 1978; *Little Books/Indians*, Roof, 1980; *Nijole's House*, Potes & Poets Press, 1981; *Code Poems*, Open Book, 1982; *Sixteen*, Awede, 1983; *Spoke*, Sun & Moon Press, 1984; *Written in/the Zero One*, Post Neo, 1985.

I believe that the community of writers around St. Mark's Church stimulated me and kept my writing on its toes. The readings by various members inside and outside the community also kept me aware of what was happening in writing around the country as well as in New York City and made me aware of what was necessary in my own work.

— **HW**

WELISH, MARJORIE. Born in New York City in 1944. Author of *Handwritten*, SUN, 1979; *Two Poems*, Z Press, 1981.

Bothered by what I called the personality within the poems, I became determined to hear John Ashbery read to see if I could overcome this obstacle to understanding. It happens I caught his reading at St. Mark's. Drawn to the poems' intelligence, I nevertheless remained essentially baffled until the thought "It's consciousness speaking in dialects" sprung to mind; and with this conceptual breakthrough, I began reading him on my own. But the experience left me impatient with the decorum I had previously accepted as poetry's verse—it now seemed comprised of small skills a writer learns on the way to accomplishing some greater vision of literature. I still look to St. Mark's to frustrate and inspire me significantly.

— MW

WHALEN, PHILIP. Born in Portland, Oregon, in 1923. Author of *You Didn't Even Try*, Coyote, 1967; *On Bear's Head*, Harcourt, Brace & World, 1969; *Scenes of Life at the Capital*, Grey Fox Press, 1971; *Off The Wall*, Four Seasons, 1978; *The Diamond Noodle*, Poltroon Press, 1980; *Heavy Breathing*, Four Seasons, 1983.

I'm sorry, but I have no anecdotes about St. Mark's in the Bowery beyond saying that I had a hard time finding the men's room in the newly renovated building. But I must express my gratitude for the very kind reception my work has had there, not to mention the kindness and care extended to me on my visits by Anne Waldman and her successors as director of the poetry program.

— PW

WIENERS, JOHN. Born in Milton, Massachusetts, in 1934. Author of *Pressed Wafer*, Gallery Upstairs Press, 1967; *Asylum Poems*, Angel Hair Books, 1969; *Nerves*, Cape Golliard/Grossman, 1970; *Behind the State Capitol or Cincinnati Pike*, Good Gay Poets, 1975; *Selected Poems, 1958–1984*, Black Sparrow Press, 1986.

WINCH, TERENCE. Born November 1, 1945, in New York City. Author of *Luncheonette Jealousy*, Washington Writers Publishing House, 1975; *Nuns*, Wyrd Press, 1976; *The Attachment Sonnets*, Jawbone, 1978; *Total Strangers*, Coffee House Press, 1982; *Irish Musicians/American Friends*, Coffee House Press, 1986 (winner of the Before Columbus Foundation's American Book Award); *Contenders*, Story Line Press, 1989. Two LPs on the Green Linnet label with Celtic Thunder: *Celtic Thunder* (1981) and *The Light of Other Days* (1988). Currently working as an editor at an art museum in Washington, D.C.

WOOLF, DOUGLAS. Born in New York City in 1922. Author of *Wall to Wall*, Grove Press, 1961; *Ya! and John-Juan*, Harper & Row, 1971; *On Us*, Black Sparrow Press, 1977; *Future Preconditional*, Coach House Press, 1978; *The Timing Chain*, Tombouctou, 1985; *Loving Ladies*, Zelot Books, 1986.

In the mid-seventies the St. Mark's Poetry Project invited me to give a reading, the first public reading I considered seriously—I'd always felt what little free time I managed should be spent in writing, not reading my writing. But I had a new young wife who thought it was time I learned to "read," and we could use the money. We'd been wandering the U.S. for over a year, thus it was not difficult for us to pass through New York on the appointed Wednesday. But when I awoke in a New Jersey motel that morning, I whispered hoarsely to my wife that my voice was gone. She laughed. After some food and drink, I found myself talking volubly and vociferously. For a good part of the day she sat on the bed listening to me tempt a heart attack which refused to happen. When we finally reached New York in late afternoon, we roamed through a snowstorm to some East Side taverns I knew from a recent two years spent alone in town, trying to numb all good judgment with Chablis and popcorn; by now my wife was as near apoplectic as I was. We did not get to the church on time, found gathered there a small and restless audience sensing snowbound. We ducked down two or three hundred steep stairs to a dungeon restroom for more Chablis from a canteen I carried. When at last we ascended from that limbo, we were surprised to find the audience waiting patiently—they must have known a nearer restroom—a congenial and attentive little group of listeners. What to do? She sang, I "read," an hour or so later I came to in euphoric shock, at having "done" it. Later I was even invited back, and occasionally when passing through I've heard others read whom I might not have elsewhere.

Greetings anew, dear old St. Mark's, may you long beckon the bashful Muses.

— **DW**

WRIGHT, JEFF. Born in Wilmington, Delaware, in 1951. Author of *Employment of the Apes*, Hard Press, 1982; *Two: Poems & Drawings* (with Yvonne Jacquette), Toothpaste Press, 1983; *Take Over*, Toothpaste Press, 1983; *All in All*, Gull Books, 1986.

Reform school . . . full of saints. St. Mark's Poetry Project "totally" made it for a lot of people.

Readings. You got to hear poets and you could go to open readings. And eventually be a featured reader. Your poem could be in an anthology.

Workshops.

You could be asked to spend time collating *The World* or someone's book. Part of very independent, very perky, bright gang des gangs.

Community, audience, support system. Space. Event. Celebration. New Year's Benefit. Town Hall. Better, older poets got to hear your work. They'd come often. Their doors were open.

St. Mark's advanced the notion of amusing lyricism, of keeping ghosts alive and very up-to-date. New York School filtered down and we all wrote a million sonnets before long.

It was a fun place to drink beer and talk shop. Alma mater.

— **JW**

WRIGHT, REBECCA. Born August 25, 1942, in Chicago. Author of *Elusive Continent*, Telephone Books, 1972; *Brief Lives*, The Ant's Forefoot, 1974; *Ciao Manhattan*, Telephone Books, 1977.

YAU, JOHN. Born in Lynn, Massachusetts, in 1950. Author of *The Sleepless Night of Eugene Delacroix*, Release Press, 1980; *Broken Off by the Music*, Burning Deck, 1981; *Corpse and Mirror*, Holt, Rinehart & Winston, 1983; *Cenotaph*, with drawings by Archie Rand, Chroma Press.

Ron Padgett, who was then the director of The Poetry Project, asked me to edit an issue of *The World*. His instructions were simple: "Do it the way you want." For me, Ron's generosity typifies what is best about The Poetry Project. I went to many of the Monday and Wednesday readings, read the *Newsletter*, and attended a workshop run by Bill Zavatsky on a fairly regular basis.

After moving to New York from Boston in the mid 1970s, I found in the Project a community of people writing and caring about that act. Like all communities, there were things I liked and disliked. More important, however, was that the Project—its gathering of people—gave you a way to find your own way.

— JY

YORTY, DON. Born in Lebanon, Pennsylvania, in 1949. Author of *A Few Swimmers Appear*, Eye & Ear Press, 1980; *Poet Laundromat*, Eye & Ear Press, 1983.

I first saw St. Mark's Church being rebuilt in the spring of '78 I guess it was (I'd brought a magazine from Philly called *Hybris* to put into bookstores, could find no poets at the church, only workmen, but I saw Ted Berrigan on the street and gave him a copy). When I moved to New York, I liked to stand at the back (when you entered from the west), where you could smoke a cigarette and come and go as you wanted (remember Ted Berrigan there and Eileen Myles, among others). Attended a workshop run by Maureen Owen that put some much needed spontaneity in my writing and Ron Padgett's French workshop (I liked that). Enjoyed innumerable readings within those walls. Once, after a Philip Whalen reading, I argued with Corso at the Ukrainian bar over who was a better poet, Keats or Shelley, coming to no conclusion (though I read "Prometheus Unbound" as a result of that discussion). I later told Corso something he didn't know: Hart Crane was shark shit. Corso started to laugh, the vision of which still makes me chuckle when I think of it. I also met Bernadette Mayer at St. Mark's (we've been translating Catullus together). St. Mark's is a place to recharge my batteries in, an oasis. And oh yes, it was a lot of fun performing in Auden's "Paid on Both Sides" there, with Bob Holman directing, (and it was nice getting a check).

— DY

YOURGRAU, BARRY. Born in South Africa in 1949. Author of *The Sadness of Sex*, Whale Cloth Press, 1979; *A Man Jumps out of an Airplane*, Sun Press, 1984.

When I first came to New York, I was very interested in the music of Buck Owens and the Buckeroos, and in a certain kind of poetry. The appeal of the poetry—or rather, this *ethos*—was for me its strong vernacular American-ness, cross-bred to French modern manners— antics and beauty, dadism and surrealism, an intoxicating connection to painting and art—and all of this wreathed, in my mind, with the fumes of venerable Bohemianism. (Understand I was quite young at the time; all my notions sprang from books; I had only just been released from prison hospital.)

Anyway . . . this poetry, this *ethos*, had its own version of the Grand Old Opry, as it were. And this was the St. Mark's Poetry Project.

— BY

ZAVATSKY, BILL. Born June 1, 1943, in Bridgeport, Connecticut. Author of *Theories of Rain and Other Poems*, SUN, 1975; *For Steve Royal and Other Poems*, Coalition of Publishers for Employment, 1985. Translated, with Ron Padgett, *The Poems of A. O. Barnabooth* by Valery Larbaud, Mushinsha, 1977.

Near the end of 1968 (I *think*) I was sitting attentively in Ron Padgett's poetry workshop at the St. Mark's Poetry Project while the Fillmore East was burning down the street—in all senses of the phrase "burning down." My wife and I were able to use that night's canceled tickets to hear the Who a couple of days later; Ron would become a friend and collaborator. Anyhow, the point is that *something* was always happening down on the Lower East Side in those years, and for me (living up near alma mater Columbia in Morning-side Heights) most of it had to do with the enormous energy being thrown off at St. Mark's. Several years later I got a chance to sit in Ron's chair and teach two years of workshops at the Project, an opportunity that allowed me to stroke and bite the hand that fed me. That is, even in those years when I was making friends with poets like Paul Violi and Charles North and avidly attending Project readings and reading *The World* and anything I could find by writers associated with it or the "New York School," I was torn between Blake's dictum that "Energy is eternal delight" and the use that was being made of that energy by the friends and contemporaries whose writings fill these pages. Someone someday will write a brilliant memoir tracing what was and was not permissible in the poetry of the "New York School," how its unspoken but forceful ideology stunted or vaunted us, what was truly nurturing in the experience, and what shifts and turns our directions took because we had a place to dream in or kick against. I have dreamed and I have screamed, but I have never been sorry that The Poetry Project was *there*, or that it continues to flourish.

— **BZ**